TSQ Transgender Studies Quarterly

Volume 3 * Numbers 1–2 * May 2016

Trans/Feminisms

Edited by Talia M. Bettcher and Susan Styker

1 **General Editor's Introduction**
Paisley Currah

5 **Introduction: Trans/Feminisms**
Susan Stryker and Talia M. Bettcher

15 **Trans Men Engaging, Reforming, and Resisting Feminisms**
Miriam J. Abelson

22 **An Affinity of Hammers**
Sara Ahmed

35 **Transfeminist Genealogies in Spain**
Aitzole Araneta and Sandra Fernández Garrido

40 **Francophone Trans/Feminisms:**
Absence, Silence, Emergence
Alexandre Baril

48 **Pregnancy:**
Reproductive Futures in Trans of Color Feminism
micha cárdenas

58 **Transmasculine Insurgency:**
Masculinity and Dissidence in Feminist Movements in México
Daniel Brittany Chávez

65 **Of *Huachafería*, *Así*, and *M' e Mati*:**
Decolonizing Transing Methodologies
Pedro Javier DiPietro

74 **Hacking the Body:**
A Transfeminist War Machine
Lucía Egaña and Miriam Solá

81 **One-Eyed Dog**
A. Finn Enke

84 **Transfeminism:**
Something Else, Somewhere Else
Karine Espineira and Marie-Hélène/Sam Bourcier

95 **Pauli Murray's Peter Panic:**
Perspectives from the Margins of Gender and Race in Jim Crow America
Simon D. Elin Fisher

104 **Transfeminist Crossroads:**
Reimagining the Ecuadorian State
Claudia Sofía Garriga-López

120 **Passing Torches?**
Feminist Inquiries and Trans-Health Politics and Practices
Christoph Hanssmann

137 **Women-Identified Women:**
Trans Women in 1970s Lesbian Feminist Organizing
Emma Heaney

146 **Birth of Transfeminism in Brazil:**
Between Alliances and Backlashes
Hailey Kaas

150 **On Being the Object of Compromise**
Cael M. Keegan

158 *Khwaja Sira* **Activism:**
The Politics of Gender Ambiguity in Pakistan
Faris A. Khan

165 **The Emergence of Transfeminism in Russia:**
Opposition from Cisnormative Feminists and Trans* People
Yana Kirey-Sitnikova

175 **From Queering to Trans*imagining:**
Sookee's Trans*/Feminist Hip-Hop
Terence Kumpf

185 **Reading Trans Biology as a Feminist Sociologist**
Riki Lane

192 **Conditions of Critique:**
Responding to Indigenous Resurgence within Gender Studies
Scott L. Morgensen

202 **Discussing Transnormativities through Transfeminism:**
Fifth Note
Ruin

212 **Looking Back on "Queering the Center"**
Naomi Scheman

220 **Transfeminism and Decolonial Thought:**
The Contribution of Brazilian *Travestis*
Joseli Maria Silva and Marcio Jose Ornat

228 **Trans*feminist Intersections**
reese simpkins

235 **Broadening the Gendered *Polis*:**
Italian Feminist and Transsexual Movements, 1979–1982
Stefania Voli

246 **The Woman Question**
Lori Watson

254 **Radical Inclusion:**
Recounting the Trans Inclusive History of Radical Feminism
Cristan Williams

259 **Reconstructing the Transgendered Self as a Feminist Subject:**
Trans/feminist Praxis in Urban China
Shana Ye

266 **Mortal Life of Trans/Feminism:**
Notes on "Gender Killings" in Turkey
Aslı Zengin

DOCUMENTS

272 **African Trans Feminist Charter**

276 **A Collective Editorial**
The *Tide* Collective

INTERVIEWS

278 **Radical Queen:**
An Interview with Tommi Avicolli Mecca
Susan Stryker

285 **A Conversation with Jeanne Córdova**
Talia M. Bettcher

294 **Another Dream of Common Language:**
An Interview with Sandy Stone
Susan Stryker

FASHION

Two Interviews by Tania Hammidi

306 **Unapologetically Rain: Interview with Fashion Model Rain Dove Dubilewski**

311 **She Ain't Taking It: Interview with Suit Consultant Vanessa Craig**

BOOK REVIEWS

315 **Venezuelan Beauties**
Review of *Queen for a Day: Transformistas, Beauty Queens,*
and the Performance of Femininity in Venezuela, by Marcia Ochoa
José Quiroga

321 **Still Here: Gender, Ballroom, and HIV/AIDS**
Review of *Butch Queens Up in Pumps:*
Gender, Performance, and Ballroom Culture in Detroit, by Marlon Bailey
Rinaldo Walcott

326 **Rearward Trajectories**
Review of *A View from the Bottom: Asian American Masculinity*
and Sexual Representation, by Nguyen Tan Hoang
Helen Hok-Sze Leung

General Editor's Introduction

I n the last decade, movements for transgender equality appear to have advanced with astonishing speed, while other issues of concern to women's movements have largely stalled, either making little progress (equal pay) or suffering real set-backs (abortion access). From policy reforms to public opinion trends, it seems that the situation has changed faster, and in a more positive direction, on issues char-acterized as "transgender rights" than it has on those understood as "women's rights." This apparent gap may be exacerbated in the United States: at the con-clusion of the culture wars of the last forty years, the almost inseparable bond between movements for sexual and gender freedom that marked liberationist discourse of the 1970s has been torn asunder, reconstituted through the logic of an identity politics that affirms the demands for recognition of sexual and gender minorities but finds the misogyny that still structures all women's lives largely unintelligible, outside the scope of the liberal project of inclusion. One poll, for example, found that 72 percent of the millennial generation in the United States favor laws banning discrimination against transgender people—a proportion very close to the 73 percent who support protections for gay and lesbian people. But only 55 percent of this generation, born between 1980 and 2000, say abortion should be legal in all (22 percent) or some (33 percent) cases (Jones and Cox 2015: 42, 3). In a three-month period ending July 31, 2015, when this introduction was written, the *New York Times* editorial board came out in support of transgender issues seven times—and that number does not include the several almost uni-versally positive op-ed contributions published during the same period. (*Almost* denotes the exception of Elinor Burkett's op-ed "What Makes a Woman?" dis-cussed by Susan Stryker and Talia Bettcher in their introduction to this special issue.) Describing "transgender Americans" as "among the nation's most mar-ginalized citizens," the lead-off editorial outlined the topics to come in this series documenting "heartening stories" of acceptance as well as the policy challenges still facing this newest "civil rights movement" (*New York Times* 2015). During the

TSQ: Transgender Studies Quarterly ★ Volume 3, Numbers 1-2 ★ May 2016   **1**
DOI 10.1215/23289252-3334115   © 2016 Duke University Press

same three months, which included the passage of restrictions to abortion and contraception potentially affecting millions of people, the *Times* published only four editorials on the subject of access to reproductive services.

Given the apparent disparity between the velocities of the feminist and trans movements, it is not entirely surprising that a certain generational grouchiness toward trans people has emerged from a few redoubts of second-wave feminism, which Stryker and Bettcher document in their introduction. No doubt, this reaction is partly bound up with larger histories of feminist movements. To some, it must seem as if second-wave feminism was surpassed by the next wave before it had time to realize its goals: eliminating or radically reorganizing the economic structures (targeted by Marxist and socialist feminists) and institutions and norms (targeted by cultural feminists) responsible for the subjugation of women. But burdened internally by the racial and class hierarchies it reproduced, limited by an analytical framework that invariably prioritized the workings of the sex/gender binary over other oppressive processes, and confronted externally by emerging neoliberal technologies of governance that could accommodate new articulations of social difference without having to modify the fundamental algorithms for the distribution of inequality, second-wave feminism was not equipped to succeed. Certainly, the long-term transformative potential of the sex positive, trans-affirming, racially engaged, and more politically ecumenical third wave remains unknown, but there is some promise in the ways it has departed from the various grand narratives of the European Enlightenment, which include the third wave's refusal to accede to the ontological priority of any particular group; its capacity to make visible the effects of power on vastly different scales, from the molecular to the global; and its general rejection of traditional political forms (the nation, the party, legal institutions) in favor of situating resistance in cultural moments and provisional events.

The persistence of limited but recurring outbursts of feminist transphobia, however, cannot be explained away simply as a displacement of a more generalized generational antipathy between the second and third waves of feminism. Nor is it useful to dismiss these outbursts as minor atavistic eruptions in the greater march toward gender equality. Those who construe trans women as a part of a patriarchal assault on women, those who assign false gender consciousness to trans people, are certainly contesting the meanings of sex and gender that have gained so much currency as a result of third-wave feminism and trans activism and scholarship. But their insistence on the rigidity and stillness of the categories has other effects that we need to attend to. In the present political moment, we find ourselves stuck in the gridlock of a seemingly unmovable identity politics, one in which the very intelligibility of the categories we find ourselves fighting over masks the processes that distribute the possibilities, potentialities, and life chances to bodies. Indeed, the narrative described in this introduction's opening paragraph, which compared political gains for "transgender people" with losses for "women," illustrates this faulty logic. It is vitally important that both feminists and communities now legible as trans also remain open to processual indeterminacies and the possibility that new formations, attachments, and opportunities for alliance might be more useful than insisting on a distinction based on whether one is in some way gender nonconforming or not. Indeed, we may have reached the point at which the transgender–cisgender binary (which implicitly structures the logic of the distinctions on which that feminist transphobia depends), the grid of intelligibility that has recently come to dominate much trans studies and advocacy, now may obscure more than it reveals. Indeed, as a category of increasing cultural currency in the language of diversity, "transgender" stitches together people whose principal commonality is that their gender didn't turn out as expected, given the sex to which they were assigned at birth. That "trans" or "transgender" purports to describe people who are so very differently situated in relation to their vulnerability to violence, to incarceration, to illness, to homelessness, and to slow death seems like one of the more miraculous feats of identity politics. For example, micha cárdenas's article in this issue, "Pregnancy: Reproductive Futures in Trans of Color Feminism," demonstrates very concretely how a capacious understanding of reproductive justice can't be contained within the usual dividing lines—between trans and cis, between trans men and trans women, between men and women—that have tended to organize thought around access to abortion and to reproductive futures.

In the title of this issue, guest editors Talia Bettcher and Susan Stryker (who is also of course one of the journal's general coeditors), mark the trans/feminist relation with a slash, which signals both the connections and disjunctions between these two categories. The expansive collection of articles they've curated revisit, reframe, interrogate, unpack, upend, and confound expectations for both terms. But enough philosophizing on the question of trans's relation to feminism—all writers know the imperative is "Show, don't tell!" Take a look at the remarkable range of work collected in this issue of TSQ and find there, hopefully, something that helps further elaborate trans/feminist practices in positive new directions.

Paisley Currah teaches political science and women's and gender studies at Brooklyn College and the Graduate Center of the City University of New York and is general coeditor of *TSQ: Transgender Studies Quarterly*.

References

Jones, Robert P., and Daniel Cox. 2015. "How Race and Religion Shape Millennial Attitudes on Sexuality and Reproductive Health." Public Religion Research Institute. publicreligion .org/site/wp-content/uploads/2015/03/PRRI-Millennials-Web-FINAL.pdf.

New York Times. 2015. "Transgender Today." May 4.

Introduction

Trans/Feminisms

SUSAN STRYKER and TALIA M. BETTCHER

This special issue of *TSQ: Transgender Studies Quarterly* on trans/feminisms profiles the remarkable breadth of work being carried on at the intersections of transgender and feminist scholarship, activism, and cultural production, both in the United States as well as in many countries around the world. It emerged from discussions within the journal's editorial board about how to respond—if at all—to the April 2014 publication of Sheila Jeffreys's *Gender Hurts: A Feminist Analysis of the Politics of Transgenderism*. As feminist scholars ourselves, we were concerned that Jeffreys's work, published by a leading academic publisher and written by a well-known feminist activist and academic who has expressed hostility toward trans issues since the 1970s, might breathe new life into long-standing misrepresentations of individual trans experience and collective trans history and politics that have been circulated for decades by Mary Daly, Germaine Greer, Robin Morgan, Janice Raymond, and like-minded others. We wanted to trouble the transmission of those ideas—but how best to do so?

We were concerned as well that Jeffreys's book would add momentum to a wave of antitransgender discourse that has recently been gaining greater strength in certain corners of academia, some feminist circles, and in pockets of the mainstream liberal press.

We understand the current wave of antitransgender rhetoric to be in reaction to recent gains for transgender human and civil rights, a concomitant rise in visibility for transgender issues, and the vague sense that public opinion is shifting, however haltingly or unevenly, toward greater support of trans lives. Those of us who are old enough remember a similar wave in the early 1990s when the contemporary queer and trans movements first emerged in the United States; those of us who are older still, or who have studied our history, can speak of other antitransgender backlashes in the early 1970s—when the women's movement, gay

TSQ: Transgender Studies Quarterly ∗ Volume 3, Numbers 1–2 ∗ May 2016
DOI 10.1215/23289252-3334127   © 2016 Duke University Press

liberation, and the sexual revolution were all accelerating, and the role of trans people in these movements became a divisive issue. Simply put, we understand there to be a relationship between antitransgender scholarship and the concrete manifestation of antitransgender politics, such as the well-known controversy surrounding trans women's exclusion from the Michigan Womyn's Music Festival that had raged beginning with Nancy Jean Burkholder's forcible expulsion in 1991 until 2015, the final year of the festival.

Whatever the cause, over the past few years we have indeed witnessed an escalating struggle over public speech, perhaps most vitriolic in the United Kingdom, in which transgender opposition to what many consider harmful speech from some feminists is perceived by others as an abrogation of the right to free speech by feminists hostile to transgender issues—a debate that engages arguments similar to those advanced regarding what some consider to be the disparagement of Islam within the context of what others consider to be protected political speech in the West. We have seen liberal publications such as the *New Yorker* magazine and the *Guardian* newspaper run features that characterize transgender people as censorious zealots when they protest the animus directed against them by some feminists. We have seen more than three dozen well-known feminists—including novelist Marge Piercy, black cultural studies scholar Michele Wallace, French feminist icon Christine Delphy, and radical feminist foremother Ti-Grace Atkinson—sign an open letter titled "Forbidden Discourse: The Silencing of Feminist Criticism of 'Gender'" (Hanisch 2013) that complains, as does Jeffreys's book, that the very concept of gender (which they see as a depoliticizing substitution for the concept of sexism) is an ideological smokescreen that masks the persistence of male supremacy and oppression of women by men, and assert that "transgender" is the nonsensical and pernicious outcome of this politically spurious set of beliefs (a stance that places them in odd congruence with the conservative Christian position, espoused by the last three popes, that opposes the "ideology of gender," which they have seen as offering support for unnatural interventions into reproductive biology, improper social roles for men and women, and assaults on heteronormative family life [McElwee 2015]). More recently, in the wake of the Caitlyn Jenner media barrage, the *New York Times* published an op-ed piece by Elinor Burkett, "What Makes a Woman?," in which the author, a feminist filmmaker, assumed she was entitled to answer that question in a way that prevented transgender women from being included in her definition—for which feminist biologist Anne Fausto-Sterling, author of the widely taught *Sexing the Body*, unexpectedly tweeted her enthusiastic support.

Given the broader context of a backlash against recent transgender gains among some feminists for which Jeffreys's *Gender Hurts* might conceivably become a standard-bearer or cause célèbre, it seemed important for *TSQ* to somehow address that book and thereby intervene in the conversation about the vexed relationship between transgender and feminist movements, communities, and identities. We asked the editorial board: should the book be critiqued, reviewed, editorialized against, or simply ignored?

After we actually read Jeffreys's text, the prevailing opinion was that the work lacked scholarly merit (a view shared by the few reviews that the book has garnered in academic journals). It completely ignores the question of transgender agency—that is, of trans people making conscious, informed choices about the best way to live their own embodied lives—and instead represents trans people as having no will of their own; for Jeffreys, they serve only as tools or victims of a patriarchal conspiracy to destroy feminism and harm girls and women. Rather than review or editorialize against *Gender Hurts*, the board suggested, we should instead publish a special issue on feminist transgender scholarship that recontextualizes and reframes the terms of the conflict. Rather than cede the label *feminist* to a minority of feminists who hold a particular set of negative opinions about trans people, and rather than reducing all transgender engagement with feminism to the strategy embraced by some trans people of vigorously challenging certain forms of antitransgender feminist speech, we should instead demonstrate the range and complexity of trans/feminist relationships. Rather than fighting a battle on the same terrain that has been contested in Anglo-US feminist movements and in English-language feminist literature for decades, we should contextualize the battle lines within a far richer and more complicated world history of trans/feminist engagement. As white North American anglophone feminist scholars, we see promoting a more global perspective on trans/feminisms as being particularly important for decentering the linguistic, cultural, racial, and national hegemony of anglocentric trans studies and politics. So that's what we set out to do.

As noted in our call for papers (CFP):

> In *Trans/Feminisms*, a special double-issue of *TSQ*, we will explore feminist work taking place within trans studies; trans and genderqueer activism; cultural production in trans, genderqueer, and nonbinary gender communities; and in communities and cultures across the globe that find the modern Western gender system alien and ill-fitting to their own self-understanding. Simultaneously, we want to explore as well the ways in which trans issues are addressed within broader feminist and women's organizations and social movements around the world. We want this issue to expand the discussion beyond the familiar and overly simplistic dichotomy often drawn between an exclusionary transphobic feminism and an inclusive trans-affirming feminism. We seek to highlight the many feminisms that are trans inclusive and that affirm the diversity of gender expression, in order to document the reality that feminist transphobia is not universal nor is living a trans

life, or a life that contests the gender binary, antithetical to feminist politics. How are trans, genderqueer, and non-binary issues related to feminist movements today? What kind of work is currently being undertaken in the name of trans/ feminism? What new paradigms and visions are emerging? What issues still need to be addressed? Central to this project is the recognition that multiple oppressions (not just trans and sexist oppressions) intersect, converge, overlap, and sometimes diverge in complex ways, and that trans/feminist politics cannot restrict itself to the domain of gender alone.

We could not be more pleased with the response to this CFP, or with the thirty-four feature article authors from seventeen different countries we have been able to publish.

Perhaps the clearest theme to emerge in reviewing and selecting this work is the tremendous worldwide effect of "intersectional" feminisms promulgated by US feminists of color in the 1980s. Although Kimberlé Crenshaw is most often cited as the point of origin and point of departure for the concept of inter-sectionality, we could not help but think—when reflecting on the rationales by means of which trans people, particularly trans women, have been excluded from feminism—of the Combahee River Collective Statement; after first criticizing "how men have been socialized to be in this society" and "what they support, how they act, and how they oppress," the collective went on to note:

> We do not have the misguided notion that it is their maleness, per se—i.e., their biological maleness—that makes them what they are. As Black women we find any type of biological determinism a particularly dangerous and reactionary basis upon which to build a politic. We must also question whether Lesbian separatism is an adequate and progressive political analysis and strategy, even for those who practice it, since it so completely denies any but the sexual sources of women's oppression, negating the facts of class and race. (Combahee River Collective [1977] 1983)

In foregrounding the necessity of attending to class and race as well as sex and gender, intersectional feminism raised the question of whether "woman" itself was a sufficient analytical category capable of accounting for the various forms of oppression that women can experience in a sexist society, which in turn opened the question of whether it was sufficient to talk about sexual "difference" in the singular, between men and women, or whether instead feminism called for an account of multiple "differences" of embodied personhood along many different but interrelated axes. This intersectional version of feminism laid the foundation for transfeminist theories and practices in the 1990s and subsequently. Another clear theme to emerge was the importance of queer and poststructuralist approaches to gender and feminism that enabled a more varied understanding of the complex and ever-shifting processes through which identity, embodiment, sexuality, and gender can be configured.

Clear, too, is the recognition that transfeminist perspectives have a decades-long history within intersectional feminisms and were crucial to early formulations of transgender studies. As one contribution to this issue of *TSQ* notes, trans issues played a role in the life of Dr. Pauli Murray, a black gender-nonconforming woman who explored hormonal masculinization in the 1940s, and whose legal activism in the 1950s and 1960s helped lay a conceptual foundation for intersectional feminist theory; other contributors note that trans people played active roles in second-wave feminist groups in the 1960s and 1970s, many of which were actively welcoming of trans people.

Angela Douglas, for example, founded the Transsexual/Transvestite Activist Organization (TAO) in 1970 in Los Angeles, while "crashing" for a few months at the Women's Center, where she immersed herself in the feminist literature in the center's library, attended classes, and participated in the Lesbian Feminist organization that met in the building—noting (with her characteristic self-aggrandizement), "To some, I was a walking monument to the women's movement, a man who had voluntarily given up male privilege to be a woman—and was now fighting for women's rights" (Douglas 1983: 31). In 1973, when Sylvia Rivera—Stonewall veteran and cofounder of the Street Transvestite Action Revolutionaries (STAR)—fought her way onto the stage of the Christopher Street Liberation Day rally in New York, after having first been blocked by anti-trans lesbian feminists and their gay male supporters, she spoke defiantly of her own experiences of being raped and beaten by predatory heterosexual men she had been incarcerated with, and of the work that she and others in STAR were doing to support other incarcerated trans women. She chastised the crowd for not being more supportive of trans people who experienced exactly the sort of gendered violence that feminists typically decried and asserted, with her own characteristic brio, that "the women who have tried to fight for their sex changes, or to become women, *are* the women's liberation" (Rivera 1973). The point here is not to debate how well or how deeply early trans radicals like Douglas and Rivera understood or engaged with feminism and the women's movement, but rather simply to document that second-wave feminist spaces in the United States could be inclusive of trans activism, and that radical trans activism drew upon tenets of the women's movement, perhaps even more than it did from gay liberation rhetoric.

Suzan Cooke, one of the first peer counselors at the path-breaking National Transsexual Counseling Unit established in San Francisco in 1968, moved to Los Angeles in the mid-1970s and became a staff photographer at the *Lesbian Tide*, a lesbian feminist publication. Early US female-to-male community organizer Lou Sullivan ([1974] 2006) tackled feminist transphobia head-on in his 1974 article "A Transvestite Answers a Feminist," while Margo Schulter (1974, 1975a, 1975b, 1975c), a self-proclaimed lesbian feminist transsexual living in Boston in the late 1960s and early 1970s, penned a series of remarkably astute articles in the gay and feminist press on what she called "the lesbian/transsexual misunderstanding." As the next decade dawned, Carol Riddell, a feminist transsexual woman and radical professor of sociology at Lancaster University, authored *Divided Sisterhood*, published in 1980, the first feminist rebuttal of Janice Raymond's notorious 1979 publication *The Transsexual Empire: The Making of the She-Male*. Riddell's leftist scholarship—such as a 1972 conference paper titled "Transvestism and the Tyranny of Gender," which characterized the two-gender system as an oppressive feature of capitalism—influenced Richard Ekins and David King, two of the leading academic researchers of transgender phenomena in the 1980s and 1990s (*Gender Variance Who's Who* 2008).

It is, however, Sandy Stone's "Posttranssexual Manifesto" ([1992] 2006) often credited as the founding document of contemporary trans studies, that most fully activates the protean relationship between trans and feminist theorizing. Written in response to the trans-exclusionary radical feminist activism that resulted in Stone's leaving the Olivia women's music collective where she had been working as a recording engineer in the 1970s, Stone's manifesto integrated many different strands of feminist, queer, and trans analysis into a potent conceptual tool kit that remains vital for the field today. The manifesto, first published in 1991, was originally presented at "Other Voices, Other Worlds: Questioning Gender and Ethnicity," a conference on intersectional feminism held in 1988 at the University of California, Santa Cruz, where Stone was then a doctoral student in the history of consciousness at a time when that program boasted such faculty members as Angela Davis, Gloria Anzaldúa, Donna Haraway, and Teresa de Lauretis. It bears mentioning that Stone's formulation of a "posttranssexual" politics took shape in the same milieu that generated Anzaldúa's "new mestiza," Haraway's "cyborg," and de Lauretis's coinage of *queer theory*. Like its contemporaneous figurations, Stone's "posttranssexual" offered a compelling new way to think in the interstices of gender, embodiment, and sexuality.

Since the early 1990s, a distinct body of transfeminist literature has taken shape. Stone's manifesto provided the impetus for Davina Anne Gabriel's *TransSisters: A Journal of Transsexual Feminism* (1993–95), which explored the underarticulated middle ground between medicalized transsexuality and radical feminism that Stone's essay had pointed toward. Other contemporary 'zines expressing similar transfeminist perspectives include Anne Ogborne's *Rites of Passage* (1991–92) and Gail Sondergaard's *TNT: Transsexual News Telegraph* (1992–2000), both from San Francisco; and Mirha-Soleil Ross and Xanthra McKay's

Gendertrash, from Montreal (1992–95). The first significant wave of peer-reviewed transgender studies scholarship to wash ashore in academia, in 1998, in special issues of such journals as *GLQ: A Journal of Lesbian and Gay Studies*, *Social Text*, *Sexualities*, and *Velvet Light-Trap*, also produced a special issue of the British feminist *Journal of Gender Studies* (guest edited by Stephen Whittle). US activists Diana Courvant and Emi Koyama are generally credited with coining the term *transfeminism* itself circa 1992, in the context of their intersectional work on trans, intersex, disability, and survivorship of sexual violence. Although various other writers were using the term by the late 1990s, including Patrick Califia and Jessica Xavier, it was Koyama's "Transfeminist Manifesto," published on her Transfeminism.org website in 2001, that gave it a greater reach. Her earlier *Whose Feminism Is It Anyway?* (2000) is also of particular note in its explicit discussion of the intersections of race and class in the debates over the Michigan Womyn's Music Festival.

The first anthology of explicitly transfeminist writing, Krista Scott-Dixon's *Trans/Forming Feminisms: Trans/feminist Voices Speak Out*, was published in 2006, a year before Julia Serano's influential *Whipping Girl: A Transsexual Woman on Sexism and the Scapegoating of Femininity* (2007) brought transfeminist concepts into even wider circulation. Since then, at least three special issues of leading English-language feminist journals have engaged with trans studies. In 2008, *WSQ* published "Trans-" (edited by Paisley Currah, Lisa Jean Moore, and Susan Stryker); in 2009, *Hypatia: A Journal of Feminist Philosophy* published "Transgender Studies and Feminism: Theory, Politics, and Gender Realities" (edited by Talia Bettcher and Ann Garry); and in 2011, Matt Richardson and Leisa Meyers, on behalf of the editorial collective of *Feminist Studies*, issued "Race and Transgender Studies." More recently, A. Finn Enke's 2013 Lambda Literary Award–winning edited volume, *Transfeminist Perspectives in and beyond Transgender and Gender Studies* (Temple University Press) has been reaching students in feminist classrooms throughout the anglophone academy. Beyond the United States, important transfeminist writings include Ray Tanaka's work on the intersection of trans and feminist concerns in antidomestic violence activism in Japan, *Toransujendā feminizumu* (*Transgender Feminism*; 2006); Miriam Solá and Elena Urko's *Transfeminismos: Epistemes, fricciones y flujos* (*Transfeminisms: Epistemes, Frictions, and Flows*; 2013), and Jaqueline Gomes de Jesus et al., *Transfeminismo: Teorias e práticas* (*Transfeminism: Theory and Practice*; 2014).

In English, *transfeminism*, written all as one word, usually connotes a "third wave" feminist sensibility that focuses on the personal empowerment of women and girls, embraced in an expansive way that includes trans women and girls. It is adept at online activism and makes sophisticated use of social media and Internet technologies; it typically promotes sex positivity (such as support for kink and fetish practices, sex-worker rights, and opposition to "slut shaming") and espouses affirming attitudes toward stigmatized body types (such as fat, disabled, racialized, or trans bodies); it often analyzes and interprets pop cultural texts and artifacts and critiques consumption practices, particularly as they relate to feminine beauty culture. In Spanish and Latin American contexts, *transfeminismo* carries many of these connotations as well, but it has also become closely associated with the "postporn" performance art scene, squatter subcultures, antiausterity politics, post-*Indignado* and post-Occupy "leaderless revolt" movements, and support for immigrants, refugees, and the undocumented; in some contexts, it is understood as a substitute for, and successor to, an anglophone queer theory and activism deemed too disembodied, and too linguistically foreign, to be culturally relevant. *Transfeminismo*, rather than imagining itself as the articulation of a new form of postidentitarian sociality (as queer did), is considered a polemical appropriation of, and a refusal of exclusion from, existing feminist frameworks that remain vitally necessary; the *trans-* prefix not only signals the inclusion of trans* people as political subjects within feminism but also performs the lexical operation of attaching to, dynamizing, and transforming an existing entity, pulling it in new directions, bringing it into new arrangements with other entities.

The "Trans/Feminisms" issue of *TSQ* includes a number of articles by authors who consider themselves transfeminist in the ways just described and that chronicle self-styled transfeminist practices and theories in the United States, Brazil, Ecuador, Mexico, Spain, France, Russia, and Turkey. By choosing the forward slash (/) to mark a break between the two halves of the neologistic portmanteau *transfeminism*, however, we intend to make space for a wider range of work that explores the many ways that transgender and feminist work can relate to one another. Some pieces are historical, looking back at trans/feminist interactions over the past half-century, in Italy as well as the United States. Others critique the contemporary upsurge of transphobia in some feminist circles, such as Sara Ahmed's analysis of the "no-platforming" debate in the United Kingdom. Still others chart the tentative emerging dialogs between established feminist cultures and newer transgender perspectives in such locations as francophone Canada, South Korea, and mainland China. Transfeminist heuristic lenses are applied to feminist science studies in the biological sciences, the relevance of the new materialism for trans studies, *khwaja sira* activism in Pakistan, radical hip-hop in Germany, grass-roots health activism in the United States and Latin America, questions of assisted reproduction for trans women of color in the United States, decolonial readings of gender diversity in South America, and the resurgence of two-spirit perspectives on erotic sovereignty. We make room as well for more disciplinary sorts of work, such as a sociological account of feminist attitudes among a cohort of trans men in the United States; whimsical cartoon artwork; work that offers personal reflections on the authors' participation in, or experience of, trans and feminist scholarship and activism; and documents of transfeminist activism.

Finally, we also include interviews—both original and archival—that help round out the scope of trans/feminisms we wish to represent. Tommi Avicolli Mecca discusses the history of the Radical Queens Collective in Philadelphia in the 1970s and their relationship with the lesbian separatist DYKETACTICS group, and long-time Los Angeles butch, lesbian, and feminist activist Jeanne Córdova recalls the 1973 Lesbian Conference that witnessed the controversy surrounding Beth Elliott's performance and discusses the trans-inclusive politic of the *Lesbian Tide*. We are also pleased to include an edited version of a 1995 interview with Sandy Stone, portions of which originally appeared in *Wired* magazine (Stryker 1996), that help document the social, political, and intellectual contexts of early transfeminist theorizing.

In bringing together this unprecedented collection of transnational trans/feminist work, we hope to counter the most vituperative and sadly persistent forms of feminist transphobia by showcasing the truly inspiring work currently being undertaken around the world under the banner of transfeminism, as well as by documenting the already long history of transfeminist activism. We hope as well to foster even more radical visions of a social order that makes room for all of us regardless of race, class, sex, gender, sexuality, ability, language, nation, or any other status that now renders us vulnerable to violence and injustice. Transfeminism is a part, but only a part, of this larger struggle.

Susan Stryker is associate professor of gender and women's studies and director of the Institute for LGBT Studies at the University of Arizona and general coeditor of *TSQ: Transgender Studies Quarterly*.

Talia M. Bettcher is a professor of philosophy at California State University, Los Angeles, and she currently serves as chair of the Department of Philosophy.

References

Bettcher, Talia M., and Ann Garry, eds. 2009. "Transgender Studies and Feminism: Theory, Politics, and Gendered Realities." Special issue, *Hypatia* 24, no. 3.

Combahee River Collective. (1977) 1983. "Combahee River Collective Statement." In *Home Girls: A Black Feminist Anthology*, edited by Barbara Smith, 264–74. New York: Kitchen Table.

Currah, Paisley, Lisa Jean Moore, and Susan Stryker, eds. 2008. "Trans-." Special issue, *WSQ* 36, no. 3.

Douglas, Angela. 1983. *Triple Jeopardy*. N.p.: Self published.

Enke, Anne, ed. 2012. *Transfeminist Perspectives in and beyond Transgender and Gender Studies*. Philadelphia: Temple University Press.

Fausto-Sterling, Anne. 2000. *Sexing the Body: Gender Politics and the Construction of Sexuality*. New York: Basic Books.

Gender Variance Who's Who. 2008. "Carol S. Riddell (?–) sociologist." December 15. zagria .blogspot.com/2008/12/carol-s-riddell-sociologist.html.

Hanisch, Carol, et al. 2013 "Forbidden Discourse: The Silencing of Feminist Criticism of 'Gender.'" *Fire in My Belly* (blog), August 19. feministuk.wordpress.com/2013/08/19 /forbidden-discourse-the-silencing-of-feminist-criticism-of-gender/.

Jesus, Jaqueline Gomes de, et al. 2014. *Transfeminismo: Teorias e práticas* (*Transfeminism: Theory and Practice*). Rio de Janeiro: Metanoia.

Jeffreys, Sheila. 2014. *Gender Hurts: A Feminist Analysis of the Politics of Transgenderism*. New York: Routledge.

McElwee, Joshua. 2015. "Francis Strongly Criticizes Gender Theory, Comparing It to Nuclear Arms." *National Catholic Reporter*, February 13. ncronline.org/news/vatican/francis -strongly-criticizes-gender-theory-comparing-nuclear-arms.

Raymond, Janice G. 1979. *The Transsexual Empire: The Making of the She-Male*. Boston: Beacon Press.

Richardson, Matt, and Leisa Meyers, eds. 2011. "Race and Transgender Studies." Special issue, *Feminist Studies* 37, no. 2.

Riddell, Carol. 1980. *Divided Sisterhood: A Critical Review of Janice Raymond's "The Transsexual Empire."* Liverpool: News from Nowhere.

Riddell, Carol. 2006. "Divided Sisterhood: A Critical Review of Janice Raymond's *A Transsexual Empire*." In *The Transgender Studies Reader*, edited by Susan Stryker and Stephen Whittle, 144–58. New York: Routledge.

Rivera, Sylvia. 1973. "Trans Activist Sylvia Rivera at the 1973 Christopher Street Liberation Day Rally." www.youtube.com/watch?v =olD75vnGc-E.

Schulter, Margo. 1974. "Notes of a Radical Transexual." *Gay Liberator*, no 41: 8.

———. 1975a. "The Lesbian/Transsexual Misunderstanding." *Gay Community News* 2, no. 33 (February 22): 6–7.

———. 1975b. "Transsexual Birds and Birds." *Gay Community News* 3, no. 2 (July 5): 15.

———. 1975c. "The Transsexual/Misunderstanding, Part II." *Gay Community News* 2, no. 38 (March 15): 8.

Scott-Dixon, Krista. 2006. *Trans/forming Feminisms: Trans/feminist Voices Speak Out*. Toronto: Sumach.

Serano, Julia. 2007. *Whipping Girl: A Transsexual Woman on Sexism and the Scapegoating of Femininity*. Berkeley, CA: Seal.

Solá, Miriam, and Elena Urko. 2013. *Transfeminismos: Epistemes, Fricciones y Flujos* (*Transfeminisms: Epistemes, Frictions, and Flows*). Barcelona: Txalaparta.

Stone, Sandy. (1992) 2006. "The *Empire* Strikes Back: A Posttranssexual Manifesto." In *The Transgender Studies Reader*, edited by Susan Stryker and Stephen Whittle, 221–35. New York: Routledge.

Stryker, Susan. 1996. "Sex and Death Among the Cyborgs." *Wired*, May: 134–36.

Sullivan, Lou. (1974) 2006. "A Transvestite Answers a Feminist." In *The Transgender Studies Reader*, edited by Susan Stryker and Stephen Whittle, 159–64. New York: Routledge.

Tanaka, Ray. 2006. *Toransujendā feminizumu* (*Transgender Feminism*). Tokyo: Impact.

Trans Men Engaging, Reforming, and Resisting Feminisms

MIRIAM J. ABELSON

Abstract A number of trans-masculine people have written about their efforts to integrate feminism with masculine and trans identities, yet there are fewer stories of those who have more ambiguous relationships or actually resist feminism. This article illustrates the multiple ways trans men engage with feminism, in some cases resisting and in some cases adopting feminist practices or politics, by drawing from in-depth interviews with sixty-six trans men from across the United States. These interviewees' accounts show that they were more likely to take on feminist identities and trans feminism as a key site of solidarity when they understood feminism as varied. Others reported little interest in feminism because they thought of it as limited or that it did not align with their own views or practices. This offers important insights for understanding why some trans-masculine people engage in feminist and trans movements and others do not.
Keywords transgender, trans masculinities, feminisms, trans men, feminist men

During a discussion of trans men and masculinity, Jeffrey paused, sighed, and then explained, "My biggest beef about trans men is that I see so many that allow such misogynist dialogue all around them and don't ever speak up and don't call themselves feminists anymore. How can you turn out that way? It's really hard for me to understand."[1] This was a common sentiment among feminist-identified trans men whom I interviewed across the United States. It was these very questions from trans men that prompted the analysis that follows and addresses the question of how a range of trans men engage, reform, and resist feminisms.

Trans men and trans masculinities have the potential to greatly impact both feminist and transgender politics, particularly in achieving the movements' goals of dismantling dominant sex and gender discourses and undoing gender hierarchies that favor masculinities and devalue femininities (simpkins 2006). There have been important works from academics (Hale 1998; Noble 2006; Rubin 1998; Ziegler 2012) and other writers (Doubek 2014; Young 2014) in which

TSQ: Transgender Studies Quarterly ∗ Volume 3, Numbers 1–2 ∗ May 2016   **15**
DOI 10.1215/23289252-3334139   © 2016 Duke University Press

trans-masculine people use first-person narrative to address both the tensions and necessities of integrating trans masculinities and feminisms in their lives. This article builds on this effort by drawing from semistructured in-depth interviews with sixty-six trans men from the US West, South, and Midwest completed between 2009 and 2013, to present how some trans men engage with feminism in multiple ways and how others resist adopting feminist practices or politics.[2] The sample was gathered using a snowball method with multiple starts. The interviews used an open-ended modified life history approach focusing on respondents' time living socially as men, starting with the experience of transition. These interviewees' accounts show that when trans men understand feminism as varied, they are more likely to take on feminist identities and trans feminism as a key site of solidarity. For others, there was little interest in feminism because they thought of it as limiting or not aligning with their own views. However, it's crucial for the further development of trans feminisms for us to better understand not only how some trans-masculine people embrace feminisms but also why they resist them as well.

Feminist Engagements

A majority of the interviewees in this project identified as feminists, though the individual form of that feminism was highly varied. Like many trans-masculine people who have written about their relationship to feminism, most of this group spent part of their lives in feminist- or women-centric communities. These men embody Bobby Noble's (2006) framing of trans-masculine people as "sons of the movement." The "sons" do not infiltrate feminist movements but are instead a vibrant part of the movement, acting as emissaries to bring feminism into the rest of the world through masculine bodies. This group of feminist interviewees saw feminist politics as central to their trans identities. There was little conflict between their identities as men or masculine people and their feminist politics because they developed alongside and through one another. That is not to say that these men did not have conflicts with other feminists or some aspect of feminist politics, but their personal articulations of feminist commitments meshed with trans and/or masculine identities.

For Saul, positive encounters with feminism and his development of a feminist identity were made possible through time living as a woman and strengthened through his experience in trans politics and communities. He said, "I think if I had been born male I would have been a chauvinist like my father (laugh) but it's like I had this other experience and other exposures and that was a really good thing." This is a commonly reported route to feminist identity for trans-masculine people (e.g., Hale 1998), but it certainly does not guarantee an individual's investment in feminist or trans politics.

The key for many of these men in maintaining a feminist identity was their ability to recognize that there is not one definition of feminism or way to be a feminist, but instead there are *feminisms*, through which to build politics and identity. As such, I do not offer a particular definition of feminism in this article because interviewees defined it in multiple ways, and the definition varied between individuals. Men who took on feminist identities and those who did not certainly had different views of what feminism is, but the crucial difference was their ability to see multiple ways of being a feminist versus a singular understanding.

Regardless of any lack of conflict between feminist and other identities, many men had experiences with feminists who were hostile to trans men. Some feminists denied that trans men were or could possibly be men, and others ostracized them from organizations and larger communities because they were either transgender or men, or both. When some feminists saw them solely as men, even if this did validate their identities, it denied the ways that their trans identity and their time living as girls or women modified their experiences as men (Hale 1998). Several men reported that other feminists were quite cruel to them early in transition. According to Alan, another trans man in his community was pushed toward suicide after engaging with a group of feminists who said that he could never be a man and implied that taking testosterone would make him hurt women. Though Alan worked to resist this group's ideologies, he did not see all feminists as bad. He explained, "It's only a small subset of feminists that do that, but there's enough of them and they're loud enough and they put that agenda out there. But there are other feminists that are like, 'I don't care what you are as long as you treat everyone fair.'" Like Alan, many of the men I interviewed clearly understood that no one group represented all feminists.

Second wave versus third wave was the most common way these men generationally distinguished among feminisms. The second wave was described narrowly as the "militant lesbian feminism" that emerged in US contexts in the 1970s. Men often rejected this kind of feminism, even if it was the framework that began their feminist consciousness, because they disagreed with its essentialist understandings of sex and gender and poor treatment of both transgender and masculine people. Instead, they embraced a constellation of feminisms that they loosely defined as third wave. These feminisms, rooted in queer activism and the punk aesthetic of riot girl, include queer and transgender theories and politics and are more attentive to intersectional understandings of race, gender, class, and sexuality. This generational tension mirrors larger feminist discourses that may erase difference within these waves (Aikau, Erickson, and Pierce 2007) or ignore problems of periodization (Thompson 2002), but it does offer at least a rhetorical strategy to identify alternative feminist possibilities.

Trans feminisms were another fruitful site for differentiating among feminist possibilities. Theoretically, their trans feminisms included topics ranging from the possibilities of trans-species analytics to radical transsexual politics of embodiment. In practice, trans feminisms centered on solidarity with other trans people, particularly trans women. For example, several men talked about their direct actions to push for formal access for trans women at places such as women's colleges. As Jeffery said, "I generally have a rule for myself where if my trans ladies aren't welcome there, then I'm not welcome there." He reported that witnessing other feminists' hurtful treatment of trans women is the only thing that had ever made him question his feminist identity. It was recognizing the possibilities of trans feminisms that allowed him to maintain his feminist identity.

Finally, recognizing men's or masculine people's feminism as legitimate was key for several men in maintaining or developing their feminist identities. This often meant learning to renegotiate how to enact their feminist ideals in everyday life now that others recognized them as men. It entailed not wanting to appear as threatening to women and being conscientious of taking up too much space in various contexts. For others, being feminist men primarily emerged through maintaining egalitarian heterosexual relations with women partners. The most common expression of being a feminist man was to critique and intervene in the misogynist behavior of other men, with a particular focus on other trans men.

Resisting Feminisms

Trans men who were suspicious of or rejected feminism represented about one-third of the interviewees. Aaron said, "I think I'm a small minority, but I have a really negative reaction to feminism." Some of these men cited the explicitly transphobic positions of some feminists, but this group of men also tended to distance themselves from feminism because of the meanings they attached to the label itself. The interviewees who resisted feminism were less likely to have come up through feminist communities or have held feminist identities in the past, although some certainly had. Like many men, this group was not particularly interested in feminism or taking on a feminist identity for themselves.

These interviewees often saw feminism as a monolithic political orientation that represented the interests of the narrow subject position of women who were cisgender, white, and class privileged. In some ways, this echoes the many critiques of feminism from women of color feminists that form the basis for intersectional feminist analyses (Combahee River Collective [1977] 1983; Crenshaw 1989). The women-centered nature of some feminist spaces also represented a conflict with their masculine identities. For example, Aaron said he resented that his feminist mother had taken him to women's meetings because being in those spaces conflicted with his male identity. He reported, "There's a zillion women and then me." This shows both the limits of particular streams of feminism that focus on essentialist understandings of women and the problems of exclusion of people who are not women. In contrast to the men who could identify as feminist through a conceptualization of feminisms, the experience of this group illustrates both the limits of individuals with a narrow view of feminist possibilities and the limits of feminist movements that are accessible only to a narrow constituency.

In line with common mainstream postfeminist discourses (McRobbie 2004), some men distanced themselves from feminism because they thought feminism was too strident or no longer necessary. For example, in describing a character in his favorite novel, Silas said, "I commend the author for having her get in touch with her feminine side and also making her a very strong character, but not to the point where she was stuck up like feminist characters that are off-putting." Like some other men, Silas appreciated strong women but thought feminists and feminism went too far. Although some agreed with some basic feminist principles, they characterized feminists as man-hating, angry women who did not understand what it was like to be a man. A few of the men, particularly those who had formerly identified as feminists, said that feminists really did not understand men's lives or what it's like to deal with the demands of contemporary masculinity. David explained, "I feel a very limiting factor of feminism is that there really isn't room for men to tell their side of the story . . . and the gender box is just smaller." Though statements like these could have produced fruitful insights into the construction of masculinity in the contemporary United States, they more often resembled men's rights discourses, which argue that men as a group are the most truly oppressed in contemporary gender systems (Messner 1998).

In the end, a few of the men resisted feminism because their views on gender and women conflicted with basic feminist principles. In contrast to those who expressed their trans feminism through solidarity with trans women, these men questioned the presence of trans women in women's spaces and engaged in other forms of trans misogyny. While this was a relatively small group, the views of these men should be of particular concern for feminist and trans politics. With the increasing visibility of trans lives, young trans men are likely to transition earlier in life than men like Saul. Though many young trans men continue to build feminist and trans movements, it is possible that more will take on this sort of trans normativity if they spend less time in explicitly feminist or trans communities. This is not to say that all trans men should be feminists or feminist and trans communities are the only paths to social justice activism, but rather that it should be a concern for feminists when they are not.

By looking across the range of experiences of sixty-six trans men, we see a broader picture of how and why trans men engage with or resist feminisms. Like most feminists, feminist trans men struggle to define and enact their own feminist ideals in their everyday lives. Some trans men resist taking on a feminist identity, owing to negative understandings of what feminism is or because their own views on gender put them at odds with feminist principles. Trans men have a place in feminist movements and can do valuable work as "sons of the movement," particularly by creating new trans feminisms and ways to be feminist men. We must continue to highlight the ways individual trans men negotiate multiple identities in the political realm but also continue to examine the men who do not take on social justice projects to the detriment of these movements. In the end, the onus is on feminists to create broader movements that address the needs of an even wider swath of marginalized peoples.

Miriam J. Abelson is an assistant professor of women, gender, and sexuality studies at Portland State University. Her areas of research are masculinities, LGBTQ youth, and intersections of race and sexuality. She has published work on masculinities and violence, intersectionality and gendered fear, and language in social psychology.

Notes

1.   All interviewee names are pseudonyms.
2.   As a gender-nonconforming woman doing research with trans men, my goal throughout the research and writing process has been to represent the multitude and variety of trans men's voices through focusing on interviewees' own meanings and the issues that were important to them.

References

Aikau, Hokulani K., Karla A. Erickson, and Jennifer L. Pierce. 2007. *Feminist Waves, Feminist Generations: Life Stories from the Academy*. Minneapolis: University of Minnesota Press.

Combahee River Collective. (1977) 1983. "Combahee River Collective Statement." In *Home Girls: A Black Feminist Anthology*, edited by Barbara Smith, 264–74. New York: Kitchen Table.

Crenshaw, Kimberle. 1989. "Demarginalizing the Intersection of Race and Sex: A Black Feminist Critique of Antidiscrimination Doctrine, Feminist Theory, and Antiracist Politics." *University of Chicago Legal Forum*, no. 140: 139–67.

Doubek, Anthony. 2014. "Transmen and Feminism: Gender Inequality Is Everyone's Issue." *Boxers and Binders*, September 23. boxersandbinders.com/2014/09/transmen-and-feminism-gender-inequality-is-everyones-issue.html.

Hale, C. Jacob. 1998. "Tracing a Ghostly Memory in My Throat: Reflections on Ftm Feminist Voice and Agency." In *Men Doing Feminism*, edited by Tom Digby, 99–129. New York: Routledge.

McRobbie, Angela. 2004. "Post-feminism and Popular Culture." *Feminist Media Studies* 4, no. 3: 255–64.

Messner, Michael A. 1998. "The Limits of 'The Male Sex Role': An Analysis of the Men's Liberation and Men's Rights Movements' Discourse." *Gender and Society* 12, no. 3: 255–76.

Noble, Bobby. 2006. *Sons of the Movement: FtMs Risking Incoherence on a Post-queer Cultural Landscape.* Toronto: Women's Press.

Rubin, Henry. 1998. "Reading Like a (Transsexual) Man." In *Men Doing Feminism*, edited by Tom Digby, 305–24. New York: Routledge.

simpkins, reese. 2006. "Feminist Transmasculinities." In *Trans/Forming Feminisms*, edited by Krista Scott-Dixon, 79–86. Toronto: Sumach.

Thompson, Becky. 2002. "Multiracial Feminism: Recasting the Chronology of Second Wave Feminism." *Feminist Studies* 28, no. 2: 336–60.

Young, Andrew J. 2014. "Are You Doing Your Work? White Transmen Holding Ourselves Accountable to Audre Lorde's Legacy." *Feminist Wire*, February 20. www.thefeministwire .com/2014/02/are-you-doing-your-work-white-transmen-holding-ourselves-accountable -to-audre-lordes-legacy/.

Ziegler, Kortney Ryan. 2012. "How My Past as a Black Woman Informs My Black Male Feminist Perspective Today." *Blac(k)ademic*, June 22. www.blackademic.com/how-my-past-as-a -black-woman-informs-my-black-male-feminist-perspective-today/.

An Affinity of Hammers

SARA AHMED

Abstract This article offers a critique of the claim made by trans-exclusionary radical feminists that transphobia is being misused as a way of silencing or censoring critical feminist speech. The article suggests that transphobia works as a rebuttal system, one that, in demanding trans people provide evidence of their existence, is experienced as a hammering, a constant chipping away at trans existence. The article suggests that transphobia within feminism needs to be understood in relation to cis privilege: not having to come into contact with this hammering. It offers a model of political hope resting on "an affinity of hammers"; that is, affinity can be acquired through the work of chipping away at the system.
Keywords: affinity, censorship, harassment, transphobia

We learn about worlds when they do not accommodate us. Not being accommodated can be pedagogy. We generate ideas through the struggles we have to be in the world; we come to question worlds when we are in question. When a question becomes a place you reside in, everything can be thrown into question: explanations you might have handy that allow you to make sense or navigate your way through unfamiliar as well as familiar landscapes no longer work. To be thrown by a question is to be thrown into a world that can be hostile as well as startling. Another way of saying this: when we are not at home, when we are asked where we are from or who we are, or even what we are, we experience a chip, chip, chip, a hammering away at our being. To experience that hammering is to be given a hammer, a tool through which we, too, can chip away at the surfaces of what is, or who is, including the very categories through which personhood is made meaningful—categories of sex and gender, for instance, that have chipped away at us.

This reciprocal hammering can be thought of as an affinity. I want to explore my relationship to transfeminism as an affinity of hammers. Why use the term *affinity* here? Let's assume that transfeminisms are built from or out of trans experiences in all their complexity and diversity. I write then of "affinity" as a way of recognizing that I write from a position of cis privilege. I am writing of how I came into contact with a hammering I did not directly experience because of that privilege. The question of how we can account for that privilege is one that I will keep live throughout this piece.

A starting point is the point from which we proceed, from where a world unfolds (Ahmed 2006). We have many starting points. I write this contribution as a cis lesbian who has experienced gender norms as alienating insofar as gender norms are so often heteronorms: rules of conduct that direct girls toward boys and that render heterosexuality the right or best or happiest destination. I write this contribution as a woman of color who finds that gender norms so often remain predicated on an unremarkable whiteness: the evocation of a fragile female body who needs to be defended from various racialized as well as sexualized others. Intersectionality is *this*. It is about ups and downs, stopping and starting; how we pass through at one moment while being stopped at another, depending on who is receiving us, depending on what is being received through us. An affinity of hammers does not assume we will automatically be attuned to others who are stopped by what allows us to pass through, even when we ourselves have the experience of being stopped. We have to acquire that affinity. It is what we work toward.

The Letter

I want to account for the problem of trans-exclusionary radical feminism, the problem of how it is within some feminist spaces, that this hammering is happening. I will start with a letter, even though the letter in question is not the starting point of a certain kind of feminism that has long been chipping away at trans lives. On Sunday, February 1, 2015, a letter denouncing the tactics used by trans and sex-worker activists to contest speech they perceived as violent toward them was published in the *Guardian* under the headline, "We Cannot Allow Censorship and the Silencing of Individuals," followed by a subheading, "Universities Have a Particular Responsibility to Resist This Kind of Bullying" (Campbell et al. 2015). It was signed by 130 prominent feminists, academics, and activists and became the most recent flash point of a long-running conflict regarding the relationship of transgender issues to feminism. Four examples are mentioned as evidence of this worrying trend: the cancellation of Kate Smurthwaite's comedy show at Goldsmiths, University of London; the calls for the Cambridge Union to withdraw its speaking invitation to Germaine Greer; the pressure on the Green Party to "repudiate" Rupert Read after he "questioned the arguments put forward by some trans-activists"; and the "no platforming" of the "feminist activist and writer" Julie Bindel by the National Union of Students.

I will not rehearse some of the wider problems with this letter that I have discussed elsewhere (Ahmed 2015). I want to focus instead on how trans comes up.

The word *trans* is mentioned both as a description of activists and as a style of accusation: the letter refers to "a worrying pattern of intimidation and silencing of individuals whose views are deemed 'transphobic' or 'whorephobic.'" The statement then says, "Today [no platforming] is being used to prevent the expression of feminist arguments critical of the sex industry and of some demands made by trans activists." Put the sentences together and you have the picture: feminists who are critical of some of the demands of trans activists (which demands? one wonders[1]) are accused of transphobia, which is how they are silenced. A summary: the accusation of transphobia is a means by which critical feminist voices have been silenced.

The sentences in the letter work to create a figure of the trans activist who is making unreasonable demands and arguments, and who is using the accusation of transphobia as a means to silence feminists. Indeed, if words like *silencing*, *bullying*, and *intimidation* cluster around the figure of the trans activist, then words like *critical*, *questioning*, and *democratic* cluster around the figure of the cis feminist.[2] The letter does not have to make an argument explicit: it works to create an impression that is sticky; trans activists are bullying the feminists, and universities are allowing this bullying to happen. The letter does not have to say explicitly that critical feminists and trans activists are distinct camps, one of whom is silenced and intimated by the other, to carry the point.

The letter uses the language of free speech; in a way it both insists on free speech while announcing that free speech is under threat. In the United Kingdom, all speech is understood as free speech, with the exception of speech that is an "incitement to violence." Free speech is increasingly mobilized as an ideological weapon by the creation of a clear distinction between offensive statements and "incitements to violence." Let me offer an example. On March 15, 2015, a leading Black public figure, Trevor Phillips, the former head of the Commission for Racial Equality, released a documentary, *Things We Won't Say about Race That Are True* (Cooper 2015), which ends up defending racism as a form of free speech. The claims made are familiar, though they are more usually articulated in the right-wing press. Antiracism or political correctness is inflated as if it is a hegemonic discourse that has prevented "us" from being able to speak the truths (things we cannot say). The story goes something like this: we cannot ask legitimate questions about immigration because will be branded "racist." The very accusation of racism is understood as what stops us from asking legitimate questions. Paradoxically, then, racism is now incited by being understood as prohibited or minority speech. In such an account the very act of being offensive or causing offense (often through articulating stereotypes about others) speaks to how we assert our national character (as being tolerant of different views) as well as our freedom.[3] In such a schema, dominant views become rearticulated as if they are minority views that we have to struggle to express. Racism is enacted by the claim that we are not free to be racist.

Let's return to our letter. I do not think the letter justifies the freedom to be "critical of . . . some demands made by trans activists" as the freedom to be offensive; rather, what is being implied is that trans activists, by labeling critical feminist speech as offensive (through the liberal use of the illiberal word *transphobia*), are intending to impose a restriction on feminist speech. In other words, being offended is registered as an imposition on the freedom of others. The real offense is caused by those who are offended. This is how the very use of the word *transphobia* is heard as an attempt at censorship. We might note that the claim to be censored can be generative of speech. The example of Germaine Greer mentioned by the letter is a case in point: she was not stopped from speaking at all. She did speak: as did transfeminist activists at another event organized by the LGBTI Society and the Women's Society (speakers included Roz Kaveney and Sarah Brown).[4] If anything, the evidence here points to the opposite of what the letter claims: protests about who is speaking have led to the proliferation rather than prevention of discourse.

When the letter says that critical feminists are being silenced, it is implying that "being critical" of the "demands of trans activists" is a legitimate form of feminist speech. In other words, the letter relies on the assumption that we can distinguish "critical feminist speech" from "incitement to violence," and that there is censorship because others have failed to make that distinction. Behind the letter I can hear these sentences uttered in unison: "It is not racist to ask critical questions about immigration; it is not transphobic to ask critical questions about the demands of trans activists." But this distinction between critical speech and incitement to violence breaks down, which is how an incitement to violence is justified *as* freedom of speech.

Let me give an example of how this distinction breaks down. At a Reclaim the Night march that took place in London in November 2014, a pamphlet entitled "Not Our Sisters" was distributed by trans-exclusionary radical feminists.[5] On one side of the pamphlet is written text. It begins by describing Reclaim the Night as "protesting male violence against women." It then describes trans women as "male transgenders" and suggests that "male transgenders" commit violence against women "at exactly the same rate as non-transgender males." This violent misgendering enables trans women to be positioned as imposters within a feminist march, as perpetrators rather than victims of male violence. On the other side of the pamphlet are four photographs of trans women who are given a story that is not theirs: they have committed violence against women; they have tried to hide that violence by describing themselves as trans or not men. The photographs are used to retell a story, to abbreviate and condense the associations made by the written text: trans women are "male transgenders," trans women are men; as men they use *trans* as a mask to commit and conceal violence; trans women as men injure, rape, and murder women.

To abbreviate and condense an association in the form of an equation:

Trans = violence and death.

I was on Facebook when someone's status update caught my attention. The person spoke of how, sadly, a peaceful feminist march was interrupted by "trans activists." Outrage about violence becomes the cause of a disturbance and not the violence itself. In the next section, I will return to the issue of how disruption is located and narrated. When I wrote in response to that update of my own outrage about the pamphlet, one of the people named in the letter referred to above responded, "So are you saying it is as bad as the Holocaust." By "it" I think she was referring both to the pamphlet that I had described as hate speech and to the more general domain of antitrans feminist speech. It would take us a long time to unpack what is wrong with this statement. But just note the implication that violence against trans people is "relatively" minor, a footnote in a much more horrifying history of human hatred. And it is this very implication that was carried by the letter: "'No platforming' used to be a tactic used against self-proclaimed fascists and Holocaust-deniers. But today it is being used to prevent the expression of feminist arguments critical of the sex industry and of some demands made by trans activists." So this comparison ("it" is not like the Holocaust) is already in use not only to present feminists critical of "some demands made by trans activists" as unjustly censored but also to recast that critical speech as not as violent or offensive as other kinds of speech. I make this point just to make clear that even if those who signed up to the letter might argue that critical feminist speech can or should be separated from the kind of speech represented by the pamphlet, the terms of the letter point to such speech: it is exactly this kind of speech that becomes justifiable as a relatively minor form of offense, or even, as no offense at all.

How often: some forms of violence are understood as trivial, or not as violence at all. How often: violence is reproduced by not being understood as violence. So much violence directed against groups (that is, directed against those perceived as members of a group) works by locating that violence as coming from within those groups. Thus minorities are often deemed as being violent, or as causing violence, or even as causing the violence directed against them. To give an account of trans people as causing violence (by virtue of being trans) is to cause violence against trans people. We are most certainly talking about lives and deaths here; and we are most certainly talking about incitement to violence.

The letter tells a tale: that to take offense at "critical feminist speech" is a wrong (the offense taken is heard as antifeminism) that leads to more wrongs. To take offense at the letter would thus be judged as enacting the very problem described by the letter. Those who protested against the letter were indeed understood not as expressing their freedom of speech but as displaying their desire to restrict freedom of speech in the very act of "being offended" by it. There is an economy of speech at work here. Some protests are judged as stifling free speech while other protests (such as the letter itself) become expressions of free speech. We learn that free speech has become a political technology that is used to redefine freedom around the right of some to occupy time and space. Whenever people keep being given a platform to say they have no platform, or whenever people speak endlessly about being silenced, you not only have a performative contradiction; you are witnessing a mechanism of power.

A Rebuttal System

When I first read the letter, I remember thinking that one of the worst consequences of it would be the new legitimacy it would give to antitrans and trans-exclusionary feminism. I thought at first I was indeed witnessing an increase of such speech. But once I began to work through the networks that supported that letter, mostly on social media, I began to realize that what I first heard as a turning up of the volume was just more of the same thing that had been going on all along for many trans people: that volume switch was already stuck on full blast. My cis privilege was, until then, not having had to notice that harassment or not having had to hear the sound of that blast.

In order to explain how this letter was taken up, we need an account of how privilege is affective as well as effective. When I think of affectivity I think of skin: a border that feels. Privilege could be thought of as rather like contact dermatitis: we are inflamed by something when or because we come into contact with it. Privilege is also thus: being able to avoid contact with the cause of an inflammation. We could contrast contact dermatitis with eczema, which is often called a "basket category," used to describe skin conditions in which the cause of the inflammation is not known. With eczema it can feel as if you are the cause of your own inflammation, whether or not you are the cause, because there is no safe externality; nothing that can be eliminated to heal the skin or the situation.

Like all analogies, this one is imperfect, but I want to use it to dramatize how causality becomes a contact zone in everyday social experience. Let's think of an inflammation as a conversation. Let's say when you enter the room, things become inflamed. If this keeps happening, then you can feel like the cause of that inflammation, whether or not you are. You learn that you cannot stop an inflammation even if you begin to try to "tone things down." So much racism feels like this: the volume turns up when race is mentioned, or the volume turns up when you turn up as a person of color. Racism is precisely how a body of color becomes the cause of tension. I always learn from bell hooks's description of how "the atmosphere will noticeably change when a woman of color enters the room" (2000: 56). A joyful atmosphere, an atmosphere of warm solidarity is lost. It becomes tense. Given that wherever you go, your body goes with you, it can end up feeling like you cause the loss of a good atmosphere. You become tense.

Privilege can be what does not come up when we turn up. This letter was signed by many academics and activists who I do not think would endorse the kind of pamphlet I described in the previous section. So why did they sign such a letter? How could they sign it? I suspect they did not hear the "point" of the letter. Many of those who supported that letter have not been in contact with the relentless nature of the harassment against trans people. They do not have to come into contact with harassment; this is what makes privilege a privilege. Privilege is what can allow a world to recede. When someone brings something up, it can then seem they are bringing something into existence that would otherwise not have been there.

Something I have learned from my work on my blog *Feministkilljoys* is how people witness a reaction as the beginning of something because they do not notice what people are reacting to. Think of a twig that snaps under pressure. A snap sounds loud, and it seems like a sudden movement. But the snap would only seem the start of something, or as the beginning of violence, if you did not notice the pressure on the twig. Pressure is hard to notice unless you are under pressure. A system can put some bodies under pressure without that pressure being experienced, let alone witnessed by others who are not under that pressure.

A snap is not the starting point even if a snap is a start of something. Violence does not originate with the one who snaps. But so often: the exposure of violence is perceived by the privileged as the origin of violence. But so often: when the exposure of violence is perceived as the origin of violence, the origin of the violence that is exposed is not revealed. The figure of the bullying trans activist circulates because of what is not being revealed: that everyday relentless hammering at the house of trans being. Following T. L. Cowan (2014), we could think of this figure of the bullying trans activist as the transfeminist killjoy. The killjoy is without doubt a violent figure: to point out harassment is to be viewed as the harasser; to point out oppression is to be viewed as oppressive. Part of the work of the killjoy is to keep pointing out violence. In making these points, killjoys are treated as people who originate violence. This is the hard work of killjoys. They are up against it!

Transfeminist killjoys expose hammering as a system of violence directed against trans people, including from some of those who identify as radical feminists. Some of the hammering might seem on the surface quite mild because it appears as an instance: a joke here, a joke there. And jokiness allows a constant trivializing: as if by joking someone is suspending judgment on what is being said.

She didn't mean anything by it; lighten up. A killjoy knows from experience: when people keep making light of something, something heavy is going on.

Something heavy *is* going on. Many of these instances might be justified as banter or humorous (the kind of violent humor that feminists should be familiar with because feminists are often at the receiving end). So much of this material makes trans women in particular the butt of a joke. Following Julia Serano (2007), I would describe much of this material as trans misogyny: what is evoked is the figure of the hyper-feminine trans woman as a monstrous parody of an already monstrous femininity. In January 2013, for example, British feminist journalist Suzanne Moore published a piece on women's anger that makes casual reference to the figure of the "Brazilian transsexual" as the "ideal body shape" that most women are angry about because they do not have it (Moore 2013). This statement could be understood as a form of casual racism as well as trans misogyny: the other over there is a means by which a subject here is given contour and definition, a "we" takes shape from what we are not. Another journalist, Julie Burchill, then writes a piece defending Moore against trans activists (quickly described as the "trans lobby"—another inflationary mechanism) whose protests against Moore's statement are called "bullying," a piece that deploys as weapons such violent phrases as a "bunch of dicks in chick's clothing."[6] These two pieces, one much more extreme than the other, are not simply related through a citational chain; they are both part of what I would call a "rebuttal system."

A rebuttal is a form of evidence that is presented to contradict or nullify other evidence that has been presented by an adverse party. A rebuttal is a form of evidence that is directed against evidence that has already been presented. What if you are required to provide evidence of your own existence? When an existence is understood as needing evidence, then a rebuttal is directed not only against evidence but against an existence. An existence can be nullified by the requirement that an existence be evidenced. The very requirement to testify to your existence can end up being the very point of your existence.

To be treated as a being who needs to provide evidence of being is also to be treated as an adverse party. The word *adverse* implies opposing. But it is often used to create a stronger impression, to convey a sense of hostility or harmfulness. To present evidence that nullifies that presented by an adverse party might be how a party is treated as adverse in the first place: you direct evidence to the one who is deemed to be opposing something in the very manner of their existence. Words can be teachers. The word *rebuttal* derives from *butt* and is often used in the sense of a target or aim, as in the butt of a joke. Trans women are made into the butts of jokes. When materials such as those described above make trans women into butts, they are functioning as a rebuttal system, which is to say, they are working together to target an existence. Jokey comments and exchanges have become a significant part of this system. And other, more qualified forms of speech might use of other kinds of "buts" to create a softer impression: I am not saying trans women are not women, *but*. What follows this "but" can contradict what precedes this "but." To qualify an argument can be how an argument is made. We learn to hear the "but," how it is pointed at someone because it has been repeated, over and over again.

Words do not always do what they say. The expression "gender critical" is now used by trans-exclusionary radical feminists to describe their own commitments. ("Trans-exclusionary radical feminism" [TERF] is regarded by this group as an antifeminist and even misogynist slur.) Of course, the implication of this expression is that trans activism (or trans existence) requires being gender *un*critical, thus nullifying the long and varied critiques of the category of gender (including as a diagnostic category) made within trans communities.[7] Putting the problem of this expression to one side, I think we need to treat these arguments about gender as techniques of rebuttal, different ways of rebutting an existence, different ways of saying, for instance, that trans women are not women, that trans women are imposters in women's spaces and the feminist movement.

Different ways of saying: how something keeps being said. This is why the criteria being used to exclude trans women from "women" keep changing. When content (a woman is *x*) is being used as an end (you are not *x*), ideas have already become weapons. At the present moment, "biology" has become weaponized in feminism. This is quite odd and actually rather striking: there are some who hold onto rigid ideas of biological sex, but I do not expect feminists to be among them. When I hear people refer in code to "biology 101," meaning the scientific basis of female and male sex difference, to claim that trans women are not "biologically women," I want to offer in rebuke, "Biology 101? Patriarchy wrote that textbook!" and pass them a copy of Andrea Dworkin's *Woman Hating*, a radical feminist text that supports transsexuals having access to surgery and hormones and challenges what she calls "the traditional biology of sexual difference" based on "two discrete biological sexes" (1972: 181, 186). To be so-called gender critical while leaving traditional biology intact tightens rather than loosens the hold of a gender system on our bodies. But if we start engaging with arguments on these terms, the target will move. Trans women will become not women because they were socialized as boys and men, or for some other reason that has yet to be invented.

When people use such criteria to decide who counts, that criterion has already become a technique for exclusion because it is not a criterion that will be shared by others. Criteria have become points: they are pointed at someone; they are aiming to do something; they are sharpening an edge. The criteria will change if the rebuttal is rebutted because the criteria have become the basis of exclusion. The target is thus a moving target: the policing of the boundaries of woman will take place on whatever basis can be found. In our collective feminist histories, the policing of who are "women" has been about how a specific group of women have secured their right to determine who belongs within feminism (whiteness being a key mechanism for policing feminism). The policing of the boundaries of "women" has never *not* been disastrous for feminism.

It is in this context that we need to think about invitations addressed to trans activists to have a dialogue with trans-exclusionary feminists. Invitations can function as part of a rebuttal system. A dialogue is not possible when some people exercise arguments as weapons by treating others as evidence to be rebutted. When you are asked to provide evidence for your existence, or when you are treated as evidence, your existence is negated. Transphobia and antitrans statements should not be treated as just another viewpoint that we should be free to express at the happy table of diversity. There cannot be a dialogue when some at the table are in effect (or intent on) arguing for the elimination of others at the table. When you have "dialogue or debate" with those who wish to eliminate you from the conversation (because they do not recognize what is necessary for your survival, or because they don't even think your existence is possible), then "dialogue and debate" becomes a technique of elimination. A refusal to have some dialogues and some debates is thus a key tactic for survival.

The very expectation that a conversation with trans-exclusionary radical feminists is possible is evidence of what people have not yet come into contact with. It is an expectation that derives from privilege, of not having been worn down by the relentless questioning of your being. Even that hopeful liberal question, "can't we just have a conversation?" can become another kind of hammering. It makes those who refuse to participate in a conversation into the problem, the cause of a division: so those "trans activists" who are making demands, who are not listening, not engaging, who are using "transphobia" to block feminist critique become those who are getting in the way of the liberal promise of reconciliation, the promise that we can move forward by getting along.

Conclusion: Hammering away at the System

Survival becomes a project when your existence is the object of a rebuttal. You have to survive a system that is constantly chipping away at your being. A feminism that participates in that chipping away is not worthy of the name.

Chipping away is something we too can do. Transfeminism is a form of diversity work. In *On Being Included: Racism and Diversity in Institutional Life* (2012), I discuss diversity work in two senses: the work we do when we aim to transform an institution (often by opening it up to those who have been historically excluded), and the work we do when we do not quite inhabit the norms of an institution. These two senses often meet in a body: those who do not quite inhabit the norms of an institution are often those who are given the task of transforming those norms. We can think of gender, too, as an institution. We can think of gender norms as places in which we dwell: some are more at home than others; some are unhoused by how others are at home. When we are talking about the policing of gender, we are talking about walls, those ways in which some are blocked from entry, from passing through. We might say that all women, including cis women, have to pass through the category of women: no one is born woman; we must be assigned to her. An assignment is what is received by others, how we exist in relation to others. But we don't all experience ourselves as passing. If you do not constantly have your legitimacy thrown into question, if you are not asked whether you are a woman, constantly, repeatedly, if you do not have the door shut in your face when you try and enter the room, then you do not have to pass through "women" in the same way.

We notice norms as palpable things when they block rather than enable an entry. If you do not conform to an idea of woman—of who she is, how she comes to be, how she appears—then you become a diversity worker in both senses. For to exist as a woman would require chipping away at the walls that demarcate who resides there, who belongs there. And this is what diversity workers come up against: walls. An institutional wall is not something that we can simply point to: there it is, look! An institutional wall is not an actual wall that exists in front of everyone. It is a wall that comes up because of who you are or what you are trying to do. Walls that are experienced as hard and tangible by some do not even exist for others. And this is how hammering, however exhausting, can become a tool. Remember, it is through hammering that these walls become tangible. We can direct our attention toward those institutions that chip away us. We chip away at those walls, those physical or social barriers that stop us from residing somewhere, from being somewhere. We chip away at those walls by trying to exist or trying to transform an existence.

We learn from political labor because of the resistance we encounter: walls come up because of what we are trying to bring about. The effort to transform a world is hopeful, not only or always because of what we do bring about (we might fail, we do fail) but also because of what (and who) we come into contact with. Contact gives us a chance. We don't have to take that chance. We can retreat. We can turn away and build fortresses around our own bodies. Feminism too can be turned into a fortress, which is another way of saying that feminism too is where hammering is happening. This is why when I use the word *affinity* I am pushing against another wall. That word is often used to indicate a natural attraction, a natural tendency. An affinity of hammers is an affinity that is acquired; we become attracted to those who chip away at the worlds that accommodate our bodies. I think of the potential as atomic: an attraction or force between particles that causes them to combine. We have to take a chance to combine our forces. There is nothing necessary about a combination. In chipping away, we come into contact with those who are stopped by what allowed us to pass through. We happen upon each other. We witness the work each other is doing, and we recognize each other through that work. And we take up arms when we combine our forces. We speak up; we rise up.

Chip, chip, chip: an affinity of hammers is what we are working toward.

Sara Ahmed is professor of race and cultural studies and director of the Centre for Feminist Research at Goldsmiths, University of London. Her work is concerned with how power is lived, enacted, and challenged in everyday life as well as institutional cultures. Recent publications include *The Promise of Happiness* (2010), *On Being Included: Racism and Diversity in Institutional Life* (2012), and *Willful Subjects* (2014).

Notes

1.   The example of Rupert Read might allow us to specify the demands: his comments related to trans women's use of public toilets.

2.   The use of *critical* is of special interest to me: I think "critical of" also evokes "gender critical," which as an expression is used to mask antitrans sentiment as feminist argument. See the following section on how arguments become part of a rebuttal system.

3.   The documentary is premised on a misunderstanding of the nature and function of stereotyping. The point is that some generalizations "stick" because they naturalize an association between groups and qualities (often but not only negative qualities). Racism works by rendering some problems into problems of culture. So when Pakistani men are found guilty of child abuse, that comes to express a quality of Pakistani or Islamic culture (or even immigrant culture), while when white men commit child abuse, that violence is understood as individual and idiosyncratic.

4.   See Sarah Brown's own discussion of the problems in Brown 2015.

5.   You can see the pamphlet itself as well as a discussion of what happened at the march on GenderTrender, a UK-based, trans-exclusionary radical feminist website. For the pamphlet, see Reclaim the Night 2014a. For the discussion, see Reclaim the Night 2014b.

6.   This piece was originally published by the *Observer* but was removed and republished in the *Telegraph*. See Burchill 2013.

7.   See Tim R. Johnston's patient review of Sheila Jeffreys's equation of "transgenderism" with being uncritical of gender. He writes, "To the contrary, there have been many transgender people and allies who have used the resources of social constructionism to question both the medicalization of transgender identity and the social forces that constructed the diagnostic criteria for gender identity disorder (GID) and gender dysphoria" (Johnston 2014).

References

Ahmed, Sara. 2006. *Queer Phenomenology: Orientations, Objects, and Others.* Durham, NC: Duke University Press.

———. 2012. *On Being Included: Racism and Diversity in Institutional Life.* Durham, NC: Duke University Press.

———. 2015. "You Are Oppressing Us." *Feministkilljoys* (blog), February 15. www.feministkilljoys .com/2015/02/15/you-are-oppressing-us/.

Brown, Sarah. 2015. "Whatever This Nonsense Letter Is Complaining About, It Is Not Censorship." *Sarah Brown's Blog*, February 14. www.sarahlizzy.com/blog/?p =293.

Burchill, Julie. 2013. "Here Is Julie Burchill's Censored *Observer* Article." Posted on Toby Young, *Politics* (blog), *Telegraph*, January 14. blogs.telegraph.co.uk/news/tobyyoung/100198116 /here-is-julie-burchills-censored-observer-article/.

Campbell, Beatrix, et al. 2015. "We Cannot Allow Censorship and Silencing of Individuals." *Guardian*, February 14. www.theguardian.com/theobserver/2015/feb/14/letters-censorship.

Cooper, Vicki, dir. 2015. *Things We Won't Say about Race That Are True.* Trevor Phillips, presenter. Outline Productions and Pepper Productions. Aired on Channel Four Television Corporation, March 25. www.channel4.com/info/press/programme-information/things-we -wont-say-about-race-that-are-true.

Cowan, T. L. 2014. "Transfeminist Kill/Joys: Rage, Love, and Reparative Performance." *TSQ* 1, no. 4: 501–16.

Dworkin, Andrea. 1972. *Woman Hating.* New York: E. P. Dutton.

hooks, bell. 2000. *Feminist Theory: From Margin to Centre.* London: Pluto.

Johnston, Tim R. 2014. Review of *Gender Hurts: A Feminist Analysis of the Politics of Transgenderism*, by Sheila Jeffreys. *Hypatia Reviews Online.* www.hypatiaphilosophy.org/HRO/reviews /content/214.

Moore, Suzanne. 2013. "Seeing Red: The Power of Female Anger." *New Statesmen*, January 8. www .newstatesman.com/politics/2013/01/seeing-red-power-female-anger.

Reclaim the Night. 2014a. Flyer. GenderTrender, www.gendertrender.wordpress.com/2014/11/22 /breaking-news-reclaim-the-night-london-2014/ (accessed July 1, 2015).

Reclaim the Night. 2014b. "Reclaim the March! Statement from Radical Feminists on What Occurred at London Reclaim the Night 2014." GenderTrender. www.gendertrender .wordpress.com/2014/11/24/reclaim-the-march-statement-from-radical-feminists-on-what -occurred-at-london-reclaim-the-night-2014/ (accessed July 1, 2015).

Serano, Julia. 2007. *Whipping Girl: A Transsexual Woman on Sexism and the Scapegoating of Femininity.* Emeryville, CA: Seal.

Transfeminist Genealogies in Spain

AITZOLE ARANETA and SANDRA FERNÁNDEZ GARRIDO

Translated by MICHAEL BRASHER

Abstract Tracing genealogies is a profoundly political and creative matter. The authors' commitment is to seek and recognize where these genealogies are located. This article blends the authors' experience, dependent on other stories and vulnerability, which together over time becomes a genealogy. For analytical purposes, this article divides the history of the transfeminist movement into two periods: the emergence and consolidation of the trans-depathologization movement (2006–10) and the consolidation of the transfeminist movement (2010–13).
Keywords trans, depathologization, transfeminism

We ask ourselves, "How can it be that it is *we* who write about this history?" How do we meet the challenge of (re)writing a genealogy of something that is currently viewed as fragmented, something in which we have been involved, both in its successes and failures?

Our paths crossed and then diverged. We were together during the birth of the trans movement in Madrid, but afterwards, around 2010, we separated—one of us cleaved closer to a nascent transfeminism and the other to the trans-depathologization movement. Our challenge is to tell a story that makes present those absences arising from this apparent fragmentation. Drawing on our different experiences, and taking advantage of the fact that sufficient time has passed for a kind of distance, but not too much time to forget, we have attempted to tell this story.

First Period: Rise and Consolidation of the Trans-Depathologization Movement
In this article, we are concerned with three main sets of political actors or agents: the trans-depathologization movement, the transfeminist movement (more or less differentiated from one another according to the objectives of any given moment), and the transsexual or LGBT collectives that we call "officialist," given

that some parameters of their struggle are determined by their dialogue with established social institutions and/or political parties.

The beginnings of the trans-depathologization movements in Spain are rooted in the struggles of radical and critical queer feminists.[1] They originate from groups making sweeping denunciations of all conditions that oppress the marginalized (commodification, institutionalization, and depoliticization of the LGBT movement, immigration regulations, expropriation of sex worker rights, and so on). The emergence of the *Guerrilla Travolaka* in Barcelona in 2006, along with the new political articulations that began to take shape thereafter, mark the birth of the contemporary Spanish trans movement. In making the trans fight a centerpiece of its activism, the nonidentarian Guerilla Travolaka loosely united many autonomous protest movements, explicitly framing trans politics as the struggle against heteropatriarchy.

What became Stop Trans Pathologization (STP) in 2012 originated in 2008 as the informal Network for Trans Depathologization. The network undertook limited efforts regarding depathologization and depsychiatrization within officialist LGBT spaces, and advanced the view that trans people were mentally healthy. The proliferation of identities under the trans umbrella, however, provoked a political shift. By embracing a politics of self-naming, and by denouncing transphobia particularly as it is institutionalized within health care (as the professionals still assume that real identity is provided by genes, genitals, and gonads), the network moved from promoting the idea that trans issues were legitimate medical concerns to advancing a position that entirely rejected the politics of legitimation, and instead critiqued and confronted hegemonic medical practices and knowledges. In doing so, we helped undermine the authority of the medical profession on the matter of transsexuality. At the international level, we concentrated our efforts on expanding the annual Trans October events, which grew from being held in only three cities in 2007 (Paris, Barcelona, and Madrid) to taking place in more than fifty cities on several continents by 2012, with more than eighty organized groups participating.

Aside from this, the trans movement vindicated itself from the politics of self-naming and the denunciation of transphobia, one of whose institutionalized expressions is creating pathologies within health care. Medical legitimacy was politically disputed, creating a scenario in which hegemonic medical practices and knowledges were confronted.

Another evolution took place at Spain's annual state feminist conference, held in Granada in 2009, in which various trans groups and independent activists also participated that year. While participation at that conference was less diverse than we might have hoped for, as the voices of the officialist trans movement were not heard at all, the event nevertheless helped develop the relationship between trans movements and feminisms. We highlight three ideas discussed at length by the participants at the 2009 conference:

1. That feminists participate in the depathologization movement and make their own demands in the name of feminism regarding trans-depathologization.

2. Mutual interrogation of trans and feminist discourses and agendas regarding the silence of feminism on trans issues and the failure of the trans movement to acknowledge its feminist roots.

3. The reaffirmation of transfeminism as addressing issues prior to and more fundamental than traditional feminism based on binary thought. This was epitomized by the public reading and explication of the "Manifesto for a Trans-feminist Insurrection."

Only after the depathologization movement became consolidated, around 2010, did the political question of identity within the trans movement resurface again with force, this time emerging from the ground of autonomous radical feminist perspectives. A question: must we unmake ourselves (as women) as political subjects in order to challenge the oppressions of gender? The question of identities and whether to go through the identity politics route was a big one that unfolded in the following events.

Second Period: Consolidation of Transfeminism
and the 2012 International STP Campaign

By the end of 2010, a new period of the transfeminist movement took shape in Spain, involving different movements and different local social agents, distinct from what would become the 2012 Stop Trans Pathologization campaign. At the same time the STP campaign became independent, the Network for Trans Depathologization, with its focus on the Spanish state, emerged onto the international stage with a new, more transnational agenda.[2] Meanwhile, the campaign for the STP depathologization, previously rooted in the framework of the state, eventually settled on the international stage where, henceforth, it would build its framework.

The grassroots work of the campaign in this period aimed, almost exclusively, at five objectives developed in 2009 by the Spanish Network for Trans Depathologization: the removal of gender identity disorder from such international diagnostic manuals and tools as the *Diagnostic and Statistical Manual of Mental Disorders* (*DSM-5*) and the World Health Organization's International Classification of Diseases (ICD-11); the elimination of sex designation on official documents; the abolition of surgical genital "normalization" practices that impose binary gender on intersex infants; free access to hormones and surgery for trans people without psychiatric monitoring; fighting transphobia through education, and working toward full inclusion of trans people in society and the workplace (Stop Trans Pathologization 2012). Meanwhile, the transfeminist network endorsed more transgressive demands by focusing on the different forms of gender-based violence that operate simultaneously with, and blend into, other forms of social oppression. Thus, activism concerning migrants, decolonization, or sex work, for example, became central concerns within transfeminist networks.

Unfortunately, at the same time, "officialist" transsexual groups engaged with specific institutions and political groups have begun to moderate the radical demand for trans-depathologization. What might have been a powerful articulation of a right to health derived from a clear commitment to diversity is instead being converted into a mere request for depsychiatrization, and not total depathologization.

Third Period: The Current Situation

Beyond and outside "officialist" political discourses and strategies, those of us committed to trans-depathologization and transfeminism now find ourselves in a pluralist political context that traces its genealogy to a common origin. Transfeminist and trans-depathologization movements sometimes overlap in terms of participants and actions at certain times and in certain regions, or in certain groups such as Trans Pandi, while at other times they are clearly differentiated by their different objectives and the other interests that inform various events and actions. This complexity can provoke mutual self-questioning and self-critique, which can be highly productive.

Challenges remain for both the trans-depathologization movement as well as for transfeminism. One challenge for the former concerns which trans identities get to be depathologized and which do not. How shall we manage the tension between obtaining recognition—in the form of changes within psychiatric manuals, health-care policies, and so forth—while not reducing gender diversity? There is no doubt that a transfeminist politic could help here. One challenge for the latter concerns the articulation of a critical nonbinary theory and politics, rooted in our lived realities, even when the lived realities of this "we" may be more local, and less diverse or numerous, than one might hope. In this respect, it may be that the international reach of the depathologization campaign through STP can help broaden and enrich the transfeminist movement as well.

Perhaps, then, it is not a shared genealogy that now keeps us together but, rather, a common belief in a story that can include divergent paths and that can thereby promote mutual self-examination and self-critique.

Aitzole Araneta holds an MA in sexology and gender studies and was the coordinator of the international campaign Stop Trans Pathologization 2012. Araneta is an international consultant for the International Lesbian, Gay, Bisexual, Trans and Intersex Association (ILGA Europe), Transgender Europe, and Global Advocates for Transgender Equality. Araneta is the coorganizer of various seminars and conferences and has authored many articles in collections.

Sandra Fernández Garrido has a degree in biology and postgraduate training in gender studies and is currently in the field of medical anthropology. Fernández Garrido was part of the LGBTQ movement for over ten years as a member of different groups and as an independent critical activist.

Notes

1.   Roughly, "trans-butch-dykes."—Translator
2.   In the last few years, it has reached a presence in international arenas such as the European Parliament (2010), Transgender Europe (2010), and Encounter of ILGA World (2010), taking a more institutionalized route.

Reference

Stop Trans Pathologization. 2012. "Objectives." www.stp2012.info/old/es/objetivos (accessed July 24, 2015.

Francophone Trans/Feminisms
Absence, Silence, Emergence

ALEXANDRE BARIL

Translated by CATRIONA LEBLANC

Abstract In this essay, the author draws on his experience as a trans, francophone, feminist researcher to share his reflections on the difficulties encountered within francophone contexts in the development of knowledge that moves beyond what the *TSQ* editors call "the familiar and overly simplistic dichotomy often drawn between an exclusionary transphobic feminism and an inclusive trans-affirming feminism." Without reducing the work of the few francophone researchers interested in trans/feminisms, including the author's, to the fight against exclusionary, transphobic feminist theories, policies, and practices, he demonstrates how problematic it is to articulate their work in terms other than the exclusion/inclusion of trans people within feminism. The author offers as a case study the 2015 Seventh International Conference of Francophone Feminist Research, currently the world's most important francophone feminist conference, to illustrate the near total silence on trans issues that reigns in francophone feminist communities.

Keywords trans feminisms, francophone communities, feminist research/studies, exclusion/inclusion

A s I read *TSQ: Transgender Studies Quarterly*'s call for papers on trans/feminisms, I was quickly overcome with the same strong, contradictory emotions I often feel as a francophone researcher working at the intersection of gender, trans, queer, and disability studies. One part of me was very excited by the opportunity to discuss the value of work in which trans and feminist perspectives both contribute to and challenge one another. I was particularly inspired by the statement, "We want this issue to expand the discussion beyond the familiar and overly simplistic dichotomy often drawn between an exclusionary transphobic feminism and an inclusive trans-affirming feminism" (*TSQ* 2015). The work I have published over the last few years in English-language journals reflects my desire to move beyond precisely this reductive conception. As the call so eloquently articulates, not only has the time come to complexify this binary vision, but the last two decades have already proven that research conducted from trans/feminist perspectives extends well beyond questions of exclusion and inclusion.

Another part of me, however, the part grounded in a linguistic, cultural, and national tradition different from the Anglo-US context in which the journal is situated,[1] nonetheless reacted with ambivalence to the passage cited above. What are the linguistic, cultural, and national conditions required to move beyond debates between feminists and trans activists rooted in the notorious dichotomy between inclusive and exclusionary/transphobic feminisms? Does not the very idea of going beyond this dichotomy reflect what is theoretically, conceptually, and politically conceivable in one or more specific linguistic, cultural, and national contexts (in this case, an Anglo-normative one), without it necessarily being intelligible, or intelligible in the same way or with the same depth, in other contexts? Drawing on my experience as a trans,[2] French-Canadian, feminist researcher, I would like to share a few critical reflections on the current (im)possibility of moving "beyond the familiar and overly simplistic dichotomy often drawn between an exclusionary transphobic feminism and an inclusive trans-affirming feminism," or at least the great difficulty of doing so.

Without reducing the work of the few francophone researchers interested in trans/feminisms, including mine, to the fight against trans-exclusionary feminist theories, policies, and practices, I will show how problematic it is to articulate our work in terms other than the exclusion/inclusion of trans people and issues within francophone feminist contexts by offering as a case study the 2015 edition of the 7e Congrès international des recherches féministes dans la francophonie (Seventh International Conference of Francophone Feminist Research), currently the most important international conference in francophone feminist studies and research, equivalent to the US National Women's Studies Association (NWSA) conference. It therefore presents an excellent case study for demonstrating the difficulty francophone communities seem to face not only in conceptualizing the possibility of moving beyond the rift between transphobic and trans-inclusive feminists but also in simply addressing trans issues within various activist, community, institutional, and academic feminist spaces. Although this example does not provide an exhaustive account of the theorization of trans/feminisms in the "Francosphere," it is nonetheless illustrative of the current situation and, in my opinion, an accurate representation of the relationship between most francophone feminists and trans activists.

The 2015 conference, which took place in Montreal, Quebec, Canada, in August 2015, shortly before this issue of TSQ went to press (and well after the submission deadline), was hosted by the Institut de recherches et d'études féministes (IREF, Institute of Feminist Research and Studies), the Réseau québécois en études féministes (RéQEF, Quebec Network of Feminist Studies), and the

Université du Québec à Montréal's Service aux collectivités (SAC, Community Services). I submitted two proposals to present my most recent work. My reflections on the complete absence of trans issues and inclusive policies for trans people in this conference began long before I considered submitting a manuscript to this special issue of *TSQ*. Indeed, I had been struck by the conference's lack of consideration for trans people on my very first reading of its call for proposals in 2014. The language used in the call and on the conference website makes a clear statement: feminine forms are used whenever possible, the masculine form is erased, and the mixed form often used in French to refer to both men and women is not employed. The conference's documentation explicitly refers to *women* professors, researchers, students, and so on. On the website, the organizing committee describes the event as follows: "In continuity with the six previous gatherings, the Conference will create a privileged space for feminist researchers(f), students(f), researcher(f)-practitioners(f), artists, stakeholders(f), and activists(f).[3] Particular effort will be made to attract the largest possible number of participants(f) from every francophone country throughout the world" (CIRFF 2015b). As an activist, teacher, and participant in francophone feminist circles for nearly fifteen years, I am aware that certain feminist spaces in French Canada (by which I mean primarily the province of Quebec) are explicitly women-only environments that deliberately exclude trans people, including trans women. Therefore, for me, the use of feminine forms on the website and in the call for proposals—a practice that, with the exception of explicitly trans-exclusive separatist events like the Michigan Womyn's Music Festival, seems entirely obsolete in anglophone contexts—immediately raised questions about whether the event was reserved for cisgender women or whether cisgender men, transsexual and transgender (trans) men and women, and people who identify as queer, genderqueer, nonbinary, nongendered, intersex, two-spirited, and so forth, could participate.

As a trans man, I made sure to consult the conference's published admission criteria before submitting a proposal and found the answer to my question in the FAQ section of the site (its very presence there leading me to believe that I am not the first to question the conference's use of feminine forms). In response to the question "Is this event reserved for women only?" the organizing committee writes, "Everyone is welcome and any person involved in feminist research is invited to propose a paper, seminar, or special session. The text of the call for proposals is feminized because the vast majority of individuals interested in our activities are women. For us, the use of the feminine includes the masculine" (CIRFF 2015a).[4]

Although the FAQ section provided me with an answer, it also left a sour taste in my mouth. First, I have never favored the simple reversal of perspectives as a minority empowerment strategy; strategies like fighting violence with violence, countering insults with insults, and claiming that feminine forms include the masculine in order to combat linguistic sexism merely reproduce the same attitudes, ideas, and behaviors we denounce. For many decades now, francophone feminists have condemned the French language's sexist practice of granting the masculine precedence over the feminine on the pretext that the masculine includes the feminine; yet this international francophone feminist conference uses the same argument to justify the use of exclusively feminine language and terms such as *women researchers* (*femmes chercheures*) and *women activists* (*femmes militantes*). Second, suggesting that the feminine includes the masculine is, at minimum, dismissive of the many identities that do not fit into these binary categories. For people who are trans, intersex, queer, genderqueer, nonbinary, nongendered, or who otherwise reject identification in terms of masculinity or femininity, the language chosen by the organizers (who are cisgender women) is problematic. Yet, as a trans person and activist, it is not the choice of words that disappoints me the most. More worrisome still is the silence surrounding the very existence of all the people who fall outside the traditional spectrum of masculinity and femininity in the conference's answer to the question "Is this event reserved for women only?"

From my perspective as a researcher who has participated in dozens of international conferences, including in anglophone contexts, at a time when intersectionality and the desire to consider the multiple components of identity are commonplace, it was clear to me that this question asks not only about the participation of cisgender men but that of trans, intersex, genderqueer, and other gender-nonconforming people as well. Nevertheless, these people's existence is never mentioned, not in the FAQs where one might expect to find it, in any other section of the site, or in the call for proposals. Given that this conference aims to host an "event that takes into account accessibility for all(f)" (note that *all* [*toutes*] includes only people whose gender is feminine; CIRFF 2015b), it is not misplaced to say that accessibility for trans, intersex, and genderqueer people is lacking in terms of language (choice of words, linguistic gender, and pronouns, etc.) and space (e.g., gender-neutral or trans-inclusive restrooms). Furthermore, the conference's call for papers uses concepts and definitions that create a chilly climate for these marginalized communities. For example, sections describing the conference themes, used to structure the call for proposals and the website and consisting of more than two thousand words of text, repeatedly refer to the diversity of women in terms of race, class, age, and sexual orientation, among many other components, but trans issues are never mentioned. The organizing committee is careful to remind us to take into account the needs of all women, including the most marginalized, without once mentioning trans people. Although I appreciate the impossibility of always including a detailed enumeration that would avoid the embarrassing "etc." described by Judith Butler (1990: 143), it is nonetheless interesting to note that trans, intersex, genderqueer, and other gender-nonconforming people are not once mentioned on the website.

The problem is that, generally speaking, trans issues are systematically ignored in francophone feminist works otherwise concerned with including *all* women, as they so often remind us. This is even more worrying given that trans issues are currently very visible both in international news and within the national contexts in which francophone feminist research is grounded. Over the last five years, Quebec, along with the rest of Canada, has witnessed the introduction of new bills, adoption of new legal provisions, and transformation of existing legislation affecting trans communities, not to mention the significant social and political mobilization of trans communities and the growing presence of trans voices in the media, culture, and social movements, including lesbian, gay, bisexual, and queer movements. Despite this, Canadian francophone feminist communities remain largely silent on trans issues.[5] As I discuss elsewhere (Baril, under review), francophone feminists' silence on trans issues is evident: French-language publications about feminist intersectional analyses rarely mention trans realities; students in feminist studies in francophone universities have difficulty finding supervisors sufficiently familiar with the topic; and many workshops, social activities, and other events in francophone feminist circles do not address trans issues. The theoretical, political, cultural, linguistic, and economic dimensions of the significant differences between francophone and anglophone feminist approaches to trans issues are very complex, however, and beyond the scope of this article.

Does this mean that no trans/feminist research is being conducted in the Francosphere? No, of course not. A few isolated trans or cisgender researchers, like Sam/Marie-Hélène Bourcier ([2001] 2006, 2005, 2011), Karine Espineira (2015), and myself, work in French on the intersections between trans and feminist issues, as well as other topics.[6] However, for the small number of researchers working in these fields, opportunities to ground their teaching and research and disseminate their work in French-language journals and conferences are few and far between. Reading the call for proposals and website of the most important international francophone conference in feminist studies left me wondering whether my trans/feminist work even fits into the event. This conference should feel like my "home," but, for me and other researchers interested in trans/feminist issues, it does not. This raises serious questions about the possibility of linking our work to other francophone feminist research and feeling that our perspectives are not just tolerated by our colleagues but recognized and valued as well. I would like to invite francophone feminist scholars and activists to engage with anglophone feminists and trans scholars whose research over the last twenty years has produced many valuable reflections on trans feminist issues (e.g., Enke 2012).

TSQ's call for papers rightly states that "feminist transphobia is not universal," and this is true in anglophone and francophone communities alike (*TSQ* 2015). Nevertheless, researchers working at the intersection of trans and feminist issues in these two communities face radically different obstacles and challenges, a reality confirmed by my experience as a professor and researcher who teaches, publishes, and works in French in francophone-majority contexts (like Quebec) and francophone-minority environments (like Ontario), as well as in English in Canada and the United States. Although francophone trans/feminist research certainly cannot be reduced to questions around the exclusion of trans people from and their experiences within feminist circles, nor to an agenda fighting for their inclusion, it would be premature to assume that francophone trans/feminist theories are therefore poised to move beyond discussing issues of exclusion and inclusion. Like my anglophone trans studies colleagues, I am engaged in the development of new paradigms, ideas, and concepts situated beyond that dichotomy—such as investigating the intersections between trans and disability studies, and between trans and disabled people—in my publications in English. This is possible, however, only because trans issues, theories, politics, and studies are at least minimally present and somewhat legitimated within the anglophone (primarily US and Canadian) academy and recognized there as being a part, however marginalized, of feminist scholarship. This is not the case in francophone circles. When feminist theorists such as Christine Delphy, who has been without question one of the world's leading francophone feminists since the 1970s, do not perceive trans issues as political, and they state that by addressing them that "we lose sight of the feminist fight for the eradication of gender" and that transgender does not represent "a political battle, in the sense that it does not propose changing societal structures" (Merckx 2013, original translation), we can hardly be surprised by the lack of theorization of trans issues by francophone feminists. Given this reality, and as surprising as this may be to many anglophones, the latest "developments" in trans/feminisms in francophone feminist communities consist of simply affirming the existence of trans/feminist perspectives, attempting to "prove" their validity and heuristic value, fighting for their recognition, and encouraging the majority of francophone feminist communities to consider trans people and issues in their language, theories, policies, political action, and activist spaces—in short, simply including them within the realm of possibility. Within these linguistic, cultural, and national contexts, moving beyond the dichotomy between inclusive and exclusionary/transphobic feminism is a largely unintelligible undertaking, difficult to conceive on epistemological and conceptual levels. Theorizing the absence of these discussions and this dichotomy is actually the next step necessary for the emergence of francophone trans/feminist voices capable of breaking through the silence.

Alexandre Baril is an assistant professor at the University of Ottawa. He has published numerous articles in journals such as *Hypatia: Journal of Feminist Philosophy*, *Annual Review of Critical Psychology*, *Disability, and Society*, and *Journal of Literary and Cultural Disability Studies*.

Acknowledgments

A previous version of this article was presented in French at the Seventh International Conference of Francophone Feminist Research in August 2015. I would like to thank participants at this conference for their questions and comments. I would like to thank the two anonymous reviewers of this article for their helpful insights; Susan Stryker for her attentive reading, editing, and valuable suggestions; and the Social Sciences and Humanities Research Council (SSHRC) of Canada for its generous support.

Notes

1. Despite the clear demonstration of transnational and linguistic sensitivity, a journal cannot be separated from its context.
2. I have been working on feminist issues since 2003 and on trans issues since 2008, when I began my own female-to-male transition.
3. The abbreviation *(f)* indicates that the feminine form of a word was used in the original French. The spelling of *artists* in French (*artistes*) is invariable and can therefore denote either gender. All passages quoted from the website are original translations.—Translator
4. The questions and answers in the FAQ have been completely revised since the conference was held in August 2015. It is perhaps not unreasonable to assume that the present critique, as well as others, presented at the conference may have influenced this decision.
5. It is worth mentioning that, despite the presence of important trans scholars like Viviane Namaste in Quebec, who discusses trans and feminist issues in one of her books in English (Namaste 2005), I published what I believe is the first French article in Canada addressing trans/feminist issues (Baril 2009). My intent is not to be pretentious but to show the scarcity of trans/feminist reflections in the French-Canadian context despite numerous analyses on these same topics in English-Canadian contexts.
6. Presently, there is a growing interest in trans/feminist perspectives in francophone contexts. For example, two new projects on these questions are Thomas, Grüsig, and Espineira 2015 and Ribeiro and Zdanowicz 2015.

References

Baril, Alexandre. 2009. "Transsexualité et privilèges masculins: Fiction ou réalité?" ("Transsexuality and Male Privilege: Fact or Fiction?"). In *Diversité sexuelle et constructions de genre (Sexual Diversity and Gender Construction)*, edited by Line Chamberland, Blye W. Frank, and Janice Ristock, 263–95. Quebec: Presses de l'Université du Québec.

———. Under review. "Intersectionality, Lost in Translation? (Re)thinking Inter-sections between Anglophone and Francophone Intersectionality."

Bourcier, Marie-Hélène. (2001) 2006. *Queer Zones: Politique des identités sexuelles et des savoirs (Queer Zones: Politics of Sexual Identity and Knowledge)*. Paris: Éditions Amsterdam.

———. 2005. *Queer Zones 2: Sexpolitiques (Queer Zones 2: Sexpolitics)*. Paris: La Fabrique.

————. 2011. *Queer Zones 3: Identités, cultures, et politiques* (*Queer Zones 3: Identities, Cultures, and Politics*). Paris: Éditions Amsterdam.

Butler, Judith. 1990. *Gender Trouble: Feminism and the Subversion of Identity.* New York: Routledge.

CIRFF (Congrès international des recherches féministes dans la francophonie; International Conference of Francophone Feminist Research). 2015a. "FAQ." cirff2015.uqam.ca/faq .html#pourquoi-toutes-les-communications-se-font-elles-au-féminin (accessed February 3, 2015).

————. 2015b. "Mot de bienvenue" ("Welcome"). cirff2015.uqam.ca (accessed February 3, 2015).

Enke, Anne, ed. 2012. *Transfeminist Perspectives in and beyond Transgender and Gender Studies.* Philadelphia: Temple University Press.

Espineira, Karine. 2015. *Transidentités: Ordre et panique de Genre: Le réel et ses interprétations* (*Trans Identities: Order and Gender Panic: Reality and Its Interpretations*). Paris: L'Harmattan.

Merckx, Ingrid. 2013. "Un entretien avec Christine Delphy" ("An Interview with Christine Delphy"). Le blog de Christine Delphy, November 14. www.delphysyllepse.wordpress.com /2013/11/14/un-entretien-avec-christine-delphy-politis/.

Namaste, Viviane K. 2005. *Sex Change, Social Change: Reflections on Identity, Institutions, and Imperialism.* Toronto: Women's Press.

Ribeiro, Kira, and Ian Zdanowicz, eds. 2015. "Transféminismes: Politiques des transitions féministes" ("Trans Feminisms: Politics of Feminist Transitions"). Special issue, *Revue comment s'en sortir?*, 1, no. 2.

Thomas, Maud-Yeuse, Noomi B. Grüsig, and Karine Espineira, eds. 2015. *Transféminisme(s)* (*Trans Feminism[s]*). Cahiers de la transidentité 5. Paris: L'Harmattan.

TSQ: Transgender Studies Quarterly. 2015. "Call for Papers, *TSQ: Transgender Studies Quarterly* Volume 3, Issue 1: Trans/Feminisms." www.lgbt.arizona.edu/content/tsq-31 (accessed October 11, 2015).

Pregnancy

Reproductive Futures in Trans of Color Feminism

MICHA CÁRDENAS

Abstract The author's hybrid poetry/bioart project, *Pregnancy*, presents a vision of trans Latina reproductive futures, based on her experiences of cryogenic tissue banking, aka sperm banking, after having been on hormones for many years. At the 2014 Civil Liberties and Public Policy Conference, Morgan Robyn Collado stated that violence against trans women of color is a reproductive issue because they are prevented from living long enough to realize their dreams of having children. Trans women of color want more than just to live. Existing literature on transgender pregnancy and family planning focuses almost exclusively on transgender men. Books such as *Trans Bodies, Trans Selves* focus almost entirely on trans men, while making only the most brief reference to the fact that trans women can bank their sperm. This reproduces a trans-misogynist dynamic in which trans men are highly valued by queer communities and transgender women's concerns and existence are erased.
Keywords trans of color, bioart, interdisciplinary, praxis, reproduction

20141201_163491.mov

A blizzard of hormones,
for months,
undersea volcanoes spewing hot affects
tectonic emotional swings
intense food cravings
my body is foreign to me
it's changing, in ways I don't like,
shape, texture
and so many little blacks hairs coming back,
despite being tortured out of existence,
on my cheeks, in my cleavage,
I have to wear baggy clothes,
all my underwear was too tight
for gamete making temperatures,

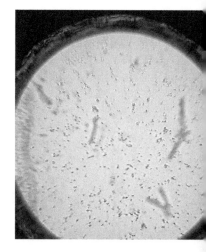

TSQ: Transgender Studies Quarterly ★ Volume 3, Numbers 1–2 ★ May 2016
DOI 10.1215/23289252-3334187 © 2016 Duke University Press

I have to take my vitamins every day,
all to make a baby.
I'm a trans woman
and I'm pregnant.

20141219_165451.mov

I am no testo junkie,
this is no experiment,
these are not drugs, they're my body.
I take hormones every day of my life out of necessity,
just to have a body I can live in,
to avoid death,
to survive,
both to avoid my own suicidal ideations,
that appear in my mind unwillingly, instantly, surprisingly,
usually with a painful, slowly resonating ache,
as I looked at some beautiful woman,
or some everyday woman,
going about her life,
a life I thought I could never have,
though now, mostly, in my own way, I do.
And to avoid death at the hands of others,
the constant promise of necropolitics
that I face everyday,
knowing that as a trans woman of color,
I'm not likely to survive until my
next dream is realized,
my next poem is written,
my next performance is danced and spoken,
my next city, country welcomes me,
my next surgery date comes,
or, this time,
until I see the eyes of my bright screaming beautiful baby come into this
        dimension
and join us with her cries of creation.
I'm not taking hormones, now, out of necessity,
the feeling of urgency of reproducing in the face of a world that wants me dead,
and wants my dearest loved ones,
from south asia, palestine, colombia, dead,

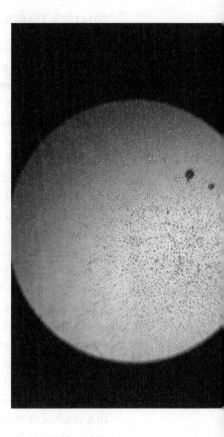

or from here,
Mississauga New Credit territory, dead.
And we will fight back these genocidal projects, by making life, family, love and
      joy,
by making babies with our queer trans bodies.

20141223_154845.mp4

Instead of a becoming woman or becoming animal
or even becoming parent
this feels like becoming asshole.
I hate testosterone,
there are many reasons why I take estrogen
and spironolactone to block my testosterone.
I feel the edge back in my mind,
the edge of impatience, of being quick to anger,
the old version of myself seeps in,
in my voice, which sounds so deep and strange to me.
My friends who've done this told me to take Xanax,
but I prefer the tincture of motherwort I got
from my crazy femme witch poet friend Leah,
she gave it to me when my mother almost passed.
It's the only thing saving my life right now, and my relationship,
after weeks of solid fighting,
mostly over my inability to understand my new emotional waves, rhythms and
      tempos
my partner and I thought we might break up,
because of the chemical changes in my neuronal activity,
that resulted in weeks of
mean, mean fights.
But I did this,
so we can make a baby,
together.
Now the motherwort is
doing its magic,
I feel it in the corners of my eyes, like sleepiness
relaxing my anger and anxiety,
finally giving me, for the first time in weeks,
tiny moments of the sense of peace,
that I feel from estrogen.

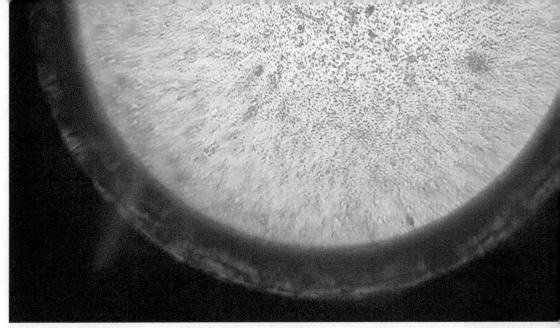

20141227_195816.mp4

While I once thought taking hormones was a good experiment
an ethico-aesthetic experimental life act in the spirit of Deleuze and Guattari,
now I realize what a masculinist, colonialist dream that was,
and I don't like that old self of mine.
Some of us write out of need,
for some of us, this is not a luxury, as Lorde said.
Now, after so many years of taking them,
I realize that in these pills there is a home for me,
these pills, and all the changes they've brought to my body and life,
have brought me to a place of commitment to building a home and a family,
to heal the deepest wounds in myself,
to care for myself and those I love,
by creating stability,
by being careful with our hearts and our lives.
Funny that my Colombian father's whole way of raising me,
was to teach me to be the man, the breadwinner,
and it didn't work at all,
but absolutely rejecting man in the deepest way I could
brought me full circle to want to create and protect my family,
in a way that dad
will one day appreciate.
They told me I would be sterile,
the doctors and brochures,
that I couldn't do this,
what I'm doing.
But they don't know,
and they lied to me,

and other trans women
have done it.
I mourned the loss of my children and family,
and I've heard my friends mourning them too,
but the truth is that even after 8 years on estrogen and t blockers,
you only have to go off your hormones for a few months
to make gametes.
Other trans women taught me how to do it.
Sadie said, get a microscope,
don't pay hundreds of dollars for doctor visits to check your semen,
with a $50 kids microscope,
you can see sperm,
morphology and motility.
I did, I can and I do,
see hundreds of sperm squirming their way across the field of view,
clearly swimming in a line,
I shared with the other women a short video I made,
and they exclaimed:
you've got swimmers!

20141228_155803.mp4

Whose language is this?
The logos of cis-heteropatriarchy?
I am writing this,
the hormonal chemistry I was born with bubbling up in my body,
it feels so foreign,
like I'm in here looking out of these eyes,
but this mind isn't mine,
these words, this rhythm, all feels so foreign, so not me.
When Anzaldúa says "I am again an alien in new territory . . . I have another set of
        teeth in my mouth . . . the heart in my cunt starts to beat"
I think she knows much of what I'm feeling, yet still
I don't think she imagined this particular mystery,
of growing face and chest hair again,
of the erotic being transformed into
the crassest instant desire for any hot woman I see on the street,
the intense quick urge to orgasm that is calling me to masturbate every day,
an urge I can barely resist.
Yet this is my experience, as a mixed race mujer,
a woman pregnant with life.

20150109_123554.mp4

Aching
just dim morning winter grey light on the bricks outside the window,
aching so hard, a slow pulsing, I don't want to get out of bed,
and my girlfriend doesn't like me and no one likes me and I don't like me
but that was last week,
but we decided to do this together,
to go the biological route,
because adoption seems almost impossible,
for two sick brown queer and trans women,
with histories of mental illness and poverty in both our families,
you know, just the usual for QTPOC.
The legal rights you have to your baby,
are more tenuous if you don't have a biological input,
and I don't want another trauma at an international border,
and the cost of IUI, ICSI and IVF are in the tens of thousands,
oh the privilege of
cis-hetero reproduction!
Everything happens through a haze,
I feel slow,
thinking is hard,
putting words together is a struggle,
the cold is biting, the sun is so shy
and the sun lamp's light is so white.
I need to just sit here, and write.
and jerking off helps
my mood for a minute
and meditating and tarot give me something larger to hold on to
and I just have to hold on, for a few more weeks, or months,
of pregnancy.

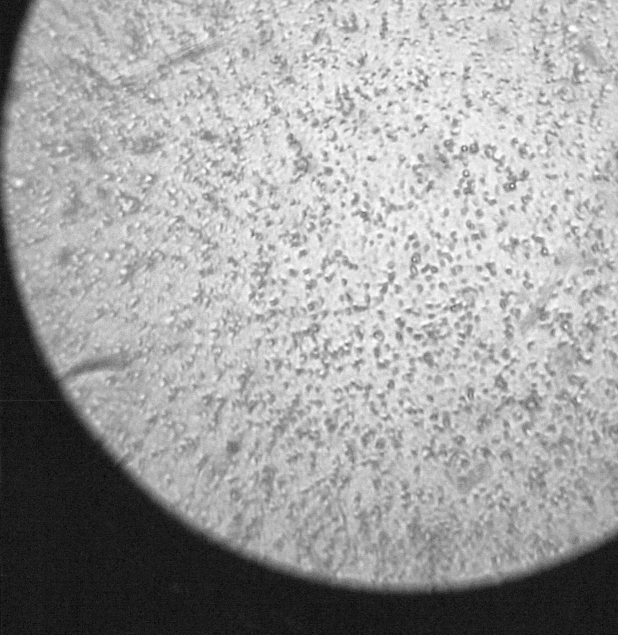

20150111_123705.mp4

Gloria says "something pulsates in my body, a luminous thin thing that grows
       thicker every day. Its presence never leaves me. I am never alone."
I see the sperm under the microscope,
each one swimming, with its own intention,
each one it's own possible life,
and I feel the strangeness of this mind and these feelings,
brought to the surface by hormones,
and I wonder
how many people are inside me?

* * *

Trans of color feminism is a feminism that responds to the violence done to trans women of color, and the historical absence of trans women in both white and women of color feminism. Trans of color feminism learns from and extends women of color feminism and queer of color critique. Additionally, the broader field of transfeminism must include the reproductive rights of trans women in its concerns.

Toward these ends, my bioart project, *Pregnancy*, presents a vision of trans Latina reproductive futures, based on my experiences of cryogenic tissue banking, aka sperm banking, after having been on hormones for many years. At the 2014 Civil Liberties and Public Policy Conference, Morgan Robyn Collado stated that violence against trans women of color is a reproductive issue because we are prevented from living long enough to realize our dreams of having children (Collado 2014). *I want more than just to live.* Existing literature on transgender pregnancy and family planning focuses almost exclusively on transgender men, reproducing the transphobic practice of conflating trans men with women by including them in women's spaces, such as books on lesbian parenting. Further, books such as *Trans Bodies, Trans Selves* (Erickson-Schroth 2014), which claims to be "for the transgender community," focus again almost entirely on trans men and their feelings, while making only the most brief reference to the fact that trans women can bank their sperm if they want to have children. This reproduces a trans-misogynist dynamic in which trans men are highly valued by queer communities and transgender women's concerns and lives are erased.

Queer theory has historically used trans women of color as the image of death and our desires for family as a symptom of heteronormative false consciousness, such as in Judith Butler's discussion of Venus Xtravaganza (Butler 2011). Additionally, queer theorists such as Lee Edelman (2004) have often presented reproductive desire as anathema to queerness. Yet books dealing specifically with transgender experience have reproduced this as well, such as Judith Halberstam's *In a Queer Time and Place* (2005), which defines queer time and space by their difference from life time lines structured around reproduction. Recent work by trans of color scholars counters this, which is not surprising, given the history of people of color's reproductive rights being taken away from them. In an interview that appeared in *Captive Genders*, Reina Gossett points to the fact that trans women in prison can only have the safety of being housed with people of their own gender if they submit to surgical procedures that are a form of sterilization (C. Gossett 2011). The present model of trans women sperm banking is not supported by insurance companies, in my experience, and therefore leaves trans reproductive rights only for those who can afford them.

The failure of queer and feminist theory and culture to envision futures for trans women of color underscores the importance of our writing our own futures. Fields such as science-fiction film, new-media art, digital technology, and speculative design still reproduce forms of misogyny and racism, and as such they have far to go to reach transfeminist consciousness. Given this, the question of who gets to write the future is even more urgent. I was able to succeed in this process only with the aid of other trans women who used social media to create their own space. On a popular social media website, I found a closed group for trans women's fertility. The group was small, with only eight members, about half of whom actively post. Yet it was here that I learned that I could simply buy a microscope to monitor my own fertility, and that I absolutely had to wear baggy clothes if this was going to work. I made all the images and videos in this piece myself, of my own sperm samples, with a microscope and slides I prepared with a pipette. *Pregnancy* is in dialogue with bioartists who engage with the tools and technologies of biology to create artworks. The project responds to bioartists such as Orlan who claimed, "I am a woman to woman transsexual act," a statement that, coming from a cisgender woman, erases the experience of transsexual women (Akman 2006). Instead, *Pregnancy* continues my research into the science of the oppressed—reimagining science in the interest of oppressed people—and into trans of color poetics, developing a poetics that may reduce the violence faced by trans people of color.

In some ways, I am living a trans Latina future so far from the experience of important elders such as Sylvia Rivera. Partly, this is because of my privilege as a light-skinned Latina whose immigrant father made sure she made it through college. In California, I had access to a trans-woman endocrinologist and a trans-woman surgeon. Under the Affordable Care Act, passed in 2010, it became illegal for insurance companies to discriminate against transgender people (Quinn 2014). Soon after this, I was able to get my surgery costs partly covered by my insurance companies, despite my doctor's and surgeon's office staff telling me they had never seen that happen before. Now, surgeons who perform gender reassignment surgery such as Dr. Marci Bowers describe having an unprecedented demand for their services. Yet there is still so much to be done to make sure that trans women of color can even live long enough to realize their dreams.

In these poems, I ask how many people there are inside me. I wrote these poems during a period of months in which I was off my hormones. I consciously shifted my body's hormone levels back to those common to male bodies. I wrote these poems in that state. The project represents an example of shifting as a material and conceptual operator of trans of color poetics, which I have described elsewhere (cárdenas 2015). By shifting my body's state, I was able to produce new knowledge and new material output. In the end, I was able to bank nine "straws" of gametes, nine million sperm. How many people are inside me? Multitudes.

micha cárdenas is an artist/theorist who creates and studies the trans of color movement in digital media, in which movement includes migration, performance, and mobility. cárdenas is an assistant professor of interdisciplinary arts and sciences at the University of Washington Bothell.

References

Akman, Kubilay. 2006. "Orlan and the Work of Art in the Age of Hyper-mechanical Organic Reproduction." *International Journal of Baudrillard Studies* 3, no. 1. www2.ubishops.ca/baudrillardstudies/vol3_1/akman.htm.

Butler, Judith. 2011. *Bodies That Matter: On the Discursive Limits of "Sex."* New York: Routledge.

cárdenas, micha. 2015. "Shifting Futures: Digital Trans of Color Praxis." *Ada: A Journal of Gender, New Media, and Technology*, no. 6. doi:10.7264/N3WH2N8D.

Collado, Morgan Robyn. 2014. "CLPP 2014: Morgan Robyn Collado, Poet." Presentation at the Civil Liberties and Public Policy Conference, Hampshire College, Amherst, MA, April 11–13. www.youtube.com/watch?v =66g_lR-I9AY.

Edelman, Lee. 2004. *No Future: Queer Theory and the Death Drive*. Durham, NC: Duke University Press.

Erickson-Schroth, Laura, ed. 2014. *Trans Bodies, Trans Selves: A Resource for the Transgender Community*. Oxford: Oxford University Press.

Gossett, Che. 2011. "Abolitionist Imaginings: A Conversation with Bo Brown, Reina Gossett, and Dylan Rodríguez." In *Captive Genders: Trans Embodiment and the Prison Industrial Complex*, edited by Eric A. Stanley and Nat Smith, 323–43. Oakland, CA: AK.

Halberstam, Judith. 2005. *In a Queer Time and Place: Transgender Bodies, Subcultural Lives*. New York: New York University Press.

Quinn, Melissa. 2014. "How Obamacare Affects Transgender People." *Daily Signal*, August 31. dailysignal.com/2014/08/31/obamacare-affects-transgender-people/.

Transmasculine Insurgency

Masculinity and Dissidence in Feminist Movements in México

DANIEL BRITTANY CHÁVEZ

Abstract In this brief essay, the author explores what it has been like to transition as a transmasculine person in Chiapas, México, with all its contradictions and complexities. The author contends what it can mean to decolonize masculinity and what his role as a transmasculine and transfeminist person has been in an almost exclusively bio-woman feminist space. What does trans presence mean in fiercely antitrans spaces? What can the power of Audre Lorde's erotic do in transforming feminist communities toward transfeminist power?

Keywords transmasculinity, transfeminism, México, decolonizing masculinity, Lorde's erotic

I begin this brief thought experiment with the open provocation, "Can masculinity be decolonized?"

In 2014, I uprooted my life in the United States and now find myself living in San Cristóbal de las Casas, Chiapas, México. My motivations for this relocation were personal, professional, emotional, political, and existential. This place has become an important transit space for me, whether it becomes a more permanent home space or not. The doors that have opened by coming here are astounding, even though or perhaps because of what those of us residing in this country have experienced in the last year. This is particularly the case for me as a transmasculine transgender individual who has no desire to be pathologized within US medical institutions that require permission letters to authorize treatment of my "dysphoria" and to define how and what "transgender" is. With the encouragement of my former partner, far from bio-family and friends I have always known, I have finally felt for the first time the freedom to explore my transmasculinity without fear of the rejection or bullying I experienced during my butch lesbian days. Here, I have been cared for by a cisgendered female doctor who works out of a home clinic, has never had a transgender patient, yet who does not flinch at ordering

TSQ: Transgender Studies Quarterly ★ Volume 3, Numbers 1–2 ★ May 2016
DOI 10.1215/23289252-3334199 © 2016 Duke University Press

laboratory tests for liver function (based on information sent by a transmasculine friend in North Carolina) to determine whether my endocrine system is healthy enough to use testogel safely. She makes home visits, free of charge, to drop off *recetas* (prescriptions), no insurance required. I can order testogel here for far below US market price without a doctor's note, prescription, side-glance, or insurance coverage. Well-fitting men's clothing costs the equivalent of five to ten dollars for shirts and pants that last far longer than more flimsily made women's wear. I have a local male barber who has never questioned why I cut my hair with him, who charges about $1.50 a cut. In the United States, all these experiences of transformation would have cost thousands of dollars and required months of waiting, many doctor's visits, multiple diagnoses, interminable social hell, and isolation. In México, these experiences have become an integral part of my social, personal, and political life as a community member of Chiapas. A dear friend and colleague who is a photographer did a photo shoot with me at home for *Foto-performance decolonial X.1: Transgresiones transfeministas desde Abya Yala con amor* (*Decolonial Photoperformance X.1: Transfeminist Transgressions from Abya Yala, with Love*) in which I explored transmasculine performativity (Chávez 2014). I also performed a piece called *(Trans)itos Transmasculinos* (*Transmasculine Transits*) as one of the invited artists for the second annual Postporn Festival in Tuxtla Gutierrez.

I begin with these anecdotes because they help narrate a complex social and political terrain. México has become a hypervigilant, militarized state dominated by the police and narco-power, where precarity and violence are quotidian realities. I, however, have the privilege of a US passport and the freedom to leave, without question, as long as I have a return ticket or my student visa—a privilege that does not extend to those traveling in the reverse direction, particularly *compañer@s* deemed "undocumented" by the state. Because of the incredibly strictly enforced gender roles prescribed for male and female appearance in México, I almost always pass as a *joven* (young man) or muchacho among all but those most intimate to me, which is key to my daily safety. Yet, within feminist movements here, there is a strong alliance to cisgendered realities as the only realities, with feminism always-already being equated with womanism, particularly in Chiapas. Within this feminist framework, my masculine physical presentation is made to represent patriarchy, violence, machismo, "wanting to be a man," succumbing to the enemy, and much more. These complex social and political realities not only determine my personal gender experience in México but also frame the larger landscape of work required of trans activism here.

I have quickly become a vocal presence for transmasculine politics in Chiapas and for bringing the "T" more meaningfully into local LGBTSTGNC identities.[1] In February of 2015, a well-known journalist in Chiapas, Patricia Chandomí, asked to interview me about transmasculinities. I eagerly accepted this invitation, given the drive I feel to debunk the prejudice around transmasculine identities, while also striving to be inclusive of the transfeminine and intersex identities that have been the source of tremendous division rather than alliance for feminists in the region.

The interview was prompted by a Facebook conversation initiated after I was tagged in an announcement for a "radical lesbian feminist" gathering. A transfeminine friend who had also been tagged had posted a response to ask if transfeminine people would be allowed to attend (given that the location was not publicly announced, and one needed to write for permission to access the space). I commented directly below this post, asking if a transmasculine presence would be honored, only to receive a retort from one of the speakers that if trans people want into these spaces so much, "they" should make their own spaces. This comment made very clear what I had always heard about feminism in Chiapas: it is inclusive of bio-women only, and anyone else will be not only rejected but also treated as outsiders and "others" who need their own spaces because feminist spaces simply cannot absorb our presence. This clarified for me two significant points: first, that feminist advances in multigender inclusion travel very differently between the global North and the global South; and second, that gender binaries have determined feminist practices in Chiapas up until now. What was my responsability for, and my "response-ability" with, this information?

I have found myself deeply nourished by the writings of transfeminists from Barcelona (see especially *Transfeminismos: Epístemes, fricciones y flujos* [*Transfeminisms: Epistemes, Frictions, and Flows*], by Miriam Solá and Elena Urko [2013]), as well as by my contemporary generation of performance artists, particularly those working in México, Brazil, and Spain, who are radically transfeminist and engage in gender-exploding body practices.[2] The ways we have found to work in collaboration have been filled with so much love, along with our transgressive breaking of gender norms. The reality of feminism = womanism that I have found in Chiapas has created a significant cognitive dissonance with my transfeminist communities elsewhere in México, the rest of Latin America, and in Europe. Simultaneously, I recognize, and celebrate, that movements such as Zapatismo and the feminism within it have created tremendous pathways for indigenous bio-women to have powerful leadership positions in Chiapas, but I contend that this should not come at the expense of diverse gender and sexual positions, identities, and politics, which also exist in the region. This is the bridge that has yet to be crossed here.

Mestiza lesbian feminists have followed their own trajectory, one that parallels in many ways the advances made by indigenous women's feminism, and they, too, have an exemplary history that a rigorous feminist genealogy of Chiapanecan geopolitics simply cannot deny. But then again, these same mestizo lesbian feminists can be the biggest perpetrators of machismo and patriarchal politics when they disparage transmasculine and transfeminine identities, engage publicly and privately in transphobic hate speech, and actively exclude us from feminism by investing their energies in spaces exclusively for bio-women, without ever expressing interest in an open dialogue. While of course I understand that it is crucial for bio-women to contest violence perpetrated against them by bio-men, and while I recognize their widespread lack of access to such essential needs as contraception and safe space from domestic abuse, I also recognize that transgender individuals need not be targeted as part of those problems. I thus began to question the way feminist communities can perpetuate transphobic exclusion and violence, especially given the fierceness and radicalism of my many itinerant performance and transfeminist communities, which offered such a powerful contrast to the conservatism I was facing in my current home space in Chiapas.

I continue to explore these lived contradictions through any number of practices. After my performance in the Postporn Festival, for example, a young woman from the master's program in cultural studies at the university in Tuxtla Gutierrez approached me about writing her thesis on my *historia de vida* (a sharing of life history similar to my own oral history work), focusing on my masculinity and transition. We have since conducted many thoughtful interviews that have deepened my self-reflexivity and self-positioning in Chiapas. I have also found space and inspiration, through my quotidian body practices, to write a book chapter about sovereign erotics and the decolonization of transgender and two-spirit identities through the reclamation of First Nations' worldviews of gender, and through diasporic identity and performance (Driskill 2004; Chávez 2015).

The ultimately relatively solitary space I have had to *devenir* (to become) in the fullness of my two-spirited self has happened in a place that is politically and socially hostile to such identities and yet is so hands off regarding the medical management of this transition that the possibilities are many.[3] The coming-to-fruition of such possibilities has connected me to a global network of transfeminist performance and activist communities that, perhaps if they could be lived out on a more permanent basis, would have their own tendencies toward suffocation and intercommunity violence—but perhaps they might also allow for new ways of becoming that would in turn allow for better ways of life. Still, I have learned not to romanticize notions of "community" or "coherence" and to find deep pleasure in this becoming, when there is a personal sovereignty over the process. This allows for endless transformations.

The one axis of community that I have encountered in Chiapas that has never challenged, undermined, or been hateful toward my transmasculinity is the one of African descent, which has become part of my chosen family here. In fact, the dialogue between feminist leaders in the Afro-descendant community of

Chiapas and me as a transmasculine person who claims African descent has helped to create a sense of intimacy, bonding, and friendship within the broader community of Afro-diasporic people here that all of us need. This reality has driven me to a deep, soul-sourced thinking through, primarily through Audre Lorde's erotics, of what a decolonizing masculinity might be. I have come to think about the exclusionary politics that characterizes some of my social world in Chiapas as being not innocent of, or separated from, the erasure of blackness. This is not to say that black feminism has necessarily always been trans inclusive (in fact, within the multiplicity of black feminisms, trans exclusion has often been present), but it is to say that in this space, for me in Chiapas, being black and being trans are not mutually exclusive, nor does the Afro-descendant community here practice a trans-exclusionary body politics toward me.

Drawing from the wisdom of Audre Lorde's erotics offers a starting place for considering transgender and transmasculine identities as practices of decolonization. Lorde's understanding of the erotic is not to be confused with the merely sexual, which she claims to be diametrically opposed to the erotic (Lorde 1984: 55). The erotic opens us up to the full capability of our sensing self (the five senses) in our capacity to enjoy our physical bodies and the world around us that interacts with it. Given, sexual pleasure is one small facet of the full capacities of our sensing and feeling world. Granted, Lorde speaks quite specifically about the erotic as a power held by bio-women. However, I do not interpret her words as applying exclusively to bio-women, nor do I think Lorde meant for her ideas to be an exclusionary gesture. She puts it this way: "The erotic is the measure between the beginning of our sense of self and the chaos of our strongest feelings. It is an internal sense of satisfaction to which, once we have experienced it, we know we can aspire. For having experienced the fullness of this depth of feeling and recognizing its power, in honor and self-respect we can require no less of ourselves" (Lorde 1984: 54). There is much to be recovered from Lorde's erotics that allows us to theorize the full power of our beings and the pleasures of our existence, and that can challenge medicalizing, pathologizing, and violent discourses against trans people, even (perhaps especially) within feminist circles. While sometimes this work lies in insisting that feminist and other communities expand our existing ways of seeing and being together, at other times the work insists that we decolonize the violating ways we improperly understand—or fail to see at all—the real difference of the other.

I consistently see masculinity being equated with the worst of patriarchy and colonial violence, yet in my own increasingly masculine embodiment, accomplished through the periodic use of testogel, masculinity consists of nothing more than the scent of my loins, the cut of my pants, the line of abdominal muscles, the style of my hair, and the squareness of my jaw. It is a clitoris larger than the typical female's that requires different methods of stimulation. I feel a feeling of physical strength in masculinity, but then again, I never had any problem associating physical strength with being female. I still enjoy my cycles and my swollen breasts when the natural estrogen in my body returns. These pleasures in the fullness of being will never make me less trans, less feminist, less masculine—but they are not what I currently emphasize.

Transmasculine erotics is attuned to a "yes" within ourselves. It is the choice, the risk, of fully embodying the expressions and desires our internal compass points us toward (granting, of course, that "fully embodying" for oneself traverses a spectrum from zero physical intervention to full medicalized transition). Here I understand embodiment as a way of being present, both physically and spiritually, in space. This is not about privileging masculine gender expressions over femme ones or arguing that masculine gender expressions participate in femme erasure. Rather, it is seeing others, as Lorde suggests, in accordance with the erotics present in their own embodiment, their own lives, and the embodiment of their lives.

I think of transgender and two-spirit identities as reclaiming indigenous worldviews stolen from us through hundreds of years of colonization—worldviews expressed through a language of spirituality that much of the secular West ignores or obliterates. It is important to recognize the spiritual dimension of the inalienable erotic capacity that lies within us, which is likewise always on the brink of theft by the persistence of colonial power. Asserting transmasculinity is thus an act of insurgency, a rebellion against this ongoing robbery—it is an assertion of the sense that our erotic power belongs to us alone. While it is undoubtedly important to assert that being transmasculine does not make you any less feminist, or that masculinity is not always-already a replication of patriarchy or the desire for it, there is, perhaps, a more pressing work to be done regarding the decolonization of masculinity in both *cuir* (queer) and hetero spaces through the manifestation of a sovereign transmasculine erotics.

Dissenting from feminism's normalizing practices in Chiapas has meant embodying sovereign erotic power and allowing a sense of true accountability to self and others to become our inner guide. The term "sovereign erotic" comes from Quo-Li Driskill's (2004) revolutionary work on First Nations two-spirit and decolonizing identities that also borrows from Lorde. What I intend here is to use the sovereign erotic as an important theoretical-praxical conversation about transmasculine identity in particular. After all, our gender expressions need to be guided by this erotic power, rather than by dominant social definitions of gender dysphoria. Such framings are illusions that serve only to create hatred of self, and of others. When we learn to encourage erotic fullness from our sisters and brothers in our feminist movements, then we can begin to think about true alliances. Gender expressions will then not be automatically equated with the ever-present hierarchies of colonial logic that divide us. Our energies can then shift from attack and reaction to affirmation and solidarity, from divisive exclusions to opportunities to share encounters with the fullness of our beings, across drastically different landscapes of embodiment. The erotic will force us away from judging others for the decisions (or nondecisions) they make regarding which body modification practices (if any) will fulfill their erotic needs, and it will compel us all to recognize and honor the erotic within the other. Only then, when we have known the changes that full attention to the erotic will bring to our feminist communities, can true trans/feminist alliances come into existence.

Daniel Brittany Chávez is a transgender, two-spirit, Afro-descendant, Cherokee artist-scholar-activist. He is a PhD candidate in performance studies at the University of North Carolina at Chapel Hill and a core troupe member of La Pocha Nostra.

Notes

1.   LGBTSTGNC stands for lesbian, gay, bisexual, two-spirit, trans, and gender non-conforming as used by the Audre Lorde Project (Audre Lorde Project 2015).
2.   Some of the performance artists of my generation include Felipe Osorino (Lechedevirgen Trimegistro, México), La Fuliminante (Nadia Granados, México and Colombia), Sara Panamby (Brazil), Dani d'Emilia (Brazil and Spain), Anuk Guerrero (México), Joyce Jandette (México and Spain), Lia La Novia (México), La Bala Rodriguez (México), Julia Antivilio (Chile and México), and Post-Op (Spain), among numerous others.
3.   While this currently quite solitary nature of my *devenir* is fine for now, it most likely will lead me to choose a different home space where I can find another trans chosen family (meaning nonblood family of trans individuals going through their own transitions), a phenomenon that at times has been called "sexilio."

References

Audre Lorde Project. 2015. alp.org (accessed May 1).

Chávez, Daniel Brittany. 2014. *Fotoperformance decolonial X.1: Transgresiones transfeministas desde Abya Yala con amor (Decolonial Photoperformance X.1: Transfeminist Transgressions from Abya Yala, with Love).* hysteria.mx/fotoperformance-decolonial-x-1-transgresiones-transfeministas-desde-abya-yala-con-amor/#prettyPhoto.

———. 2015. "Devenir performerx: Hacía un erótico soberano descolonial niizh manitoag" ("Becoming a Performer: Toward a Decolonial Niizh Manitoag Sovereign Erotic"). In *Andar erótico decolonial (Erotic Decolonial Walkings)*, compiled by Raul Moarquech Ferrera-Balanquet, 83–98. Buenos Aires: Ediciones del Signo.

Driskill, Qwo-Li. 2004. "Stolen from Our Bodies: First Nations Two-Spirits/Queers and the Journey to a Sovereign Erotic." *Studies in American Indian Literatures* 16, no. 2: 50–64.

Lorde, Audre. 1984. "Uses of the Erotic: The Erotic as Power." In *Sister Outsider: Essays and Speeches*, by Audre Lorde, 53–59. New York: Crossing.

Solá, Miriam, and Elena Urko. 2013. *Transfeminismos: Epístemes, fricciones y flujos (Transfeminisms: Epistemes, Frictions, and Flows).* Barcelona: Txalaparta.

Of *Huachafería, Así,* and *M' e Mati*

Decolonizing Transing Methodologies

PEDRO JAVIER DiPIETRO

Abstract Trans, transing, queer, and queering are typically represented as sharing in the anti-normalizing labor that concerns material bodies. In the vein of decolonial feminism, this essay looks at three renderings of transing methodologies for what they teach us about: the geopolitical tension between transing and queering; genealogies of feminist, gay and lesbian, queer, and trans studies; the collusion of Euro-centered thought with trans research; and the social ontology of transing embodiments.

Keywords transing methodologies, decolonial feminism, transgender studies and women of color feminisms

Loretta Ross, cofounder of SisterSong, Women of Color Reproductive Justice Collective, claims that the designation *women of color* since its inception in the late 1970s cannot possibly rely on a biological "basic identity" (Ross 2011). Against a Westernizing gender system in which man is central (Wynter 2003: 288), and in response to invisibility, immobilization, and having been historically subjected to the dominant scripting of racial and gender identities (Hammonds 1994), the "uplifting" of identity/embodiment performed by women of color unfolds in a double movement: (1) recognizing shared histories of being rendered genderless as not-women/women of color (Lugones 2007), and (2) reclaiming embodiments as a way of reconstituting carnality within non-Western arrangements of being in the midst of each other.

Feminist, gay and lesbian, queer, and transgender studies are concerned with channeling activisms against the normalization of material bodies. Whether as social constructionists or new materialists, they contest regulatory norms through which sex is materialized. Like scholars of transgender studies argue, these activisms illustrate myriad "ecologies of embodied difference" (Stryker, Currah, and Moore 2008: 12) while simultaneously undoing categories that render embodiments legible (Fausto-Sterling 2000: 253; Stryker, Currah, and Moore 2008: 13).

Not unlike critiques advanced by women of color, trans struggles and theorizing foreground the social ontology of embodiment.[1] What overwhelmingly differs between transgender studies and women of color theorizing are the material bodies they each favor for research. Whereas feminisms of color focus on bodies whose histories of "nonbeinghood" produce anatomies of nonpeople, transgender and queer studies have usually taken for granted that bodily variations, their queering and transing, are materialized in and through the zero degree of human flesh.[2]

The constitutive contingencies of flesh under coloniality, race making fused to sex making, have only recently begun to receive much-needed attention within trans studies (Green 2015;[3] Snorton and Haritaworn 2013). Whenever race is made to operate only as cultural technology to signify embodiments,[4] the materiality of flesh is destined to lend an objective type to the subject of dominant trans epistemologies (Roen 2006: 658–59, 663). Therefore, studies combining racialization and gender nonconformity tend to further marginalize racialized embodiment as always already an aftereffect of social life, a mix and match of body parts and bodily stylizations in which the racial axis plays a role in vesting bare flesh with power to do race work, eroticizing, magnifying, diminishing, and/or altering gender.[5]

As Julian Gill-Peterson (2014) argues, drawing from the field of "somatechnics" (Stryker and Sullivan 2009), decolonial feminisms, critical race theory, and critical trans studies work within enriching and yet incomplete frameworks of hybridity and intersectionality. Pointing beyond these epistemologies, in this essay I enact transing methodologies by performing epistemic disobedience in a decolonial vein. At the intersection of philosophical and (auto)ethnographic ways of learning/knowing the social, I seek to establish distinctions that, associated with linguistic and cultural practices, help us to elucidate the decolonizing reality of transing embodiments or their social ontology.[6] Specifically, I consider three renderings of transing research for what they teach us about epistemic disobedience: Giancarlo Cornejo's "For a Queer Pedagogy of Friendship" (2014), Gloria Wekker's *The Politics of Passion* (2006), and my "Decolonizing *Travesti* Space in Buenos Aires" (DiPietro 2015).

Cornejo provides a critique of modernist accounts of trans materialities and identities but fails to decolonize Euroamerican models of envisioning erotic subjectivity and nonnormative embodiments. Beginning with an ethnography of the survival of Italo, "a 'queer' subject, specifically a trans child" (Cornejo 2014: 352) from one of Lima's marginal quarters in Peru, he demonstrates that the child's resilience despite homo- and transphobia expands an archive of working-class affectivity among nonheterosexist possibilities. The trans child is known as both Itala and Italo, the feminine and masculine variations of the same name in

Spanish. In turn, Itala/o underscores the relative positioning of embodiment with utterances that describe her/him as "[being] gay with gays, and *travesti* with *travestis*" (352). Although committed to subverting ethnography, Cornejo carves his authorial place by blocking any direct citation of Itala/o's voice (353) or citing Itala/o but always translated into English, a transliteration upon which Cornejo does not elaborate. The quotation marks incorporate Itala/o translated twice over, first, for what Cornejo can make of Itala/o's variation of Spanish and linguistic competence and, second, for the social ontology—the basic distinctions about trans embodiment—called upon by Cornejo's translating Itala/o into English.

In what concerns the first transliteration, Cornejo obliterates Itala/o's Limeño Spanish and her/his linguistic register. Even when Itala/o's childhood was spent among both upper and lower strata of Lima, her/his use of the English term *gay* would be considered by some, particularly by the whitened elite of coastal Peru, a *huachafo* or inadequate attempt by those from lower social ranks to access higher ones (Niño-Murcia 2003: 126). Racial stratification in Peru today encompasses subtle forms of cultural segregation through which geographical origin, class, and educational status are policed (de la Cadena 2000; Quijano 1978). Linguistic variation is inscribed within broader racial connotations, and the use of anglicisms such as *gay* accrues dubious linguistic capital when uttered in Lima's marginal quarters by *un maricón*, a term that refers to varying degrees of *faggotry* among the lower class. Whereas Itala/o favoring *gay* to highlight her/his own stylization of embodiment may work as a ruse embracing an ironically trashy sense of self, Cornejo's translation of Itala/o's voice contracts a colonizing register (Rafael [1988] 1993) by muting Itala/o's *huachafería* or paradoxically failed attempt at crossing class boundaries.[7]

The second transliteration consists of Cornejo's borrowing Itala/o's wisdom only to the extent that transparency is assumed between third-world vernaculars and the supracultural coherence of queer language. The snappy playfulness of *las conchitas*, the network of life-affirming friends in which Itala/o thrives, invokes the provincial notions of *gay* and *travesti* that Cornejo suggests. And yet, for him, as shown by the use of italics, *travesti* is the only term opaque enough to warrant the bracketing of the social ontology advanced by queer language. Furthermore, *gay* remains within the transparency of queerness as the lingua franca. In this second transliteration, *travesti* is to be uttered as foreignization but in Cornejo's voice as translator, conflating queer language from the south with the working-class Limeño Spanish of Itala/o, which is thereby domesticated.[8] His method remains under the thumb of colonizing epistemology inasmuch as it leaves the ethnographer removed from transcultural and multilingual interanimations. Finally, by deploying *queer* and *queering* as injunctions of nonnormative practices in describing Itala/o's networks of friends, Cornejo partakes in transnormative globalizing imperatives (Snorton and Haritaworn 2013: 67).

In *Contracting Colonialism*, Vicente Rafael ([1988] 1993: 28) reminds us that within colonial translation, not only the linguistic transactions between minoritized source language and ruling target language are of importance but also the "special status accorded" to the colonizing language. In Cornejo's transliteration, queerness is accorded the status of cross-cultural object (353, 363), disciplinary study (353–54), and method (356–57). It occupies nonnormative global domains while enabling translation to strategically codify provincial vernaculars—*mariconería* and *travesti*, among others—according to Euroamerican queer theory. In collusion with such epistemic traditions, *las conchitas* could not possibly be queen theorists of their own right but a network of friends whose existence is to be explained by Michel Foucault's notion of "friendship,"[9] Judith Butler's psychic life of power, and Julia Kristeva's abjection. Anticolonial and decolonial critiques highlight the pitfalls of remaining loyal to this constellation of Euro-centered thought (on Kristeva, see Ahmed 2004; on Butler, see Alcoff 2006 and Hames-García 2011; on Foucault, see Ross 2005). Women-of-color feminisms and queer-of-color theory in the United States, and more recently, multicultural feminisms in Latin America,[10] refuse to contract colonialism. That is, by refusing to submit to the logic of a colonizing grammar that positions itself not only as superior but also as more encompassing and universal than vernacular meanings and practices. In that vein, to turn away from Cornejo's *queer touch* (354) involves shifting this inquiry toward the locus of decolonial thinking I just mentioned.

Gender and sexuality studies approach language use mostly for its way of conveying social positioning across power differentials (Cameron and Kulick 2003; Leap 1996). Seldom do they encounter languages as the realities that they are (Arteaga 1994) and what they contribute to the study of social ontologies or the understandings-meanings of the basic entities of our realities. I now turn to this type of engagement with *travesti* embodiments in Argentina and Gloria Wekker's rendering of *mati* work in Surinam.

Travestis perform "brothel-like" (*prostibular*) stylizations of their bodily presentations (Fernandez 2004). This esthetic domain in the sex trade, in which they find a livelihood to avoid endemic poverty, realizes material culture at its most intimate scale, corporeality. It points to dissident racialized ways, actualizing an imaginary of hypersexualization among the lower and racialized classes in Latin America. The protoeugenicist foundation of Argentina's civilizing project toward the end of the nineteenth century cast the *lunfardo* underworld of immigrants and racialized internal exiles as the threatening environment where the unruly ethos of tango spawned: petit-thief schemes, cabarets, brothels, single entrepreneurial women, and flamboyant pimps.[11] Not unlike gauchos arriving from the country's interior at the end of that century, *travestis* from the Northwest settle in today's *zona roja* (vice zone) in the Palermo quarter of the city of Buenos Aires. The Afro, indigenous, and criollo roots of *milongas* (tango clubs), bordellos, and cabarets reflect a *travesti* esthetic, sustaining forms of embodiment in opposition to feminine bourgeois docility. Silicone-injected buttocks, padded hips, fishnet stockings, and six-inch stilettos are but a few of the markers fashioning the esthetic of *traviesa* (naughty) and *minón*. The term *minón* in Spanish represents the superlative of the *lunfardo* word *mina* (precious metal mine), which, over a century after its inception, still refers to the ambiguity of femininity among the lower classes. Both slang words signal embodiments that *travestis* aspire to shape and, in turn, are pushed to achieve.

Milongas at the turn of the twentieth century valued working-class women who were known as prostitutes, cabaret performers, and entrepreneurs. They entered the "low life," securing resources as waitresses, entertainers, and tricksters. This relative autonomy slipped into the *lunfardo* lexicon by way of *mina*, giving birth to new subjectivities. Gender and racial codes are meshed into a brothel-like esthetic, with which contemporary slang imbues the noun *traviesa* (naughty) in order to name *travesti* embodiment. This neologism plays on the sound "trav" shared by both words.

A native of the Argentinean northwest, Lohana Berkins is a well-known activist and 2003 Felipa de Souza awardee. With respect to the stylization of *travesti* embodiments, Berkins enables a transing methodology to contend against the contradictions of coloniality. Rather than asserting that *travesti* embodiments are anchored by mimicking femininity or marking the flesh this or that way with chemical or surgical modifications, she encounters bodily possibilities in the midst of others, in an intersubjective fashion that she calls *así* (like that). The Spanish modal adverb "*así*" translates into English by making visible within the target language a demonstrative pronoun, *eso* (that), which remains implicit in the source language. Drawing upon *eso*, Berkins linguistically marks her relative positioning, proximity, and distance among nonnormative embodiments.[12] She did not know how they had become *eso*, but the very first time she ran into them, Berkins knew that she was motivated to become "like that" (*así*). This modality of becoming points to histories of carnality, reassembled by linking togetherness with dissident racialized ways, enmeshed in the making of *lunfardo* intimacies.

On the decolonial modalities of language use, Gloria Wekker offers inspiring research on West African grammatical principles that undergird Creole spoken among Afro-Surinamese working-class women. She focuses on the *mati* work, an Afro-diasporic institution of intimate belonging that contests monogamous heterosexuality among subaltern subjects. Her ethnography captures non-Western ways of living and being with others, webs of erotic selfhood materially produced through activity and connectivity.

Citing one of her interactions with Mis' Juliette, an eighty-four-year-old partaker in *mati* work, Wekker refers to her learning curve with Sranan Tongo, the Creole spoken in Surinam. At first trying to anchor the *mati* work to a "dominant Euro-American" model of envisioning sexual identity (2006: 13), Wekker asked Mis' Juliette if she was a mati ("Juliette na wan matisma, no?"). Wekker's interlocutor replied, almost annoyed at this failure of cross-cultural translation, by stating, "Ma di m' e srib' nanga umasma, dan m' e mati" (But since I'm sleeping with women, then I mati). This emphasis on action and positioning, in which *mati* enacts subjectivity, goes beyond the mere performative ontology of postmodern selfhood. It decolonially steers this conversation by foregrounding embodiments in their carnal porosity, no longer dependent on the zero degree, the human universal, of the psychic life of power but instead dependent on histories of power differentials wherein the human/nonhuman distinction is paramount. For Afro-Surinamese Creole women, the decolonizing turn involves engaging the Winti religion, with its principles of multiplicitous selfhood and nondichotomous contiguity between the worldly/nonworldly. For racialized *travestis* of the Andes, it involves Aymara- and Quechua-infused worldviews.[13] For *las conchitas*, it may be worth exploring whether indigenous thinking underwrites their *huachafería* style.

In the vein of women of color's epistemic disobedience, this essay engaged transing methodologies through which a queer touch may be revealed as colonizing violence. Mis' Juliette and Berkins, *m' e mati* and *así*, respectively, call on us to dwell in the opacity of non-Western distinctions of the real, those able to animate realities in which the metaphysics of events, doing rather than being, connectivity rather than individuality, degrees of differentiating rather than either/or divides, belong in and across always already vernacular histories and ecologies of embodied difference.

Pedro Javier DiPietro is an assistant professor in the Department of Women's and Gender Studies at Syracuse University. He works at the intersection of decolonial feminisms, women-of-color thought, and critical theories of race and sexuality.

Notes

1.   For an account of social ontology, see Alcoff 2007.
2.   Stryker, Currah, and Moore (2008) articulate the critical potential of transing epistemologies and methodologies.
3.   Kai Green's subversion of the ethnographic genre in "The Essential I/Eye in We" (2015) is a powerful invocation of shared accountability. It performs a call to sustain "trans*" as intersubjective negotiations. Although attuned to sending waves across rather than to or

from trans(ing)(s), the notion of liminality pertaining to "masculine of center (MoC) people of color" (188) collapses into "androgyny" as point of self- and collective restructuring (194–95). The rather limited review of Toni Cade Bambara's reflections on Black alterities beyond masculine/feminine dimorphism requires a deeper engagement with not only Black feminist thought but also with historiography on both Afro-diasporic principles of self-formation and African American urban and nonurban restructurings of nonbeinghood. This tension is heightened by the voice-over on the filmic version (DrGreen85 2011) of Green's essay, repeating for about thirty seconds the shifting phrase "These are the moments where there's nothing (else) (left) (but) to say but so much more *to be*" (my emphasis).

4.   For an approach to racialization and its assembling of flesh and anatomy beyond the modernist mind/body split, see Weheliye 2014.

5.   Judith Halberstam follows this additive framework. For instance, in "Mackdaddy" (1997), masculinity is not quite an articulated category. Instead, it is intersected with race (104), "inflected" (106), constricted by race (106), and in confluence with race (117).

6.   The plurality of embodiments that bring me to decolonizing praxis are produced within networks of *travesti* belonging in the Andean northwest of Argentina and networks of queer-of-color belonging in the Latina/o counterculture of the San Francisco Bay area. Most but not all in the Andean networks identify as *travestis*, while those in the bay area as *jotas* and *jotos*. By *jotas* and *jotos*, mostly Mexican Americans and Chicanas/os signal nonheteronormative subjective positionings. Both networks cultivate subjectivities irreducible to modern sexual identities.

7.   Amalia Mesa-Bains (1999) and Laura Pérez (2007) theorize esthetic strategies of minoritized Chicana/o cultural production such as *rasquache* and *domesticana rasquache*. Although perceived as tacky by the mainstream, *rasquache* affirms delegitimized Chicana/o culture, an attitudinal disposition imbued by barrio sensibility. Comparatively, in the worlds of Itala/o, does *huachafería* belong within a realm of cultural affirmation resisting transliteration into "queerness"?

8.   *Domestication* and *foreignization* describe translation strategies. Choosing either is linked to the linguistic status of the languages that translation interweaves (see Machali 2012: 75).

9.   Cornejo provides no rationale for translating "un désir-inquiétude" into "queer" on Foucault's interview about friendship.

10.   For a representative selection of this scholarship, see DiPietro 2015.

11.   *Lunfardo* is a slang developed by criminals in the late nineteenth century. Created to remain unintelligible before policemen, it combined the Italian dialect *Lombardo* with elements from Quechua and African languages and Gaucho speech.

12.   This marking of relative positioning resembles Itala/o's reference to being *gay* with *gays* and *travesti* with *travestis*.

13.   For an initial conversation about racialization, indigeneity, and *travesti* embodiment, see DiPietro 2015.

References:

Ahmed, Sara. 2004. "Declarations of Whiteness: The Non-performativity of Anti-Racism." *Borderlands* 3, no. 2. www.borderlands.net.au/vol3no2_2004/ahmed_declarations.htm.

Alcoff, Linda. 2006. *Visible Identities: Race, Gender, and the Self*. New York: Oxford University Press.

———. 2007. "Comparative Race, Comparative Racisms." In *Race or Ethnicity? On Black and Latino Identity*, edited by Jorge Gracia, 170–88. Ithaca, NY: Cornell University Press.

Arteaga, Alfred. 1994. "An Other Tongue." In *An Other Tongue: Nation and Ethnicity in the Linguistic Borderlands*, edited by Alfred Arteaga, 9–33. Durham, NC: Duke University Press.

Cameron, Deborah, and Don Kulick. 2003. *Language and Sexuality*. Cambridge: Cambridge University Press.

Cornejo, Giancarlo. 2014. "For a Queer Pedagogy of Friendship." *TSQ* 1, no. 3: 352–67.

de la Cadena, Marisol. 2000. *Indigenous Mestizos: The Politics of Race and Culture in Cuzco, Peru, 1919–1991*. Durham, NC: Duke University Press.

DiPietro, Pedro. 2015. "Decolonizing *Travesti* Space in Buenos Aires: Race, Sexuality, and Sideways Relationality." *Gender, Place, and Culture*. doi.org/10.1080/0966369X.2015.1058756.

DrGreen85. 2011. "No Name." YouTube video, 9:08. February 28. www.youtube.com/watch?v=0W75GXIXP0s.

Fausto-Sterling, Anne. 2000. *Sexing the Body: Gender Politics and the Construction of Sexuality*. New York: Basic Books.

Fernandez, Josefina. 2004. *Cuerpos desobedientes: Travestismo e identidad de género* (*Unruly Bodies: Transvestitism and Gender Identity*). Buenos Aires: Edhasa.

Gill-Peterson, Julian. 2014. "The Technical Capacities of the Body: Assembling Race, Technology, and Transgender." *TSQ* 1, no. 3: 402–18.

Green, Kai M. 2015. "The Essential I/Eye in We: A Black TransFeminist Approach to Ethnographic Film." *Black Camera* 6, no. 2: 187–200.

Halberstam, Judith. 1997. "Mackdaddy, Superfly, Rapper: Gender, Race, and Masculinity in the Drag King Scene." *Social Text*, nos. 52–53: 104–31.

Hames-García, Michael. 2011. "Queer Theory Revisited." In *Gay Latino Studies: A Critical Reader*, edited by Michael Hames-García and Ernesto Javier Martínez, 19–45. Durham, NC: Duke University Press.

Hammonds, Evelyn. 1994. "Black (W)holes and the Geometry of Black Female Sexuality." *differences* 6, nos. 2–3: 127–45.

Leap, William L. 1996. *Word's Out: Gay Men's English*. Minneapolis: University of Minnesota Press.

Lugones, María. 2007. "Heterosexualism and the Colonial/Modern Gender System." *Hypatia* 22, no. 1: 186–209.

Machali, Rochayah. 2012. "Cases of Domestication and Foreignization in the Translation of Indonesian Poetry into English: A Preliminary Inquiry." *Language and Culture* 3, no. 4: 72–84.

Mesa-Bains, Amalia. 1999. "Domesticana: The Sensibility of Chicana Rasquache." *Aztlan: A Journal of Chicano Studies* 24, no. 2: 157–67.

Niño-Murcia, Mercedes. 2003. "'English Is Like the Dollar': Hard Currency Ideology and the Status of English in Peru." *World Englishes* 22, no. 2: 121–42.

Pérez, Laura Elisa. 2007. *Chicana Art: The Politics of Aesthetic and Spiritual Altarities*. Durham, NC: Duke University Press.

Quijano, Aníbal. 1978. *Imperialismo, clases sociales y estado en el Perú, 1890–1930: El Perú en la crisis de los años 30* (*Imperialism, Social Class, and State in Peru, 1890–1930: Peru during the Crisis of the 1930s*). Lima: Mosca Azul.

Rafael, Vicente. (1988) 1993. *Contracting Colonialism: Translation and Christian Conversion in Tagalog Society under Early Spanish Rule*. Durham, NC: Duke University Press.

Roen, Katrina. 2006. "Transgender Theory and Embodiment: The Risk of Racial Margin-alization." In *The Transgender Studies Reader*, edited by Susan Stryker and Stephen Whittle, 656–65. New York: Routledge.

Ross, Loretta. 2011. "The Origin of the Phrase 'Women of Color.'" 2011. YouTube video, 2:59. February 15. www.youtube.com/watch?v =82vl34mi4Iw.

Ross, Marlon. 2005. "Beyond the Closet as Raceless Paradigm." In *Black Queer Studies: A Critical Anthology*, edited by E. Patrick Johnson and Mae G. Henderson, 161–88. Durham, NC: Duke University Press.

Snorton, C. Riley, and Jin Haritaworn. 2013. "Trans Necropolitics: A Transnational Reflection of Violence, Death, and the Trans of Color Afterlife." In *The Transgender Studies Reader 2*, edited by Susan Stryker and Aren Aizura, 66–76. New York: Routledge.

Stryker, Susan, Paisley Currah, and Lisa Jean Moore. 2008. "Introduction: Trans-, Trans, or Transgender?" *WSQ* 36, nos. 3–4: 11–22.

Stryker, Susan, and Sullivan, Nikki. 2009. "King's Member, Queen's Body: Transsexual Surgery, Self-Demand Amputation, and the Somatechnics of Sovereign Power." In *Somatechnics: Queering the Technologisation of Bodies*, edited by Nikki Sullivan and Samantha Murray, 49–61. Farnham, UK: Ashgate.

Weheliye, Alexander G. 2014. *Habeas Viscus: Racializing Assemblages, Biopolitics, and Black Feminist Theories of the Human*. Durham, NC: Duke University Press.

Wekker, Gloria. 2006. *The Politics of Passion: Women's Sexual Culture in the Afro-Surinamese Diaspora*. New York: Columbia University Press.

Wynter, Sylvia. 2003. "Unsettling the Coloniality of Being/Power/Truth/Freedom: Towards the Human, after Man, Its Overrepresentation—An Argument." *New Centennial Review* 3, no. 3: 257–337.

Hacking the Body

A Transfeminist War Machine

LUCÍA EGAÑA and MIRIAM SOLÁ

Translated by MICHAEL BRASHER

Abstract In this article, the authors address the relationship between artistic production and political activism in Barcelona's transfeminist scene, by reflecting on the first stage of their joint research project, *War Machines: Transfeminist Practices of Representation*, which maps and interprets the past ten years of transfeminist cultural production there. Transfeminist art practices, the authors argue, offer new strategies that supplement the operational logic of more traditional activisms by also acting in and through creative processes, principally by conceiving the body itself, in relation to technology, as a site for political transformation.

Keywords postpornography, transfeminism, Barcelona

*W*ar Machines: Transfeminist Practices of Representation is a work in process that maps transfeminist cultural production in Barcelona over the last ten years.[1] It is a work that inverts the gaze, turning back to document the emergence of transfeminism there from the concrete activist practices of local feminisms, modes of creative expression, and specific artistic productions, and at the same time to propose situated methods for visual research. This research is a result of the trajectories of our personal lives, as well as our experiences in activism, cultural production, and *trans-marica-bollo-feminist* thought—underlying inspirations that don't always manifest in clear and distinct forms in the work itself. We investigate the interaction between art and politics in the context of transfeminism, while at the same time playing active roles in diverse spaces of militancy.

Transfeminism in Barcelona

Since the first decade of the twenty-first century, queer theories and sociopolitical movements have materialized in Barcelona primarily through the postporn and transfeminist movements. Through the concept of "transfeminism," which closely

TSQ: Transgender Studies Quarterly ★ Volume 3, Numbers 1–2 ★ May 2016
DOI 10.1215/23289252-3334223   © 2016 Duke University Press

approximates the notion of a "queer feminism," some feminist organizations have claimed a word that feels more embodied and more meaningfully contextualized for them than *queer*.[2] At the same time, the concept has allowed the articulation of an entire series of new minority discourses, and of new political-cultural practices that are emerging in feminist, *okupas*,[3] lesbian, anticapitalist, fag, and transgender communities. Such collectives are based on fragmented visions of the subject of feminist representation, and they focus on kinds of individuals that traditional feminism hasn't fully addressed as political subjects, such as transsexual or transgender people, dykes, butches, sex workers, fags, and people with functional diversity, to name but a few.

Little by little, transfeminism has woven a network between groups both within and beyond Catalonia, working through such questions as pornography and sex work; trans depathologization; squatting; migrant resistance; economic precarity; the critique of state feminism; the institutionalization of the LGBT movement; open-source software, copyleft, creative-commons licensing, antisurveillance and data obfuscation strategies; self-training and peer-to-peer education that allows more access to technology for more kinds of people who have been excluded from it; and performance and the body. It is within these multiple contexts that the idea of a transfeminist alliance first began to take shape, a vision first expressed during the Granada Feminist Conference of 2009 and with the publication of the "Manifesto for the Transfeminist Insurrection" (Ideadestroyingmuros 2010). A few months later, this alliance definitively crystallized through the "Transfeminist Conference: Under Construction," held in the squatted Can Vies Social Center, Barcelona, in April 2010.

Mixing Research, Friendship, Activism, and Life

In this work, we address the production of art within activist movements, without seeking to legitimize it as activism per se.[4] The cross between artistic creation and artistic criticism, between political action and cultural action, seems to us an appropriate place to focus on dissident micropolitical practices. This allows us to reassess the cultural production present in any political activity, rather than ascribing legitimacy only to institutional art spaces—an analytical cut that hierarchizes the dichotomy of formal and informal production. We therefore propose a research agenda that doesn't follow the standard protocols of heteronormative academia, not only in terms of its content but also regarding its styles of research: an investigation by proximity, taking as its subjects some friends and companions in activism; and a process of open, inconclusive research that provides its findings as they happen, and as they are produced. Rather than proposing and proving a formal hypothesis, this research seeks to actively contribute to cultural and creative production, to its documentation and interpretation.

First, we conducted three interviews in video format with key activists and colleagues in Barcelona who have transfeminist art practices. These conversations allowed us to discern two articulated axes of analysis:

1. Dissident bodies and representations of gender and sexuality: Along this axis we grouped cultural, visual, and performative works that operate principally through the body as a locus for political work. This includes work that explicitly focuses on sex and sexuality (postporn); representations of bodies considered by the dominant culture to be abject and/or deviant (disabled, trans, intersex, fat); and works that use the body as a basis for resistance to normalized hetero-binary strategies of gender, sex, and sexuality.

2. Technologies, free software, transfeminist machines, and networks: The practices included in this line of analysis are related to projects, spaces, and works of cultural production that address technology as a site for feminist and transfeminist activism. Such works emphasize autonomy, self-instruction, DIY (do-it-yourself), peer networking, and empowerment, among other themes.

In our desire to implement other ways of doing research, we constructed a series of graphs of ideas—conceptual maps—drawn from the conversations we conducted. This exercise allowed us to perform analysis and interpretation and, at the same time, to deploy a critical and creative methodology. Alongside these conceptual maps, we made some collages from textual works discussed in the literature review that provided the theoretical framework for our project. For us, the collage was something playful that helped us materialize theory, that let us grasp it in an embodied form, departitioning it from objects, and giving it another order of meaning. These artisanal techniques—something like making a fanzine—also linked us with methodologies of production specific to DIY culture and, ultimately, to spaces where knowledge is produced in a manner parallel to the circuits of academic knowledge production. All the materials generated through this process of creation-research (video interviews, graphical maps of concepts, and collages of theoretical texts) are freely available on a website with a creative-commons license.

Postpornographic Machines

Artistic and cultural production has been fundamental to transfeminist politics (Sentamans 2013: 31–44). As Marisela Montenegro, Joan Pujol, and Nagore García point out, a number of artistic movements exist in metropolitan Barcelona that are strongly influenced by queer theories and are articulated with feminism and lesbian culture; they also question sexual categories, thereby opening "a space of recognition within cultural innovation in the area of sex-gender" (2011: 157). These movements are part of a tradition that seeks to destabilize sex/gender in a politically productive way, by opening up possibilities for the empowerment of sexual practices, bodies, and identities marginalized and disparaged by the dominant culture.

In keeping with this politico-aesthetic sensibility, one of the key arenas for transfeminist artistic expressions in Barcelona has been postpornography. Postpornography, according to María Llopis, is "queer politics, postfeminist, punk, DIY, but also a complex view of sex which includes an analysis of the origin of our desire and a direct confrontation with the source of our sexual fantasies" (Llopis 2010: 22). Postporn practices develop forms of sex-gender-sexuality representation that problematize the male/female binary and compulsory heterosexuality, using the body as a support for visibilizing abject, antinormative, and pathologized sexualities. In this sense, postpornographic practices further elaborate creative and theoretical work on bodies and technologies, articulating them together in an extended manner.

Postpornographic sensibilities materially express themselves in various ways: video production, performance, photography, creative writing, and a lot of online activity through blogs, websites, and social networks. Some common features persist in many postpornographic works. As Elena Urko (2014) says, "Some years, there was a very specific style because we all worked together, we were friends. So many of the productions of those years have a style that could be characterized as the style of Barcelona: bizarre practices, including BDSM, with a lot of DIY and cyberpunk props." We see in these works how Barcelona has become, almost by chance, a place of reference for that to which radical and politicized postpornographic production refers. This is because of a number of elements that have coincided in the same place: migration from multiple regions, a strong *okupas* (squatting) and hacker scene in the first decade of the new millenium, conditions of economic precariousness that make it difficult to survive, and accessible institutional art spaces capable of accommodating postpornographic work (Ziga 2009; Llopis 2010; Torres 2010).

Different kinds of postporn practices take place in dissimilar kinds of spaces throughout the city, ranging from DIY to the more institutional art spaces, from social centers occupied by museums to the public space of the street, from large parties to intimate domestic spaces. It is difficult to ascribe postporn practices to any particular kind of environment, precisely because they treat dynamics that are interwoven with life and sexuality and with the body itself, as bodies and sexualities go everywhere. What is clear is that, since the second half of the 2000s, postpornographic politics and aesthetics have constructed a space in which minority practices and discourses now run alongside dominant cultural geographies. Proposals that emerge from museums and other cultural institutions coexist with an infinity of autonomously organized proposals that emerge from social movements, such as Muestra Marrana, which has taken place almost every year since 2008, the TransMarikaBollo Video Festival, and Queeruption 8, to name but a few of these self-organized events (for more references and history of postporn in Barcelona, see Egaña 2011).

Barcelona also provides a particular intellectual and theoretical context in which the politics of the body and technology are closely linked to postporn sensibilities. As Klau Kinki (2014) argues, "Postporn treats gender itself as a technology, the body as technology, and opens up a channel for relating to it directly." This preoccupation with the body and the construction of sexuality results in a composite of artistic practices and machinic processes, grounded in new understandings of sovereignty as it pertains to the body and to machines. Such positions grant agency to the technological—a perspective that really has not been considered much within other political movements, in which technology functions only as an instrumentality. Within transfeminism, however, we can observe how the technological is, together with the body, a space from which to transform reality. Such a social transformation requires autonomy, construed as being able to count on one's own abilities, in which we can "rely less on patriarchal and hegemonic structures," as well as having access to "free servers" where "they do not control or censor us." "To know the tools," Kinki reminds us, and to be able to solve for ourselves the technical problems necessary for making technology more accessible to more people, "is also a political thing."

In this sense, the hacker and open-source software movement has served not only as a means of technical support for transfeminist production but also as metaphors that exemplify the practices transfeminists attempt to carry out. Open-source software offers a set of liberties that private software restricts: freedom to use, copy, modify, and distribute at will. Transferred to the field of gender politics, these ideas provide a new framework for thinking, manipulating, and modifying bodies and desires outside the framework of compulsory heterosexuality.

Conclusion

After completing the first stage of our research, it is quite clear to us that our local transfeminisms successfully enact new corporeal practices of knowing and knowledge production through creative expression. They make new uses of the body and technology, which are themselves arenas for political action. Transfeminist politics and artistic-cultural production feed off one another. This politico-aesthetic relation is key to generating new imagery that directly informs the ways in which people with nonnormative genders and sexualities build their identities and subjectivities, perhaps in a more liberatory and autonomous manner, while also helping to create new social and cultural space for them to exist within.

Lucía Egaña is a Chilean artist and activist, with a license in visual art from Pontificia Universidad Católica de Chile, a diploma in aesthetics from Universidad Diego Portales (Chile), and a master's in creative documentary from Universidad Autónoma de Barcelona, where she is currently completing a doctorate in audiovisual communication. Lucía co-organizes the Muestra Marrana festival and is the author with Josefa Ruiz-Tagle of the book *Encyclopedia of Love in the Time of Porn* (2014).

Miriam Solá studied philosophy in Murcia and gender studies in Barcelona. A researcher and activist, Miriam recently edited the anthology *Transfeminisms: Epistemes, Frictions, and Flows* with Elena Urko.

Notes

1. *Máquinas de guerra* is the name of the project whose first stages were carried out between September 2014 and February 2015 by Miriam Solá and Lucía Egaña (see Egaña and Solá 2014).

2. The word *queer* in Spanish doesn't have any meaning. The question about its translation is an open debate not without conflict because, among other things, of the colonial relationship between English and Spanish. The word *queer* is a recent anglicized word, the use of which is restricted to academia, and does not refer to stigma, insult, or a history of violence, let alone the possibility of reappropriation or redefinition of injury. Therefore, its use in Spanish is stripped of all subversive potential.

3. Variously, the squat movement and/or, post-2011, the Occupy movement.—Translator

4. The translator and managing editor were not entirely clear about the intent of this sentence when translating: "En este trabajo nos propusimos abordar la producción cultural como una parte del activismo, y no buscar desde/en las producciones legitimadas como arte los componentes activistas."—Trans.

References

Egaña, Lucía, dir. 2011. *Mi sexualidad es una creación artística* (*My Sexuality Is an Art Creation*). Spain, self produced.

Egaña, Lucía, and Miriam Solá. 2014. *Máquinas de guerra* (*War Machines*). Políticas transfeministas de la representación (Transfeminist Politics of Representation). www.politicas transfeministas.wordpress.com (accessed November 7, 2015).

Ideadestroyingmuros. 2010. "Manifesto per un'insurrezione transfemminista" ("Manifesto for the Transfeminist Insurrection"). January 1. ideadestroyingmuros.blogspot.com.es/2010/01 /manifesto-per-uninsurrezione.html.

Kinki, Klau. 2014. "'Máquinas de guerra': Entrevista a Klau" ("'War Machines': Interview with Klau Kinki"). Vimeo video, 32:48. December 30. www.vimeo.com/115642829.

Llopis, María. 2010. *El postporno era eso* (*Postporn Was This*). Barcelona: Melusina.

Montenegro, Marisela, Joan Pujol, and Nagore García. 2011. "Reconstruccions dels cossos lesbians: Aspirema un circuit postpornogràfic" ("Reconstruction of Lesbian Bodies: We Aspire to a Postporn Circuit"). In *Accions i reinvencions: Cultures lèsbiques a la Catalunya del tombant del segle XX-XXI* (*Actions and Reinventions: Lesbic Cultures in Catalonia in the Twentieth and Twenty-first Centuries*), edited by Meri Torras. Barcelona: UOC-UAB.

Sentamans, Tatiana. 2013. "Redes transfeministas y nuevas políticas de la representación sexual (I): Diagramas de flujos" ("Transfeminist Networks and the New Politics of Sexual Representation [I]: Flow Chart"). In *Transfeminismos, epistemes, fricciones y flujos* (*Transfeminisms, Epistemes, Frictions, and Flows*), edited by Miriam Solá and Elena Urko. Tafalla, Spain: Txalaparta.

Torres, Diana J. 2010. *Pornoterrorismo* (*Pornoterrorism*). Tafalla, Spain: Txalaparta.

Urko, Elena. 2014. "'Máquinas de guerra': Entrevista a Urko" ("'War Machines': Interview with Elena Urko"). Vimeo video, 15:21. January 9, 2015. www.vimeo.com/116365079.

Ziga, Itziar. 2009. *Devenir perra* (*Become a Bitch*). Barcelona: Melusina.

One-Eyed Dog

A. FINN ENKE

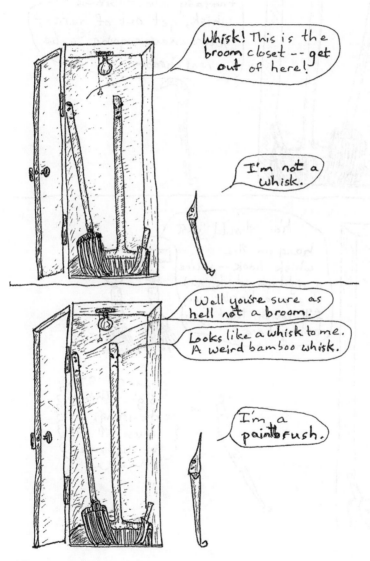

Figure 1. Ink and watercolor on paper

TSQ: Transgender Studies Quarterly * Volume 3, Numbers 1–2 * May 2016
DOI 10.1215/23289252-3334235   © 2016 Duke University Press

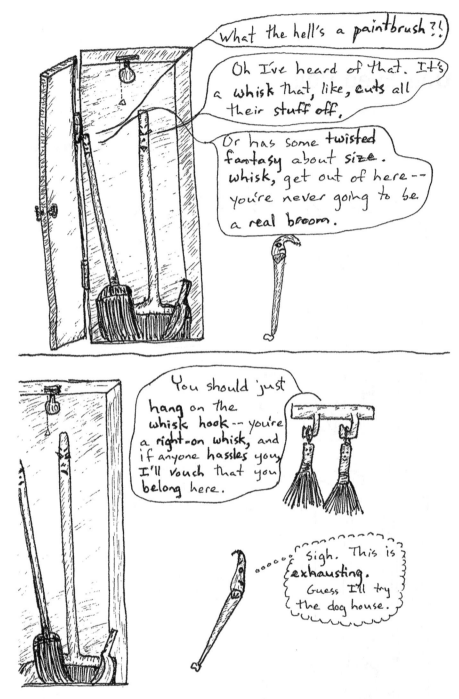

Figure 2. Ink and watercolor on paper

Figure 3. Ink and watercolor on paper

Finn Enke is professor of gender and women's studies, history, and LGBTQ studies at the University of Wisconsin–Madison. Finn is currently working on a graphic novel, "With Finn and Wing: Growing Up Amphibious in a Nuclear Age."

Transfeminism

Something Else, Somewhere Else

KARINE ESPINEIRA and MARIE-HÉLÈNE/SAM BOURCIER

Abstract The aim of this article is to trace genealogies of transfeminism in France and in Spain. It examines the relationship of transfeminism alongside third-wave and second-wave feminist political objectives, the struggle against transpathologization, and the resistance to the binary sex/gender system. It also addresses the politics of translating *queer* in the European context, showing how transfeminism is a critique of Anglo white queer theory and its capacity for disembodiment. The postporn movement—a distinctive feature of Spanish transfeminism—is offered as a productive use of the body as a means to resist biopower through creative counterproduction and space occupation. The authors argue that transfeminism is about not only resignification but also rematerialization and is a way of getting away from English as an imperialistic language and a reaction against the theoretical excesses of US first-wave white queer theory.
Keywords postporn, transpathologization, queer, translation, sex dualism, biopolitics, Outrans, Le Zoo

Transfeminism started in France in the late 1990s and formally went public when the trans collective Outrans published a statement, "Transfeminismes," first in 2009 and again in revised form in 2012 (Outrans 2009, 2012, 2013). Transfeminism first entered public discourse in Spain at about the same time, in the context of a state conference on feminism in Cordoba in 2000. This article discusses the recent, interrelated development of transfeminist politics and perspectives in these two countries.

Outrans

As stated in the Outrans declaration, "transfeminism is a major opportunity to build a politics of resistance and alliance, because we consider domination to be a multilayered system that produces cross-oppressions, including transphobia. Our analysis is a feminist one, drawing from third-wave feminism, queer feminism, and postidentity feminism" (Outrans 2012). Within this coalitional politics of resistance, we see two fights that are specific to trans people: the battle against the

TSQ: Transgender Studies Quarterly * Volume 3, Numbers 1–2 * May 2016
DOI 10.1215/23289252-3334247   © 2016 Duke University Press

medical and psychiatric control of trans lives, and resistance to the totalizing and compulsory system of two exclusive binary genders. Regarding the first struggle, against transpathologization, Outrans aligns itself with Stop Trans Pathologization (STP), an emancipationist group that seeks to abolish the various diagnostic classifications of trans people, whether in the *Diagnostic and Statistical Manual of Mental Disorders* of the American Psychiatric Association or in the World Health Organization's (WHO) International Classification of Diseases.[1] STP is a broad coalitional movement that has managed to unite three hundred collectives on five continents, and it has contributed in a major way to thinking transfeminism in Spain. Regarding the latter struggle, in favor of gender proliferation, Outrans embraces the growing tendency to deploy such self-defining terms of identification as *FtX*, *Ft**, *FtU*, *trans'*, *trans**, *transsexual*, *trans woman*, *trans men*, *trans boy*, *trans variant*, or *gender fluid*—to name but a few of those documented by recent research (Espineira 2012; Giami, Beaubatie, and Le Bail 2010).[2] We consider this position to emerge from a feminist critique of the sex/gender system that, on the one hand, interrogates the power relationship between men and women and, on the other hand, supports the production of new gender formations that reject and move beyond compulsory heteronormativity and its enabling gender norms (Rubin 1975, 1984). We are answering Patrick Califia's (2003: 221) call to "trash the clinic and burn down the beauty parlor" and liberate ourselves from the apparatuses that manufacture standardized femininities and masculinities.

French Transfeminism as an Offspring of Third-Wave Feminism

Third-wave feminism foregrounds "a new understanding of the power of women and girls," the "politicization of popular culture and new technologies of communication," and "the claiming of a positive sexuality open to all experience" (Mensah 2005: 15). Transfeminism's special contribution to the third wave is its insistence that a specifically transfeminist subject be included within feminism, and its demand for accountability regarding the changes that this insistence brings to feminist thinking and organizing. In her 2003 "Transfeminist Manifesto," Emi Koyama wrote that while transfeminism is certainly open to queers, intersex people, trans men, and nontrans women, it is "primarily a movement by and for trans women who view their liberation to be intrinsically linked to the liberation of all women and beyond" (Koyama 2003: 245). Four years later, Julia Serano wrote in *Whipping Girl: A Transsexual Woman on Sexism and the Scapegoating of Femininity*, "Because anti-trans discriminations is steeped in traditional sexism, it is not simply enough for trans activists to challenge binary gender norms (i.e., oppositional sexism)—we must also challenge the idea that femininity is inferior to masculinity and that femaleness is inferior to maleness. In other words, by necessity, trans activism must be at its core a feminist movement" (Serano 2007: 16).

Outrans shares this perspective and also insists on coalitional practices and intersectional analyses that expand the subject of feminism—another point of view that draws heavily from anglophone third-wave feminist traditions. Transfeminism aims to counter the homogeneity of the white, straight, and abstract subject of feminism. As did lesbian feminists, feminists of color, queer feminists, and cyber feminists before us, trans people are fighting feminism's exclusionary tendencies (Dorvil 2007). Since no definition of "oppression applies to all women any time, in any place and in any situation" (Blais et al. 2007: 143), the transfeminist paradigm relies on intersectional approaches such as Kimberlé Crenshaw's articulation of gender, race, and class (1994), and recent elaboration of intersectionality in the French context by Christine Delphy (2006), Elsa Dorlin (2008), and others.[3]

Multiplicity, variety, and hybridity remain key organizing concepts in the effort to build a feminism inclusive of ethnic, cultural, sexual, and economic minorities; women of color; lesbians; prostitutes; transsexuals; transgender people; and other marginalized groups. More recently, queer anarcho-feminist critics of capitalism have added their voices to this transfeminist call for an inclusive feminism that also encompasses antiliberals, antiracists, and anarchists. J. Rogue notes in *Queering Anarchism* that, while "the feminist movement has a history of internal hierarchies" and that the "movement as a whole has not resolved these hierarchical tendencies," a number of groups have persistently spoken up regarding their marginalization within feminism, "in particular, transgendered women" (Rogue 2009).[4] Rogue insists that differences must be discussed rather than rejected; she explains that "one cannot address the position of women without also addressing their class, race, sexuality, ability, and all other aspects of their identity and experiences," including transgender status. All forms of oppression and exploitation are "intimately related and reinforce each other" and attempting "to address them singly (i.e., 'sexism' divorced from racism, capitalism, etc.) does not lead to a clear understanding of the patriarchal system."

Earlier French Transfeminism: Another Genealogical Thread

Transfeminism cannot be reduced to a single definition, single perspective, or single trajectory of theoretical development—even when tracing its roots in a tendency as diffuse as the feminist third wave. Excavating the history of Le Zoo—the first French queer group, founded in 1996—reveals another genealogy from which feminism entered French trans politics. Le Zoo's Q seminars (1996–2003), organized by Marie-Hélène/Sam Bourcier, helped raise feminist consciousness for many trans people doing trans politics, especially those who resisted inclusion in the *transidentités* movement they considered more normative and assimilationist, who then began to borrow concepts from feminist thought (Bourcier 1998). It was crucial for participants in Le Zoo to think through concepts of sexual difference and inequality as a basis for deconstructing gender binarity. As Maud-Yeuse Thomas noted when the *transidentités* movement was in its infancy, many assimilationist trans people did not want to be grouped together with homosexuals, prostitutes, transvestites, or the new transgender movement, and they sought instead to simply be accepted as members of a society they did not want to change (Thomas and Espineira 1998).[5] Those of us who sought to distance ourselves from this sort of trans identity politics constructed a different political and theoretical framework. We sought to disengage from the politics of binary sexual difference, which we felt could only reinscribe inequalities. We did this through trans identifications and trans practices, and by not worrying anymore about complying with the compulsory order of gender or caring whether we were either only women or only men. As two self-identified trans lesbians and their allies in Le Zoo said, "We identify as trans because we are doing politics, not because of our transsexualism" (Espineira, et al. 1998: 114).

One root of French transfeminism begins in this milieu. Drawing from Monique Wittig's (1992) critique of heterosexuality as a political regime that oppresses women, as well as Judith Butler's (1990) gender performativity paradigm and her strategy of gender proliferation as resistance to the sex/gender system, Le Zoo focused on queer theory, subcultural expression, and the "epistemopolitics" of self-identified faggots, dykes, trans, bi, and queer people. The aim of Le Zoo's Q Seminar was to "widely circulate knowledge of the historical, social, political, and cultural construction of homosexuality, heterosexuality, bisexuality, transsexuality, and gender," to "highlight work that provides a hyperbolic critique of the formation and location of normative sexual and gender identities," and "to deconstruct foundational knowledges that naturalize the disciplining of bodies" (Andrieu 2008: 5). Since a new trans politics arrived on the French feminist scene via Le Zoo, a transfeminist perspective has influenced many different groups and collectives. Nowadays, all the French anarchist, antiassimilationist, and antisexist groups fight against patriarchy and see sexual difference as the origin of inequality.

Transfeminism in Spain: A Geopolitical Translation of *Queer*

The term *transfeminism* first appeared on the Spanish scene during the Jornadas Feministas Estatales (an annual national feminist conference) held in Cordoba in 2000; by the 2009 conference, it had become a familiar and persistent expression for reclaiming space for feminist trans people excluded from feminist circles and for building up a feminism based on a coalition of microgroups and identities, including "*okupas*, lesbians, anticapitalists, *maricas*, transgender people, and sex workers" (Solà 2013: 19).

More often than not, throughout the late twentieth century, both radical feminism and institutional feminism, as well as assimilationist lesbian and gay movements, have denied rights, agency, empowerment, and subcultural expression to trans people. Feminism typically reinscribes trans lives within hegemonic masculinities and femininities and, consequently, denies trans people the capacity to be feminist subjects. They may even consider trans people to be actual enemies of feminism. Transfeminism in Spain resists such feminist practices of exclusion and objectification by appropriating the term *feminism* itself, and by using the prefix *trans-* to signify a feminist trans subject or identity.[6] The *trans-* prefix is also meant to signal the process of crossing over or moving through the current impasses of feminist thought, rather than calling for "post-" feminism, as if there were no longer a need for feminist activism or analysis.

Many factors contribute to the strategy of feminism's abjected subjects' appropriating feminism for themselves, instead of subverting and transforming an insulting epithet, such as *queer* or its equivalents in Spanish. One such factor is the progress made by institutional feminism and its reformist politics of gender mainstreaming; another is the mainstreaming of the gay and lesbian movement in Europe. Queer collectives such as Smachieramenti in Bologna have made the same move, in order to make clear that the exclusion of trans people from feminism is now over (Smaschieramenti 2011; SomMovimentonazioAnale 2012).[7] Another factor has to do with translations of *queer* in different cultural and geopolitical contexts that aim to get rid of Anglo white queer theory and English as an imperialistic language:[8] "Sin embargo, en un gesto de desplazamiento geopolitico, pero cercano a los postulados queer, el concepto 'transfeminista' està siendo reivindicado por algunos colectivos trans-bollo-marica-feministas surgidos en los últimos años en el Estado español. Un conjunto de microgrupos han reclamado esta palabra que suena mejor en castellano que el término queer" (Solà 2013: 19).[9] A similar strategy has been adopted in Brazil, where "palabra queer" is being translated as "pos-pornôs, transfeministas, loucas" (Lopes 2015).

Transfeminism might also be understood as a reaction against the theoretical excesses of first-wave white Anglo queer theory, whose poststructuralism promoted an abstract concept of political subjectivity. Transfeminism in Spain seeks to avoid this theoretical disembodiment of the political subject by consistently referencing the body and its ongoing transformations as the main means of resisting biopower through creative biopolitical production and counterproduction. A new focus on the body through trans and crip bodies, along with a new focus on sexuality through the postporn movement, takes transfeminism where queer theory failed to go (Bourcier 2012).[10]

Postporn as a Transfeminist Praxis against Capitalism and Sex Dualism

In contrast to the Anglo queer constellation of the 1990s, transfeminism offers a new admixture of perspectives: a blend of Foucaldian biopolitics and feminist materialism rooted in the resurgence of Marxism after the recent violence of the economic crisis, and the subsequent programs of austerity and debt restructuring imposed on Spain by European and international institutions after the collapse of the financial markets. Transfeminism's political horizon is not abolitionist; rather, it is counterproductive: a material proliferation of new femininities and masculinities, of "abnormal" and monstrous bodies inserted into biopolitics, which overflow the fictional but foundational dualism at the heart of capitalist modernity—so-called "sexual difference." Transfeminism is not an abstract critique of this theoretical dualism. Rather, it traffics in actually existing nonbinary lives, bodies, identities, and genders on a collective social level. Collective "artivism," especially a performance-oriented politics of representation and enspacement, plays a crucial role in transfeminism precisely because it makes visible the lie of sexual dualism. Postporn performance activism in particular has become a distinctive feature of European transfeminism—countering the neoliberal reprivatization of the sexual sphere by publicly exposing the many ways in which the logic of binary sexual difference routinely fails.

Neoliberal politics, whether it emanates from the state or from private corporations, produces neoliberal subjectivities in part by reconfiguring the relationship between private and public, sexual and social. It demands the death of embodied subjects that defy this segregation of life into incommensurably separate spheres—of physical bodies that might otherwise produce new social formations and subcultures and, therefore, new bodies politic. Trans and queer urban space-making practices can counter the neoliberal spatial politics of zoning laws, social segregation, and gentrification. Many transfeminist collectives such as Quimera Rosa (2003), Post-op, ORGIA, and Ideadestroyingmuros[11] 2005, as well as individual artists such as Diana Pornoterrorista, work against the spatial logic of neoliberalism that manifests in most cities worldwide today. In 2010, many of these artists staged a collective performance in Barcelona called "Oh-Kaña" (Post-op et al. 2010), a tribute to José Pérez Ocaña, who used to walk naked in the streets of Madrid to protest Francisco Franco's dictatorship. Through this performance they brought prosthetized, gender-fucked, and cyborg bodies; queer bodies in fetish and leather gear—that is to say, monstrous antineoliberal embodied subjectivities produced in queer sex subcultures—into such public spaces as Las Ramblas and La Boqueria.

Transfeminist bodies stand today with the freaks, the crips, and the naked queers. They share the common project of reclaiming bodies that matter precisely because they are "unproductive" bodies capable of becoming bodies of pleasure dedicated to nonreproductive forms of sex, microsocial bodies that can reclaim and reconfigure space; they offer resistance to a neoliberal subjugation that aims to put bodies to work in worse conditions than ever before. Disruptive practices of embodiment have been lived by sexual minorities since at least the 1970s. Postporn practices today draw upon this resource produced by gay, lesbian, and queer BDSM cultures of the past. The passivity, anal objectification, cutting, and fist fucking that were practiced in dungeons and clubs by lesbian SM groups in the 1980s (such as Samois in San Francisco, and the Lesbian Sex Mafia in New York City) are now openly performed in the streets of Spanish cities by postporn transfeminist activists who know how to concretize and reenact their sexual and economic situations, and thereby to analyze the naturalizing and depoliticizing mechanisms at work in them.

"Queer" lately has been the target of harsh criticisms for its multiple perceived failures: internal racism, false promises of intersectionality, class privilege, the still burning issue of feminism. Chicana feminist Gloria Anzàldua has been given a postmortem footnote in the US academy as the person who first appropriated and subverted the pejorative term *queer* (Alarcon 1990), but in Europe, queer of color feminism is routinely excluded by the queer academic jet-setters who keep asking for obscene conference fees in the middle of one of the worst economic crises we have ever faced.[12] Transfeminism in Europe, whether in Le Zoo in Paris in the 1990s or in Bologna or Barcelona today, has thus come to play the vital role of advancing a critique of queer theory and politics—a critique necessitated first by the transnationalization of "queer" along the progressivist trajectory of US modernity and, second, by the refusal within Europe to adopt the anti-identitarian stance required by first-wave US queer theory.

Is this queer corpse worth reanimating, or should we let it die? In *Animacies*, the linguist Mel Y. Chen (2012) suggests that if such a thing as queer liveliness still exists, it is to be found in *queer*'s verbal and adjectival forms rather than its deadly nominal one. *Feminism* is a noun without a verb form, but *trans* is grammatically polymorphous. *Trans* is not about resignification; rather, it is about rematerialization. It can be a noun as well as a prefix that attaches to and dynamizes other words, providing new directions for them, bringing both feminism and queerness into new assemblages (*reagencements*). *Trans* works as well in French, Spanish, Italian, and many other languages as it does in English. What are we to make of the mobility of this little unit of grammar, its ability to animate, to cross, to "quare" (Johnson and Henderson 2005)? To quote Chen:

> Queer . . . while it continually re-animates in new formations—thanks particularly to queer of color, transnational, disability, and trans scholarship—has also achieved nominal fame as an identity; but it has simultaneously coalesced, gotten sticky, inertial, lost its animation and its drive in the context of the United States. Its nominal terminus along certain semantic paths has led it to an atemporal staticization, a lack of cognitive dynamism, an essential death, and a future imaginable only according to its modification by something else. (Chen 2012: 82–83)

Transfeminism is that "something else," and it is happening somewhere else than white Anglo feminism and queer theory in the United States.

Marie-Hélène/Sam Bourcier, queer activist and theorist, teaches at the University of Lille 3 in France. He is the author of the *Queer Zones* trilogy — *Queer Zones: Politique des identités sexuelles et des savoirs* (2001), *Queer Zones 2: Sexpolitiques* (2005), and *Queer Zones 3: Identités, cultures, politiques* (2011) — and *Comprendre le féminisme* (2012). All his books and articles are available on academia.edu.

Karine Espineira is a research fellow at the University of Nice-Sophia Antipolis and University of Paris 8, where she studies gender models and the representations of trans people in the media. She is the author of *Transidentités: Ordre et panique de genre* (2015), *Médiacultures: La transidentité en télévision* (2015), and *La transidentité* (2008).

Notes

1.   Stop Trans Pathologization: "A campaign for the depathologization of trans identities. The main goals of the Campaign are the removal of the categories of 'gender dysphoria'/ 'gender identity disorders' from the diagnosis manuals (DSM of the American Psychiatric Association and ICD of the World Health Organization), as well as the fight for trans health rights." See Stop Trans Pathologization 2012.
2.   See also the survey for the report on transphobia conducted by Arnaud Alessandrin and Karine Espineira in 2014 (Alessandrin and Espineira 2015).
3.   It should be underlined that Delphy's definition of intersectionality does not include trans people and that she accuses them of ruining the feminist project to abolish gender.
4.   See also Rogue 2012.
5.   See also Espineira et al. 1998. At the time, we thought of many Zoo members (gays, lesbians, bis, queers, etc.) as virtual trans identities, which, later on, proved to be true.
6.   The term *Spanish* is not used in a nationalistic sense here. A lot of transfeminists living in Spain are Italian.
7.   Regarding Smaschieramenti, see Smaschieramenti 2010, and regarding the call for a "transfeminist block" in the demonstration against austerity in Rome on October 15, 2011, see Smaschieramenti 2011. See also the collective A/matrix based in Rome, who identified as transfeminist, write, "A/matrix è unprogetto post, trans, pop, cyber,neo, ultra, meta, iper femminista. Anche se non sembra, siamo piuttosto concrete: è la discriminan-te fondamentale per non imploderee/o faregomitolo" (A/matrix is a post, trans, pop, cyber, neo, ultra, meta, hyper feminist. We are more concrete than we look: being concrete is crucial for not imploding or becoming a tangle[Sconvegno 2008]). Many thanks to Alessia Acquistapace for the resources and the translation.
8.   See, for instance, Lawrence La Fountain-Stoke's (2009) play on words "Queericans."
9.   In Latin America, *queer* has also been translated as "*cuir*" in order to break with Anglo imperialism.
10.   On the crucial part of workshops, see Bourcier 2013.
11.   See "Capitalism Is a Shit" and "Pornocapitalismo" in Ideadestroymuros 2005.
12.   See, for example, the infamous conference on sexual nationalism in Amsterdam in 2011 (Stelder 2011).

References

Alarcon, Norma. 1990. "The Theoretical Subject(s) of This Bridge Called My Back and Anglo-american Feminism." In *Making Faces, Making Souls, Haciendo caras: Creative and Critical Perspectives by Feminists of Color*, edited by Anzaldúa Gloria, 356–69. San Francisco: Aunt Lute Books.

Alessandrin, Arnaud, and Karine Espineira. 2015. *Sociologie de la transphobie (Sociology of the Transphobia)*. Bordeaux: Maison des Sciences de l'Homme d'Aquitaine.

Andrieu, Bernard. 2008. "Entretien avec Marie-Hélène Bourcier." *Dilecta corps*, no. 4: 5–11. www .cairn.info/revue-corps-dilecta-2008-1-page-5.htm.

Blais, Mélissa, Laurence Fortin-Pellerin, Ève-Marie Lampron, and Geneviève Pagé. 2007. "Pour éviter de se noyer dans la (troisième) vague: réflexions sur l'histoire et l'actualité du féminisme radical." *Recherches féministes* 20, no. 2: 141–62.

Bourcier, Marie-Hélène/Sam, ed. 1998. *Q comme queer: Les séminaires Q du Zoo (1996–1997)*. Lille, France: Éditions GayKitschCamp.

———. 2012. "Cultural Translation, Politics of Disempowerment, and the Reinvention of Queer Politics." In "European Culture/European Queer," edited by Lisa Downing and Robert Gillett, special issue, *Sexualities* 15, no. 1: 93–109.

———. 2013. "Bildungs-post-porn: Notes sur le post-porn, un des futurs du féminisme de la désobéissance sexuelle." *Rue Descartes: Revue du Collège international de philosophie*, no. 79: 42–60.

Butler, Judith. 1990. *Gender Trouble: Feminism and the Subversion of Identity*. New York: Routledge.

Califia, Pat. 2003. *Sex Changes: The Politics of Transgenderism*. 2nd ed. San Francisco: Cleis.

Chen, Mel Y. 2012. *Animacies, Biopolitics, Racial Mattering, and Queer Affect*. Durham, NC: Duke University Press.

Crenshaw, Kimberlé. 1994. "Mapping the Margins: Intersectionality, Identity Politics, and Violence against Women of Color." In *The Public Nature of Private Violence*, edited by Martha Albertson Fineman and Rixanne Mykitiuk, 93–118. New York: Routledge.

Delphy, Christine. 2006. "Antisexisme ou antiracisme? Un faux dilemme." *Nouvelles questions féministes* 25, no. 1: 59–83.

Dorlin, Elsa. 2008. *Sexe, genre, et sexualités (Sex, Gender, and Sexualities)*. Paris: Presses universitaires de France.

Dorvil, Henri, ed. 2007. *Théories et méthodologies de l'intervention sociale*. Vol. 4 of *Problèmes sociaux*. Quebec: Presses de l'Université du Québec.

Espineira, Karine. 2012. "La construction médiatique des transidentités: Une modélisation sociale et médiaculturelle" ("The Media Construction of Trans Identities: A Social and Media-Cultural Modelling"). PhD thesis, Université de Nice Sophia Antipolis.

Espineira, Karine, et al. 1998. "Q comme questions." In Bourcier 1998: 112–21.

Giami, Alain, Emmanuelle Beaubatie, and Jonas Le Bail. 2010. "Caractéristiques sociodémographiques, identification de genre, parcours de transition médicopsychologiques et VIH/sida dans la population trans: Premiers résultats d'une enquête menée en France en 2010." *Bulletin épidémiologique hebdomadaire*, no. 42: 433–37.

Ideadestroyingmuros. 2005. "Who We Are." www.ideadestroyingmuros.info/bio/chi-siamo/ (accessed April 12).

Johnson, E. Patrick, and Mae G. Henderson. 2005. "Introduction: Queering Black Studies/ 'Quaring' Queer Studies." In *Black Queer Studies: A Critical Anthology*, edited by E. Patrick Johnson and Mae G. Henderson, 1–20. Durham, NC: Duke University Press.

Koyama, Emi. 2003. "The Transfeminist Manifesto." In *Catching a Wave: Reclaiming Feminism for the Twenty-First Century*, edited by Rory Dicker and Alison Piepmeier, 244–59. Boston: Northeastern University Press.

La Fountain-Stokes, Lawrence. 2009. *Queer Ricans: Cultures and Sexualities in the Diaspora.* Minneapolis: University of Minnesota Press.

Lopes, Denilson. 2015. "Gender and Sexuality Turn/Queer Turn." Paper presented at the seminar "Forms of Affect," King Juan Carlos Center for Latin American and Caribbean Studies (CLACS), New York University, New York, April 14.

Mensah, Maria Nengeh, ed. 2005. "Une troisième vague féministe au Québec?" In *Dialogues sur la troisième vague féministe*, 11–27. Montréal: Éditions du Remue-Ménage.

Outrans. 2009. "Trans et féministe, nos corps nous appartiennent." News release, March 6.

———. 2012. "Transféminismes." www.outrans.org/infos/articles/transfeminismes/ (accessed December 2012).

———. 2013. "Le transféminisme." L'Observatoire des transidentités, April 2. www.observatoire -des-transidentites.com/page-8618633.html.

Post-op, et al. 2010. "Oh-Kaña." Vimeo video, 11:43. June 14. vimeo.com/12566813.

Rogue, J. 2009. "Strengthening Anarchism's Gender Analysis." *Northeastern Anarchist*, no. 14. Common Struggle. www.commonstruggle.org/index.php?q=node/2484.

———. 2012. "De-essentializing Anarchist Feminism: Lessons from the Trans-Feminist Movement." In *Queering Anarchism: Addressing and Undressing Power and Desire*, edited by C. B. Daring, J. Rogue, Deric Shannon, and Abbey Volcano, 39–50. Oakland, CA: AK.

Rubin, Gayle. 1975. "The Traffic in Women: Notes on the 'Political Economy' of Sex." In *Toward an Anthropology of Women*, edited by Reiter Rayna, 157–210. New York: Monthly Review Press.

———. 1984. "Thinking Sex: Notes for a Radical Theory of the Politics of Sexuality." In *Pleasure and Danger*, edited by Vance Carole, 143–78. New York: Routledge and Kegan Paul.

Serano, Julia. 2007. *Whipping Girl: A Transsexual Woman on Sexism and the Scapegoating of Femininity*. Berkeley, CA: Seal.

Sconvegno. 2008. "Le inclassificabili." In *Futuro Femminile. Passioni e ragioni nelle voci del femminismo dal dopoguerra a oggi*, edited by Reale Lorella, 19–32. Bologna, Luca Sossella Editore.

Smaschieramenti. 2010. "Manifesto per un'insurrezione PutaLesboNeraTransFemminista." Blog, January 1. smaschieramenti.noblogs.org/manifesto-per-uninsurrezione-putalesbonera transfemminista/.

———. 2011. "Appello per uno spezzone putatransfemministaqueer nella manifestazione del 15 ottobre." Blog, October 8. www.smaschieramenti.noblogs.org/post/2011/10/08/appello -per-uno-spezzone-putatransfemministaqueer-nella-manifestazione-del-15/.

Solà, Miriam. 2013. "Pre-textos, con-textos y textos." In Solà and Urko 2013, 15–30.

Solà, Miriam, and Urko Elena, eds. 2013. *Transfeminismos, epistemes, fricciones y flujos (Transfeminisms, Epistemes, Frictions, and Flows)*. Tafalla, Spain: Txalaparta.

SomMovimentonazioAnale. 2012. "Una giornata di co-spirazione lesbica, frocia, trans e femminista nella crisi—Bologna, 15 dicembre." Blog, December 15. www.sommovimentonazioanale .noblogs.org/post/2012/12/15/una-giornata-di-co-spirazione-lesbica-frocia-trans-e -femminista-nella-crisi-bologna-15-dicembre/.

Stelder, Mikki. 2011. "Start with Amsterdam! An Alternative Statement on the Sexual Nationalisms Conference." *QueerIntersectional* (blog), February 16. queerintersectional.wordpress .com/2011/02/16/start-with-amsterdam-2/.

Stop Trans Pathologization. 2012. "Welcome." www.stp2012.info/old/en (accessed April 20, 2015).

Thomas, Maud-Yeuse, and Karine Espineira. 1998. "Deux lesbotrans se posent des Q." In Bourcier 1998, 100–104.

Wittig, Monique. 1992. *The Straight Mind and Other Essays*. Boston: Beacon.

Pauli Murray's Peter Panic

Perspectives from the Margins of Gender and Race in Jim Crow America

SIMON D. ELIN FISHER

Abstract This article investigates the history of intersectional feminism and demonstrates that the theory is grounded in a trans-of-color analysis of the racial caste system known as "Jim Crow." In 1944, Pauli Murray, an African American activist, journalist, and lawyer, coined the term *Jane Crow*, which critiqued the simultaneous structural and affective impacts of white supremacy and male supremacy. These hegemonies divided individuals into binary categories of race and gender, categories that were naturalized and violently upheld. Murray lived on the margins of these classifications as a light-skinned African American who expressed a trans gender and desired medical transition. S/he was read as a variety of genders and races and observed others' attempts to discern her/his "true" identity. From this perspective, Murray scrutinized this quotidian yet fundamental process of categorization, analyzed the operations of race and gender subjectification, and crafted an intersectional feminist analysis s/he called "Jane Crow."

Keywords intersectionality, Civil Rights movement, transgender history, passing, Pauli Murray

Intersectionality argues that racism and sexism cannot be treated separately as single oppressions, especially when considering the lives of black women (Crenshaw 1989). The history of intersectional feminism demonstrates that the theory is grounded in a trans-of-color analysis of the racial caste system known as "Jim Crow." In 1944, Pauli Murray, an African American activist, journalist, and lawyer, began exploring the simultaneous structural and affective impacts of "white supremacy as well as male supremacy" (Murray 1947: 5). Murray argued that Jim Crow, a system of binary racial categorization, social segregation, violence, and political and economic repression, had a companion: "Jane Crow" similarly classified humans into two binary gender categories, segregated the groups and violently policed their intimate interactions, and restricted the economic and political possibilities of those labeled "woman" (Panic 1944; Murray 1947, 1950; Murray and Eastwood 1965). For three decades, Murray wrote

TSQ: Transgender Studies Quarterly ★ Volume 3, Numbers 1–2 ★ May 2016   **95**
DOI 10.1215/23289252-3334259   © 2016 Duke University Press

prominent legal briefs and policy recommendations about Jane Crow and the negative effects it had on women of color, and when Murray moved from law to the priesthood in the 1970s, Jane Crow's perilous affects became the focus of a number of spiritual tracts and sermons.

This article explores Murray's writing on Jane Crow, but instead of charting the progression of Murray's thesis forward through the Civil Rights and feminist movements, I look backward. I build upon the historiography of Civil Rights activists that connects an individual's early encounters with racist oppression and their radical thoughts and actions, and I examine Murray's experiences as a person whose racial appearance and gender expression fell outside black/white and female/male binaries. Jane Crow was developed out of Murray's early navigations of Jim Crow gender and racial categories. At times, Murray purposefully played with the norms that shifted as s/he[1] moved across geographies and institutional settings, but s/he was acutely aware that the power to name her/his race and gender was rarely in her/his hands. Following Kenneth Mack (2012), I ask, how does a life of navigating these hegemonic binaries shape one's analysis of their operation and effects? Through exploring this question, I highlight the trans-of-color analysis of and resistance to Jim Crow central to the historical and theoretical development of intersectional feminism.

Pauli Murray was born in 1910 in Baltimore, a child of what s/he calls "my dual family heritage" (Murray 1987: xiv). Descended from a free woman and freeman, an enslaved woman and her owner, Murray was light-skinned but did not pass as white in the strict racial binaries constituted by Jim Crow. Especially salient to Murray was her/his childhood experiences of segregation that split her/his own family. Out of six siblings, only Murray and one other did not pass as white, separating the siblings in both the public spaces they could inhabit and the social statuses they were afforded. Even with light skin, Murray was designated as black and was "very, very conscious" that her/his movements were regulated and restricted throughout her/his childhood in the South (Murray 1976: 6).

Therefore, from a young age, Murray was a keen observer of the processes of racial categorization, in which, in any (and every) given situation, a more powerful white individual could observe and determine her/his race and admit or refuse her/him entrance into these local, privileged spaces. Murray was simultaneously also restricted by contemporary binary gender norms that insisted each individual be demarcated as either female or male. S/he expressed a pronounced masculine sense of self throughout childhood, and during her/his twenties and thirties, Murray (1937a) wrote that s/he "desired experimentation on the male side." In 1939, s/he clipped an article from the African American *Amsterdam News* reporting that experiments with testosterone "transform[ed] effeminate males into normal men, strong and virile" (*New York Amsterdam News* 1939). S/he immediately visited the hospital where the experiments were conducted, inquiring whether "the clinic would experiment" on her/him "with the male hormone" (Murray 1940).

Recently, and finally, historians (Azaransky 2011, 2013; Gilmore 2009; Mack 2012) have begun to read Murray's archive using a trans-analytical lens, refuting the conflation of her/his identification as a heterosexual male with internalized homophobia in an era before the modern gay liberation movement. From this perspective, Murray was attempting to align her/his physical body with her/his sense of normative male gender (described as her/his sexual attraction to feminine women, drive to compete in "men's" occupations, a desire to partner with a woman in a monogamous marriage, and "wearing pants" [Murray 1937a]). Even though Murray implored endocrinologists for treatment, stating that her/his "desire to be male was so strong," s/he was rejected—it was recommended s/he "accept treatment using female hormone[s]" instead (Murray 1940). Murray pursued testosterone therapy until at least 1944; there is no record that her/his numerous appeals were ever fulfilled.

During this period, Murray was hospitalized three times, each for "emotional breakdowns" from a combination of intense overwork, heartbreak, and the struggle to normalize her/his gender and sexuality through testosterone therapy (Azaransky 2011: 23). Murray's personal notes (1937a, 1937b, 1938, 1940) from these episodes are centered on these "conflicts," and her/his race, and others' perception of it, is always in play. In one document (1937a), s/he wonders if part of this inner turmoil is not also racial—that being "hemmed in" by Jim Crow "restrictions" adds additional strain on her/his precarious gendered life. S/he wonders why, since s/he is so eager to become more masculine to ease this "conflict," s/he does not desire to pass as white, or make efforts to do so: "Why is [it] I am proud of my Negro blood?" While considering these critical questions, hospital staff "palmed [her/him] off as Cuban" so that s/he might receive a higher level of treatment.[2] Murray (1937b) simply left "the race question in the open" and let others decide what racial category to place her/him into.

Murray spent a great deal of time and energy observing the operations of racialization and gendering at work as those surrounding her/him tried to categorize her/him for their own purposes. In her/his 1938 poem "Mulatto's Dilemma," Murray writes:

> Oh God! My face has slipped them . . .
> Can I endure the killing weight of time it takes them
> To be sure? (Murray 1938)

Although the poem centers on the "killing" wait while others attempt to identify Murray as either black or white, her/his gender was simultaneously appraised. Racial and gender nonnormativity explicitly crossed paths on Murray's body, and as s/he walked through the world, others were always taking measure of this dual nonbelonging.

I argue that it is this trans perspective, not only Murray's experience "as a black woman" as others have concluded (Hartmann 2002: 75; Lewis 1977), that led to her/his first formulation of *Jane Crow*. Murray first introduced the term in a short 1944 *Los Angeles Sentinel* article, "Little Man from Mars: He's All Mixed Up," penned under the name Peter Panic (Panic 1944). The nom de plume is a nod to the character Peter Pan, traditionally played onstage by a woman. But Murray isn't Pan—s/he is Panic, perhaps referencing her/his failed quest for masculinization therapy and gender alignment. The article itself centers not on this gender tension but rather on the panic over the arbitrary violences of Jim Crow. Published in the largest African American newspaper on the West Coast, it is told from the perspective of a "little man from Mars" who observes the processes of racial and gender categorization from above. The martian literalizes Jim Crow as a bird that bites "culud" people, giving them "something like an itch" that "nearly drives them crazy." Keeping the words "culud folks" and "white folks" in quotation marks demonstrates that it is actually the bite of the bird and its harmful effects that demarcates who is "culud" and who is "white," not a physiological "truth" that stands outside processes of subjectification.

The martian rarely sees the bird, but humans erect "certain signs" that delineate not only space but also the people within it. Describing the infamous "white only" signs that littered the public spaces of the South, including the cemeteries, Murray/Panic writes, "If you get buried with the wrong sign on you, they dig up your bones, put the proper label on you, and bury you in the designated graveyard." To the martian, this represents the extreme in racial categorization, in that even without skin, proper racial binaries must be retained. While these strictures might hold in the daylight, at night, "sometimes they're careless and forget to put up their signs . . . then everybody gets mixed up." Alluding to the interracial intimacies, consensual and not, that occur throughout segregated communities, Murray/Panic is also connecting these hidden relationships within her/his own ancestry. Intimacies that cross racial lines leave people "all mixed up," just like the man from Mars is. Murray writes, "Being changeable color—green-and-blue—I don't know which sign to choose" (Panic 1944).

In the last paragraphs, the martian introduces Jim Crow's mate, Jane Crow. Although Murray/Panic does not expound upon Jane Crow's "bite," it is clear that Murray sees similarities between their operations and effects. Articulating an early form of social constructionism, s/he argues that both racialization and gendering are violent binary systems imposed from without—"the bite"—rather than from truths that emerge from the body. Those that are "bit" by these birds, those labeled black and/or woman, suffer both the internalized sense of inferiority—the "itch" that "drives them crazy"—and the material effects of systemic racism and sexism. However, as exemplified by the little man from Mars, Peter Panic, and Pauli Murray herself/himself, there are those who do not easily fit into these binarized categories and are themselves "all mixed up."

During this period, Murray took several interstate trips, sometimes in the company of a lover. S/he carefully recorded others' perceptions of her/his race and gender, which changed as s/he traveled through different parts of the country. In 1940, Murray, dressed in men's clothes, and her/his partner Adelene MacBean were arrested in Virginia during the first recorded utilization of Gandhian nonviolence in the struggle against Jim Crow. While some reports of the incident describe Murray and MacBean as two women, another describes one of the arrestees as "a young colored girl" and the other as a "young man . . . lighter than she, of slight build" (Gilmore 2009: 322). In the South, Murray was read as black regardless of gender.[3] But upon leaving the region, the perception of Murray's racial identity was more fluid, as was the case during Murray's hospitalization in 1937. For example, on a 1935 hitchhiking trip through Illinois, one woman thought Murray "was a Boy Scout," while another "thought [s/he] was Indian" (Murray 1935).

Contemporary trans and critical race scholarship (Omi and Winant 1994; Serano 2009; Snorton 2009) invites us to see Murray as passed rather than passing. Instead of the responsibility for identification falling solely on the individual, it rests on the racial and gender norms that shape the way they are assessed. One's visible and audible embodiments are read through governing hegemonic categories, and the identification of the individual as a particular race and gender is created through that process. In this way, the experiences of people who are passed as more than one race and/or gender can teach us about the structural norms of that historical moment. Each time the individual is read and then categorized as one singular race and gender, the local racial and gender norms are exposed. Witnessing this quotidian yet fundamental process can build comprehension of complex hegemonic discourses.

Murray was labeled in ways that changed day to day and place to place. This, then, is a set of experiences that sets Pauli Murray apart from most of her/his movement activist counterparts—other "race women" who made black women's experiences a central focus of their racial justice work. While race women spent the majority of their time in the public sphere, most kept the details of their intimate lives well hidden. Darlene Clark Hine (1989: 914–15) argues that many black women who "desire[d] to achieve personal autonomy" developed a "culture of dissemblance" wherein they denied whites and black men access to their interior psychic and sexual selves. This was crucial for black women in leadership positions, toward whom stereotypes about black female sexual excess was explicitly and implicitly directed. Race women crafted personas of "openness" while "actually remaining an enigma," allowing them to inhabit culturally held white heteronormative ideals of virtuous womanhood, industriousness, emotional regulation, and gender respectability.

A long historiographical conversation regards the negative impact of the culture of dissemblance on black women, lesbians, and gender-nonnormative people. Hine highlights black middle-class women's attempted management of poor women, nonmonogamous women, and sex workers. Evelynn Hammonds (1999: 101) argues that lesbian and queer black women have been and are among those labeled as "traitors," in that not only do they invite additional scrutiny, but their expression of queerness enunciates their nonnormative sexual desires. Fearing that revelation might displace them from their racial community, black queer women police themselves, furthering the silences surrounding black women's intimacies.

Matt Richardson (2003) uses Hine's analytic to understand the absence of transgender people from black history. He cites her research on Cathy Williams, who lived under the name William Cathy, was read consistently as a black man, and served as a buffalo soldier in the late nineteenth century. Richardson argues that what is missing from Hine's analysis is the connection between Cathy's race and gender expression and the racial and gender norms in which Cathy was read and categorized. Separating William Cathy from the historical governing hegemonies results in the relegation of her/his gender and sexual nonnormativity to a biographical aside, rather than a lens through which to view the historical effects of changing cultural discourses.

Hammonds and Richardson argue that scholars perpetuate the culture of dissemblance in two ways. First, dissemblance maintains a closet for historical figures, denying queer and trans African Americans a place in the historiography. Second, it refuses the likelihood that one's sexuality or desire for gender self-definition is woven into one's race work, even if it is not spoken outright. Murray's crucial role in the histories of Civil Rights activism and intersectional feminism has been marginalized because both disciplines have yet to fully include transgender as a category of analysis that offers a distinct perspective on systemic operations of subjectification. Only a handful of scholars have recognized Murray's transgender history, and only Mack (2012) has begun to unpack how those experiences shaped Murray's theoretical analysis of Jane Crow.

Making her/his way through Jim Crow's strict racial and gender norms, Pauli Murray had plenty to Peter Panic about. Before studying law at Howard

University, Murray was rejected from the University of North Carolina on account of her/his race; after graduating from Howard as valedictorian, s/he was rejected from Harvard Law School on account of her/his sex. In response to this latest exclusion, Murray famously wrote, "Gentlemen, I would gladly change my sex to meet your requirements, but since the way to such change has not been revealed to me, I have no recourse but to appeal to you to change your minds. Are you to tell me that one is as difficult as the other?" (Mayeri 2013: 87).

Just one month later, Murray introduced Jane Crow to an African American readership rapidly coalescing into a national civil rights movement. S/he articulated what would be intimately resonant to many: white supremacy and male supremacy operated in tandem, and their combined effects fell squarely across the bodies and psyches of African American women. As the analysis gained popularity among Murray's colleagues and friends, s/he used her/his full name when writing about Jane Crow, and by the mid-1960s, Murray was regarded as the legal expert on the civil rights of black women. But the bird's first sighting was by Peter Panic—the spirited boy played by a woman, and a little man from Mars—a color-changing observer from another planet. These caricatures represent Murray's sense of nonbelonging in a social world built on racial and gender binaries, and these outsider observations became the theoretical foundation of intersectional feminism. Murray's trans gender is more than a biographical aside in feminist and Civil Rights historiography; these experiences informed Murray's racial justice work and shaped her/his analysis of hegemonic racism and sexism.

Simon D. Elin Fisher is a doctoral candidate in the Department of History at the University of Wisconsin–Madison. His dissertation, "Nonviolence, Queer Intimacies, and the Making of the Civil Rights Movement," is in progress.

Acknowledgments
An earlier version of this article was presented at the Sixteenth Annual Graduate Student Conference in African American History at the University of Memphis, February 13, 2015. I wish to thank Jessi Lee Jackson for her careful reading and astute comments in preparation for publication.

Notes

1. I use *s/he* pronouns for Murray to both accentuate Murray's internal sense of male/masculine gender during the 1930s–1950s and also Murray's identification with female experience after this period until her death. My desire is to use a third-gender pronoun; yet I feel the contemporary *they* is ahistorical. As scholars continue to consider the lives of gender-nonconforming people living before the availability of a transgender/transsexual identity, a more uniform system of pronoun usage will likely emerge.

2.   It is unclear whether the Long Island Rest Home (Amityville, New York) excluded African American patients at this time, but regardless of the admittance policy, a light-skinned Cuban client would likely receive better treatment than an African American.

3.   This has much to do with the discursive expansiveness of the racial category "colored," constituted as such to maintain white racial purity and enfold the greatest number of individuals into a politically and economically subordinate position.

References

Azaransky, Sarah. 2011. *The Dream Is Freedom: Pauli Murray and American Democratic Faith.* Oxford: Oxford University Press.

———. 2013. "Jane Crow: Pauli Murray's Intersections and Antidiscrimination Law." *Journal of Feminist Studies in Religion* 29, no. 1: 155–60.

Crenshaw, Kimberlé. 1989. "Demarginalizing the Intersection of Race and Sex: A Black Feminist Critique of Antidiscrimination Doctrine, Feminist Theory, and Antiracist Politics." *University of Chicago Legal Forum* 140: 139–67.

Gilmore, Glenda Elizabeth. 2009. *Defying Dixie: The Radical Roots of Civil Rights, 1919–1950.* New York: W. W. Norton.

Hammonds, Evelynn M. 1999. "Toward a Genealogy of Black Female Sexuality: The Problematic of Silence." In *Feminist Theory and the Body: A Reader,* edited by Janet Price and Margrit Shildreck, 93–104. New York: Taylor and Francis.

Hartmann, Susan M. 2002. "Pauli Murray and the 'Juncture of Women's Liberation and Black Liberation.'" *Journal of Women's History* 14, no. 2: 74–77.

Hine, Darlene Clark. 1989. "Rape and the Inner Lives of Black Women in the Middle West." *Signs* 14, no. 4: 912–20.

Lewis, Diane K. 1977. "A Response to Inequality: Black Women, Racism, and Sexism." *Signs* 3, no. 2: 339–61.

Mack, Kenneth W. 2012. *Representing the Race: The Creation of the Civil Rights Lawyer.* Cambridge, MA: Harvard University Press.

Mayeri, Serena. 2013. "Pauli Murray and the Twentieth-Century Quest for Legal and Social Equality." *Indiana Journal of Law and Social Equality* 2, no. 1: 80–90.

Murray, Pauli. 1935. Travel Diary, April 27–May 24. Box 1, Folder 25, Pauli Murray Papers (PMP), Schlesinger Library, Cambridge.

———. ca. 1937a. "Interview with Dr. _____." Box 4, Folder 71, PMP.

———. ca. 1937b. "Questions Prepared for Dr. Titley." Box 4, Folder 71, PMP.

———. 1938. "Mulatto's Dilemma (A Poem)." *Opportunity* 16: 180.

———. 1940. "Summary of Symptoms of Upset—Pauli Murray. March 8, 1940." Box 4, Folder 71, PMP.

———. 1947. "Why Negro Girls Stay Single." *Negro Digest,* July: 4–8.

———. 1950. *States' Laws on Race and Color.* Athens: University of Georgia Press.

———. 1976. "A Legal Activist Discusses Her Work in the Civil Rights and Women's Liberation Movements." Oral History Interview with Pauli Murray, February 13, 1976. Interview G-0044. Southern Oral History Program Collection (#4007): Electronic Edition. docsouth .unc.edu/sohp/G-0044/G-0044.html (accessed January 29, 2015).

———. 1987. *Proud Shoes: The Story of an American Family.* New York: Harper and Row.

Murray, Pauli, and Mary O. Eastwood. 1965. "Jane Crow and the Law: Sex Discrimination and Title VII." *George Washington Law Review* 34, no. 2: 232–56.

New York Amsterdam News. 1939. "Sex Tablets Stir Medics." November 11.

Omi, Michael, and Howard A. Winant. 1994. *Racial Formation in the United States: From the 1960s to the 1990s.* New York: Taylor and Francis.

Panic, Peter [Pauli Murray]. 1944. "Little Man from Mars." *Los Angeles Sentinel*, July 14.

Richardson, Matt [published as Mattie Udora Richardson]. 2003. "No More Secrets, No More Lies: African American History and Compulsory Heterosexuality." *Journal of Women's History* 15, no. 3: 63–76.

Serano, Julia. 2009. *Whipping Girl: A Transsexual Woman on Sexism and the Scapegoating of Femininity.* Berkeley, CA: Seal.

Snorton, C. Riley. 2009. "'A New Hope': The Psychic Life of Passing." *Hypatia* 24, no. 3: 77–92.

Transfeminist Crossroads

Reimagining the Ecuadorian State

CLAUDIA SOFÍA GARRIGA-LÓPEZ

Abstract This article provides an account of transfeminism as a grassroots political project rooted in material politics that has led to significant changes on transgender issues in Ecuadorian public policy over the past decade. Ecuadorian transfeminist activists firmly believe that feminist theory and practice are critical tools in the struggle for trans liberation, and that the social oppression of transgender people is intimately connected with the larger structures of patriarchy that feminisms seek to counteract. Their praxis has worked its way up from walking the streets with "working girls," to drafting articles for the constitution based on the knowledge learned during nightly street patrols, and later garnering the necessary support for successful inclusion of these articles in the constitution. "Transfeminist Crossroads" follows the trajectory of the My Gender on My ID campaign to highlight the role of transfeminist activism in changing public opinion and pushing new legislation in one of the flagship countries of the Latin American "left turn." The unfolding of this campaign demonstrates the dynamic flux and fluidity of state formation as transfeminist activists respond to President Rafael Correa's call for a "citizen revolution" and geopolitical forces reconfigure relationships between social conservatism, left populism, adaptive neoliberalism, and new regimes of state security.

Keywords feminism, transgender, Ecuador, queer, rights

Transgender as an expression of gender identity, and transfeminism as a mode of politics, are increasingly visible within academic debates about gender and sexuality. Transfeminism exists in the "contact zone" between feminism as an analytic lens for a broad set of cultural phenomena and a series of interventions that aim to move transgender issues from the margins to the center of feminist theory, debates, and activism (Pratt 2007: 4). Transfeminists in Ecuador are working to transform the material conditions of people on the street, to affirm their right to exist outside conventional norms of gender and sexuality in public spaces, and to strengthen the self-organization of working-class trans Ecuadorians. This article follows the trajectory of the My Gender on My ID campaign to highlight the role of transfeminist activism in changing public opinion and pushing new legislation in one of the flagship countries of the Latin American "left turn." It is grounded in the imperative not only to analyze new state formations in relation "to or against colonial and neocolonial capitalism" but also, crucially, to "read them within a racialized and gendered developmentalism" that produces specific citizen-subjects as agents of social change and nation building (Saldaña-Portillo 2003: 7).

Grassroots Transfeminism

The history of transfeminism in Ecuador precedes the election of President Rafael Correa in 2006 and the establishment of a new constitution in 2008. Transfeminism is a practice and ideology that has worked its way up from walking the streets with "working girls," to drafting articles for the constitution based on the knowledge learned during nightly street patrols, and later garnering the necessary support for successful inclusion of these articles in the constitution. What follows is a brief overview of the emergence of the Legal Patrol as the starting point of an explicitly transfeminist politics in Ecuador.

Founded by Elizabeth Vasquez in 2002, Legal Patrol is a grassroots organization that supports the social, civil, and economic empowerment of trans sex workers in Quito, working toward reducing police abuse through various strategies, including direct interventions during altercations with the police, public denouncements of police abuse, police sensitivity trainings, and the inclusion of guidelines for proper treatment of trans people in the police human rights handbook. Patrol members walk the streets in areas frequented by trans sex workers to educate and dialogue with them about their rights.[1] The Legal Patrol is grounded in a transfeminist standpoint—they believe that feminist theory and practice are critical tools in the struggle for trans liberation, and that the social oppression of transgender people is intimately connected with the larger structures of patriarchy that feminisms seek to counteract. They emphasize what they call the "subjacent symmetries" between trans sex workers and the people they share the street with: other sex workers, clients, members of the Latin Kings gang, goths, and punk rockers, as well as street vendors and neighbors (Almeida and Vasquez 2010: 19). This approach aims to cultivate "intersectional coalitions constructed through analogies of oppression" (Castellanos 2014: 203).

Vasquez founded the Legal Patrol when she was a law student taking evening courses, and twice a week, she would walk home late at night through the Mariscal zone, where her route took her past a group of trans sex workers on the other side of the street. She soon decided to approach them. In a statement that stands as something of an origin story for transfeminism in

Ecuador, Vasquez recalls her first encounter with trans sex-worker community leader Yelina Lafayette:

> I crossed over, and there was a girl whose back was turned to me, I tapped her shoulder and she turned around. I was startled, and she was startled, and I said "hello" and she said "hello" and we began to talk. And this was Yelina, and that night I spoke with her until three in the morning. She introduced me to her collective: the Lafayette Girls, named after the hostel where they lived. And she also introduced me to all the other groups of trans girls from the Mariscal, but the Lafayette Girls were certainly the most glamorous. They were the first to use cell phones for sex work, so in that sense this group was in the lead. And Yelina and Valeria were at the top of the hierarchy. They took care of younger coworkers. They were already twenty-two and twenty-three, which in the world of trans sex work meant that they were quite experienced. They had coworkers who were sixteen and seventeen. They had the trust to show me everything about their experience as trans girls.[2]

Transfeminism in Ecuador thus started on the street, in the night, in grassroots dialogue and consciousness-raising between trans sex workers and a feminist, quite literally when a young law student decided to cross over to a parallel path and interact with trans sex workers, and when outspoken, politically minded, street-smart trans sex workers decided to trust and educate a young nontrans woman who came to them, to share with her their experiences of violence at the hands of the police, their clients, and society at large.

Tragically, Yelina Lafayette was murdered in 2004 in an apparent hate crime. This loss marked Elizabeth Vasquez deeply but ultimately strengthened her resolve to work toward trans empowerment. After Yelina's death, Vasquez trained a new cohort of paralegal activists in the techniques and methods that had been developed by the Legal Patrol over the previous year. Among these new recruits was Geovanni Jaramillo, the first openly transmasculine activist and the first trans-licensed attorney in Ecuador. As is the case in other Latin American countries, trans women in Ecuador tend to be more visible than trans men within the LGBT community and in activist circles, and, historically, organizing efforts around trans issues have focused more attention and resources on trans women than on other gender-variant people. Jaramillo's involvement in the group was part of a concerted effort to increase the visibility of trans men, and it signaled an expansion of transfeminism as a conceptual tool for transmasculine analysis and empowerment.

In many ways, transfeminism gives a name to practices and analyses that Jaramillo had already engaged in for many years. He had participated in feminist conferences, meetings, health forums, and social campaigns, and he was a founding member of one of the first lesbian and gay organizations that had worked toward the decriminalization of homosexuality in 1998. During our interview, Jaramillo recalled his years working with feminist groups with great affection; he smiled as he told me about being the only guy at various feminist meetings and conferences and proudly insisted on his commitment to feminism beyond his own experience as a trans man. Jaramillo's story demonstrates that transfeminism is not a one-way flow of solidarity from nontrans feminists toward trans people; rather, trans activists have been at the forefront of feminist and LGBT struggles for many decades, and the category of "transfeminism" signals the articulation of these practices into a cohesive political standpoint (pers. comm., March 15, 2014).

The combined effect of the work of the Legal Patrol, litigation against the civil registry, and active participation in the 2007 Constitutional Assembly resulted in a remarkable expansion of rights, activism, and visibility for trans people. For example, once gender was included as one of the protected categories within the constitution's antidiscrimination clause, and once the civil registry recognized trans people's right to legally change their names in accordance with their gender identity, there was a boom in the number of trans people who obtained formal state IDs, which in turn had many important repercussions— like allowing trans students to be admitted into universities. A "first generation" of trans students thus entered the university system in 2009. Such advances were not the natural outcome of the election of a leftist government, or of Rafael Correa's policies as president, but rather of the persistent work of activists to build coalitions with other urban groups, to educate elected officials as well as police officers walking the streets, to subvert and work within conventional legal frameworks, and to act swiftly and strategically during periods of political opportunity.

Correa in Context

President Rafael Correa took office in 2007 following a decade of antineoliberal mobilizations by indigenous, black, environmentalist, feminist, student, and LGBT social groups. The Ecuadorian state reestablished itself through a constitutional assembly process that resulted in one of the most progressive legal frameworks in Latin America. Correa defaulted on debt agreements with the World Bank, created social support programs, invested in health care and education, increased governmental efficiency, and built highways and other public infrastructure. These projects were mainly funded through revenues from record-high oil production and development loans from China. However, Correa's administration has been unable to diversify the Ecuadorian economy, and when the oil prices drop, as they did in January 2015, the country is hit hard, resulting in decreased wages and increased taxation for much of the population.

Correa is a media-savvy strong-arm politician who has enjoyed considerable popularity throughout his presidency. He hosts a weekly presidential program, in the style of Hugo Chavez, which he uses as a platform to promote his administration and combat his critics. In many ways, he is emblematic of the confluence of leftist populism, adaptive neoliberalism, and social conservatism that Paul Amar identifies with the emergence of new security regimes in the global South (Amar 2013).[3] Over the years, he has alienated many of the social movements that initially brought him to power, notably, indigenous and environmentalist groups whom he openly derides as "infantile leftists" and "economic terrorists," as well as feminist groups that decry the heavy criminalization of abortion under his administration. His critics from both the Left and the Right increasingly oppose his authoritarian governance practices. In the lead-up to the 2015 visit by Pope Francis, conservative groups held some of the largest anti-government demonstrations in recent years, which compelled Correa to back down on a proposed real-estate inheritance tax increase and to shore up the support of his remaining allies. In this tense political climate, Correa revised his position on a legal proposal that would allow people to change their gender designation on their official IDs and state documents.

Correa's announcement of support for the My Gender on My ID campaign demonstrates that, even within a socially conservative Christian political environment, there are important openings for trans empowerment and increased rights. His support represents a significant reversal of his previous position, which had been heavily criticized by feminist and LGBT activists for being both sexist and transphobic. I examine Correa's initial statements against the My Gender on My ID campaign here in order to trace the arc of activism that led to his current support for the proposed reform, within the rapidly shifting national political landscape.

My Gender on My ID

Missing or inadequate identity documents limit a person's ability to enter into formal contracts, attend schools, cash checks, or travel; lacking proper documentation exacerbates poverty and unemployment, raises suspicion of fraud, creates a pretext for arrest, and denies basic rights such as voting; Dean Spade identifies these systematic and structural practices as "administrative violence" (2011). The amalgamation of these exclusions constitutes transphobia as a state practice, and, like state-sanctioned racism, produces a "heightened vulnerability to premature death" for those affected (Gilmore 2007: 28). Transfeminist legal reform efforts like the My Gender on My ID campaign intervene against purportedly neutral administrative norms that marginalize and harm trans people.

The My Gender on My ID campaign began on June 6, 2012, when the activist groups Transgender Project, CONFETRANS, Building Equity, and Silueta

X proposed that the civil registry be amended to allow people to change their gender designation on their official state documents. Their proposal strategically calls for a distinction to be made between gender as a public identity and sex as a private biological trait, suggesting that a person's gender, not their sex, should be registered on public documents and identification cards in accordance with their gender identity. A sustained campaign increased public awareness, built support among feminist and LGBT groups, educated assembly members on trans issues, and provided political education to trans people on the need for this kind of reform.

The My Gender on My ID proposal received a hearing with the Commission for Autonomous Governments and the Decentralization of the National Assembly on July 23, 2012, at which various trans activists testified about the negative impact of not having an ID that adequately reflects their gender identity, while others simultaneously protested outside the building. The commission approved the proposal after its first hearing. The next step in the ratification process was to hold a debate within the full assembly, and if approved again the proposal would become law. In an effort to prevent further debate on the My Gender on My ID proposal, President Correa vowed to veto it if it was approved in the second hearing. This move effectively derailed the debate within the National Assembly for three years.

Correa's promise to veto My Gender on My ID is one of many recent instances in which ostensibly leftist, morally conservative politicians have zeroed in on issues of gender and sexuality, primarily by making opposition to gay marriage and abortion their signature concerns. Correa in fact justified his opposition to My Gender on My ID by characterizing it as a back-door strategy to obtain the right to same-sex marriage—a narrative that builds upon a "queer criminal archetype" that represents trans people as inherently deceptive and untrustworthy criminals with intent to commit identity fraud or theft (Mogul, Ritchie, and Whitlock 2012: 24).

On December 28, 2013, Correa dedicated a segment of his weekly television program to discussing gender identity and the state of feminist politics in Ecuador. He began by laying out some of the feminist accomplishments of his administration, such as higher numbers of women holding elective office and political appointments, and declared Ecuador to be in the vanguard of women's struggles in South America as well as globally. He warned his audience, however, against celebrating these accomplishments too quickly, given that there was still a long way to go regarding ongoing problems such as domestic violence, wage discrimination, and the uneven distribution of household labor. He emphasized the limits of legislative reform in the face of cultural acceptance of sexism and argued that in order to move beyond formal equality it would be necessary to transform the culture at large. Correa then shifted from celebrating feminist advances to cautioning against feminist excesses:

> We all struggle for equal rights between men and women, but that's different from fundamentalist feminist movements that seek for men and women to be the same, and I insist to you—that ideology is very dangerous. They are teaching about gender identity to our youth in the schools, basically saying that there is no natural man or woman, that it is not sex that determines if we are a man or a woman but rather social conditions, that man and woman are a social construction, and in order to liberate ourselves from those conditionings a woman can choose to be a man, and a man can choose to be a woman. (Correa 2013)

Correa establishes a dichotomy between a commonsense feminism that everyone can support, which works toward equal rights, and what he calls a "fundamentalist" feminism that aims to radically transform gender relations. In doing so, he draws upon a concept of "gender ideology" common to conservative Christian critics of LGBT activism, as well as to "gender-critical" antitransgender feminists. Anticipating critiques from those who view him as a socially conservative politician rather than an authentic leftist, Correa tried to explain, sometimes stumbling over his words and expressing himself with apparent difficulty:

> Ideology is constructed above all on material conditions, modes of production, et cetera. It is also constructed sometimes on moral issues, but these issues are . . . they have me . . . they imply so much discussion. So they are going to call me a conservative because I believe in the family. I don't believe in this ideology of gender, in these novelties, that destroy the conventional family, which is, and happily will continue to be, the foundation of our society. (Correa 2013)

Correa builds here on a leftist legacy that prioritizes questions of material production and political economy above struggles over representation and identity. Lisa Duggan describes this conceptual distinction between leftist political economy and identity politics as a "ruse of capitalist liberal discourse" that obscures the ways in which class is lived through the categories of race, ethnicity, age, gender, sexuality, and religion. She notes that since the 1970's, socialist feminists have analyzed the ways in which "sexual regulation is a core component in historically changing modes of economic distribution," and warns that this ruse "produces an implicit hierarchy where no explicit one exists, by stripping 'cultural' critique or identity politics of their capacity to engage and transform the economy" (Duggan 2003: 81–83). Correa's verbal stops and starts make evident how difficult it is to actually separate gender and sexuality from materiality and means of production, even as he tries to position himself as a rational leftist executive decision maker tasked with filtering out *novelerias* from the real questions of political economy.[4]

Despite these setbacks, trans activists continually placed the My Gender on My ID campaign at the forefront of their political efforts. In early 2014, a coalition of trans activists formed Trans Pact, a national steering committee that strategized about national policy objectives in a series of closed-door meetings. Elizabeth Vasquez, the author of the My Gender on My ID proposal and a main organizer of Trans Pact, points out that the proposed reform does not enable same sex-marriage because it retains sex as an administrative category of state (while rendering it private, recorded only on the birth certificate).[5] The Ecuadorian state could thus forbid same sex-marriage while also allowing a change of gender on state-issued IDs by requiring marriage applicants to provide their birth certificates. Calling for a legal distinction between sex and gender, rather than the elimination of sex as an administrative category, was carefully considered in relation to how it might affect other feminist and LGBT legislation that depends on sex. As Vasquez notes:

> If the civil distinction between men and women were eliminated, many legal questions would emerge: what would happen, for example, with the classification of present day "sexed" crimes; such as *femicide*, on the protective end, or abortion, on the repressive end? How would political parity between men and women on electoral legislation be interpreted? How would the segregation by sex of persons deprived of liberty in the prison system function? How would the rules about sex and gender-based violence be applied? (Vasquez 2015: 207)

Beyond this effort not to disrupt other feminist social justice legal reforms already in place or under way, and not to be stymied by the juridical challenge of eradicating sex altogether from state records, Vasquez contends that the simultaneous use of both gender and sex as administrative categories forces the state to reckon with the complexity and variability of people's combined gender, sex, and sexuality, claiming that this approach has a "pedagogical effect" on the legal system by demonstrating that "on certain occasions sex is important, many other times gender is what's important, and sometimes they are both important as a fusion embodied in each person " (Vasquez 2015: 211).

While conservative political positions on marriage and abortion are firmly fixed, there are openings through which activists can push for increased rights when no rigid party line has been handed down to religious and conservative leaders regarding other specific social issues. Efforts to reduce employment discrimination for trans people, or to increase access to gender-affirming health care and higher education, are topics that the Catholic church and other conservative leaders have not taken a strong position against, and these can be successfully advocated for on the basis of a call to equality. It remains to be seen whether the principle of equality will provide "enough of an open container for the nonnormative, the excessive, and multiply situated sexual and affective expressions" (Gómez-Barris and Fiol-Matta 2014: 497), yet transfeminism represents an emerging possibility for maneuvering within the constraints of a liberal rights discourse to disrupt the state's management of gender, sex, and sexuality.

Turning to Transfeminism

Since August 2014, Correa has held an unprecedented series of meetings with LGBT activists to establish objectives for policy reform, organized by the executive director of Silueta X, Diane Rodriguez. The fourth meeting took place days before nationwide LGBT pride celebrations and the arrival of Pope Francis to Ecuador in 2015, amidst a political frenzy of nightly right-wing antigovernment protests along one of the main avenues of the city. In this context, Correa came out in support of the My Gender on My ID proposal in his weekly television program on Saturday, June 27, 2015. He explained that he is still unlearning homophobia and described the kinds of humiliation, confusion, and exclusion that administrative violence produces. He asked his audience to reflect on how hard it must be "on a human level" to experience this kind of discrimination and constructed a narrative in which brave trans people resisted victimization and, in the face of adversity, had expressed good will toward the government by engaging in a series of high-level policy meetings. This was in contradistinction to the "stubborn" and "ungrateful" same-sex marriage advocates who were wearing down his administration and making possible the return of right-wing governments (Correa 2015). Despite Correa's rhetorical attempt to pit trans rights against same-sex marriage—even despite the fact that Correa's closest trans ally, Diane Rodriguez, publicly distanced her organization from same-sex marriage advocacy—the My Gender on My ID campaign has widespread support within the larger LGBT and feminist communities.

On the one hand, these latest developments demonstrate the loyalty that Correa demands from those he favors, requiring them to endorse his stance on controversial topics such as same-sex marriage, abortion, and oil extraction as the price of his support. On the other hand, they demonstrate the dynamic flux and fluidity of state formation, as transfeminist activists respond to Correa's call for a "citizen revolution" and opportunistically test different strategies for getting the state to do what they need under emergent political conditions. They are doing the work of state making and expanding notions of citizenship and agency. The My Gender on My ID campaign, located at the intersection of an ongoing history of transfeminist activism and the reimagining of the Ecuadorian state, exemplifies the current moment in which geopolitical forces are reconfiguring relationships between social conservatism, Left populism, adaptive neoliberalism, and new regimes of state security—a moment in which the future remains very much up for grabs.

Addendum: Gender for All

After this article was accepted for publication in mid-2015, Ecuador experienced a remarkable milestone in the administrative history of identity management. In October 2015, the ruling Alianza País party made public a draft proposal to overhaul guidelines and regulations governing the civil registry—a bill known as the Organic Law of National Identity and Civil Data Management. The proposed law contained 103 articles covering a wide range of issues including the listing of blood type and other medical information on state-issued IDs, provisions of IDs for children, the elderly, foreigners, migrants, and refugees, guidelines for what names are permissible for registration, and the removal of marital or civil union status from state-issued IDs, to name but a few of the proposed areas of change. Given the breadth and depth of the proposed reforms, virtually every sector of the population would be affected by the new guidelines and regulations.

Trans activists were disappointed to find that while the Organic Law of National Identity and Civil Data Management included some of the principles of their My Gender on My ID proposal, it significantly undermined their underlying rationale because sex, as a biological category, rather than gender, as a social identity, would remain the default administrative category on state-issued IDs. Article 94 of the new bill would establish the right to apply for an alternate ID without a sex designation, which would instead list the cardholder's gender as either masculine or feminine. There would be no requirement to disclose personal or medical information to the civil registry staff in order to apply for the alternate ID or to change one's official gender designation.[6] The bill would also add the stipulation that persons who officially change their names to one with a different gender designation than the sex/gender assigned at birth would be required to obtain an alternate ID and to change their official gender designation. Name and gender would be changeable only once, irreversibly. The proposed bill contained several other conservative provisions, such as Article 44, which stipulates that only married heterosexual couples would be eligible to adopt children and denies the right of adoption by single people of any gender identity or sexual orientation. The bill would also prohibit the recognition or registration of same-sex parents for children, regardless of the couple's civil status or whether the child was conceived through assisted reproduction. Articles 44 and 94 both represent conservative political efforts to stabilize the sex/gender categories that underpin heterosexuality in the face of transgender fluidity and to push back against the advancement in rights for LGBT families.

As the early draft of the reform bill began to circulate among LGBT and feminist activists, many criticized the proposal's overt sexism and homophobia as well as the creation of a separate ID system for trans people. They pointed to Article 67 in the Constitution, which establishes the right to and recognition of diverse family structures, and Article 68, which confers the same rights to children of civil unions as those born within heterosexual marriages. Activists from Trans Pact held several press conferences and demonstrations throughout the months of October and November 2015 to denounce the changes made to the original proposals of My Gender on My ID and to renew their calls for gender, rather than sex, as the standard administrative category for everyone. They established a new social media campaign, Gender For All: We All Have Gender, which once again made the case that sex is a private biological trait while gender is a public identity that all people experience and which is not unique to trans people. In an effort to reinstate the language of the original My Gender on My ID proposal, members of Trans Pact met with assembly members who supported the proposal in its original form to request that they speak out against the creation of separate IDs for trans people. Campaign activists forcefully articulated a more nuanced account of gender as a person's culturally intelligible and recognizable, socially constructed individual identity. They also recirculated social media memes from the earlier campaign, featuring national IDs with photos of male and female genitals instead of faces, to emphasize how the current ID system violates privacy.

The Gender for All campaign steered clear of discussions of gender fluidity and instead heavily emphasized the right of trans people to maintain their privacy with respect to their biological sex as a means of preventing discrimination. This narrative framing reflected transfeminists' pragmatic efforts to navigate within what Christine (Cricket) Keating (2013: 246) has called "state homoprotectionism," a conservative political terrain characterized by a complex "interplay between state homophobia and policies geared toward the protection of sexual minorities." In spite of their strategic use of rights discourse, transfeminists' repeated insistence on a clear distinction between sex as a private biological trait and gender as a socially constructed public identity, and their insistence upon understanding gender as a universal experience, worked its way into the national psyche and political vocabulary in a profound manner, setting the terms for what will now be considered progressive LGBT positions in Ecuador.

On December 10, 2015, after two months of spirited public discussion, the national assembly met to debate and vote on the Organic Law of National Identity and Civil Data Management. A group of thirty trans activists were present in the mezzanine of the assembly, the great majority of them members of Trans Pact, whose mood was less than celebratory. Over the course of the previous weeks, a significant conflict had emerged between activists who wanted to reject the new proposal and those who argued that it would be more strategic to accept it while continuing to work toward the use of gender as the standard administrative category for all people. This conflict created deep divisions among activists who until that point were working together toward the passage of the original proposals of My Gender on My ID. On the day of the debate, two different representatives of the trans community spoke to the assembly, Nua Fuentes on behalf of the members of Trans Pact and Diane Rodriguez, President Correa's most partisan and high profile transgender supporter, in her new capacity as the appointed president of the Ecuadorian Federation of LGBT Organizations, which is a coalition formed by the national assembly in September 2015 following a series of meetings between Correa and a select group of invited LGBT activists.

Fuentes criticized changes to the original legislation brought forward by Trans Pact and once again made the case for gender as a "universal" experience. She conceded that the option to change one's gender designation on official IDs would in some ways be an advance for trans people's rights, but in other ways it would be detrimental. She argued that rather than conferring full equality, inclusion, and privacy on trans people, the proposed bill would create an "abstract equality that does not necessarily have an impact on real life." A person with an alternate ID would be assumed to be trans and could be discriminated against on that basis. In her closing remarks she stated:

> This is why today we ask you to pass legislation on gender not in an optional way but in a universal way, so the rights of our group do not remain abstract recitations but are concretized, so I can go into society and exercise my right to privacy without fear of violence, without fear that my identity will be violated. My rights are not optional, they are constitutional, they are universal, like gender is universal. Gender is for everyone, and that is why we ask you today to approve gender for everyone. It is our right, not a privilege. Gender for all, thank you very much. (Fuentes 2015)

Diane Rodriguez (2015) followed this address with a speech that sowed further division within the LGBT community and demonstrated her allegiance to Correa's Alianza País party, at a time of renewed and increased political repression against antigovernment protesters, saying:

> The rights of trans populations—that is to say *travesti*, transgender, transsexual, and intersex populations—have been used and frequently mocked by cisheteronormative people and even by some bad gay and lesbian elements in our community, who unfortunately base their activism on their hatred of a political project that has brought [positive] changes and wellbeing.

Rodriguez's derision of "bad gay and lesbian elements" is not in reference to lesbian or gay activist groups that opposed the My Gender on My ID campaign but rather to those critical of the "citizen revolution" spearheaded by President Rafael Correa and the Alianza País party, specifically those same-sex marriage and adoption advocates whom the president had deemed dangerously "stubborn" and "ungrateful" when he announced his support for the My Gender on My ID campaign in the summer of 2015. Throughout her speech, Rodriguez created a narrative of Ecuadorian exceptionalism, characterizing Ecuador as the first country in the world to recognize gender identity in its constitution in 2008 and as a vanguard nation in LGBT rights. She further argued that the proposed Organic Law would be the most advanced legislation in the world with respect to the recognition of trans identity, because unlike Argentina, Colombia, Italy, and Denmark, these new IDs would list gender instead of sex and would not create what she characterized as an "incorrect" third gender category as do newly available forms of state ID in Nepal, India, and Australia. Though she vowed to continue working towards "universal gender," which by this point had become a shorthand for the original My Gender on My ID reform proposal, Rodriguez explained how the creation of a new alternate ID would not actually be dis-criminatory, because it would be available to all people.

Despite the numerous criticisms leveled against the proposed legislation by LGBT activists and some Alianza País assembly members for how it under-mined the intent of the My Gender on My ID proposal, few members of the ruling party felt obliged to respond to these criticisms. When speaking out against the alteration of the original text of the proposal, assembly members María Soledad Vega, Noralma Zambrano, María Alexandra Ocles, and Diego Veintimilla of the Alianza País party all used the language of Trans Pact activists about the uni-versality of gender and the vulnerabilities faced by trans people if a separate ID system were to be implemented. A few members of the assembly simply stated that the bill represented an advancement in rights for LGBT people. Many assembly members did not mention the topic of gender at all, focusing instead on questions raised by the sprawling piece of proposed legislation's treatment of migration status and medical history in reference to official state IDs and documents. No one explained why the changes to sex/gender classification were made, and no one defended the retention of sex as an administrative category. In effect, the only person who defended the changes in the proposal against the criticisms made by trans activists was Diane Rodriguez.

The national assembly passed the Organic Law of National Identity and Civil Data Management on December 10, 2015. Transfeminist activist Elizabeth Vasquez characterized the passage as a "bittersweet victory," given that the bill contained many advances in civil rights but not fully inclusive state-issued IDs for trans people (*Diario Extra* (Guayaquil) 2015). This struggle will require more cycles of activism and political engagement. Many anticipate that there will be problems associated with the alternate IDs, such as logistical difficulties with sex-segregated voting lines, or instances of discrimination against trans people by potential employers or landlords because their alternate IDs out them as trans. Trans activism will continue work toward the use of gender as a standard administrative category for all state-issued IDs and will use whatever problems emerge from the current legislation to build the case for the full inclusion and equality of trans people within the civil registry and society at large.

Claudia Sofía Garriga López is a doctoral candidate in American studies at the Department of Social and Cultural Analysis of New York University.

Acknowledgments

I would like thank the editors of this special issue, Susan Stryker and Talia Bettcher, as well as two anonymous peer reviewers for their critical and thoughtful feedback, and managing editor Abraham Weil for his guidance. Many thanks to Elizabeth Vasquez and Ana Almeida, who generously imparted their political experiences and welcomed me into transfeminist activism. Geovanni Jaramillo also shared valuable historical information and serves as a model for an expansive transfeminist practice. Jennifer Flores Sternad, Marcela Di Blasi, and Brian Ray read early drafts of this work. Flor Bermudes, Yadira Perez-Hazel, and Paula Saunders have shown me immense kindness and support over the last year, for which I am eternally grateful. Edgar Rivera-Colón guided my methodological approach and provided invaluable counseling as well as close feedback on early drafts of this text. Macarena Gómez-Barris and Santiago Castellanos provided on-site advice and encouragement during the research and writing period, while Salvador Vidal-Ortiz invited me to dream big about the future of transfeminism. Maritza Stanchich and A. J. Bauer kindly read this article in its final iterations and aided me in crafting the title and subtitles. Lastly, I'd like to thank María Josefina Saldaña-Portillo for her exceptional mentorship and unwavering support. This article is dedicated to my sister Adriana María Garriga-López, trans-feminist activists in Ecuador, and everyone working to combat police violence in the Americas. Sections of this article were presented at the Latin American Studies Association Conference in 2015. I personally translated quotes by Elizabeth Vasquez, President Rafael Correa, Nua Fuentes, Diane Rodriguez, and Santiago Castellanos. When possible, I directly translated the names of activist organizations into English, such as the Legal Patrol (Patrulla Legal), Transgender Project (Proyecto Transgénero), Building Equality (Construyendo Igualdad), and Trans Pact (Pacto Trans).

Notes

1.   The Legal Patrol has had twelve different incarnations since its initial formation in 2002. It is not a recognized nongovernment organization, nor is it active year-round, rather it operates intermittently as an activist group spearheaded by Elizabeth Vasquez.

2.   This passage was transcribed and translated from a self-produced documentary film on the Legal Patrol (Palacios 2011).

3.   Security politics relies heavily on a Christian conservative morality and produces discourses that simultaneously promote a nationalist and decolonial struggle and seek full incorporation into global markets.

4.   This term translates into "novelties" but also references the culture of telenovelas as a kind of melodramatic feminist politics.

5.   The proposal states that at the age of sixteen all card holders be granted the right to change their gender designation and that until an individual decides to change their gender designation, the system will use the sex designations as a kind of default guide to establishing gender designations on subsequent state records, documents, and IDs.

6.   On January 13, 2016, President Correa implemented a partial veto on the Organic Law of Identity and Civil Data Management that altered 61 out of the 103 articles in an overhaul reform bill passed on December 10, 2015. Among the changes in the articles, Correa added that in order to apply for a new ID which lists gender instead of sex, a person must have the support of two witnesses.

References

Almeida, Ana, and Elizabeth Vasquez. 2010. *Cuerpos distintos: Ocho años de activismo transfeminista en Ecuador* (*Different Bodies: Eight Years of Transfeminist Activism in Ecuador*). Comisión de Transición Consejo Nacional de Mujeres y la Igualdad de Género (Transitional National Commission for Women and Gender Equality), Quito, Ecuador.

Amar, Paul. 2013. *The Security Archipelago: Human-Security States, Sexuality Politics, and the End of Neoliberalism*. Durham, NC: Duke University Press.

Castellanos, Santiago. 2014. "Sexualidades no-normativas, diferencias racial y la erótica del poder: Escenarios de deseos queer en el Ecuador del siglo XXI" ("Nonnormative Sexualities, Racial Difference, and the Erotics of Power: Scenes of Queer Desire in Twenty-First-Century Ecuador."). In *Resentir lo queer en América Latina: Diálogos desde/con el sur* (*Resenting/Feeling-again Queer in Latin America: Dialogues from/with the South*), edited by Diego Falconí Trávez, Santiago Castellanos, and María Amelia Viteri, 195–212. Barcelona: Egales Editorial.

Correa, Rafael. 2013. "Enlace ciudadano nro. 354 desde Monte Sinaí—Guayaquil" ("Citizen Link No. 354 from Monte Sinaí—Guayaquil"). YouTube video, 3:31. December 28. www .youtube.com/watch?v=qkw_fRi8xUE.

———. 2015. "Enlace ciudadano nro. 430 desde guasmo sur, guayas 27/06/2015" ("Citizen Link No. 430 from Guasmo South in Guayas 06/27/2015"). YouTube video, 4:01. Streamed live June 27. www.youtube.com/watch?v=JoAPcpPU7Cs.

Diario Extra (Guayaquil). 2015. "Un éxito 'agridulce' para los GLBTI" ("A Bittersweet Success for LGBTI"). December 12.

Duggan, Lisa. 2003. *The Twilight of Equality: Neoliberalism, Cultural Politics, and the Attack on Democracy*. Boston: Beacon.

Fuentes, Nua. 2015. "Tod@s Tenemos Género: Género para Tod@s" ("Gender for All: We All Have Gender"). Opening remarks for the National Assembly debate and vote on the Organic Law of National Identity and Civil Data Management, Law ID no. 233646, December 10.

Gilmore, Ruth Wilson. 2007. *Golden Gulag: Prisons, Surplus, Crisis, and Opposition in Globalizing California*. Berkeley: University of California Press.

Gómez-Barris, Macarena, and Licia Fiol-Matta. 2014. "Introduction: *Las Américas Quarterly*." *American Quarterly* 66, no. 3: 493–504.

Keating, Christine (Cricket). 2013. "Conclusion: On the Interplay between State Homophobia and Homoprotectionism." In *Global Homophobia: States, Movements, and the Politics of Oppression*, edited by Meredith L. Weiss and Michael J. Bosia, 246–54. Urbana: University of Illinois Press.

Mogul, Joey L., Andrea J. Ritchie, and Kay Whitlock. 2012. *Queer (In)Justice: The Criminalization of LGBT People in the United States*. Queer Action/Queer Ideas. Boston: Beacon.

Palacios, Mariangeles. 2011. *Patrulla legal . . . El derecho en la calle* (*Legal Patrol . . . The Right to the Street*). DVD. Ecuador: Namaste, Luna Films, and Twenty-One Film. Trailer on Vimeo, 3:32. February 2, 2012. www.vimeo.com/36121692.

Pratt, Mary Louise. 2007. *Imperial Eyes: Travel Writing and Transculturation*. 2nd ed. New York: Routledge.

Rodriguez, Diane. 2015. "Género opcional en DNI—Cédula hecho histórico" ("Optional Gender in the National Identification Document [DNI]—Cédula Historic Event"). Opening remarks for the National Assembly debate and vote on the Organic Law of National Identity and Civil Data Management, Law ID no. 233646, December 10. www.facebook.com/DianeRodriguezZ/videos/953840111336666/?pnref=story.

Saldaña-Portillo, María Josefina. 2003. *The Revolutionary Imagination in the Americas and the Age of Development*. Durham, NC: Duke University Press.

Spade, Dean. 2011. *Normal Life: Administrative Violence, Critical Trans Politics, and the Limits of Law*. New York: South End.

Vasquez, Elizabeth. 2015. "Mi género en mi cédula: Un concepto nuevo por una puerta vieja" ("My Gender on My ID: A New Concept through an Old Door") In *Queering Narratives of Modernity*, edited by Maria Amelia Viteri and Manuela Picq, 197–214. Bern, Switzerland: Peter Lang.

Passing Torches?

Feminist Inquiries and Trans-Health Politics and Practices

CHRISTOPH HANSSMANN

Abstract This article offers an empirical and theoretical inquiry into how the emergent field of trans health can be productively read with and through feminist health formations. It explores connections (tense and otherwise) between trans health and feminist health, and it brings critical theorizing of feminist health practices to bear on how trans health is currently fashioned, situated, and represented. It asks how trans studies might begin to map health, technoscience, and medicine in ways that extend or exceed the medicalization critiques that form cornerstones of scholarship in trans studies, as they did in feminist women's health. In so doing, it draws upon feminist theorizing of technoscience and reproductive health as generative sites for reflection and analysis. The article employs data from an ethnographic study of trans-health providers and activists in metropolitan areas in the United States and Argentina.

Keywords transgender health, reproductive health, feminist science and technology studies, biomedicine, activism and social movements

S itting alongside forty medical and health-professional students enrolled in a transgender health elective, I listened to a physician and trans-health advocate deliver a lively lecture on the history of transgender health.[1] Densely mapping early sexology through LGBT community-based health and contemporary policies, he portrayed an emergent and politicized health-care practice gradually prevailing over its detractors. Key actors in the history of trans activisms, however, were missing from his narrative. Elisions are inevitable in the course of a fifty-minute lecture,[2] but I left the classroom with a curious sense of omission: where was feminist health?

This particular exclusion is not unique to this lecturer. In the United States, the popular historical narrative of transgender health goes a bit like this: US and European sexological nosology gave way to the interdisciplinary field of transsexual medicine in the mid-twentieth century, which soon came under the watchful eye of psychiatry and professional authority. A power struggle between providers and patients eventually reached a fever pitch, and trans patients rebelled in ways both subtle and brazen—following in the footsteps of LGBQ health activists. Queer-community health formations[3]—sometimes, and sometimes reluctantly—provided both the signal boost and the clinical sites for meeting and forging broader demands regarding trans policies and practices. After gathering strength and momentum, transgender health now stands on its own. A slightly more textured map might include mention of HIV care and research or cite a "depathologization" template offered by gay activists demanding the 1974 removal of "homosexuality" from the *Diagnostic and Statistical Manual of Mental Disorders*, second edition (*DSM*-II, American Psychiatric Association 1974).[4] Yet in these popular histories, feminist health—particularly in its language of "self-possession" and its emphasis on the politicization of clinical practice (Murphy 2012)—is conspicuously absent.[5]

To address this lacuna, here I explore the ongoing convergences, tensions, and resonances of feminist and trans health. I argue that reflecting on the varied instantiations of trans health as a partial reassembly of certain feminist health formations offers insights on how to think through their proximity. I suggest that looking to feminist theorizing—particularly analyses of reproductive health and technoscience[6]—may extend and reformulate how trans studies theorizes health care and biomedicine. Drawing from my training as a feminist sociologist of science and medicine, and leveraging concepts from feminist ST&MS (science, technology, and medicine studies), I ask how trans studies might analyze bio-medical practices to interrogate the sometimes-obscured or overly flattened politics of clinical knowledge and care.[7]

Placing trans and feminist activism and scholarship in conversation is hardly novel. Nonetheless, it is remarkable how often these are positioned along parallel but separate rails or in antagonistic tension. In the United States, analyses often rehearse a narrative of antipathy dating from at least the 1970s. Transfeminist approaches contradict this tendency, emphasizing constitutive crossings, mutual imbrications, and solidarities in the connections and convergences of trans and feminist theories and projects (e.g., Hale 1998; Bettcher and Garry 2009; Bettcher 2007; Koyama 2003; Salamon 2010; Enke 2012; cárdenas 2015; Heyes 2003; Snorton and Haritaworn 2013; Stryker 2008). Tensions remain, however, and anxiously (re)animate debates concerning themes ranging from gendered restrooms to sexualized labor (Heyes 2003; Spade 2006; Goldberg 2014; Pecheny 2010).

Examining the mutual positioning of these politics need not conclude that trans and feminist politics and scholarship are necessarily or obviously allied, nor that they ought to be indistinguishable. Rather, I suggest that focusing on their convergences and points of tense contact might generatively texture an understanding of prior and existing relations that goes beyond well-rehearsed if not tired animosities. This ambition pursues paths forged by a growing number of activists and scholars (Koyama 2003; Heyes 2003; Bettcher and Garry 2009; Audre Lorde Project 2012; cárdenas 2015; Stryker, Currah, and Moore 2008). My emphasis on interrogating concrete practices, especially clinical practices, offers a distinctive analytic angle and focuses nuanced attention on the manifold differences often subsumed in characterizing projects and positions as either "feminist" or "trans."

Last year saw the publication of *Trans Bodies, Trans Selves* (*TBTS*, Erickson-Schroth 2014). Advanced by US-based activists and practitioners as a singular community resource, clinical handbook, and service guide by and for trans communities, its title nods directly to the classic feminist health resource, *Our Bodies, Ourselves* (*OBOS*, Boston Women's Health Book Collective [1971] 2011). *TBTS* pointedly renarrates trans health as a feminist health legacy rather than simply as queer health's most immediate progenitor. A split-panel illustration in the book depicts this connection with a hand passing *OBOS* to a receiving hand grasping *TBTS*. The caption reads, "Passing the torch." This metaphorical kindred-but-distinct relation marks a slightly tense homage and cagey distinction between these ostensibly distinct communities of concern and historic activism. I argue, though, that feminist health—in many different forms—constitutes something more than merely a parent or predecessor for contemporary trans studies and movements.

Trans Health in Plural Form

Despite its increasing ubiquity, precisely what "trans health" intends to signal or describe remains unclear. While some informants, for example, described their relation to trans health as one of biomedical expertise, others described it more broadly. One provider proclaimed that his "self-taught endocrinology" expertise authenticated his credibility in trans health. Another asserted that disproportionate rates of HIV in trans communities indicate the racialized and classed failures of health-care systems and reveal the need to improve care for trans people in health systems writ large. For one activist, trans health was "the starting point for beginning to think . . . about what it would take to turn back the tide on neoliberalism" and to "rebuild [what a] democratic, egalitarian welfare state could look like." An activist in the global South explained efforts to craft regional trans-health policies that resisted US "medical and psychiatric imperialism" and that instead institutionalized "nonhegemonic gender relations" in care practice.

These wildly ranging aspirations of trans health find resonance in the multiplicity of feminist health formations in the United States and transnationally. As Michelle Murphy (2012) asserts in her work on particular US feminist health movements in the 1970s, "feminisms"—decisively in the plural—ranged greatly in their tactics, composition, and politics (Murphy 2012: 6, 184). Some of these strategies involved cultivating highly technoscientific approaches to care—such as "menstrual extraction kits" that sidestepped abortion regulations or in vitro fertilization (IVF). Advancing the term *counter-conduct* rather than *resistance*, Murphy describes how feminists sought at once to disassemble the hegemonic and to (re)fashion nonhegemonic modes of practice, even while these novel forms of conduct remained "conditioned by and entangled with the hegemonic" (184). That is, technological innovations rendered life alterable in new ways, and many feminists seized upon and translated such tools and practices in ways uniquely organized by feminist politics. However, as Franklin (2013) points out, feminists did not adopt this position unanimously. Some rejected technological innovations such as IVF and amniocentesis as inherently patriarchal. For others, technologies provoked ambivalence and raised concerns about power relations, access, and agency—but incited engagement rather than rejection. While few doubted the patriarchal, militaristic, eugenic, and/or capitalist impulses initially shaping such technologies and their development, many feminists were (and are) interested in their subversion and repurposing.

Thus the notion of trans health elicits wide-ranging political, strategic, and conceptual questions about the very configurations of biomedicine. Does trans health amend biomedical practices to "tailor" clinical care, in the sartorial language of cultural-competency regimes (Truong, Paradies, and Priest 2014)? Or does it transfigure health and biomedicine at the level of materiality and ideology? One way to understand the scale, scope, and content of various transformations might be to ask what is being reorganized, in what ways, and with what effects.[8] Stryker, Currah, and Moore (2008: 13) describe "transing" as "a practice that takes place within, as well as across or between, gendered spaces." Relevant to health care, these spaces may compose the clinic, the diagnostic manual, and/or treatment protocols. As a "practice that assembles gender into contingent structures of association with other attributes of bodily being, and that allows for their reassembly," transing might exert varying forces on clinical practice (13). In the empirical field of trans health, it is possible to examine the distinct pressures and effects of these varying forces, and to analyze how trans health might at once challenge and reinforce biomedical relations of power.

If trans health "transes" biomedicine then, it does so by introducing radical contingency with respect to sexed or gendered bodies and their need for clinical care. Trans-health providers describe various technical and technoscientific strategies through which they realign biomedical practices beyond obvious modes of body modification. Some of these include retooling language and reminder systems regarding prostate or cervical cancer screenings to ensure that they are appropriately directed to trans people, introducing notions of self-determination and bodily autonomy to practices of care, or revealing how health systems may be detrimental or deadly to trans and other gender-nonnormative people.

These strategies evoke some of the innovations and refusals of anti-medicalization strategies of feminist health movements. Quotidian practices of feminist health care, for example, have foregrounded autonomy and contested standardized clinical care, engaging the notion that sexed and gendered embodiment fail to predict particular modes of conduct. As such, trans health's political plurality and its technical and epistemological capacities to realign and reassemble bodily being are shared by nonhegemonic feminist health-care formations since the 1970s and 1980s. That trans health is conceived and practiced in such varying ways reveals both biomedical entanglements and engagements in what Alondra Nelson (2011: 5) calls the "powerful and elastic political lexicon" of health.

Trans-Health Practice after the Diagnostic Battlefield

From its inception, trans studies has critically theorized surgical, psychiatric, and other facets of clinical care. One major strand problematizes gender non-normativity as an appropriate object of medical or psychiatric classification and scrutiny (Aizura 2010; Burke 2011; Cabral and Viturro 2006; Namaste [2005] 2011; Prosser 1999; Singer 2006; Stone 1992; Stryker 2008). While many of these are nuanced, certain critiques tended to flatten or underanalyze medical authority, viewing it as monolithic and geographically untethered rather than "local" or specifically situated (Lock 1993).

In her "posttranssexual manifesto," Sandy Stone (1992) classically describes the clinical encounter as a "diagnostic battlefield" across which "transsexuals and clinicians continue to face off" (298). In the near quarter century since Stone's publication, trans health has shifted in a variety of ways, and some of its very critiques have even been repeated by health-care providers. Some providers now advocate, for example, "rejecting psychopathological models" and "including community perspectives" in shaping care protocols (Center of Excellence 2011; Drescher 2010; Drescher, Cohen-Kettenis, and Winter 2012; Feldman 2008; Gorton 2013). Updated and revised diagnoses and protocols for care now state the importance of diagnostic and treatment flexibility, patients' desires, and access to primary and transition-specific care (Bagby 2011; Center of Excellence 2011; Drescher 2010; Drescher, Cohen-Kettenis, and Winter 2012; Coleman, et al. 2012).[9] Trans providers, lawyers, and activists increasingly shape policies and protocols. As views and practices on the landscape of care provision shift, corollary changes also take place in arrangements of authority, with implications for the politics of knowledge.

Such shifts are neither consistent nor complete. Nonetheless, my interviews with providers who claimed particular expertise in trans health—certainly disproportionately supportive of their patients compared to providers overall—portrayed a landscape much changed from the scorched-earth scene of Stone's diagnostic battlefield. These providers often explained how their own embeddedness within queer and trans communities informed their practices, describing how this precipitated their decision to work in health-care provision. Some were particularly adamant about sidestepping pathologizing and diagnostic frameworks, including the provider who remarked, "Now I'm getting more comfortable just speaking from the heart, and not using that language, but still participating. [That] feels more real . . . [than when] it's like a textbook is talking." Here, he refuses the standard lexicon of diagnosis to engage in conversations with colleagues about his patients. For this provider, communicating "from the heart" rather than through diagnoses or from "a textbook" constitutes a more supportive form of care provision.

Such ruminations raise questions about how biomedical ideologies and privileged forms of knowledge circulate within shifting relations of clinical care and community practice. Sheryl Burt Ruzek (1978: 144) describes feminist interventions on health as having "the potential to deinstitutionalize medical authority" in part by "transform[ing] authority relationships between patients and practitioners." As such, feminist health movements leveraged patient expertise to contest hegemonic medical practice, "linking a systematic critique of patriarchal institutions to a concrete praxis of self-help" (Epstein 1996: 9–10). Feminist health activists advocated various strategies in undertaking these objectives: self-help at home, "politicized" nurses and nurse practitioners infiltrating medical practice; ownership and operation of explicitly feminist clinics; and so on (Morgen 2002; Ruzek 1978, 1980). Partnership, collectivity, and trust were key themes in these efforts to restructure clinical practice settings. Similarly, in the case of trans health, it is not only patients but also those whom I call "insider-providers" that presently seem to drive these ideological and practical challenges and refigurings. For example, a queer-identified nurse working in an LGBT clinic expressed skepticism about a new hospital-based trans-health program: "I don't feel like they care about us. I'm highly suspicious." Expertise in trans health, for this provider, requires alignment with or membership within "the community," which encompasses both patients and providers in the embrace of the "us." For insider-providers, community membership is key to good care.

In another case, a nurse practitioner had long pressured a prison in which she worked to enhance access to hormone treatment for incarcerated trans women, among other forms of care. She was surprised to find that this was a far easier victory than her two-year fight to get women inside the men's prison access to bras:

> You have this system that says, we'll give you estrogen, we'll feminize you, and we will harass you when we can see your breasts, but we won't allow you the courtesy or the dignity to have a [bra] to be a little more modest. Or we'll still make you shower with the [men] . . . or we won't give you condoms, when we know you're having sexual activities. . . . [T]he whole thing . . . would sound like a horror movie if it wasn't reality.

The punitive measures this provider described—which, as far as prison administration was concerned, fell outside the bounds of adopted trans-health policy—definitively imperiled incarcerated trans women's health and survival. In this mode, narrowly defined trans-health practices were turned back on themselves and deployed vindictively, much to the indignation and fury of the provider who initially pressured the prison administration to adopt standards guiding care.

While US-based trans-health activism often advances a depathologization framework through guidelines and diagnostic interventions, certain strategies elsewhere in the world increasingly encode this imperative into law (Suess, Espineira, and Walters 2014; GATE 2015). In Argentina, for example, the activist-led passage of the 2012 Gender Identity Law incorporated depathologization at the level of federal legislation (Salum 2012). While providers throughout the world typically require a diagnosis and several letters of approval or support for trans patients seeking gender-confirming care, Argentina's law obviates these requirements (at least for trans adults). The act of diagnosis in this regard, as one activist coyly reminded me, "is actually illegal now." Here, the law trumps medical expertise, and the "expressed desire" of trans patients is the sole requirement to access covered forms of treatment—including in public hospitals. Nevertheless, regulatory problems have disparately limited its actualization, especially among those without private insurance, resulting in racialized and classed stratifications in access to care. But such infrastructural delays have not slowed inspiration for similar legal developments elsewhere in Latin America and Europe, including in Malta, Colombia, Norway, and Chile (Ministry of Health 2015; Lee 2015; Transgender Europe 2015; Duarte 2015).

The sites of struggle through which trans health takes shape worldwide have thus shifted, but unevenly so. Medical authority is understood as far from singular; it is diffuse and capricious, whether ostensibly supportive or putatively violent. Focusing simultaneously on multiple empirical sites of trans-health practices—always attending to the who, what, where, when, why, and for whom—resists flattening both the "trans" and the "health" in trans-health practices. From within this detailed process of accounting, it is possible to map how feminist politics of self-help, counter-conduct, autonomy, and ideological struggle persists in contributing to trans health—even as feminist epistemologies too often remain ignored or relegated to the past. I argue that foregrounding feminist interventions helps to tease out some of the submerged dynamics and relations of power embedded in trans-health practice and politics—to the benefit of trans health.

Tangling with Feminist Health

Anthropologist Rayna Rapp (1999) examines feminist health practices to unpack a set of elisions within "reproductive health" that resonate with similar condensations in "trans health." Rapp (2011: 10) draws from Shellee Colen (1995) and Dorothy Roberts (1997) in her discussion of "stratified reproduction" to query "how, why, and with what consequences the reproductive aspirations, practices, and outcomes of one group of people are valorized, while the parenthood of another is despised or unsupported." Rapp (1999) argues that the technical management of pregnancy reproduces varying forms of social and economic hierarchy. Extending this analysis, Khiara Bridges's (2011) ethnography of a public hospital in New York City suggests that pregnancy's management is not solely a reproduction of power relations but is indeed a discernible site of racialization. Describing pregnancy as a "racially salient event," Bridges (10) details how processes of racialization unfold in the very activities of delivering clinical care to patients defined as "high-risk" in and through their encounters with the hospital and state agencies or policies. The providers that Bridges observed differentially employed medical testing during pregnancy for poor, black pregnant patients in a public hospital in marked contrast to wealthy, white pregnant patients in a nearby private hospital. Such tests do not serve the intended purpose of ascertaining health; rather, they enact a suspicious classed and racialized surveillance at the level of the body.

As ST&MS scholars show, those who interact with and utilize technologies and institutional guidelines do so in ways that may differ radically from their intended uses (Clarke and Fujimura 1992; Casper and Clarke 1998). In employing testing technologies, the health-care providers that Bridges observed reiterated the racial logics that produce differentiated "vulnerabilities to premature death," to employ Ruth Wilson Gilmore's construction of racism (2007: 28). Such quotidian practices demonstrate in part why reproductive justice activists argue for a politics that transcends health access based on "choice" (Silliman et al. 2004). Instead, these activists respond to racialized conditions of stratified reproduction not only by foregrounding the distinct conditions of biological reproduction and medicine (e.g., being subject to forced sterilization as particularly gendered and sexualized black, Latina, or Native people) but also by linking sexuality, reproduction, and bodies to broader problems of racialized social and political divestment (e.g., exposure to environmental toxins; Silliman et al. 2004; Murphy 2013; Ross 2006).

These analyses aptly demonstrate what Clarke and colleagues call "stratified biomedicalization": an "increasingly complex, multisited, multidirectional processes of medicalization, both extended and reconstituted through the new social forms of highly technoscientific biomedicine" (Clarke et al. 2003: 161; Clarke et al. 2010: 41). Clarke and colleagues (2010: 29) emphasize biomedicalization's "unequal (and sometimes unintended) effects," as well as "how these may exacerbate rather than ameliorate social inequalities across many different dimensions." As Janet Shim (2010: 226) asserts, biomedicalization processes actually frame problems in particular ways, "such that notions of stratification become embedded into our 'biomedical common sense.'" For Clarke and Oleson (1999: 3), feminist analysis "ruptures" the prevailing commonsense arrangement of "biomedicalized frameworks of women's health," enabling a "revisioning" of new modes of perception and organization about women's and feminist health. Indeed, the content of "biomedical common sense" more broadly is precisely at stake in the ideological challenges to biomedical practice presented in these and other critical accounts of feminist health, reproductive health, and trans health.

Even through the shared lens of reproductive and health practice more generally, various instantiations of feminist and reproductive politics have emerged with distinct racial, sexual, and class politics. Viewing these as "entangled and yet discrepantly realized," Murphy (2012: 35, 47) traces how whiteness—as a historical and social formation rather than as a "property of bodies"—circulated, differentially enrolled, and distinctly shaped varying feminist self-help projects in the 1970s. Engaging critiques of Foucauldian biopolitical power and its conspicuous omissions of colonialism, slavery, racialized segregation, and Malthusian modes of governance from its formulation (to name a few), Murphy instead suggests mobilizing a "discrepant and shifting *biopolitical topology*" (11). Rather than a particular means of linking life with population, biopolitical topology renders biopolitics an "open question about the manifold ways life became a venue for the exercise of power in a messy, multiterritorialized world" (11). This analytic is helpful in making sense of the racialized distinction between conceiving of a reproductive biomedicine that scolds or harms individuals and a reproductive biomedicine that "distributes harm" at the level of population.

I am arguing that the notion of biopolitical topology can be similarly generative in analyzing trans health. As a number of scholars point out, particularly racialized and sexualized forms of trans life are broadly linked to varying forms of state and biomedical governance in transnationally distinct, messy, discontinuous, and perpetually shifting ways (e.g., Najmabadi 2013; Hsu 2013;

Cabral and Viturro 2006). Attending to these particularities proves critical in elaborating accounts of how trans health takes shape and travels, and how it may—much like obstetric care—not only engage but also produce differential distributions of life chances (Spade 2011; Gehi and Arkles 2007). Empirically attending to the "local" (Lock 1993) concrete clinical practices of trans health can thus be critically generative for continued efforts for more equitably distributed, patient-responsive care.

Conclusion

There has legitimately been much ado about certain technophobic and biologically determinist feminist analyses, as well as the contentious theoretical instrumentalization of trans subjectivities that in part spurred the development of trans studies. Nonetheless, these need not preclude trans and feminist studies from forging a generative mutuality, even—and perhaps especially—through their tense points of contact. Many have already made this point with eloquence (e.g., Heyes 2003; Bettcher and Garry 2009; Koyama 2003; Sylvia Rivera Law Project 2012; Audre Lorde Project 2012; cárdenas 2015; Stryker, Currah, and Moore 2008; Salamon 2010; Spade 2011; Snorton and Haritaworn 2013; Enke 2012). Following these interventions, I suggest that drawing from feminist ST&MS offers engagements with some seriously undertheorized domains and addresses some of the coarser and potentially deleterious generalizations of trans health.

Trans studies of biomedicine would benefit from examining the contingencies to which feminist ST&MS attends to, palpably texturing its accounts of the entangled politics of biomedical knowledge and practice. Certain trans activists and scholars fastidiously analyze the stratifying processes of trans health in dividing ostensibly "good citizens" from "societal drains" (Spade 2011; Gehi and Arkles 2007; Spade et al. 2009; Strangio 2012; Irving 2008; Aizura 2006, 2014; Najmabadi 2013; Hsu 2013). But these analyses remain the exception rather than the rule. Feminist technoscience studies of health and reproduction offer up realms in which scholars have assiduously mapped biomedicine, technoscience, power, and the politics of knowledge while accounting for the shifting biopolitical topologies of racialization and sexualization that organize and suffuse forms of life. These analytic tools enable engagement with biomedical practices based not only on what it claims about its actions but also in what these actions actually consist, as well as their differential effects as they are routed through various organizational sites and lived bodies.

Trans Bodies, Trans Selves is cannily prescient in renarrating trans health's historical trajectory through feminist health activism. Historicizing the link between these activist fields of practice may yield new ways of thinking through trans health's emergence. Previous and ongoing struggles among feminist health activists may also provide hermeneutics for trans health through which to grapple with stratification, racialization, and other open and underanalyzed questions. Nevertheless, as I attempt to show above, relations between feminist and trans health far exceed the simple linear trajectory of torch passing. These fields are not necessarily kindred—activists and scholars must take on the analytic labor of historicizing and theorizing these fields together. Through such convergences, trans and feminist health and theorizing may contribute to new modes of organizing health-care practice and scientific inquiry in forms that can meaningfully address rather than reiterate the profound injustices of biomedical practice.

Christoph Hanssmann, MPH, is a sociology PhD candidate at the University of California, San Francisco (UCSF). His dissertation examines the emergence of trans health as transnationally mobile sets of practices, and it draws from feminist ST&MS and critical race, sexuality, and citizenship studies. He has contributed essays to *Transfeminist Perspectives* (2012) and *Trans Bodies, Trans Selves* (2014).

Acknowledgments

I thank the editors, reviewers, and staff for this issue of *TSQ: Transgender Studies Quarterly* and for improving this article for publication, especially Talia Mae Bettcher, Susan Stryker, Abraham Weil, and an anonymous reviewer. Thank you also for discussions and feedback on early drafts to Adele Clarke, Janet Shim, Alisa Bierria, Kate Darling, Martine Lappé, Sonia Rab-Alam, Zakiyah Luna, Cindy Bello, Emily Thuma, and Krista Sigurdson. It also greatly benefitted from presentation at the University of California, Berkeley, Reproductive Justice Working Group and the UCSF Science and Technology Studies Working Group. This material is based upon work supported by the National Science Foundation under Grant No. 1519292. Writing and research was also generously supported by the Social Science Research Council's Dissertation Proposal Development Fund and by UCSF's Graduate Dean's Health Science Fellowship.

Notes

1. This study (12-09175, *Trans Health: Practices, Processes, and Boundaries*) has been approved by the University of California, San Francisco, Committee on Human Research ethics board for the dates August 28, 2012, through February 25, 2016.
2. This sense of being deeply squeezed structures medical and health-professional education on transgender health and beyond. Presenters often teach pragmatically to minimize harm to future patients, despite recognizing shortcomings and gaps in their presentations.
3. This is an awkward gloss of an already complex assembly. For example, lesbian health may have more overlap with women's or feminist health formations than health care organized by and for gay men around HIV/AIDS. "Queer health" is further textured by its various instantiations vis-à-vis geopolitical location, race, class, ethnicity, ability, and other factors shaping care relations. Here, I define *LGB health* or *queer health* as the ideas

and practices of health-based groups, organizations, agencies, and institutions that presume the relevance and primacy of nonnormative sexual identity or conduct in shaping relations of health and clinical care.

4.   This is my own paraphrase of a popular US history of transgender health. By no means universal, it is a reliably repeated narrative in transgender health trainings, conferences, casual conversations, strategic planning sessions, and in my interviews with informants. While this is distinct from Argentine legacies of trans health (see Cabral and Viturro 2006), the United States' popular history is also generally familiar outside of US activist and provider settings. The reverse is not generally true; US activists and providers often know little about trajectories of trans health in Argentina.

5.   Of course, feminist health is not and has never been any one thing, and its current and historical instantiations vary widely. Writing about feminist self-help movements focused in Los Angeles, historian Michelle Murphy (2012: 40) discusses "a refracted traffic of feminisms entangled yet discrepantly realized." She emphasizes how these formations were shaped by geographies, distributions of health and vulnerabilities, and perspectives on the politics of health—all in distinctly racialized and situated ways. I follow Murphy in resisting a collapse of difference in the term *feminist health*. I also emphasize (even without space to historicize) the complex set of reassembled elements, projects, and movements that partially constitute feminisms oriented around health-care practice—from the proximal in community health and Black Panther Party health activism (Nelson 2011) to the distal, such as human relations techniques, as Murphy (2012: 58–63) also notes.

6.   While the focus on reproductive health enables a theoretical limitation of the broad field of feminist health movements, it is by no means the only relevant facet of such movements. Indeed, as Clarke and Oleson (1999: 25) assert, women's health has often been reduced to obstetric or gynecological domains while "*nonreproductive* aspects of women's health" are frequently disregarded. I do not wish to replicate this particular reduction, and I suggest that, in fact, it has been rearticulated to a large degree in trans health through the primacy of genital surgical intervention, which (while a critical domain of practice and exploration) remains problematically central in representations of both embodiment and trans-health practice. I do not have the space to analyze this in detail here, but it remains an area for exploration.

The term *technoscience* emphasizes the coconstitutiveness of sciences and the instruments, techniques, and other elements involved in the production of scientific knowledge (Latour 1988). Haraway (1997: 3) defines technoscience as "extravagantly exceed[ing] the distinction between science and technology as well as those between nature and society, subjects and objects, the natural and the artifactual, that structured the imaginary time called modernity."

7.   Studying practices emphasizes that knowledge production consists in both what people think, say, and write, but also in what they concretely do and how they do it. This approach emerges in part from anthropology, sociological symbolic interactionism, and philosophical pragmatism, and it shares intellectual ground with critical legal theorists, among others.

8.   Attorney Chase Strangio (2012) shows how deeper, epistemic reorganizations can occur in somewhat counterintuitive ways. When the *DSM* changed "gender identity disorder," (GID) to "gender dysphoria" (GD), the diagnosis shifted to emphasize distress rather than pathology. Strangio argued that this change would limit care for some:

> For many people, especially trans people of color and low income and incarcerated trans people, the diagnosis of [GID] has become a tool to resist medical and other forms of state control. . . . [F]or incarcerated transgender individuals, the availability of a GID diagnosis creates an important framework for meeting Eighth Amendment and statutory requirements for challenging the deliberate indifference of prison medical staff. The recognition and disordering of gender through the DSM has been a vital tool for incarcerated individuals to access hormones, surgery and other trans health care.

This strategic response attempts to redefine the very phenomena that medicine and psychiatry attempt to stabilize. Here, GID works to undermine and shrewdly navigate highly coercive health-care systems, rather than presuming that diagnostic revision will reduce stigma and increase access as intended.

9. T. Benjamin Singer (2006: 615) describes this paradigm shift as the move from "a model of medical pathology to a 'trans-health' model of care."

References

Aizura, Aren Z. 2006. "Of Borders and Homes: The Imaginary Community of (Trans)Sexual Citizenship." *Inter-Asia Cultural Studies* 7, no. 2: 289–309.

———. 2010. "Feminine Transformations: Gender Reassignment Surgical Tourism in Thailand." *Medical Anthropology* 29, no. 4: 424–43. doi:10.1080/01459740.2010.501314.

———. 2014. "Trans Feminine Value, Racialized Others, and the Limits of Necropolitics." In *Queer Necropolitics*, edited by Jinthana Haritaworn, Adi Kuntsman, and Silvia Posocco, 129–47. New York: Routledge.

American Psychiatric Association. 1974. *Diagnostic and Statistical Manual of Mental Disorders*. 2nd ed. Washington, DC: American Psychiatric Association.

Audre Lorde Project. 2012. "Audre Lorde Project." www.alp.org (accessed December 13, 2014).

Bagby, Dyana. 2011. "WPATH Announces New Standards of Care for Transgender and Gender Nonconforming People." *Georgia Voice*, September 25. www.thegavoice.com/index.php/news/national-news/3497-wpath-announces-new-standards-of-care-for-transgender-and-gender-nonconforming-people.

Bettcher, Talia Mae. 2007. "Evil Deceivers and Make-Believers: On Transphobic Violence and the Politics of Illusion." *Hypatia* 22, no. 3: 43–65. doi:10.1111/j.1527-2001.2007.tb01090.x.

Bettcher, Talia Mae, and Ann Garry, eds. 2009. "Transgender Studies and Feminism: Theory, Politics, and Gender Realities." Special issue, *Hypatia* 24, no. 3.

Boston Women's Health Book Collective, and Judy Norsigian. (1971) 2011. *Our Bodies, Ourselves*. 9th ed. New York: Simon and Schuster.

Bridges, Khiara M. 2011. *Reproducing Race: An Ethnography of Pregnancy as a Site of Racialization*. Berkeley: University of California Press.

Burke, Mary. 2011. "Resisting Pathology: GID and the Contested Terrain of Diagnosis in the Transgender Health Movement." In *Sociology of Diagnosis*, edited by P. J. McGann, David J. Hutson, and Barbara Katz Rothman, 183–210. Bingley, UK: Emerald Group.

Cabral, Mauro, and Paula Viturro. 2006. "(Trans)sexual Citizenship in Contemporary Argentina." In *Transgender Rights*, edited by Paisley Currah, Richard M. Juang, and Shannon Minter, 262–73. Minneapolis: University of Minnesota Press.

cárdenas, micha. 2015. "We Need Trans of Color Feminism Now." Micha Cárdenas. www.michacardenas.org/we-need-trans-of-color-feminism-now/ (accessed March 15, 2015).

Casper, Monica, and Adele Clarke. 1998. "Making the Pap Smear into the 'Right Tool' for the Job: Cervical Cancer Screening in the USA, circa 1940–95." *Social Studies of Science* 28, no. 2: 255–90.

Center of Excellence for Transgender Health. 2011. "Primary Care Protocol for Transgender Patient Care." University of California, San Francisco, Center of Excellence for Transgender Health, April. www.transhealth.ucsf.edu/trans?page=protocol-00-00.

Clarke, Adele, and Joan H. Fujimura. 1992. *The Right Tools for the Job: At Work in Twentieth-Century Life Sciences.* Princeton, NJ: Princeton University Press.

Clarke, Adele E., and Virginia Olesen. 1999. "Revising, Diffracting, Acting." In *Revisioning Women, Health, and Healing: Feminist, Cultural, and Technoscience Perspectives,* 3–48. New York: Routledge.

Clarke, Adele E., et al. 2003. "Biomedicalization: Technoscientific Transformations of Health, Illness, and U.S. Biomedicine." *American Sociological Review* 68, no. 2: 161–94. doi:10.2307/1519765.

Clarke, Adele E., et al., eds. 2010. *Biomedicalization: Technoscience, Health, and Illness in the U.S.* Durham, NC: Duke University Press.

Coleman, Eli, et al. 2012. "Standards of Care for the Health of Transsexual, Transgender, and Gender-Non-Conforming People, Version 7." *International Journal of Transgenderism* 13, no. 4: 165–232.

Colen, Shellee. 1995. "Stratified Reproduction and West Indian Childcare Workers and Employers in New York." In *Conceiving the New World Order: The Global Politics of Reproduction,* edited by Faye D. Ginsburg and Rayna Rapp, 78–102. Berkeley: University of California Press.

Drescher, Jack. 2010. "Transsexualism, Gender Identity Disorder, and the DSM." *Journal of Gay and Lesbian Mental Health* 14, no. 2: 109–22. doi:10.1080/19359701003589637.

Drescher, Jack, Peggy Cohen-Kettenis, and Sam Winter. 2012. "Minding the Body: Situating Gender Identity Diagnoses in the ICD-11." *International Review of Psychiatry* 24, no. 6: 568–77. doi:10.3109/09540261.2012.741575.

Duarte, Andrés Rivera. 2015. "Chile's Gender Identity Bill: Two Years Later." International Gay and Lesbian Human Rights Commission (IGLHRC), May 8. www.iglhrc.org/content/chile%E2%80%99s-gender-identity-bill-two-years-later.

Enke, Anne, ed. 2012. *Transfeminist Perspectives in and beyond Transgender and Gender Studies.* Philadelphia: Temple University Press.

Epstein, Steven. 1996. *Impure Science: AIDS, Activism, and the Politics of Knowledge.* Berkeley: University of California Press.

Erickson-Schroth, Laura, ed. 2014. *Trans Bodies, Trans Selves: A Resource for the Transgender Community.* New York: Oxford University Press.

Feldman, Jamie. 2008. "Medical and Surgical Management of the Transgender Patient: What the Primary Care Clinician Needs to Know." In *Fenway Guide to Lesbian, Gay, Bisexual, and Transgender Health,* edited by Harvey J. Makadon, et al., 365–92. Philadephia: American College of Physicians.

Franklin, Sarah B. 2013. *Biological Relatives: IVF, Stem Cells, and the Future of Kinship.* Durham, NC: Duke University Press.

Gehi, Pooja S., and Gabriel Arkles. 2007. "Unraveling Injustice: Race and Class Impact of Medicaid Exclusions of Transition-Related Health Care for Transgender People." *Sexuality Research and Social Policy* 4, no. 4: 7–35. doi:10.1525/srsp.2007.4.4.7.

Gilmore, Ruth Wilson. 2007. *Golden Gulag: Prisons, Surplus, Crisis, and Opposition in Globalizing California*. Berkeley: University of California Press.

GATE (Global Action for Trans* Equality). 2015. "Making Depathologization a Matter of Law: A Comment from GATE on the Maltese Act on Gender Identity, Gender Expression, and Sex Characteristics." GATE—Global Action for Trans* Equality, April 8. www.transactivists .org/2015/04/08/making-depathologization-a-matter-of-law-a-comment-from-gate-on-the -maltese-act-on-gender-identity-gender-expression-and-sex-characteristics/.

Goldberg, Michelle. 2014. "The Dispute between Radical Feminism and Transgenderism." *New Yorker*, July 28. www.newyorker.com/magazine/2014/08/04/woman-2.

Gorton, R. Nick. 2013. "Transgender as Mental Illness: Nosology, Social Justice, and the Tarnished Golden Mean." In *The Transgender Studies Reader 2*, edited by Susan Stryker and Aren Aizura, 644–52. New York: Routledge.

Hale, Jacob. 1998. "Consuming the Living, Dis(re)membering the Dead in the Butch/FTM Borderlands." *GLQ* 4, no. 2: 311–28.

Haraway, Donna J. 1997. *Modest_Witness@Second_Millennium. FemaleMan©_Meets _OncoMouse™: Feminism and Technoscience*. New York: Routledge.

Heyes, Cressida J. 2003. "Feminist Solidarity after Queer Theory: The Case of Transgender." *Signs* 28, no. 4: 1093–1120. doi:10.1086/343132.

Hsu, Stephanie. 2013. "'Transsexual Empire,' Trans Postcoloniality: The Biomedicalization of the Trans Body and the Cultural Politics of Trans Kinship in Northeast Asia and Asian America." In "Life (Un)Ltd: Feminism, Bioscience, Race," special issue, *Scholar and Feminist Online* 11, no. 3. sfonline.barnard.edu/life-un-ltd-feminism-bioscience-race /transsexual-empire-trans-postcoloniality-the-biomedicalization-of-the-trans-body-and -the-cultural-politics-of-trans-kinship-in-northeast-asia-and-asian-america/.

Irving, D. 2008. "Normalized Transgressions: Legitimizing the Transsexual Body as Productive." *Radical History Review* 100: 38–59.

Koyama, Emi. 2003. "The Transfeminist Manifesto." In *Catching a Wave: Reclaiming Feminism for the Twenty-First Century*, 244–59. Boston: Northeastern University Press.

Latour, Bruno. 1988. *Science in Action: How to Follow Scientists and Engineers through Society*. Cambridge, MA: Harvard University Press.

Lee, Brianna. 2015. "Colombia Allows Transgender Community to Change Sex on IDs without Physical Exams." *International Business Times*, June 8. www.ibtimes.com/colombia -allows-transgender-community-change-sex-ids-without-physical-exams-1957412.

Lock, Margaret M. 1993. *Encounters with Aging: Mythologies of Menopause in Japan and North America*. Berkeley: University of California Press.

Ministry of Health and Care Services (Norway). 2015. "The Government Proposes to Make It Easier to Change Legal Gender." News release. Government.no, June 26. www.regjeringen .no/en/aktuelt/the-government-proposes-to-make-it-easier-to-change-legal-gender/id24 25069/.

Morgen, Sandra. 2002. *Into Our Own Hands: The Women's Health Movement in the United States, 1969–1990*. Piscataway, NJ: Rutgers University Press.

Murphy, Michelle. 2012. *Seizing the Means of Reproduction: Entanglements of Feminism, Health, and Technoscience*. Durham, NC: Duke University Press.

———. 2013. "Distributed Reproduction, Chemical Violence, and Latency." In "Life (Un)Ltd: Feminism, Bioscience, Race," special issue, *Scholar and Feminist Online* 11, no. 3. sfonline .barnard.edu/life-un-ltd-feminism-bioscience-race/distributed-reproduction-chemical -violence-and-latency/.

Najmabadi, Afsaneh. 2013. *Professing Selves: Transsexuality and Same-Sex Desire in Contemporary Iran*. Durham, NC: Duke University Press.

Namaste, Viviane. (2005) 2011. *Sex Change, Social Change: Reflections on Identity, Institutions, and Imperialism*. Toronto: Canadian Scholars' Press.

Nelson, Alondra. 2011. *Body and Soul: The Black Panther Party and the Fight against Medical Discrimination*. Minneapolis: University of Minnesota Press.

Pecheny, Mario. 2010. "Political Agents or Vulnerable Victims? Framing Sexual Rights as Sexual Health in Argentina." In *Routledge Handbook of Sexuality, Health, and Rights*, edited by Peter Aggleton and Richard Parker, 359–69. New York: Routledge.

Prosser, Jay. 1999. "Transsexuals and the Transsexologists: Inversion and the Emergence of Transsexual Subjectivity." In *Sexology in Culture: Labelling Bodies and Desires*, edited by Lucy Bland and Laura Doan, 116–32. Chicago: University of Chicago Press.

Rapp, Rayna. 1999. *Testing Women, Testing the Fetus: The Social Impact of Amniocentesis in America*. New York: Routledge.

———. 2011. "Reproductive Entanglements: Body, State, and Culture in the Dys/Regulation of Child-Bearing." *Social Research* 78, no. 3: 693–718.

Roberts, Dorothy. 1997. *Killing the Black Body: Race, Reproduction, and the Meaning of Liberty*. New York: Vintage.

Ross, Loretta. 2006. "Understanding Reproductive Justice." *off our backs* 36, 4: 14–19.

Ruzek, Sheryl Burt. 1978. *The Women's Health Movement: Feminist Alternatives to Medical Control*. New York: Praeger.

———. 1980. "Medical Response to Women's Health Activities: Conflict, Accommodation, and Cooptation." In *Research in the Sociology of Health Care*, edited by Julius A. Roth, Sheryl Burt Ruzek, and Dorothy C. Wertz, 335–54. Greenwich, CT: JAI.

Salamon, Gayle. 2010. *Assuming a Body: Transgender and Rhetorics of Materiality*. New York: Columbia University Press.

Salum, Alejandro Nasif. 2012. "Argentina Has Passed the Most Progressive Gender Identity Legislation in Existence." International Gay and Lesbian Human Rights Commission, May 13. www.iglhrc.wordpress.com/2012/05/13/argentina-has-passed-the-most-progressive -gender-identity-legislation-in-existence-how-did-it-happen/.

Shim, Janet K. 2010. "The Stratified Biomedicalization of Heart Disease: Expert and Lay Perspectives on Racial and Class Inequality." In Clarke et al. 2010: 218–41.

Silliman, Jael, et al. 2004. *Undivided Rights: Women of Color Organizing for Reproductive Justice*. Cambridge, MA: South End.

Singer, T. Benjamin. 2006. "From the Medical Gaze to Sublime Mutations: The Ethics of (Re) Viewing Non-normative Body Images." In *The Transgender Studies Reader*, edited by Susan Stryker and Stephen Whittle, 601–20. New York: Routledge.

Snorton, C. Riley, and Jin Haritaworn. 2013. "Trans Necropolitics: A Transnational Reflection on Violence, Death, and the Trans of Color Afterlife." In *The Transgender Studies Reader 2*, edited by Susan Stryker and Aren Aizura, 66–76. New York: Routledge.

Spade, Dean. 2006. "Compliance Is Gendered: Struggling for Gender Self-Determination in a Hostile Economy." In *Transgender Rights*, edited by Paisley Currah, Richard M. Juang, and Shannon Minter, 217–41. Minneapolis: University of Minnesota Press.

———. 2011. *Normal Life: Administrative Violence, Critical Trans Politics, and the Limits of Law*. Cambridge, MA: South End.

Spade, Dean, et al. 2009. "Medicaid Policy and Gender-Confirming Healthcare for Trans People: An Interview with Advocates." *Seattle Journal for Social Justice* 8: 497–514.

Stone, Sandy. 1992. "The *Empire* Strikes Back: A Posttranssexual Manifesto." *Camera Obscura*, no. 29: 150–76. doi:10.1215/02705346-10-2_29-150.

Strangio, Chase. 2012. "Debating 'Gender Identity Disorder' and Justice for Trans People." *Huffington Post*, December 5. www.huffingtonpost.com/chase-strangio/gender-identity -disorder-dsm_b_2247081.html.

Stryker, Susan. 2008. *Transgender History*. Berkeley, CA: Seal.

Stryker, Susan, Paisley Currah, and Lisa Jean Moore. 2008. "Introduction: Trans-, Trans, or Transgender?" *WSQ* 36, no. 3: 11–22. doi:10.1353/wsq.0.0112.

Suess, Amets, Karine Espineira, and Pau Crego Walters. 2014. "Depathologization." *TSQ* 1, nos. 1–2: 73–77. doi:10.1215/23289252-2399650.

Sylvia Rivera Law Project. 2012. "Sylvia Rivera Law Project (SRLP)." www.srlp.org (accessed December 13, 2014).

Transgender Europe (TGEU). 2015. "Malta Adopts Ground-Breaking Trans and Intersex Law— TGEU Press Release." TGEU, April 1. www.tgeu.org/malta-adopts-ground-breaking -trans-intersex-law/.

Truong, Mandy, Yin Paradies, and Naomi Priest. 2014. "Interventions to Improve Cultural Competency in Healthcare: A Systematic Review of Reviews." *BMC Health Services Research* 14, no. 1: 99. doi:10.1186/1472-6963-14-99.

Women-Identified Women

Trans Women in 1970s Lesbian Feminist Organizing

EMMA HEANEY

Abstract This essay argues that retrieval of the archive of trans women's engagement with women's liberation corrects a historical focus on the virulent trans misogyny that targeted trans women for exclusion from feminist milieus and projects beginning in 1973. This essay follows the arguments for trans exclusion into their contemporary iterations and proposes the archive of trans women's feminist work as a theoretical and political resource for countering trans misogyny.
Keywords lesbian feminism, feminists of trans experience, women's liberation, trans misogyny, trans women's autonomy

A photocopied flyer filed in the folder labeled "transsexuals" in the cabinets of the Lesbian Herstory Archive in Brooklyn invites people to the January 19, 1983, meeting of the Gay Women's Free Spirit discussion group in Greenwich Village that will feature "A Very Special Discussion with Riki Anne Wilson [*sic*] a Lesbian Transsexual and Radical Feminist" ("Gay Women's" 1983).[1] This flyer is a trace of a historical event that would seem unlikely to contemporary feminists. Conventional wisdom in trans and feminist academic, social, and political milieus remembers radical feminism for its trans misogyny, exemplified by Jean O'Leary's 1973 attack on Sylvia Rivera at the Christopher Street Liberation Day, the community pressure put on the Olivia music collective to oust Sandy Stone in 1977, and Janice Raymond's 1979 jeremiad against trans women, *The Transsexual Empire*. Nancy Jean Burkholder's ejection from the Michigan Womyn's Music Festival (MWMF) in 1991 spurred a queer and trans protest camp that hardened this political framing in queer and trans circles. When the festival, an enduring emblem of 1970s cultural feminism, instituted a "womyn-born-womyn" policy to bar trans women from participating, the factionalism between a 1970s feminism that defended the category of "woman" as the ground for autonomous organization and the new trans activists who demanded a move beyond this term of political alliance seemed intractable and generationally defined.

TSQ: Transgender Studies Quarterly ∗ Volume 3, Numbers 1–2 ∗ May 2016 **137**
DOI 10.1215/23289252-3334295 © 2016 Duke University Press

In her indispensable 2008 book *Transgender History*, Susan Stryker confirms this factionalism, writing that "most feminists [in the 1970s] were critical of transgender practices such as cross-dressing, taking hormones . . . , having . . . surgery, [which they considered] 'personal solutions' to . . . gender-based oppression," and identifies transgender feminism as part of "third wave feminism" (Stryker 2008: 2). *Transgender History*'s rich presentation of references to trans women's political work in the 1970s launched this article, which seeks to prove that Riki Anne Wilchins's 1983 discussion was not an anomaly but heir to a rich relation between women's liberation and trans feminism that has not been adequately accounted for in the periodization of feminist struggle. This erasure results from the amplified voices of trans misogynists and the resultant rise of the narrative of factionalism in the early 1990s. This relation is evident in diverse models of political work undertaken by trans-feminine people in the 1970s.[2] This article uses one example of one of these models of trans women's organizing—Beth Elliott's participation in lesbian feminist autonomous organizing—to argue for a turn away from the trans misogynists of the 1970s and today and toward an archive of feminists of trans experience.

Beth Elliott was a folksinger who was a vice president in the San Francisco Daughters of Bilitis (SF DOB) in the early 1970s, wrote for the Los Angeles–based newsmagazine *The Lesbian Tide*, and participated in the West Coast Lesbian Conference (WCLC) in Los Angeles in 1973. Her participation in the SF DOB ended in 1972 when some of the women in the organization forced her out for being trans. After learning of Elliott's presence at the WCLC, the radical feminist Robin Morgan rewrote her keynote address to feature a viciously trans-misogynist attack on Elliot's participation in the conference, and a group called the Gutter Dykes from San Francisco spearheaded the taunting of Elliott. Morgan accused Elliott of divisiveness and the metaphorical "rape" of women's space. These incidents reflect a strain of radical feminist writing that to this day targets trans women.

These incidents also reveal that Beth Elliott participated in lesbian organizing, and that she found something politically significant in these projects. Elliott's place within radical feminist practices is affirmed by the fact that many of her sisters in the DOB resigned in protest following her ouster, including the entire collective of *Sisters*, the SF DOB's newspaper. Likewise, when the organizers of the Los Angeles conference responded to Morgan and others' trans-misogynist request to kick out Elliott, two-thirds of the lesbians in attendance voted that Elliott should stay (McLean 1973: 36).[3] When Elliott was harassed while onstage, Jeanne Cordova, organizer and editor of the Los Angeles journal *The Lesbian Tide*, "walked onto the stage and grabbed the microphone and asked: 'What is the problem here?' . . . Elliott is, Cordova said again and again, 'a feminist and a sister'" (Clendinin and Nagourney 2001: 116).

After Elliott's ouster from the DOB, *The Lesbian Tide* printed a collective response that cited DOB dissenters who supported trans women (Editorial Collective 1972). The SF DOB dissenters write, "It is wrong to say that a lesbian woman in a male body is 'passing as a lesbian woman.' You don't 'pass' for something you ARE. . . . Any transsexual who considers her/himself to be a woman will be eligible for membership and participation in S.F. DOB" (21). The *Tide* writers go on to offer their own understanding of the trans women's political situation as one of exemplary radical self-determination: "Our common oppression is based on society's insistence that we perform certain roles: wife, husband, mother, father, masculine, feminine, etc. . . . We cry out 'You cannot define us. WE DEFINE OURSELVES!'" *The Lesbian Tide* concludes their publication of the letter with their own note to "advise our transsexual sisters that, if they are not welcome in the liberal city of San Francisco, they are most welcome in the city of Los Angeles" (29). In "Diary of a Mad Organizer," an article that critiques Robin Morgan's attack on Elliott, WCLC organizer Barbara McLean observes that butches often benefit from male socialization so, the question of woman's oppression could not be reduced to assigned sex (McLean 1973: 37). The solidarity of cis and gender-nonconforming lesbians reveals their analysis that the political category "woman" is internally different, with trans women as one kind of autonomy within it.

"Diary of a Mad Organizer" reveals a more important reality. While the Gutter Dykes were berating Beth Elliott, a blind woman fought her way onto the stage: "She is furious . . . pounds on the podium, insists on speaking" (McLean 1973: 38). She identifies to the audience as a trans woman and is "so emotional, trembling so bad she can hardly stand up, clutching the mike she cried out 'These women are crucifying Beth and all transsexuals. Why do they torment her? You are more oppressive than our oppressors.'" She then sits down defiantly in front of the stage and continues shouting over the din of the crowd (38). This glorious direct action defeats the Gutter Dykes, and they relinquish the microphone. The 1970s Italian feminist political group Rivolta Femminile writes that they "consider incomplete any history which is based on nonperishable traces" because "nothing, or else misconception, has ever been handed down about the presence of woman" (Rivolta Femminile 1991: 39). Morgan's keynote was reprinted in lesbian media and in her book *Going Too Far*. In contrast, the blind trans woman's insurgent act of trans-feminist resistance and solidarity lives only as a brief mention in *The Lesbian Tide* article. Retrieval of this more perishable archive is an urgent trans-feminist scholarly priority, to which this article seeks to contribute.

Another scrap of perishable history is found in an interview titled "Rapping with a Street Transvestite Revolutionary" with Marsha P. Johnson, a transliberation radical and cofounder of Street Transvestite Action Revolutionaries (STAR), a youth support service. Johnson reports her reception among the New York DOB:

> Once in a while, I get an invitation to Daughters of Bilitis, and when I go there, they're always warm. All the gay sisters come over and say, "Hello, we're glad to see you," and they start long conversations. But not the gay brothers. They're not too friendly at all toward transvestites. . . . [because]A lot of gay brothers don't like women! . . . And when they see a transvestite coming, she reminds them of a woman automatically, and they don't want to get too close or too friendly with her. (Jay 1972: 115)

Here Johnson deftly theorizes the misogyny that connects all feminine and feminized people involved in gay liberation. She also attests to the virulent everyday misogyny of gay men and the practical solidarity of cis women toward transfeminine people. Beth Elliott's experience working for years in lesbian separatist projects indicates that the receptivity that Marsha Johnson reports was not limited to New York. Elliott's experience demonstrates that lesbian separatism as a political tactic was attractive to trans women, just as her ouster demonstrates the tactic's improper execution by trans misogynists. In her 2011 memoir (Nettick and Elliott 2011: vii), Beth Elliott reflects back on her experience with separatist feminism. She speaks about the pressure exerted by a few people in "the new wave of trans advocacy, who viewed women's community as the enemy" who reached out to her to denounce the community based on how she was treated in the 1970s. Elliott writes, "I did not want my name and reputation appropriated by anyone, for any purpose. . . . I could not communicate to them that this community was my home, that I had helped to nurture and unbind it with all my heart, and that it still mattered to me" (vii–viii). To revisit the trans-feminist solidarities of the 1970s is to restore trans women's claims to feminism and women's autonomy to historical memory. The extant frame has been more apt to engage the perspective of cis women who take it upon themselves to adjudicate trans women's access to the category "woman."

Trans-Lesbian Feminism after 1973

A 1976 article in the *Journal of Homosexuality* describes lesbian feminist identifications that survived the purges of the early 1970s. "Lesbian/Feminist Orientation among Male-to-Female Transsexuals" rejects the popular image of trans women as hyperheterosexual and conservative, suggesting that lesbianism and feminist political orientation are as common among trans women as among cis. This argument is evidenced by autobiographical sketches written by "the trans-sexual coauthors of this paper," "woman-identified women (lesbians) who (as feminists) reject the traditional male-created norms of what women (and men) should be" (Feinbloom et al. 1976: 60). The form of the article, trans women narrating and theorizing their own lives, pushes against a (by 1976) hundred-year-old model of appropriating trans women's words to craft medical diagnostics that bolster the gate-keeping authority of the cis-medical establishment. The authors suggest that "the transsexual/lesbian/feminist individual must be explored in her own terms, not only as an object of biosocial forces but as a *subject* who endlessly participates in a process of choice and change" (61).

This feminist practice of self-definition takes a form particular to women of trans experience. One coauthor rejects both the diagnostic assertion that she is "trapped in the wrong body" and the suffering that the medical model uses to define transsexuality. Instead she affirms that a feminist "social environment reinforced my self-concept," leading to "little internal stress" and ensuring "freedom of self-expression" (62). She discusses the process through which she gains feminist consciousness and marks this process with her ability to say, "I am a woman." This allowed "a growing awareness and integration, into my life, of feminist thinking" (64). This women-identification was itself a feminist practice—the assertion of their identity as women in an androcentric culture was a central concern of 1970s feminist projects. Trans feminism clarifies that this concern was shared by all feminist women with a specific valence for women of trans experience whose battle to be recognized as women also included defying their assigned sex. Again, centering the voices of trans women decenters trans misogynists, and "Lesbian/Feminist Orientation among Male-to-Female Trans-sexuals," testifying as it does to the shifts in consciousness that feminism brought to the coauthors, contributes to the sources that document the many perished experiences that the historical record has inadequately indexed.

Trans Misogyny, Cis Sexism, and Feminist Factions

Close study of these events and analyses recontextualizes the spectacular trans misogyny of certain radical feminists as pushback against a 1970s trans feminism that exposed the conceptual elisions haunting radical feminist thought and practice. The first of these elisions is the status of social practices that signify "femininity" and their relation to feminism. The most iconic demonstration of radical feminism (and Robin Morgan's "coming out" action) was a protest of the Miss America pageant that included signs that read "Up against the Wall, Miss America" and "Miss America Is a Big Falsie" (Echols 1989: 96). The protest uncovered a tension within women's liberation between a "brainwashing line," which approached the trappings of traditional femininity as the formation to be resisted (a perspective that is expressed by the Miss America demonstration), and "a pro-woman line," which took women's experience as a political base and sought to reclaim feminized work and culture (Echols 1989: 92–98). A transfeminist investigation of this tension uncovers strains of cis sexism in both lines. Those who followed the brainwashing line mocked the social markers that often define femininity and focused on its artificiality. Beyond the traditional misogyny inherent in parsing femininity as false and regulating women's behavior, these disavowals carry with them a particular trans misogyny because presenting gendered markers of identity is often important for trans women who are often misgendered and because trans life is regularly presented as fake by cis people.

Pro-women advocates naturalized women's experience and didn't allow for the diversity of this experience, forwarding the racist, class-blind, and cis-sexist idea that "woman" is an internally homogenous category. Right after denouncing Beth Elliott, Robin Morgan (1973: 34) says in her keynote, "Isn't it way past time that we stopped settling for blaming each other, stopped blaming heterosexual women and middle-class women and married women and Lesbian women and white women and any women for the structure of sexism, racism, classism, and ageism, that no woman is to blame for because we have none of us had the power to create those structures. They are patriarchal creations not ours." Morgan defines the feminist milieu as a space in which differences among women are sidelined because they are "patriarchal creations" and will hinder unity among women. This definition of women's solidarity simply refuses the analyses that women of color were making within caucuses of that very conference in which they made public the racism that was present in the movement.[4] These caucuses use the language of "woman" and "sister," as do trans feminists of the period. Both groups understand these categories to be produced through the differences internal to them. Feminist solidarity is the site for the articulation and reckoning of these differences, a reckoning that may include the airing of materially produced antagonisms.

Elinor Burkett's June 2015 article "What Makes a Woman?" published in the *New York Times*, demonstrates that both kinds of cis sexism are alive and centered in mainstream discussions of trans women. Burkett echoes Morgan when she critiques Caitlyn Jenner's "cleavage-boosting corset, sultry poses, thick mascara and [excitement at] the prospect of regular 'girls' nights' of banter about hair and makeup" in Jenner's recent coming-out story in *Vanity Fair*, practices and interests that Burkett attributes to the majority of trans women. Burkett echoes a component of the pro-women line that has underwritten trans exclusion since the 1970s when she writes, "People who haven't lived their whole lives as women . . . shouldn't get to define us." This is because "their truth is not my truth.

Their female identities are not my female identity" (Burkett 2015). Burkett identifies the sexualization by male colleagues, pregnancy scares, unplanned onset of menstruation, lower pay than male partners, and fear of sexual assault as gender-defining experiences. This argument doesn't hold up when considered in relation to trans and cis women's experience: sexualization, low pay, and sexual assault are risks that women of trans experience report at high rates, and menstruation and potentially reproductive sex are not features of life for all cis women. But there is a more fundamental contradiction in Burkett's and other cis writing that advocates trans exclusion. Burkett writes that "being a woman means having accrued certain experiences, endured certain indignities and relished certain courtesies in a culture that reacted to you as one" (Burkett 2015). Burkett and the many other women who forward similar critiques present the cultural markers of femininity as the thing that women are trying to escape, but they also affirm the feminine as the condition that constitutes "woman" as a political collectivity.

This herstory and hirstory of trans misogyny and trans feminism has left us with two significant trans-feminist perspectives that (like many feminists of the 1970s) neither proscribed the kinds of gendered cultural practices that are compatible with dignity nor insisted on a false uniform women's injury. Sandy Stone's influential "The *Empire* Strikes Back: A Posttranssexual Manifesto" ([1987] 2008) represents one strain. Her manifesto responds to Janice Raymond's warning that trans women infiltrate and divide vulnerable autonomous women's spaces. In resistance to these claims, Stone proposes that "we start by taking Raymond's accusation that 'transsexuals divide women' beyond itself, and turn it into a productive force to multiplicatively divide the old binary discourses of gender" (231). Stone's suggestion that trans politics could move beyond the "old binary" was taken up in emerging queer intellectual and political circles in the early 1990s that announced their politics as a revision of 1970s feminism. But Stone's piece directly addresses trans people; she takes for granted the reality and value of trans life, including trans women's lives. We might call this an autonomous trans-feminist address in which the category "woman" is generalized (assumed of writer and audience) as a precondition to theorize its abolition.

Sandy Stone can dream this future, but she and other queer theorists can't just declare it here. The work that might establish the conditions for such a future brings us to the second strain of trans feminism. Davina Gabriel's interview with Leslie Feinberg, which addresses Nancy Burkholder's treatment at the Michigan Womyn's Music Festival, helps us to identify this second strain. Gabriel asks Feinberg, "What is your response to feminist writers such as Mary Daly who described transsexuals as 'Frankensteinian' or Janice Raymond who has stated that transsexuality should be 'morally mandated out of existence'?" (Gabriel 1993: 8). Feinberg replies, "I haven't read those specific references" and quickly pivots to emphasize her enthusiasm for the trans and cis women who returned to the festival after Burkholder's ouster to conduct a poll that found that 73 percent of women supported the right of trans women to attend the festival (8). Feinberg affirms autonomy and deemphasizes the neat factionalism between old and young and between cis women and trans people. She also, however, points out that solidarity among women of different kinds of experience requires real, material practices to address historically produced and enduring imbalances of power among women. The two strains of trans feminism that advocate, in turn, for the transcendence of gender and women's autonomy are mutually enabling political practices that confront both enforcement of gender norms and misogyny. Trans women's autonomy in all its forms is the necessary pretext for such a conversation to unfold, not between trans feminists and trans misogynists, but among feminists of trans experience and their sisters and siblings who have received the gift of trans-feminist autonomist legacies.

Emma Heaney is visiting assistant professor in the Draper Interdisciplinary Master's Program in Humanities and Social Thought at New York University. Her book, *The New Woman: Literary Modernism, Queer Theory, and the Trans Feminine Allegory*, is forthcoming.

Notes

1. This is almost certainly a misprint and actually a reference to the influential trans-feminist writer Riki Anne Wilchins.

2. This article focuses on trans women in women's liberation milieus, but it is part of a larger inquiry in progress into the various political practices and legacies of trans women's autonomous organizing in the United States in the 1970s. Such organizing took shape around a diversity of models of autonomy, including trans women who organized around shared precarities (among these homelessness, police violence, sex work and other criminalized work, trans misogyny, and homophobia with an analysis of the way race organizes each of these) and allied with those vulnerable to these precarities regardless of gender or trans experience; trans women who worked in coalition with other femme queers and allied themselves with women's liberation; and, crucially, trans women who only worked with other trans women and adjudicated alliance with cis women from a trans women's autonomous perspective.

3. *Out for Good* puts the count at "a bare majority" (Clendinin and Nagourney 2001: 166).

4. For instance, members of the Black Caucus write in their workshop report, "We, the Black lesbian women, are conscious of your racism" and make proposals to address this racism in future conferences (Black Caucus 1973: 19).

References

Black Caucus. 1973. "Black Caucus Position." *The Lesbian Tide* 2, nos. 10–11 (May–June): 19.

Burkett, Elinor. 2015. "What Makes a Woman?" *New York Times*, June 6.

Clendinin, Dudley, and Adam Nagourney. 2001. *Out for Good: The Struggle to Build a Gay Rights Movement in America*. New York: Simon and Schuster.

Echols, Alice. 1989. *Daring to Be Bad: Radical Feminism in America 1967–1975*. Minneapolis: University of Minnesota.

Editorial Collective of *The Lesbian Tide*. 1972. "A Collective Editorial." *The Lesbian Tide* 1, no. 5 (December): 21–29.

Feinbloom, Deborah Heller, et al. 1976. "Lesbian/Feminist Orientation among Male-to-Female Transsexuals." *Journal of Homosexuality* 2, no. 1: 59–72.

Gabriel, Davina. 1993. "The Life and Times of a Gender Outlaw: An Interview with Leslie Feinberg." *TransSisters*, no. 1: 4–9.

"Gay Women's Free Spirit Discussion Group." 1983. Flyer. Lesbian Herstory Archive. Folder 14730, "Transsexuals."

Jay, Karla. 1972. *Out of the Closets: Voices of Gay Liberation*. New York: New York University Press.

McLean, Barbara. 1973. "Dairy of a Mad Organizer." *The Lesbian Tide* 2, nos. 10–11 (May–June): 16–37.

Morgan, Robin. 1973. "Lesbianism and Feminism: Synonyms or Contradictions." *The Lesbian Tide* 2, nos. 10–11 (May–June): 30–34.

Nettick, Geri, with Beth Elliott. 2011. *Mirrors: Portrait of a Lesbian Transsexual*. Oakland, CA: CreateSpace.

Rivolta Femminile. 1991. "Manifesto, 1970." In *Italian Feminism Thought: A Reader*, edited by Paola Bono and Sandra Kemp, 37–40. Oxford: Basil Blackwell.

Stone, Sandy. (1987) 2008. "The *Empire* Strikes Back: A Posttranssexual Manifesto." In *The Transgender Studies Reader*, edited by Susan Stryker and Stephen Whittle, 221–35. New York: Routledge.

Stryker, Susan. 2008. *Transgender History*. Berkeley, CA: Seal.

Birth of Transfeminism in Brazil
Between Alliances and Backlashes

HAILEY KAAS

Abstract This text aims to briefly summarize the initial steps of transfeminism in Brazil, its difficulties and issues within the mainstream feminist movement, which in some ways molded the transfeminist movement, and also its support, not always free from cissexist practices. It also emphasizes intersectionality as a way out of the problem of identity politics and as a praxis to fight for human rights in general.
Keywords transfeminism, mainstream feminism, intersectionality

In 2012, almost no one within mainstream feminist activism in Brazil had heard about transfeminism—only a very few texts, blogs, and videos covering the basic premises but making no connection to mainstream feminism. It was in this context that I started reading about transfeminism on Tumblr and soon created the first transfeminism-focused group on Facebook and a blog in Brazilian Portuguese. There were no trans-exclusionary radical feminists (TERFs) in the Brazilian context at that time—at least no feminists whose activism was specifically oriented toward harming trans* people (especially trans* women). Within three years, a Brazilian transfeminist community had taken shape that enjoyed a lot of support—support won through hard work, despite a lot of hate.

This issue of *TSQ: Transgender Studies Quarterly*, in seeking to escape the dichotomy of trans*-inclusive versus trans*-exclusionary feminisms, addresses the complexity of transfeminism(s), both within networks of transfeminist allies, as well as in reference to feminisms that aim to exclude trans* people altogether. It is, indeed, a very complex situation. Even if we are able to label some part of feminism as being trans* excluding, it does not therefor follow that the rest of feminism is free from reproducing cissexism. Similarly, it does not follow that all trans*-exclusionary feminisms act in the same way.

Transfeminism in Brazil emerged not from discussions about trans* issues within feminism but over concerns with LGBT rights. After reading Kimberlé

TSQ: Transgender Studies Quarterly ★ Volume 3, Numbers 1–2 ★ May 2016
DOI 10.1215/23289252-3334307 © 2016 Duke University Press

Crenshaw's work on intersectional feminism, however, I could not stop thinking about it. If there is feminism that fights for women, and if there is an LGBT rights movement that fights for lesbian, gay, bisexual, and transgender people, then what would happen if we overlapped these two movements of marginalized identities? What about lesbians and bisexual women, who are oppressed both as women and as people who engage in same-sex sexual behavior? While wrestling with the implications of an intersectional feminism, I began to pay attention to the constant (re)affirmation in certain feminism spaces of the opinion that women cannot oppress because they are the oppressed. But if women cannot oppress, then how are we to understand the homophobia and racism of some white and straight women?

In addition, some arguments within mainstream feminism seemed, on the one hand, to deny the possibility of agency for women, eternally placing women in the role of victim, and on the other hand, giving full agency to the feminist subject, disregarding the consequences of living female in a sexist culture. The conundrum of full agency versus no agency has been a source of distress in the movement, but in time I found myself wondering whether the issue was not more complex than simply positioning oneself—and feminism—for or against agency. Only in reading Judith Butler (2004: 3), who recontextualized the debate about agency in a way that spoke to me, did I find satisfactory answers for my questions:

> If I have any agency, it is opened up by the fact that I am constituted by a social world I never chose. That my agency is riven with paradox does not mean it is impossible. It means only that paradox is the condition of its possibility.
>
> As a result, the "I" that I am finds itself at once constituted by norms and dependent on them, but also endeavors to live in ways that maintain a critical and transformative relation to them.

It was in this context that I created my transfeminist Facebook group and blog. At first, we were more concerned with educating other feminist spaces about basic trans* issues and how they related to feminism, sometimes translating texts from foreign transfeminists because of the lack of domestic material. We faced a lot of resistance, and soon enough, pages denouncing our "appropriation" of feminism appeared in the worst ways, often insinuating that arguments and theories rooted in US or anglophone histories made no sense in our cultural context and therefore could not be used to support our agenda (for example, the "cotton ceiling" argument, or Sheila Jeffrey's arguments against medicalization, which similarly don't make any sense because our medical system is completely different). We found ourselves constantly arguing about events that had never occurred here, and authors whose works were never even translated into Brazilian Portuguese, let alone referenced within mainstream feminism. In actuality, however, we constantly sought to distance ourselves from North American issues and activism because we wished to create our own transfeminism, one that could encompass the reality of the *travestis*—a category that does not exist in the United States—as we were aware of how the socioeconomic and racial issues that affect *travestis* intersect with the transphobia that also affects them.

While we faced a lot of resistance in some quarters, other feminist groups embraced transfeminism and provided a friendly environment for transfeminist bloggers in their online spaces. Such support has not always been free from contradictions. Blogueiras Feministas, for example, has been open to trans* authors and often published trans* articles in its blog, but in its Google groups, a lot of hateful and ignorant comments about trans* people flow without any intervention. Such practices are still common in some feminist environments, and we often find ourselves wondering whether it's worth contesting these spaces.

A lot has happened since 2012. Even if I had the space and time to provide a full account of everything, I would not remember it all. The fact that we somehow inspired the creation of our very own local "TERF hubs," when before there were no open TERFs whatsoever, makes clear how quickly things have moved in our favor—they are in a reactive and defensive mode, trying to turn back the tide. I consider this strong backlash to be a positive event because it demonstrates how visible we have become and how much we have changed the conversation. Previously, for example, no one knew what *cis* meant, and nowadays we see congresspersons and even government agencies using the term.

It would be unfair to point out the resistance to transfeminism within the mainstream feminist movement without similarly pointing out the resistance within the LGBT movement (usually ironically referred to as the "GGGG" movement to call attention to the predominant focus on cis gay men). Maybe this LGBT resistance is actually what makes our transfeminist alliances so diverse: the fact that we cannot count on old forms of political organization based on identities alone. Maybe the best alliances are those of and for people of different backgrounds who are eventually compelled to understand and fight for one another. These new arrangements are an effort to *do* intersectionality, to put into practice new forms of political organization that do not premise themselves solely on the politics of identity marginalization or on the belief that an identity category is sufficient for describing the kinds of oppression experienced by all members of that category. Our approach seemed validated when we received unexpected support from black feminists—most notably, the preeminent black feminist group Blogueiras Negras—not only because they, as did we, denounced racist exclusions within feminisms that resemble our own but also because we identified ourselves with the same fight they were fighting: the same plight approached from distinct fronts. One could see this as an attempt to make analogies between racism and transphobia, but it was, in fact, an engagement in some form of class solidarity, across categories. Of course, this is not a utopian alliance; unfortunately, there were and are transphobic black feminists just as there were and are racist transfeminist people. Racism, sexism, transphobia, and other forms of discrimination are not elements that one can simply erase from oneself, given that the societies and cultures that have shaped us are founded upon these very same ideologies.

In this brief piece, I've tried to describe the difficult birth of transfeminism in Brazil. Our movement is, of course, not free from the many issues that get in the way of our goal, but what we aim for is not only mutual recognition and empathy when we work together with different groups in the common goal of fighting sexism and transphobia; we also want to work on issues that we would not usually be compelled to act on, owing to the individualization of our respective plights. Intersectionality is, in my view, the only escape from the compartmentalization of politics. Class solidarity across categories is the only way to build a strong and united movement. We seek to add to, and not appropriate, feminist institutions. In Emi Koyama's words:

> Transfeminism is not about taking over feminist institutions. Instead, it extends and advances feminism as a whole through our own liberation and coalition work with all others. It stands up for trans and non-trans women alike, and asks non-trans women to stand up for trans women in return. Transfeminism embodies feminist coalition politics in which women from different backgrounds stand up for each other, because if we do not stand for each other, nobody will. (Koyama 2001)

Hailey Kaas is a Latina transfeminist born in São Paulo, Brazil. Writer and translator, she was responsible for introducing transfeminism in Brazil through one of the first Brazilian transfeminism websites, Transfeminismo. She is currently taking part in multiple initiatives to spread transfeminism in Brazil.

References

Butler, Judith. 2004. *Undoing Gender*. New York: Routledge.
Koyama, Emi. 2001. "The Transfeminist Manifesto." Eminism.org. www.eminism.org/readings
/pdf-rdg/tfmanifesto.pdf.

On Being the Object of Compromise

CAEL M. KEEGAN

Abstract The 2014 National Women's Studies Association (NWSA) conference specifically solicited trans-feminist academic work through a call for proposals subtheme entitled "Trans-Feminisms." This subtheme called for work exploring how "trans-feminist analyses help us redefine feminist politics" and discussing "opportunities for coalitions and convergences among trans-feminisms without co-opting self-chosen trans*/gender identifications and/or objectifying trans* people." Yet when trans attendees arrived at the conference, they encountered a bathroom implementation that reflected negative cultural attitudes about trans people and subjected them to gender policing and potential violence. Below, I analyze the NWSA's bathroom "compromise" as a failed strategy that compromised the safety of all conference attendees while raising serious questions about the current viability of political trans-feminist coalition.

Keywords bathrooms, NWSA, National Women Studies Association, sex segregation, feminism

I n November 2009, the Transgender Caucus of the National Women Studies Association (NWSA) submitted a letter to the NWSA leadership to request changes in bathroom implementation at the national conference—the major professional gathering for academics working in women, gender, and sexuality studies in the global anglophone North. In the letter, the caucus noted that at the 2009 conference in Atlanta, "there were no all gender/gender neutral bathrooms, nor were there any men's bathrooms on the first floor of the building, the main floor of the conference" (Transgender Caucus 2009). Anecdotal accounts from previous cochairs of the Transgender Caucus reported that all men's rooms at the 2009 conference had been converted into women's rooms, thereby leaving both cisgender and transgender men with no bathroom access on the main conference floor. Individuals requiring access to all-gender or gender-neutral restrooms were excluded altogether from the conference's imagination. The 2009 letter noted, "While we fully recognize that a large majority of conference participants are women . . . turning all of the bathrooms on the first floor into 'women's only' did not increase accessibility for all, rather it took accessibility away from certain groups to give to others." As a corrective to these conditions, the 2009 caucus

TSQ: Transgender Studies Quarterly ∗ Volume 3, Numbers 1–2 ∗ May 2016 **150**
DOI 10.1215/23289252-3334319 © 2016 Duke University Press

requested a policy ensuring that "at least one gender neutral/all gender bathroom be made available on the main floor(s) of the conference as well as announced in the conference program and depicted on the map of the conference site."

This essay is a response to requests from NWSA leadership to explain why subsequent bathroom implementation at the NWSA 2014 conference continued to be problematic, particularly for trans-feminine and gender-nonconforming members. Despite NWSA's efforts to offer gender-neutral space, bathroom design at the 2014 conference (see fig. 1) ultimately failed to ensure equal and safe participation for

Figure 1. Gender-neutral bathroom design at the 2014 National Women's Studies Association conference

NWSA members. As Judith aka "Jack" Halberstam has noted, persistence of "the bathroom problem," especially in feminist spaces, points to the "flourishing existence of gender binarism despite rumors of its demise" (1998: 22). The ongoing tensions between trans members of NWSA and the organization's attempts to incorporate us through a weak commitment to gender neutrality indicate a deeper and persistent problematic attached to the inclusion of trans people in feminist discourse.[1] That NWSA 2014 reproduced common exclusionary attitudes about bathrooms should suggest to us that major stumbling blocks remain in the effort to recognize trans people as "feminist, intellectual subjects" (Spade 2006: 317).

Below, I discuss how the compromise that NWSA's 2014 bathroom policy sought to strike between the needs of cisgender women and trans people in fact compromised the safety of all conference attendees. The repurposing of only men's rooms as "gender neutral" at the premiere academic conference for people working in US-based academic feminism is troubling. Despite a recent flourishing of trans-feminist research and theory in the Western academy, trans people still face immense barriers to the spaces in which this work is presented and discussed. That NWSA 2014 consciously solicited trans-feminist work while offering this bathroom implementation replicates a toxic anthropology in which trans people are "tragically misread" as objects of study only (Namaste 2000: 9–23) and are never thought of as feminist agents or bodies themselves.[2] NWSA's 2014 signage renders trans women and nonbinary trans people as "impossible people" (Spade 2008: 368) who cannot be made visible without presumably costing others their safety, subjectivity, or convenience.

While regarded as "obvious" (Kogan 2007: 3) by the dominant culture, bathroom sex segregation remains a ground-zero battle for trans people (Plaskow 2008: 54), whose right to enter sex-segregated facilities is challenged—interpersonally and legally—on a daily basis. Transgender politics, intersecting with disability politics, draws our attention to bathroom access as a human right: without right of entry to safe bathrooms, trans people are denied equal access to public accommodations, our bladders acting as "leashes" that restrict our social mobility and participation (Cavanagh 2011: 18, 20). Lack of access to all-gender bathrooms often forces trans people to choose between likely abuse in a gendered bathroom or potential arrest for urinating or defecating outside—charges that, if upheld in court, can permanently place us on sex offender registries. These risks are further increased by high rates of homelessness and poverty in the transgender population, leaving transient transgender people dependent upon public restrooms for their bodily needs as well as for shelter. Recent legislative attempts to prevent or criminalize transgender bathroom access in North Carolina, Utah, Minnesota, Texas, Kentucky, and Florida illustrate that this resistance may share a negative causal relationship with progress on LGB/T issues—most notably, marriage equality.

Cisgender women's physical protection from cisgender men continues to be the principal reason cited for sex segregation of bathrooms, although the current structure of most women's rooms does nothing to prevent ill-intended actors from entering them (Faktor 2011: 13). The presumed security of cis women in segregated bathrooms may actually produce increased peril in these spaces, which are assumed to be safe although they are not. Nonetheless, the "safety" of cis women is consistently deployed to illustrate why trans people (i.e., trans women) must be kept out of women's spaces. The notion that trans women are "really men" who seek legal access to women's bathrooms in order to commit sexual violence ignores both the total lack of evidence for this argument and the reality that cis women are capable of violence themselves. Assumptions that sex segregation makes cis women "safe" allow the bathroom to be used as an "icon of danger" (Cavanagh 2010: 19) that is strategically deployed to shut down transgender claims to civil equality. Objections to trans-inclusive bathroom spaces tend to insinuate that all transgender people should ideally use men's rooms, since this is the only conceivable way to segregate bodies with penises from cisgender women's urinary spaces.

While we might expect that NWSA—an intentionally feminist organization whose mission is to promote "the production and dissemination of knowledge about women and gender through teaching, learning, research, and service" (NWSA 2015)—would respond in more progressive ways to the "bathroom problem," closer examination reveals that bathroom policy at NWSA's 2014 conference in San Juan replicated the same transphobic patterns embedded in standard defenses of sex segregation. The conference identically repeated the structure of "protecting" cis women by mandating potentially dangerous bodies (i.e., bodies that might possess penises) into men's bathrooms. The guise of neutrality in NWSA's implementation offers a compromise that purports to keep cis women "safe" while obviating transphobic harm. In actuality, NWSA's bathroom policy compromises the security of cis women by producing a false sense of safety that it can only achieve by directing concentrated risk at the bodies of trans women.

Critical race theory has given us excellent reasons to be suspicious of neutrality as an antidiscrimination measure. Both Kimberlé Crenshaw and Patricia J. Williams have demonstrated that race neutrality, when designed and enforced by whites, tends to erase structural violence against people of color, thereby rescuing white people from any responsibility for the racial inequities from which they benefit. Race neutrality discourses make invisible their very reason for existing in the first place, thereby rendering racism undetectable and uncorrectable. Crenshaw notes that the enforcement of color blindness under antidiscrimination law "constitutes a formidable obstacle to efforts to alleviate conditions of white supremacy. . . . In sum, the very terms used to proclaim victory contain within them the seeds of defeat" (1988: 1347). Williams describes color blindness as "racism in drag, . . . propounded not just as a theory of equality, but as a standard of 'neutrality'" (1991: 116), which in turn limits people of color's ability to claim resistant positions without appearing biased or irrational. While not entirely synonymous with race neutrality, uncritical implementations of gender neutrality fall into similar traps: they erase the structural oppression of trans and gender-nonconforming people and enact a weak form of inclusion that privileges cis people's partial understandings of fairness and safety.

As represented in the picture I snapped at the 2014 conference (fig. 1), NWSA's bathroom policy represents gender neutrality as a compromise between cis and trans women's needs. However, this "compromise" can only be established through the double compromise of neutrality itself: the implementation mandates gender neutrality only for the men's side of the sex-segregated bathrooms, and yet also does not cover the men's signs. This implementation is insufficient for a number of interlocking reasons:

1. It traffics in the ideas of "neutrality" and "inclusion" while delivering their opposite. If all spaces are not neutral to gender designation, then no spaces are neutral. The signage engages in an "oxymoronic strategy of uncritical inclusion" (West 2010: 157) that produces effects in direct opposition to its professed intent. By not removing the men's sign, but merely placing the gender-neutral sign next to it, the appeal to "neutrality" is rendered not simply partial, but hollow.

2. It exposes those most vulnerable to violence in bathrooms, trans women, to the most risk. The signage affirms cultural beliefs that trans women are "really men" who seek to enter women's spaces to commit acts of sexual violence. Trans women are faced with an impossible choice between two potentially treacherous situations: if a trans woman seeks to avoid policing, accusations, and possible violence in the women's room, she can only do so by entering a "neutral" space that immediately outs her and may expose her to violence by men.

3. It places the convenience of cis women above the safety of trans people, especially trans women. Embedded in the repurposing of a men's room as a "gender neutral" space is the aim of creating shorter bathroom lines for cis women. Since NWSA is a space dominated by cis female bodies, this uneven application of neutrality bespeaks an underlying desire to shift the bodies of trans women into the lower-volume bathroom, thereby enhancing the convenience of cis women—who may also choose to use the "neutral" space if they so wish.

3. It ignores the clear recommendations of activist organizations on how to implement safe bathrooms for trans people: Both PISSAR (West 170) and the Transgender Law Center (2005: 13) explicitly state that repurposing men's rooms as "gender neutral" can expose trans people to heightened forms of policing and jeopardy when they enter bathrooms that are clearly marked as "special."

4. It promotes an essentialist assumption that penises, rather than misogynistic and sexist forms of socialization, are the source of physical and gendered violence. Suggesting that all people with penises should use the same restroom regardless of their varying gender identities/expressions is a form of "genital narcissism" (Juang 2006: 247) in which uniform genital morphology is enforced as a paradoxical solution to gender oppression.

5. If it purports to ensure the safety of trans women, then the signage must assume that men will not be present at the conference. There is indeed a history of this assumption at NWSA, as noted by the 2009 caucus letter.

6. It erases cis women's capacity for violence and produces a false sense of security in cis women's spaces.

7.   It maintains the culturally imposed sex binary by suggesting that there are "men," "women," and "others" who are neither women nor men. Neutrality here implies that trans people's genders are all equal in their artificiality, while cis genders get to maintain their "natural" status. The "gender neutral restroom" sign here may as well read, "Trans people go here."

Despite NWSA's intended inclusivity, its compromised approach to gender-neutral bathrooms has the same material effects on trans bodies as does outright hostility. At the 2014 Trans/Gender-Variant Caucus business meeting, caucus members expressed surprise and anger about the bathroom implementation, confusion about which bathroom to use, and fear that the bathrooms had been intentionally designed to exclude them. Some activist conference-goers moved the gender-neutral signage to the middle of the binary signs, or covered both binary signs with handmade gender-neutral placards. However, the gender-neutral signs were consistently repositioned on the men's side of the bathrooms, ostensibly by conference staff or by other attendees. Subsequent discussions between Trans/Gender-Variant Caucus cochair Rachel Reinke, NWSA leadership, and myself revealed that repurposing men's bathrooms as gender neutral is official NWSA policy.[3] Yet according to these conversations, the policy comes from no particularly invested committee and represents no specifically transphobic position. Rather, it appears that NWSA representatives were attempting to meet the requests of the 2009 Trans Caucus letter, and they were genuinely puzzled at why this implementation was problematic. Trans requests for gender-neutral space had apparently not prompted NWSA organizers to do the work of being "pedagogically thoughtful" (Cavanagh 2010: 218) about bathroom design.

As of this writing, NWSA has verbally agreed with the Trans/Gender-Variant Caucus's request to make all bathrooms at the 2015 conference in Milwaukee gender neutral. Nonetheless, the minoritized status of trans people in feminist discourse and organizing indicates that unexpected challenges are likely to emerge. The entrenched conditions of invisibility that trans attendees have faced at NWSA is evidence of the larger gap between traditional women's studies discourses and the younger fields of queer and trans studies, which often share institutional space within women, gender, and sexuality programs. That gap is itself reflected in the decades of marginalization that trans people have faced in the academy and in feminist and queer activist communities. Although increasingly receptive to trans theories and methodologies, establishment academic feminism continues to lag in its understanding of and accountability to transgender experience. By thinking more concretely about its institutional environments, and by not seeking weak compromises, academic feminism can allay the "stranger-making" effects of assuming a certain body as its norm (Ahmed

2012: 3). Until trans bodies can be present in feminist spaces without being subject to preventable forms of risk and erasure, we should question to what extent a coalitional trans-feminist praxis can exist—beyond gesture, beyond intervention, beyond compromise.

Cael M. Keegan is assistant professor of women, gender, and sexuality studies at Grand Valley State University and cochair of the Trans/Gender-Variant Caucus of the National Women Studies Association. He is currently at work on a book exploring trans aesthetics in the films of Andy and Lana Wachowski for the University of Illinois Press.

Notes

1. Anecdotal reports from long-time caucus members confirm an extended and contentious struggle over the issue of trans inclusion at the annual NWSA conference. Unfortunately, the marginalized and fragmentary nature of the caucus's history means that I have not been able to collect more than verbal accounts of this problematic prior to 2009.
2. NWSA 2014's CFP subtheme, "Trans-Feminisms," solicited work addressing a "wide range of non-cisgendered experiences and embodiments" as well as work that included "transnational, transcultural, transgenerational, and/or transspecies subjects." The CFP for this subtheme also made specific requests for work pursuing the following questions: "In what ways do trans-feminist analyses help us redefine feminist politics and epistemologies? In what ways does women's and gender studies traffic in the objects, knowledges, languages, desires, and bodies of trans-feminisms? And what are the opportunities for coalitions and convergences among trans-feminisms without co-opting self-chosen trans∗/gender identifications and/or objectifying trans∗ people?" (NWSA 2014). That the conference theoretically considered these questions without sufficiently examining its material practices in relation to the bodies of trans attendees illustrates an acute disconnect between feminist theorizing and the politics of feminist space. For the full NWSA 2014 CFP, see NWSA 2014.
3. Of course, this is not actually how the implementation was carried out, since the men's bathroom signs were not actually covered. The purported "neutrality" of the added bathroom signage was therefore entirely undercut.

References

Ahmed, Sara. 2012. *On Being Included: Racism and Diversity in Institutional Life*. Durham, NC: Duke University Press.

Cavanagh, Sheila L. 2010. *Queering Bathrooms: Gender, Sexuality, and the Hygienic Imagination*. Toronto: University of Toronto Press.

———. 2011. "You Are Where You Urinate." *Gay and Lesbian Review Worldwide* 18, no. 4: 18–22.

Crenshaw, Kimberlé. 1988. "Race, Reform, and Retrenchment: Transformation and Legitimation in Antidiscrimination Law." *Harvard Law Review* 101, no. 7: 1331–87.

Faktor, Alex. 2011. "Access and Exclusion: Public Toilets as Sites of Insecurity for Gender and Sexual Minorities in North America." *Journal of Human Security* 7, no. 3: 10–22.

Halberstam, Judith. 1998. *Female Masculinity.* Durham, NC: Duke University Press.

Juang, Richard M. 2006. "Transgendering the Politics of Recognition." In *Transgender Rights*, edited by Paisley Currah, Richard M. Juang, and Shannon Price Minter, 242–61. Minneapolis: University of Minnesota Press.

Kogan, Terry S. 2007. "Sex-Separation in Public Restrooms: Law, Architecture, and Gender." *Michigan Journal of Gender and Law* 14, no. 1: 1–57.

Namaste, Viviane K. 2000. *Invisible Lives: The Erasure of Transsexual and Transgendered People.* Chicago: University of Chicago Press.

NWSA (National Women Studies Association). 2014. "Call for Proposals." www.nwsa.org/files /NWSA%202014%20CFP_Final.pdf.

———. 2015 "About." www.nwsa.org/about (accessed May 3).

Plaskow, Judith. 2008. "Embodiment, Elimination, and the Role of Toilets in the Struggle for Social Justice." *Cross Currents* 58, no. 1: 51–64.

Spade, Dean. 2006. "Mutilating Gender." In *The Transgender Studies Reader*, edited by Susan Stryker and Stephen Whittle, 315–32. London: Routledge.

———. 2008. "Trans Law and Politics on a Neoliberal Landscape." *Temple Political and Civil Rights Law Review* 18, no. 2: 353–73.

Transgender Caucus of the National Women Studies Association. 2009. "NWSA Trans Caucus Concerns." Unpublished letter.

Transgender Law Center. 2005. "Peeing in Peace: A Resource Guide for Transgender Activists and Allies." transgenderlawcenter.org/issues/public-accomodations/peeing-in-peace.

West, Isaac. 2010. "PISSAR's Critically Queer and Disabled Politics." *Communication and Critical/ Cultural Studies* 7, no. 2: 156–75.

Williams, Patricia J. 1991. *The Alchemy of Race and Rights.* Cambridge, MA: Harvard University Press.

Khwaja Sira Activism

The Politics of Gender Ambiguity in Pakistan

FARIS A. KHAN

Abstract This essay examines an instance of media activism by members of a Karachi-based organization run by and for nonnormatively gendered people who are known as *khwaja siras*. By providing
both ethnographic analysis and a genderqueer feminist reading of the group's strategies for resisting
categorization and surveillance through practices of gender ambiguity, this essay argues for the
potential of *khwaja sira* politics to produce radical subjectivity.
Keywords *khwaja sira*, *hijra*, activism, ambiguity, resistance, genderqueer feminism, Pakistan

On a hot October Karachi evening in 2011, Payal quickly locked the office door
while Shazia and I descended the three flights of stairs to the ground floor. As
we exited the building through the rusty metal gate, we passed the exterior wall on
which Payal had recently had one of her *chelas* (students) paint the name of their
organization in a bold shade of red: Gender Solidarity Society (GSS).[1] Soon the
three of us were comfortably seated in the shuttle sent by Wave TV, en route to
the station's studio, where the activists I was accompanying had been invited to
participate in a talk show. GSS had had a rather busy week of television and radio
interviewing, which formed an important component of the organization's media
strategy, aimed at promoting a positive public image of *khwaja siras* (a category of
gender-ambiguous people). In this essay, I examine GSS's appearance on Wave
TV to argue that *khwaja sira* activists practiced gender ambiguity as a form of
resistance to categorization and surveillance by society and the state. I discuss the
potential feminist dimensions of GSS's approach and offer a genderqueer feminist
reading to suggest how *khwaja sira* politics may produce radical subjectivities.[2]

Khwaja Siras, Past and Present

The term *khwaja sira* is rooted in the medieval period of South Asian history,
when it served as a title for the chief eunuch of the Mughal court (Manucci 1906:
350). Castrated male eunuchs served as harem guards, army generals, and imperial

advisors, and they held many powerful administrative positions (Reddy 2005: 22). The term *khwaja sira* regained currency in the first decade of the twenty-first century when gender-ambiguous people, who differed from their medieval counterparts with respect to sex, gender, and sexuality, appropriated the appellation as an identity label to replace the pejorative term *hijra*. Despite the recent mainstreaming of the royal epithet *khwaja sira*, *hijra* nevertheless remains widely in use within the social networks of gender-ambiguous people.

In the contemporary period, *khwaja sira* serves as an umbrella term consisting of several overlapping sex and gender subcategories that, according to my research consultants, may include individuals with congenital genital irregularities (*khunsa*), feminine males who situationally cross-dress (*zennana*), and *zennanas* who excise their male genitalia and assume a more permanent feminine presentation (*hijra*). *Zennanas* and *hijras* alike consider themselves to have been endowed with a feminine soul since birth. They understand this soul not only to have driven them to be feminine in appearance and gender role but also to have shaped their sexual preference for men. *Khwaja siras* have a centuries-old system of social organization premised on the *guru-chela* (master-disciple) relationship through which gender-ambiguous people ritually forge alliances with one another. Most come from lower-class backgrounds, typically receive little or no formal education, and earn a living through singing and dancing, begging, and sex work.

Societal perceptions of *khwaja siras* both diverged from and overlapped with the structuring of identities within the social networks of gender-ambiguous people. Alongside the dominant belief that *khwaja siras* were physically inter-sexed was a widespread suspicion that they might also be considered biologically male individuals who were physically emasculated, innately feminine, gender dysphoric, and same-sex desiring. These varying understandings of *khwaja sira* not only were shaped by societal differences (e.g., disparities in class, ethnicity, religious belief, personal experience) but were also interlayered by a sense of uncertainty or ignorance about the corporeality and sexuality of gender-variant people, the mere presence of whom often evokes a sense of curiosity, anxiety, and confusion in the wider society.

Between 2009 and 2012, the Pakistani Supreme Court granted a number of rights and privileges to *khwaja siras* in a series of rulings, recognizing *khwaja sira* as a distinct sex/gender in addition to male and female.[3] Registrants were given the choice of entering one of three groupings for their national identity cards: male (*khwaja sira*), female (*khwaja sira*), and *khunsa-e-mushkil* (which translates roughly as a person who is born with indeterminable genitalia). Although the court did not clearly define the meaning of these official subclasses, it gave *khwaja siras* the right to self-determination in selecting their identity category of choice. In their public performances, *khwaja sira* activists availed themselves of, and further problematized, the sociocultural and legal uncertainties surrounding their bodies and sexuality.

Performing Ambiguity

Upon our arrival at the Wave TV studio, we were escorted to the hair and makeup department where two professional beauticians made Payal and Shazia camera-ready. After a brief conference with the show's host, a fashionably suited man in his early thirties, Payal and Shazia entrusted me with their handbags and strode onto the studio set. Activists Noor Vicky and Banno Ali joined the program remotely from Islamabad and Lahore, respectively, while I observed the live broadcast from behind the cameras.

Following a set of generic introductory remarks about *khwaja siras*, the host welcomed his guests and immediately began his questioning. He traced the familiar line of inquiry I had come to associate with televised *khwaja sira* interviews. In the excerpts below, I document the host's interrogation of two distinct yet imbricated areas of public anxiety concerning *khwaja sira* sexuality and corporeality. In the first extract, the activists confront the recurrent social curiosity pertaining to the sexual preferences of gender-ambiguous people. Noteworthy here is the proficient manner in which the activists confound the host by speaking in circles about the erotic desires of *khwaja siras*, thereby sustaining ambiguity about their romantic and sexual interests.

> HOST: So who are *khwaja siras* attracted to more? Men or women?
>
> (Noor laughs nervously)
>
> PAYAL: See, we like whoever treats us nicely, whether they are men or women.
>
> HOST: But we were talking about the feelings of *khwaja siras*....
>
> PAYAL: We feel for both men and women. It depends on how they treat us.... If there is a man who likes us . . . and if he's a good friend of ours . . . then what's wrong with that?
>
> NOOR: Loving is not a crime.
>
> HOST: But does this love happen with men or with women?
>
> NOOR: Our love is for men, for women, for everyone.
>
> HOST: This is a very confusing situation. Ms. Banno, what are your thoughts?
>
> BANNO: Obviously, we . . . too have a heart . . . so we too like someone or another . . . whether it's our mother, our father or some friend.

The host carefully articulated his query regarding a taboo subject by using non-sexual, euphemistic language. His inability to explicitly enunciate his questions on television enabled the activists to deploy deflective patterns of speech to frustrate his line of questioning. Throughout the conversation, statements about *khwaja sira* sexual object choice were safely couched in the idiom of "love" and "feelings," the polyvalence of which allowed the activist leaders to digress about loving relationships between parents and children, siblings, and friends. Despite being from different parts of the country and lacking a formal alliance, the activist leaders were unified in their use of verbal ambiguity to resist invasive inquiry. Their shared strategy was not so much indicative of a loose-knit coalition among activists but rather is illustrative of similarities in the subjective experiences of gender-ambiguous people from diverse Pakistani contexts.

Following this dramatic and somewhat amusing exchange, the host, now visibly frustrated, embarked on another line of questioning. His focus shifted from sexual proclivities and practices to the physical embodiments of *khwaja siras*. In the brief dialogue below, Payal responds to the host's query about somatic alterities among *khwaja siras* by delivering a convoluted and partial explanation of the state-sanctioned *khwaja sira* identity categories.

> HOST: Can you discreetly explain to me the difference between male *khwaja sira*, female *khwaja sira*, and *khunsa khwaja sira*?
>
> PAYAL: See, our relationship is with our soul. Often you hear that there was a girl but she used to . . . behave like a boy. And then later on when they did her medical test, they discovered that she was a boy from within. We have a similar condition. So *khwaja siras* will select the box [for their ID cards] that applies to them. But we have been given several options since we are neither complete men nor complete women.

Payal's intentionally obscure response about *khwaja sira* anatomies, though partially attributable to the host's request for her to be discreet, intended to evoke multiple interpretations among diverse viewers. She begins by describing *khwaja siras* as individuals who possess a soul that influences their gender performance. She then immediately offers a seemingly contradictory explanation by suggesting that the state of being a *khwaja sira* was comparable to medically verifiable sex/gender conditions. What remains unclear in her next polysemous statement, "she was a boy from within," is whether Payal was commenting on gender, genital, or hormonal ambiguities. Importantly, at no point does she explicitly describe the physiological characteristics of *khwaja siras*. Through her carefully crafted utterances, Payal successfully manages to perpetuate a veil of ambiguity surrounding the sex, gender, and sexuality of the groups she represents.

On our ride back to the GSS office from the studio, I asked Payal about her reluctance to answer some of the host's questions, to which she responded by referencing what Stephen Murray describes as the "common Islamic ethos of avoidance in acknowledging sex and sexualities" (1997: 14). She emphasized the impropriety of an open admission of one's sexual proclivities and practices by stating, "Pakistan is an Islamic country, and we cannot talk about these things on television." After a moment's pause, she added, "And why should we have to talk about our sex when ordinary men and women don't have to." On the one hand, Payal demonstrates her socially conditioned discomfort with discussing culturally licentious topics in a public forum. On the other hand, she expresses her principled stance against the injustice of singling out, interrogating, and coercing minorities to declare private details in a public forum when dominant groups are not subjected to the same standard of transparency.

Reading Realities and Potentialities

Inderpal Grewal and Caren Kaplan caution that "we cannot think of sexual subjects as purely oppositional or resistant to dominant institutions" (2001: 670). Likewise, Evelyn Blackwood notes that Western queer scholars cannot "demand that all forms of queer sexuality adhere to the same strategies and representations of sexuality" (2010: 117), disregarding the historical and cultural specificities through which activism transpires in various geographical contexts. That the *khwaja sira* practice of perpetuating ambiguity does not conform to the overt strategies of resistance that are generally assumed and asserted within US queer and trans politics should not, however, disqualify it from being understood as a form of genderqueer activism.[4] As I have demonstrated, *khwaja sira* activist strategies of obfuscation are culturally informed gestures of resistance, which have both practical political value and theoretical significance.

This obfuscation transpires precisely at the intersection of an indigenous mode of seeking justice and equal rights with the widespread Islamic cultural practice of circumventing public disclosure of private sexuality. Drawing on Michel Foucault, Blackwood has suggested that there are pleasures and powers associated with normativity, just as there are social and material losses and rewards attached to nonnormativity (2010: 24). Situated between the poles of normativity and queerness, gender ambiguity offers a form of productive power over mainstream society by preserving the mysterious aura of *khwaja siras*.

How, if at all, might a *khwaja sira* politics of ambiguity parallel or advance queer feminist agendas? The activist work described herein was not consciously performed in the name of genderqueer feminism. In fact, given their lack of access to education and resources, few of the *khwaja siras* I worked with were familiar with feminist concepts, ideologies, and praxis, or even with the term *feminism* itself. And yet their media advocacy conveys a feminist sensibility, exemplified by resistance to corporeal disciplining, sexual surveillance, biopolitical categorization, and heteronormalization. Importantly, this activism has the potential to inform genderqueer feminist politics in South Asia and beyond. Others may find the *khwaja sira* performance of ambiguity applicable to and operable within their own unique sociocultural and political circumstances. Although I do not suggest that *khwaja sira* activism is inevitably feminist, I assert that it resonates with genderqueer feminism precisely due to its potential for social and political transformation.

If the liberation of all nonnormatively gendered people is the end goal of genderqueer feminism, then empowerment may be sought in escaping the shackles of classification that bind people into fixed taxonomic categories. This approach aims to destabilize essentialist and binary assumptions about gender and sexuality that categorically thwart nonheteronormativities from taking shape. In sustaining ambiguity, *khwaja sira* activism may be understood as going beyond the articulation of multiple subject positions to abjuring categories altogether. By this logic, liberation rests in repositioning ambiguity from the margins to the center—that is, in celebrating it as a norm rather than an exception. This form of gender and sexuality activism, instead of demanding inclusion of nonnormative subjectivities into the nation's fabric, aims to collapse all sense of knowable types by obdurately reveling in and championing ambiguity in defiance of being rendered socially and legally legible. This manner of ceaselessly queering the queer is reminiscent of Geeta Patel's call to "hybridize" the center such that "queerness no longer sit[s] in for 'otherness'" but becomes a process of unsettling the self, preventing it from becoming a static and stable category (1997: 134, 138). Here, *khwaja sira, genderqueer*, and *trans* signal a perpetual state of indistinctness beyond mere traversal, transformation, and transition. Hence, from a genderqueer feminist stance, the act of sustaining ambiguity may be interpreted as a radical politics of unbecoming.

In his study of queer and black self-making in Cuba, Jafari Allen describes the politics of his project as one that "insists on recording the real while also mining those spaces for moments, experiences, and roadmaps toward freedom" (2011: 3). Allen's approach has informed my own supplementary reading of *khwaja sira* politics. In providing both an emic and genderqueer feminist reading of an activist practice, I have attempted to resolve the tension between ethnography and theory. In addition to demonstrating what the politics of ambiguity currently accomplishes for *khwaja siras*, I have used a genderqueer feminist perspective to reflect on how this technique may be further developed to create radical subjectivity. In presenting a subject position that is always in flux and never fully knowable, *khwaja sira* activists perform a mode of resistance characterized by functional efficacy, resonance with feminist and queer values, and radical transformative potential.

Faris A. Khan is a lecturer in the Department of Anthropology at Brandeis University. He is the author of "Powerful Cultural Productions: Identity Politics in Diasporic Same-Sex South Asian Weddings" (2011) and "Khwaja Sira: Transgender Activism and Transnationality in Pakistan" (2014).

Notes

1. I have replaced the names of people and the organization with pseudonyms in order to prevent them from being identified with the activist strategies detailed in this essay. Revealing the name of the organization I discuss may negatively impact not only the credibility of its members but also the efficacy of their techniques. I have, however, made up a pseudonym (i.e., GSS) that evokes a likeness in meaning to the actual name of the organization, particularly its emphasis on the relationship between genders.

2. I employ the term *genderqueer* as opposed to *trans* or *transgender*, since the former encompasses a greater diversity of gender nonnormativities and is therefore more suitable for discussing non-Euro-US subjectivities, such as *khwaja sira*. Moreover, calling *khwaja siras* "trans" may be seen as an imperialist imposition that misrepresents the experience of being a gender-nonnormative Pakistani.

3. I use *sex/gender* to indicate, as Gayle Rubin (1975) does, the link between bodies and gender attributes, particularly the lack of analytical distinction between the two categories in the Pakistani context.

4. Importantly, in their discussion of US trans politics, some theorists, such as Talia Bettcher, have endorsed "gender deception" as a "laudable tactic" while emphatically denying that "honesty is [always] the best policy" (2007: 60).

References

Allen, Jafari S. 2011. *¡Venceremos? The Erotics of Black Self-Making in Cuba*. Durham, NC: Duke University Press.

Bettcher, Talia Mae. 2007. "Evil Deceivers and Male-Believers: On Transphobic Violence and the Politics of Illusion." *Hypatia* 22, no. 3: 43–65.

Blackwood, Evelyn. 2010. *Falling into the Lesbi World: Desire and Difference in Indonesia*. Honolulu: University of Hawai'i Press.

Grewal, Inderpal, and Caren Kaplan. 2001. "Global Identities: Theorizing Transnational Studies of Sexuality." *GLQ* 7, no. 4: 663–79.

Manucci, Niccolao. 1906. *Storia do Mogor or Mogul India, 1653–1708*. London: John Murray.

Murray, Stephen O. 1997. "The Will Not to Know: Islamic Accommodations of Male Homosexuality." In *Islamic Homosexualities: Culture, History, and Literature*, edited by Stephen Murray and Will Roscoe, 14–54. New York: New York University Press.

Patel, Geeta. 1997. "Home, Homo, Hybrid: Translating Gender." *College Literature* 24, no. 1: 133–50.

Reddy, Gayatri. 2005. *With Respect to Sex: Negotiating Hijra Identity in South India*. Chicago: University of Chicago Press.

Rubin, Gayle. 1975. "The Traffic in Women: Notes on the 'Political Economy' of Sex." In *Towards an Anthropology of Women*, edited by Tayna R. Reiter, 157–210. New York: Monthly Review Press.

The Emergence of Transfeminism in Russia

Opposition from Cisnormative Feminists and Trans* People

YANA KIREY-SITNIKOVA

Abstract Trans* issues became visible in Russian feminist communities only in 2013. In Russia, transfeminism was not a reaction against the explicit exclusion of trans* people from feminist spaces; on the contrary, transphobia in feminism arose after an attempt to introduce transfeminism. Both sides currently borrow their arguments from texts by US authors, without significant adaptation to the post-Soviet context. According to the results of a survey conducted among Russian-speaking feminists, the acceptance of trans* people depends on social privilege and education, with more privileged and educated feminists being more conservative. On the other hand, the support for existing gender roles in Russian trans* communities is rather high, although it was shown to be lower than in the general population. Assaults from cisnormative feminists and trans* people, together with the tough political situation, make the survival of transfeminism questionable in Russia.

Keywords Russia, transfeminism, trans* activism

Transfeminism became well known in Russian trans* and feminist communities only in 2013. This is not surprising, given that trans* activism in general started only around 2008. From its introduction, transfeminist ideas faced strong opposition from both cisgender feminists and trans* people. In this article, I will briefly describe the historical context of recent trans* and feminist movements, and the introduction of transfeminism in Russia. I will then try to explain why it has been rejected by many trans* people and feminists alike. As a person actively involved in transfeminist activism, I will rely mainly on my memory of events in which I personally participated, which makes this article partly autoethnographic. I also rely on information from numerous online forums, surveys, and personal communications with trans* people and feminists. However, it is worth noting that my experience is limited to events that took part mainly in Moscow and St. Petersburg after 2010, and some of my observations are drawn mainly from communication with people with trans* feminine identities.

Trans* Activism

Transgender issues are scarcely known to the general public in Russia, and they did not receive any attention from mainstream political groups before 2015. If discussed at all, it was only in connection with the LGBT issues that have recently gained visibility because of antipropaganda laws, and most people do not understand the difference between transgenderism and homosexuality. From personal experience, I can say that even LGBT activists have little understanding of the needs of trans* people and regard them as less important than the problems of cisgender lesbians and gays. This is reflected in the work of LGB(T) organizations, which rarely cover any trans-related issues—when they do, it is usually by allowing one token trans* person to coordinate all the work in this area, which is not seen as a priority. The situation has slightly started to change over since the beginning of 2015, when trans* people were identified as a suitable group (different from lesbians and gays) for harassment by religious conservatives, and the authorities are picking up this trend.

Lectures and workshops on transgenderism started as early as 2008 (Sitnikova 2014). Trans* issues first appeared in a public space in a political context only in 2010, when Anno Komarov raised a banner with the slogan "My Gender Is My Choice" during Moscow Pride, organized by the radical Russian LGBT organization GayRussia. Only two street actions explicitly devoted to trans* issues have been held in Russia to date; both were part of international Stop Trans* Pathologization campaigns in 2011 and 2014, drawing only five and ten participants, respectively. More street actions included trans* slogans, including the 2011 and 2012 protests for fair elections, where transgender and genderqueer flags appeared for the first time. Other kinds of activism occur mostly in the sphere of self-advocacy while attempting to change names or legal genders, or when seeking access to hormones or surgeries. Generally speaking, self-defined trans* activists are few, centered in large cities such as Moscow, Saint Petersburg, Novosibirsk, Samara, and Arkhangelsk, rarely affiliated with organizations or institutions, and have few if any resources to influence even other oppressed groups that might conceivably become allies.

Feminism

In contrast, the Russian feminist movement has a long history that may be traced back to the nineteenth century. In 1917, the Soviet Union was among the first countries to grant women voting rights, and in 1920, abortion was legalized. The feminist movement was later suppressed along with other independent civil movements during the period of Joseph Stalin's rule, and a new law prohibiting abortion was issued in 1936, to be revoked only in 1955, two years after Stalin's death. Despite official Soviet support for equal rights, the oppression of women continued, although in a different form than in many Western countries. Women were considered equal with men in terms of ability to work and were allowed to perform heavy physical labor, but at the same time, patriarchal thinking persisted, and women were still required to do all the housework, which led to the "double burden" of women being expected to work both at home as well as at their jobs. A new wave of dissident feminism in the 1970s argued against the "unisex" model of Soviet citizenship and drew attention to the specific challenges and experiences of women (Moscow Feminist Group 2013).

After the dissolution of Soviet Union, the return of women to their "true destiny" as wives and mothers was an explicit goal of various nationalist projects (Gapova 2004: 109). Feminism is unpopular in contemporary Russia, enjoying the support of only 8 percent of the general population, with 38 percent of all Russians never even having heard the word (Public Opinion Foundation 2012). Far more than was the case for third-wave feminism in the West, post-Soviet feminism evolved in the context of virulent class stratification and economic inequality. According to feminist scholar Elena Gapova, Russian women's ignorance of or inattention to feminism stems in part from the consideration of gender inequality to be a problem secondary to economic issues more generally (Gapova 2004: 116).

Emergence of Transfeminism

Given the low visibility of both transgender and feminist communities, it is no surprise that the two groups were not interested in one another's issues and really didn't even know of one another. Because of the small number of separatist feminist spaces, hardly any trans* people ever experienced discrimination there, and trans* access to women-only spaces never became an issue. Feminism was rarely discussed among trans* communities, where conversation focused instead on hormones, surgeries, and the need to navigate within transphobic medical and social institutions.

I became interested in feminism in 2011, as a member of Yabloko, a political party, and its gender branch, which supports liberal feminism. I hadn't previously identified as a feminist, owing to what I knew of transphobia within mainstream Western feminism, and I was unfamiliar with any alternatives at that time. I first read about transfeminism in English in the summer of 2012 and was apparently one of the first persons in Russia to do so. I publicly presented on transfeminism for the first time in October 2012 at the Festival of Queer Culture (QueerFest) in St. Petersburg. I gave another lecture on transfeminism in Moscow later that same year, organized under the auspices of the Moscow Feminist Group, which became the first feminist group in Russia to organize a transfeminist event. They invited me to their separatist meetings, though I never came. A rally in Moscow on March 8, 2013 (International Women's day, an official holiday in Russia), was the first feminist street action in which transfeminist issues were publicly raised, but transfeminist activism was not confined to the capital city. I know at least two trans∗ women in Siberia (cities of Novosibirsk and Novokuznetsk) who successfully engaged with their local feminist communities. I encountered no opposition toward transfeminism at this early stage of activism, and even now there is currently only one organized feminist group in Russia whose members explicitly reject the identities of trans∗ women ("Initiative Group 'Za feminism'").

This positive start could perhaps have inspired hope that transfeminism in Russia would follow a different path than it had in the United States, where it had to struggle against feminist transphobia. Unfortunately, the reality was somewhat different. It's not that transphobia didn't exist at all in Russian feminism before the introduction of transfeminism. Reading online feminist discussions before 2013, one can certainly find posts in which commentators refer to trans∗ people as mentally ill and regard them with suspicion, but their opinions were not based on any particular feminist theory and were not different from arguments made by other (nonfeminist) people. The general attitude appears primarily to be one of curiosity, and even sympathy, toward a little-known phenomenon. The introduction of transfeminism, however, seems actually to have provoked a more explicit and deliberate transphobic response. The earlier situation changed drastically after I started blogging in online feminist communities, the largest of which was Feministki.livejournal.com, where I introduced the basic concepts of transfeminism, first by borrowing from US transfeminist authors such as Sandy Stone, Julia Serano, and Emi Koyama (Sitnikova 2013), then going on to develop my own ideas. Before long, cisgender feminists started using such concepts as "women's experience" and "male privilege" to discuss transgenderism, and their attitude toward it gradually changed from neutral to negative, or even hostile.

How did theoretical or ideological positions on transgenderism begin to appear in Russian feminism? Were they imported from the West or homemade? While Russian transfeminist perspectives indeed borrowed directly from US transgender theorists, it is less clear where Russian feminist transphobia originated. Such concepts as "universal women's experience" and "male privilege" were long known in Russian feminism, but it is difficult to determine whether the transphobic application of these to trans∗ issues was the independent invention of Russian feminists, or whether they first encountered these arguments in foreign sources. Part of the hostility toward transfeminism among some Russian feminists is undoubtedly the result of my personal style of activism, which is confrontational and uncompromising. I see this clearly when I compare comments on online posts I've made with comments made on posts by other trans∗ people. Had transfeminism been introduced in a more gradual and delicate way, the oppositional response might have been less vigorous. Whether my radical strategy was the right way to go depends on whether we as trans* people want assimilation and sympathy in a cisnormative world (including the feminist world) or whether we want to deconstruct cisnormativity. This question is highly controversial, even among members of trans* communities in Russia, who often post "don't rock the boat" comments in response to my blogs and other statements.

Who Are Trans*-Exclusive Feminists in Post-Soviet Space?

What makes some feminists trans* inclusive and others trans* exclusive? This question has been of great concern to me for some time. To satisfy my curiosity, I decided to organize an online survey, the initial results of which are published here for the first time. The language of the survey was Russian. It did not restrict participation based on the respondent's country of residence. The only requirement for participation was self-identification as a feminist. The survey was run in the first half of 2015.

Of the 639 respondents analyzed here, 54 self-identified as transgender people; their answers are excluded from the discussion that follows in an effort to reduce bias. One question I asked, which provided a key for interpreting responses to other questions, was, "People who were assigned male at birth but who identify as female are . . ." The answers included "women" (62 percent), "men" (12 percent), "an intermediate gender" (4 percent), and "depends on conditions" (18 percent). There was also a field in which respondents could enter their own answer. It was possible to select more than one answer. Answers to a similarly structured question about trans* men correlated closely to answers for the question about trans* women. The survey is not representative, and it is clearly biased by the fact that many feminists know me as an active participant in the trans* movement, which must undoubtedly contribute to underrepresentation of the opinions of "trans*-exclusive" feminists.

I compared respondents who answered either "women" or "men" to the question regarding the gender of people assigned male at birth but who identify as female, referring to these groups as, respectively, "accepting" and "rejecting" of transgender identity claims. Surprisingly, unlike the case with cisgender gays and lesbians, personally knowing trans* people was not a determining factor in accepting their identity. This result also contradicts other studies that suggest the significance of this factor in determining levels of transphobia (Hill and Willoughby 2005: 541). It should be noted that rejection of a trans* person's identity claim is not necessarily synonymous with transphobic behavior. It should also be noted that a few of the "rejecting" feminists indicated that they acquired their views only after being in communication with trans* people who were misogynist or supported existing gender norms.

The most indicative factors for the acceptance or rejection of a trans∗ persons' identity appears to be class privilege and level of education (which are not always correlated in post-Soviet states, where higher education is often free). The average salary of "rejecting" feminists is almost twice as high as the average salary of "accepting" feminists (US$1,147 and US$592 per month, respectively). The gap would be even wider if transgender respondents (all of whom fall into the "accepting" group) were included. As for education, there is a significant gap in graduate education between the two groups—40 percent of "rejecting" respondents and 24 percent of "accepting" respondents (fig. 1). These differences may be regarded in part as the consequence of age difference: the mean age for the "accepting" group was 21.8 years old, while for the "rejecting" group it was 23.5 years old. This age gap (1.7 years) is, however, too small to explain the huge difference in salary and educational level. The answers to other questions confirm that social and economic privilege is the most important indicator regarding Russian-speaking feminist attitudes toward trans∗ people.

Respondents in the "rejecting" group tend to live in larger cities: 46 percent live in cities with more than 5 million in population, compared to only 35 percent in the "accepting" group. "Accepting" respondents were more likely to report experiencing more than one form of discrimination, while the "rejecting" respondents were more likely not to experience any discrimination at all except for misogyny. There were more bisexuals and gender nonbinary people among the "accepting" group, while there were more lesbians among the "rejecting" feminists. Being a migrant, belonging to a national/ethnic minority group, and having a disability had no correlation with attitudes toward trans∗ issues

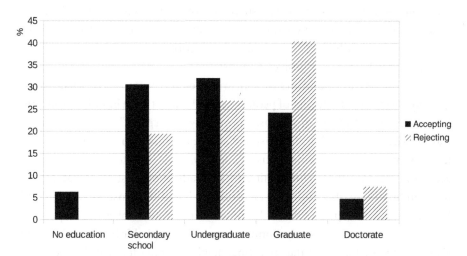

Figure 1. Respondents considered accepting and rejecting of transgender identity claims, according to their level of education

(fig. 2). The "rejecting" group appears to be more active on feminist issues and causes, with only 25 percent reporting not participating in any type of activism, compared to 37 percent of the "accepting" group not being active (fig. 3). "Rejecting" feminists were twice as likely to write articles and blogs on feminist issues or to translate texts. Participation in street protests, fund-raising, and gender studies is also higher among the "rejecting" group, owing to part to their higher levels of socioeconomic privilege and greater opportunities for activism in larger cities.

Participants were asked what most defined "female" and "male" for them. For the "rejecting" group, genitals were the primary factor (67 percent), followed by genes (49 percent). Hormones, reproductive capacity, and gender socialization were listed. Among the "accepting" group, "gender identity" was by far the leading criterion (67 percent), followed by other social factors rather than biological ones.

Rejection of trans* people's preferred gender identity is closely related to the negative attitude toward the concept of intersectionality, that is, a theory that studies intersections of oppressions and privileges in different social hierarchies. Only 18 percent of "rejecting" feminists believe this concept is useful for feminism, while 57 percent think it is harmful, and 18 percent are unfamiliar with the term. This finding is not surprising, given that many "rejecting" feminists have never experienced forms of oppression other rather than misogyny. Among the "accepting" group, 61 percent think that intersectionality is useful for feminism, while only 2 percent think it is harmful, and 29 percent have never heard of the

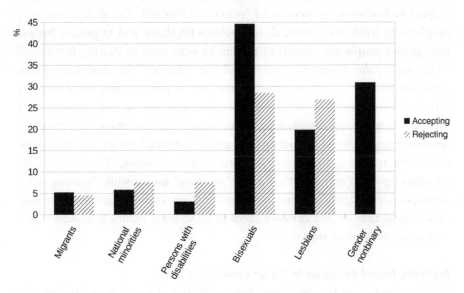

Figure 2. Respondents considered accepting and rejecting of transgender identity claims, according to their social group

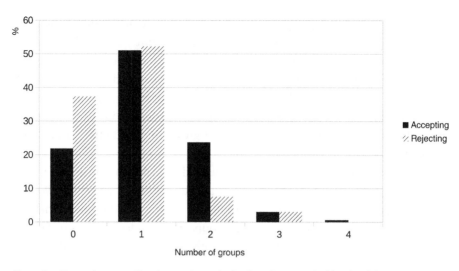

Figure 3. Respondents considered accepting and rejecting of transgender identity claims, according to the number of groups to which they belong

concept. Attitudes toward transfeminism are similarly highly correlated to rejection or acceptance of trans identities.

A few other findings are worth mentioning. Among the "rejecting" group, 39 percent opposed being able to amend gender markers on official documents at all, and 21 percent thought it should be possible to do so only once. At the same time, 27 percent believe that one should be able to change gender markers as many times as one wants. Regarding why trans* people would want to participate in feminism, 66 percent of "rejecting" feminists feel that transgender people want feminists to solve their problems for them, and 27 percent believe transgender people are "agents of patriarchy who want to destroy feminism." At the same time, however, 21 percent of the "rejecting" feminists believe that feminism and the trans* movement have similar goals. When asked whether trans* women should be included in women-only spaces, only 51 percent of the "rejecting" group opposed inclusion under any circumstances, while the remainder said it should depend on having had surgeries, having taken hormones, or visually appearing to be women. Thus, strictly speaking, "trans*-exclusive" feminists represent only about half of the "rejecting" group, while the other half is willing to tolerate trans* women in women-only spaces under certain conditions, even though they do not consider them to be women. Attitudes toward trans* men were much more tolerant.

Attitudes Toward Feminism in Trans* Community

The introduction of transfeminism specifically and of feminism more generally faces strong opposition in Russian trans* communities. Many trans* people in

Russia are very conservative with regard to upholding gender norms, and social norms more generally. They see their goal as "becoming normal," not in challenging norms, which leads to rejection of feminism as well as any public trans* activism that undermines binary gender roles. This conservative faction is very active and vocal, creating the impression of a strong trans* opposition to any form of feminism. Empirical evidence paints a different picture, however, and suggests that conservative voices do not represent a significant fraction of opinion within the trans* community. According to a survey I conducted in early 2015 among Russian-speaking trans* people (N = 358), 30 percent of respondents have a positive attitude toward feminism, and 32 percent have a positive attitude toward transfeminism. This is more than three times higher than the percentage of the general population that has a positive attitude toward feminism, as noted above (Public Opinion Foundation 2012). Only 9 percent of trans* respondents have a negative attitude toward feminism, and only 6 percent have a negative attitude toward transfeminism. Among those surveyed, 24 percent identified as feminist, and 11 percent identified as transfeminist.

While 23 percent of respondents didn't know what the word *transfeminism* meant, this is not a hopeless finding, taking into account the short history of the movement in Russia. One reason for the lack of comprehension of (trans) feminist ideas among the trans* community here is its overintellectualization and the large number of unfamiliar theoretical concepts that are often difficult for a person without higher education, or previous exposure to these concepts, to understand. Many trans* people find the discussion of these abstract concepts inappropriate at a time when more urgent practical problems remain unsolved. Unfortunately, there have been no significant attempts among Russian (trans) feminists to explain how their theories can correlate with the everyday experiences of trans* people, and, even more importantly, how these theories can help to change the political situation. Transfeminism thus remains the interest of a few college-educated middle-class activists. To some extent, this is a problem of Russian feminism in general.

Political Context

The general political climate in Russia will play a significant role in determining the ultimate fate of transfeminism. In the beginning of trans* activism here, and especially during the protests of 2011 and 2012, there was a feeling that democratization would come some day—or that at least the direction of political change was heading in that direction, though not as quickly as one might hope. Since 2012, however, the situation has only gotten worse. The Russian state tries to undermine any civil activism. Russian imperialism is on the rise. Both feminism and transgenderism are considered Western phenomena that are contrary to "traditional" Russian values, which leads to censorship, prohibition of public assemblies, and attacks from ultra-right groups. Some trans* activists are leaving the country, while others are abandoning their activism. Others, such as myself, reorient their activism to less public spheres such as theoretical writing.

Many trans* people and feminists have internalized the conservatism propagated by state media. One trans* woman told me that "propaganda of queer theory," a formulation that paraphrases the law banning "propaganda of non-traditional sexual relations," would be prohibited in the Facebook group she created. At a time of massive assaults on women's rights (for example, the recent legislative initiative against abortion or smoking for women under forty), it is easier for cisgender feminists to claim that the rights of trans* women should not be their concern, as they have more important issues to resolve. Likewise, it is easier for the general population to claim that feminism and trans* rights are not a high priority during a time of financial crisis sparked by the annexation of Crimea, the conflict with Ukraine, and international economic sanctions. Under such conditions, it is hardly surprising that the development of transfeminism in Russia has been suspended so soon after it began, and that its future in the region is so uncertain.

Yana Kirey-Sitnikova is a trans* activist and feminist from Moscow, Russia, and the author of the first book on transfeminism in the Russian language. She is also a PhD student in the field of chemoinformatics.

References

Gapova, Elena. 2004. "O gendere, nacii i klasse v postkommunizme" ("On Gender, Nation, and Class in Postcommunism"). *Gendernye issledovaniya* 13: 101–18.

Hill, Darryl, and Brian Willoughby. 2005. "The Development and Validation of the Genderism and Transphobia Scale." *Sex Roles* 53, nos. 7–8: 531–44.

Moscow Feminist Group. 2013. "Leningradskij feminizm 1970-x godov" ("Leningrad Feminism in the 1970s"). ravnopravka.ru/2013/05/leningrad_feminism/ (accessed March 2, 2015).

Public Opinion Foundation. 2012. "Zhenshhina—tozhe chelovek: Predstavleniya rossiyan o feminizme" ("Woman Is Also a Human: Attitudes of Russians toward Feminism"). www .fom.ru/obshchestvo/10611 (accessed July 16, 2015).

Sitnikova, Yana. 2013. "Transfeminism I radicalnij feminism: Kogda chastnoe stavit pod vopros publichnoe" ("Transfeminism and Radical Feminism: When the Private Calls into Question the Public"). In *Zhenshhiny v politike: Novye podxody k politicheskomu* (*Women in Politics: New Approaches to the Political*). *Feministskij obrazovatelnyj almanax* (*Feminist Educational Almanac*), vol. 3, edited by Alexander Pershai and Evgenia Ivanova, 79–88. Prague: Adliga.

———. 2014. "Transgender Activism in Russia." Freedom Requires Wings. www.freedom requireswings.com/2014/01/report-transgender-activism-in-russia.html (accessed July 16, 2015).

From Queering to Trans*imagining

Sookee's Trans*/Feminist Hip-Hop

TERENCE KUMPF

Abstract While rap music in many countries continues to asphyxiate itself on calcified sexist, cisgendered, and homo/transphobic sentiments and representations, Berlin-based hip-hop activist Sookee strives to forge queer and trans/feminist spaces to provoke dialogue, instigate action, and enable people to engage and imagine alternatives. A self-fashioned *quing* MC actively recording since 2006, Sookee's work confronts a number of issues, including sexism, heteronormativity, homo/transphobias, and neofascist/anti-immigrant paroxysms plaguing Germany today. This article provides a brief overview of the artist's work and the ways in which it opens trans/feminist spaces to foster allegiances and alliances across gender, sexual, cultural, geopolitical, and national borders.

Keywords trans*, hip-hop, activism, Germany, Europe

There's certainly no shortage of sexism or homophobia in hip-hop in Germany.[1] *Rap.de*, one of the country's predominant online and print publications, depicts a steady stream of hypermasculine fantasies of über-cisgendered men and women engaging in ever more lurid performances of heteronormativity. Cissexual exaggerations proliferate in videos by Bushido, Haftbefehl, Kollegah, Farid Bang, King Orgasmus One, and Schwester Ewa, a former prostitute of Polish descent who draws inspiration from her experiences in the commercial sex milieu, catering to audience expectations and hard-edged tastes (Aydemir 2015: 25). Even Lady Bitch Ray, a controversial artist who "casts herself as the hypersexualized ghetto bitch" to critique German rap's hyperhetero stances (Stehle 2012b: 158), seems almost coerced into using faux pornographic imagery to try and usurp power and space for women (Stehle 2012a: 94). In many instances, the commercial rap scene in Germany is asphyxiating itself on the ad nauseam recirculation of tired tropes that are hyperbolic beyond preposterous.

Underlying these representations, perhaps unsurprisingly, are deeply embedded homo/transphobias. In a scene in which epithets are the ultimate diss

TSQ: Transgender Studies Quarterly ∗ Volume 3, Number 1–2 ∗ May 2016   **175**
DOI 10.1215/23289252-3334355   © 2016 Duke University Press

(Stüttgen 2007: 134), homoerotic imagery has intentionally been used as a means to generate negative PR—to sell records, no less.[2] If a case study were needed to illustrate how the entertainment industry reifies unspoken normativizing assumptions and manipulates people in the process of re-creating sex and gender norms, mainstream German consumer rap would be a good place to start. Some intervention is required.

Enter Sookee—self-fashioned *"quing* of berlin," *Zeckenrapper* (literally "tick rapper," here meaning conscious rap), and one of Germany's preeminent critical voices exposing sexism, gender binaries, and homo/transphobias. Born Nora Hantzsch to political dissidents who fled East Germany, Sookee is a queer-feminist rapper and hip-hop activist who has been actively recording since 2006. Songs with such titles as "Quing," "Purpleize Hip Hop," "Pro Homo," "D.R.A.G.," "One Billion Rising," and "Working on Wonderland" clarify Sookee's mission: to insist upon, establish, maintain, celebrate, and promote queer/trans presences in a pop musical culture mired in suffocating conceptualizations of sexual and gendered binaries. Recorded by Berlin's Springstoff Records, Sookee's work resonates on the indie scene but also through her engagement with a variety of media outlets. The following is a brief overview of this artist-activist's concerns, efforts, and aims, as well as the prospects for creating trans/feminist spaces through such work.

Quing, Colors, and Code Switching: Purpleizing Hip-Hop

Sookee's material lyrically, visually, and thematically creates and promotes queer/trans spaces in a number of ways. First, the artist's performance persona is rooted in the concept of *"quing."* According to a 2003 *Urban Dictionary* entry, and recently reiterated by Maria Stehle (2012b: 157), *quing* constitutes a gender-neutral monarch (queen + king); however, the term equally suggests a queer/trans sovereign (queer + king); process (queering); active, critical thinking (question + ing); and possibly even the journey toward trans-consciousness (quest + ing). In the chorus to the title track of her full-length 2010 release *Quing* (Sookee 2010a), Sookee invites listeners to locate themselves in the term: "Hast du politische ziele bist motiviert unzufrieden / dann herzlich willkommen Du bist quing—dis is quing" (Do you have political goals, are you dissatisfied but motivated? / Welcome! You're quing—that's quing; Sookee 2010b). In an interview with *AVIVA-Berlin: Online Magazin für Frauen*, Sookee confirms that the term should remain open and flexible enough to allow young people who feel excluded from traditional political organizations to reflexively politicize themselves.[3] The introductory articulation of *quing* urges self-activation, social and political engagement, and activism.

Sookee asserts that purple is *quing*'s ideal optical analogy, and the concept takes on wide-ranging implications.[4] Purple is a fusion of red and blue, colors typically associated with traditional conceptualizations of femininity and masculinity, respectively. Sookee (2007: 39) claims that "quing is initially a mixture of masculine connoted blue and feminine connoted red, such that the mix ratio of feminine and masculine is altered by every nuanced shading of lilac, violet, purple, and magenta" (sie ist zunächst eine Mischung aus dem männlich konnotierten Blau und einem weiblich konnotierten Rot, wobei die genauen Michungsver-hältnisse mit jeder Nuance von Lila, Violett, Purpur und Magenta verändert werden). Sookee almost exclusively costumes herself in shades of purple and violet, thereby embodying *quing*. Where color is used to denote political affilia-tion, mixing blue and red can also be understood as an attempt to unify com-mon orientations on the political spectrum. In comparison to Republicans (red) and Democrats (blue), Germany's conservative Christian Democrats (CDU) and Christian Union (CSU) predominantly associate with blue, while red rep-resents the more liberal Social Democrats (SPD) and Left (*Die Linke*). Visually merging conservative and liberal ideals, *quing* becomes anchored in the notion of political compromise. And in hip-hop culture, in which blue and red have signified gang allegiances (the Bloods and the Crips), it becomes even clearer how Sookee's use of purple is designed to mitigate conflict and perceived dif-ference. The fusion of traditional right/left affiliations suggests third-way poli-tics based on mutual inclusivity. In this manner, Sookee's blending of colors very much coincides with Tope Omoniyi's retheorization of code switching, one that moves away from traditional understandings of language-based code mixing to include the recombination of colors and symbols (Omoniyi 2005).

Yet given that purple has long stood for the color of royalty, privilege, power, and prestige both in and outside Europe, aristocratic undertones are also at play in *quing's* color-coded visualization. The title of Sookee's 2014 album *Lila Samt (Purple Velvet)* affirms this reading, while suggesting the beatification and elevation of queer/trans symbols, aims, and concerns through *quing's* royal fe/male synthesis. Sookee's deliberate use of purple in this way lends a revolutionary dimension to her project, especially when read alongside recent European dem-ocratic movements such as Czechoslovakia's 1989 Velvet Revolution, Georgia's 2003 Rose Revolution, or Ukraine's 2003–4 Orange Revolution. Moreover, the decision to use purple and black on the highly stylized artwork of her 2011 album *Bitches Butches Dykes & Divas* illustrates Sookee's aesthetic choice to anchor her project in a much deeper global anarcha-feminist perspective, thus reflecting trans/feminist thought and thinking. Exemplifying a kind of "trans*imagining," the aforementioned aesthetic choices work to merge gender, sexual, political, and social dichotomies to enable thinking beyond normativizing binary paradigms.[5]

The opening verse of the 2011 track "Purpleize Hip Hop" (Sookee 2011a) frankly states Sookee's desire to open up new spaces in queer/transphobic soci-eties: "Nicht irgendwo irgendwann, sondern hier jetzt / Lila Basis, rosa Winkel, Regenbogen, queer rap" (Not somewhere sometime, rather here and now / Purple

Figure 1, above.
Sookee, *quing* of Berlin,
visually coded in purple and black,
the colors of anarcha-feminism.
Photos courtesy of www.sookee.de

Figure 2, right.
Covert art for *Bitches Butches Dykes
& Divas* (2011)

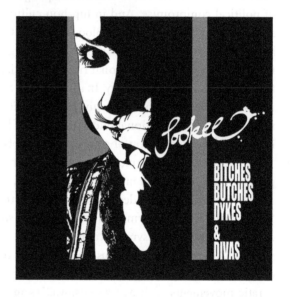

foundational, pink triangle, rainbow, queer rap; Sookee 2011b). The song's repetitive hook ("How can one purpleize hip hop? / We don't imitate—we intimidate") invites listeners to imagine such possibilities and boldly move without hesitation. By substituting the indefinite third-person singular (*one*) with nominative personal pronouns (*I*, *you*, *he*, *she*, *we*), Sookee frequently riffs on the hook in live performances to make the call for involvement more personal, intimate, and immediate (Sookee 2014e).[6]

Perhaps more importantly, the first two lines of the second verse address critics who assert that the active promotion of gender/sexual diversity and equality axiomatically leads to an aggressive hatred of cisgendered heterosexuals: "Man munkelt ich sei Hetenfeindlich—so ein scheiß! / Ich bin cool mit jeder

Hete, die Pro Homo teilt" (Some say I'm just hatin' on heteros—what bull! / I'm cool with them if they share Pro Homo; Sookee 2011b).[7] By suggesting that cisgendered heterosexuals commit to achieving equality for those in the LGBTQ movement, Sookee disarms her critics and expands the scope of her activist call. Her rhymes proselytize, engendering allies. One wonders the effect lyrics such as these have on listeners who do not see themselves as directly benefiting from the advancement of the LGBTQ cause.

Trans∗imagining: Celebrating Trans/feminisms and Community Building

On the 2014 track "Frauen mit Sternchen" ("Women with Asterisks"; Sookee 2014a), Sookee celebrates all manifestations of womanhood and femininity by expanding and extending them in trans∗ directions. The song firmly establishes at the outset an unshakeable allegiance to feminist principles: "Ich fänds unanständig keine feminist zu sein" (Sookee 2014b). This literally translates into "I'd find it rude not to be a feminist"; however, Sookee uses the somewhat more informal translation "I can't imagine not being a feminist." Signaling at once her desire to enfold every conceivable type of femininity within the feminist movement, Sookee raps "Ich shließ mich nicht ein ich shließ euch mit ein,"[8] a loaded, ambiguously worded line that can be read simultaneously as "I don't hem myself in / I don't shut myself out / I don't enclose myself" (Ich shließ mich nicht ein) and "I don't count you out / I include you / I enwomb you" (Ich shließ euch mit ein). Taken in sum, the line poetically affirms a welcoming inclusive attitude. Sookee then proceeds to cite a dazzling array of feminist figurations, including "ladies divas dykes," "Tribaden ultras amazonen" (scissorers ultras amazons), "bitches inter weiber [hags] homos," "macherinnen babes pans" (doers/makers babes pansexuals), as well as essential feminist thinkers, including philosopher Olympe de Gouges, musician Clara Schumann, critical theorist Simone de Beauvoir, and the revolutionary Rosa Luxemburg. Sookee concludes the opening verse with "Alle anders alle gleich / Alle sternchen mitgemeint" (Everyone else everyone equal / All the asterisks all people). As the song shifts into an extended instrumental, the allegiance to strong female figures resonates in an edited sample of Sarah Jones's spoken word piece "Your Revolution" (Jones 2009), thereby reaffirming Sookee's commitment to revolutionary feminism via her connection to the spoken-word performance tradition.

Yet Sookee's activities are not solely confined to writing, performing, and the recording of audiovisual material. Acting as tutor, mentor, and educator, the artist frequently leads creative writing workshops—urging, for example, young men to write original rhymes based on their own experiences in an effort to avoid the pitfalls of imitating, and thus reproducing, the cissexual assumptions, exaggerations, and homophobic impulses so common in mainstream German rap.[9] In addition, panel discussions are frequently held before concerts. For example, on the 2014 Purple Velvet Tour in Bielefeld, Germany, Sookee, Shirlette Ammons (United States), and Lex Lafoy and DJ Doowap (South Africa) discussed their individual ambitions, collaborative aims, and the creative challenges and opportunities they face as women in a highly masculine-dominated field. Taking questions in two languages from the audience, the ensuing discussion encouraged dialogue and the sharing of knowledge across three continents. Events such as these allow fans to interact with artists, which in turn fosters a sense of community that stands in stark contrast to conventional musician-fan relationships, especially if we understand the idolization of popular music stars as constituting yet another reductive binary sociocultural relationship. Where artists and labels work to destabilize and break down such artificial socialcultural constructions, one might call this the *trans*imagining* of cultural spaces, particularly when such interactions occur at a bilingual international hip-hop event.

These and similar efforts lend themselves to the growth of communities rooted in the celebration of trans/feminism, sexual and gender diversity, inclusivity, and participatory democratic practices. A stenciling workshop held on June 7, 2014, at AJZ Bielefeld (a youth center in Bielefeld, Germany) for young people who identify as lesbian, trans*, and/or intersex sought to create a space in which

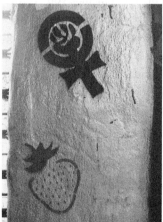

Figure 3, left.   Tour poster and stencil art outside AJZ Bielefeld, June 2014. Courtesy of Terence Kumpf

Figure 4, above.   Tour poster and stencil art outside AJZ Bielefeld, June 2014. Courtesy of Terence Kumpf

participants could develop, hone, and share their artistic skills in a safe and supportive environment. This dedication to spreading knowledge through teaching, mentorship, discussion, and the nurturing of artistic practice exemplifies hip-hop's long-standing commitment to the creation and sharing of (new) knowledge, a philosophy Sookee herself echoes in the song "Links Außen" ("Extreme Left"; Sookee 2014c). The bilingual line "Each one teach one highfly tiefgang / Alle sind anders wir feiern vielfalt" (Each one teach one fly high be deep / Everyone's something else celebrate diversity; Sookee 2014d) doubles down on Sookee's advocacy for queer/trans acceptance and, most importantly, for people to embrace, celebrate, and promote tolerance. These activities, taken together, constitute a range of cultural practices that illustrate this artist's transformative potential as a feminist hip-hop activist and advocate for queer/trans issues.

Conclusions

Germany's mainstream commercial hip-hop scene is rife with heteronormative exaggerations of gender and sexuality. Sookee's queer-feminist activist cultural work confronts sexist assumptions in Germany's hip-hop scene while building and promoting queer/trans spaces for people who do not identify with, or flatly reject, stultifying gender binaries and/or traditional sex roles. As a transformative figure, Sookee more than answers the call by Joan Morgan, Gwendolyn Pough, and Shani Jamila for hip-hop feminists to produce material with "radical and liberating potential" (Peoples 2008). As an artist-activist, Sookee explicitly advocates for building bridges and communities so that people working in and outside academic institutions can connect, interact, and work together.[10] Where she collaborates with international artists and reaches out to fans in nonhierarchical ways, Sookee's intersectional work ethic fosters trans*/feminist community activists who insist upon queer/trans equality. By working within hip-hop, by now a transnational cultural paradigm, Sookee's sociopolitical, sexual, and linguistic trans/feminist project signals an emerging trans*sectional cultural practice—the application of feminist intersectional thinking and action within the transnational and transcultural space of bilingual hip-hop.[11] I have taken to calling the figurations and advocacy in Sookee's work *trans*imagining*, but the postulations this artist puts forth hardly represent any kind of final word. Much of Sookee's material invites people to follow her lead and get actively involved. This trans/feminist political hip-hop cultural project continues.

Terence Kumpf is a PhD candidate at the Ruhr Center of American Studies at TU Dortmund University in Dortmund, Germany. His doctoral dissertation deals with bi- and multilingual hip-hop in Germany and the United States from a transnational/transcultural perspective.

Notes

1.   The lead to a July 2015 story on the absence of women in Germany hip-hop asks, "Is German hip-hop macho music? There's certainly no shortage of sexism or homophobia. This makes it tough for women to enter the scene. Time to change" (Ist deutscher HipHop Macho-Musik? Zumindest mangelt es nicht an Sexismus oder Homophobie. Das macht es Frauen nicht gerade einfach in die Szene rein zu kommen. Zeit etwas zu ändern; Elmenthaler 2015). Unless otherwise indicated, all German translations to English are my own.

2.   While researching and writing this article, the somewhat has-been rapper known as Bass Sultan Henzgt (BSH) had just released an album with cover art showing a close-up of two men about to kiss. BSH's Twitter feed and the comments section of an article at *Rap.de* blew up with all sorts of generalized homophobic aspersions. See Marquart 2015.

3.   "Because parliamentary or labor union politics remain the focus, there are relatively few opportunities for [young] people to organize themselves politically if they are not in the youth organization of some [political] party. If this understanding were to open up somewhat, then the impression of political apathy among young people would cease to exist. In this sense *quing* reflects an opportunity to politicize oneself." (Damit wird nur parlamentarische Parteipolitik oder Gewerkschaftsarbeit gedacht, aber darüber hinaus gibt es relativ wenige Gelegenheiten für Menschen, sich als politisch zu fassen, wenn sie nicht in der Jugendorganisation einer Partei sind. Ich glaube, wenn sich da das Verständnis ein bisschen öffnen würde, dann gäbe es auch nicht diesen Eindruck von Politikverdrossenheit bei jungen Menschen. *Quing* ist auch die Gelegenheit, sich zu politisieren; quoted in Adler and Meyer 2011).

4.   "Purple is the optical equivalent of quing. That means it is initially a mixture of masculine connoted blue and feminine connoted red, such that the mix ratio of feminine and masculine is altered by every nuanced shading of lilac, violet, purple, and magenta." (Diese Farbe ist die optische Entsprechung zu Quing. Das heißt, sie ist zunächst eine Mischung aus dem männlich konnotierten Blau und einem weiblich konnotierten Rot, wobei die genauen Mischungsverhältnisse mit jeder Nuance von Lila, Violett, Purpur, und Magenta verändert werden; Sookee 2007: 39).

5.   Since Sookee herself uses asterisks to promote gender and sexual openness, I follow her lead in my development of the term *trans*imagining*.

6.   During a conversation with Shirlette Ammons, Sookee explains her reasoning for modifying the song in live performances. See Sookee and Ammons 2013.

7.   In this line, Sookee self-reflexively references her track "Pro Homo," also from *Bitches Butches Dykes & Divas*. The video for the song is widely available online.

8.   The misspelling of *schließen* as "shließen" here is deliberate. Sookee sometimes leaves out the *c* in German words that have an sch prefix or suffix, that is, "shreiben" for *schreiben* (to write) or "Shwester" for *Schwester* (sister).

9.   "I arrive in the morning at a school on a workshop day and the teacher immediately says, 'Here, this is Kevin. He's our rapper.' Now Kevin is under a lot of pressure because he knows he is bad at math—he has to shine. So he takes a seat and quickly writes down a ton of words. Then I realize: this line is from Massiv [a hardcore rapper from Berlin], this one is from Haftbefehl [a hardcore rapper from Frankfurt], and the next line is from Farid Bang [a battle rapper from Düsseldorf]. Kevin's entire text is a mosaic of lines by famous rappers, but he doesn't get the chance to develop himself. . . . I tell him: Now try to write your own lyrics, without biting. The theme I give him: Me." (Ich komme an

einem Workshop-Tag morgens in die Schule, und sofort erzählt mir der Lehrer: Hier, das ist der Kevin, das ist unser Rapper. Der hat dann gleich Druck, weil er weiß, ich bin schlecht in Mathe, jetzt muss ich glänzen. Also setzt der sich hin und schreibt ganz schnell viel Text runter. Ich seh dann: Die Zeile ist von Massiv, die ist von Haftbefehl, die nächste von Farid Bang. Die bauen sich Mosaike aus Texten von bekannten Rappern zusammen, bekommen aber gar nicht den Raum, sich selbst zu entfalten. . . . Ich sage ihm: So, jetzt versuch mal einen Text zu schreiben, in dem du nicht zitierst. Das einzige Thema, das ich vorgebe, ist: Ich; quoted in Gross and Winkler 2013: 36).

10.   "To me it's important to build bridges, it's important to share, it's important to relate and be connected, but it doesn't help if just me and my ten friends know because beyond that nothing will come of it." (Ich finde es wichtig, Brücken zu bauen, ich finde es wichtig, zu teilen, ich finde es wichtig, anschlussfähig zu sein, es hilft nichts, wenn ich es weiß und meine zehn Freundinnen und darüber hinaus passiert halt nichts; quoted in Adler and Meyer 2011).

11.   I borrow the term *trans*sectional* from Dan Goodley, who uses the word to theorize how intersectionality can assist people with disabilities to insist upon their place in societies prejudiced in favor of ableism. Goodley himself echoes Robert Kulpa. For my puposes, I use the term to describe how intersectional, political artwork devised within transnational and transcultural spaces achieves an aesthetic built upon multiple notions of trans. See Goodley 2012.

References

Adler, Sharon, and Britta Meyer. 2011. "Interview mit Sookee" ("Interview with Sookee"). *AVIVA-Berlin: Online Magazin für Frauen* (*AVIVA-Berlin: Online Magazine for Women*), December 31. www.aviva-berlin.de/aviva/content_Interviews.php?id =12103.

Aydemir, Fatma. 2015. "Ich kriege das allein hin, Alter" ("I Got It Myself, Dude"). *Die Tageszeitung* (TAZ.AM Wochenende), January 3–4 (weekend edition).

Elmenthaler, Sophie. 2015. "Du willst rappen!?" ("You Wanna Rap!?"). *DRadio Wissen*, July 20. dradiowissen.de/beitrag/hiphop-berlin-label-springstoff-workshop-rapperinnen.

Goodley, Dan. 2012. "Dis/entangling Critical Disability Studies." *Disability and Society* 28, no. 5: 631–44. doi:10.1080/09687599.2012.717884.

Gross, Thomas, and Thomas Winkler. 2013. "Hau rein, denn die Welt kaputt ist." *Die Zeit*, July 25.

Jones, Sarah. 2009. "Your Revolution." *Russell Simmons Presents: Def Poetry*. Season 1, episode 3. DVD. New York: HBO Studios.

Marquart, Oliver. 2015. "Bass Sultan Hengzt löst Schwulenfeindlichen Shitstorm aus" ("Bass Sultan Hengzt Unleashes Antigay Shitstorm"). *Rap.de*, February 23. rap.de/news/54283 -bass-sultan-hengzt-loest-schwulenfeindlichen-shitstorm-aus/.

Omoniyi, Tope. 2005. "Toward a Re-theorization of Code Switching." *TESOL Quarterly* 39, no. 4: 729–34.

Peoples, Whitney A. 2008. "'Under Construction': Identifying Foundations of Hip-Hop Feminism and Exploring Bridges between Black Second-Wave and Hip-Hop Feminisms." In "Representin' Women, Hip-Hop, and Popular Music," special issue, *Meridians* 8, no. 1: 19–52.

Sookee [Nora Hantzsch]. 2007. "Sookee ist Quing" ("Sookee Is Quing"). In *Female HipHop: Realness, Roots, und Rap Models*, edited by Anjela Schischmanjan and Michaela Wünsch, 33–40. Mainz, Germany: Ventil.

———. 2010a. "Quing." *Quing.* Springstoff CD-SOQU-0026, compact disc.

———. 2010b. "Quing." Song lyrics. Transcribed by Esqua_lation. Genius Media Group. genius
.com/Sookee-quing-lyrics (accessed February 27, 2015).

———. 2011a. "Purpleize Hip Hop." *Bitches Butches Dykes and Divas.* Springstoff CD-SOBB-0032,
compact disc.

———. 2011b. "Purpleize Hip Hop." Song lyrics. Transcribed by Gripweed. Genius Media Group.
www.genius.com/Sookee-purpelize-hip-hop-lyrics/ (accessed February 28, 2015).

———. 2014a. "Frauen mit Sternchen" ("Women with Asterisks"). *Lila Samt.* Springstoff CD-
SOLS-0046, compact disc.

———. 2014b. "Frauen mit Sternchen" ("Women with Asterisks"). Song lyrics. Transcribed by
Ileana Exaras. Genius Media Group. www.genius.com/Sookee-frauen-mit-sternchen
-lyrics (accessed March 1, 2015).

———. 2014c. "Links Außen (Featuring Mal Élevé and Ben Dana)." *Lila Samt.* Springstoff CD-
SOLS-0046, compact disc.

———. 2014d. "Links Außen (Featuring Mal Elévé and Ben Dana)." Song lyrics. Transcribed by
Ileana Exaras. Genius Media Group. www.genius.com/Sookee-links-auen-lyrics (accessed March 1, 2015).

———. 2014e. "Sookee: Purpleize Hip Hop—Purple Velvet Tour." May 24. YouTube video, 5:41.
Posted by Springstoff, June 6, 2014. youtube.com/watch?v=CfLzr-qV8Pg.

Sookee, and Shirlette Ammons. 2013. "Sookee and Shirlette Ammons: Pretty Precious Cargo
Tour—Fall 2013." YouTube video, 16:32. Posted by Springstoff, May 10, 2014. youtube
.com/watch?v =6WVVJItktxA.

Stehle, Maria. 2012a. "Gender, Performance, and the Politics of Space: Germany and the Veil in
Popular Culture." *Comparative Studies of South Asia, Africa, and the Middle East* 32, no. 1:
89–101.

———. 2012b. *Ghetto Voices in Contemporary Germany: Textscapes, Filmscapes, Soundscapes.*
Rochester, NY: Camden House.

Stüttgen, Tim. 2007. "Homo(phob) HipHop: Zur Homophobie im HipHop und den Beats und
Rhymes queerer Frauen" ("Homo[phobe] HipHip: Homophobia in HipHop and the
Beats and Rhymes of Queer Women"). In *Female HipHop: Realness, Roots, und Rap
Models*, edited by Anjela Schischmanjan and Michaela Wünsch, 134–43. Mainz, Germany:
Ventil.

Reading Trans Biology
as a Feminist Sociologist

RIKI LANE

Abstract Feminist analysis has often rejected ideas that biology influences gender development as inherently reactionary. However, some trans people have found personal and political utility in making the argument that they were "born this way." This essay argues for an understanding of nature and culture that aims to supersede a division of bodies as authentic and real versus constructed and mutable—reappraising scientific understandings of sex and gender can overcome this false dichotomy. Recent biological and neurological research has shifted from linear determinism toward ideas of nonlinearity, contingency, self-organization, and open-endedness. Feminist and trans studies engagement with such research offers ways around theoretical impasses and can assist struggles for social and political change.
Keywords biological diversity, gender identity, feminism, transgender, social change

F eminist analysis generally situates biological explanations of gender as legitimating women's exclusion from public life and as justifying male dominance. Instead, the focus is on gender as a sociocultural product. Rejecting biological determinism has sometimes led to any mention of the biological body being seen as essentialist and has led many feminist researchers to ignore the details of biology, abandoning the field to biological science (Birke 2000: 29–34). This suspicion of arguments that women's brains are fundamentally different from men's is historically well grounded. However, it causes trouble for many feminists when considering some trans people's arguments that their brain is differently sexed from their body.[1] A recent example was Elinor Burkett's op-ed piece in the *New York Times* (2015), and the subsequent mini-controversy over feminist biologist Anne Fausto-Sterling's supportive tweet.

The sex/gender distinction enthusiastically taken up in the 1970s has often led feminist and other sociological researchers to view "gender as social product" as "our" field. I argue that while social constructionist analysis is important to debates about the relative weight of biological and social factors in the causation

TSQ: Transgender Studies Quarterly ★ Volume 3, Numbers 1–2 ★ May 2016
DOI 10.1215/23289252-3334367 © 2016 Duke University Press

of gender development, it cannot be equated with a socialization theory about gender development. This is a mistake commonly made by positivist scientists (McKenna and Kessler 2000: 69) but also in feminist analysis, if it automatically rejects any biological role in gender development.

Within the social sciences, a social constructionist analysis emphasizes how humans' interpretations of their physical and cultural environments are basic to social action. All human knowledge reflects its social context, and interpretations have "real" effects, including on shaping the material realities of sex/gender. Social constructionism can illuminate the gendered assumptions built into all research, and the problems with single-factor and multifactorial approaches to gender development. However, there is no necessary connection between a social constructionist methodological approach and an ontological belief in the superiority of socialization theories of gender development. Both biological determinist and socialization theories of gender have been mobilized for regressive and progressive political and social purposes. For example, biological theories were used to justify Nazi attempts to exterminate homosexual and trans people, while socialization theories have been used to justify attempts to "normalize" homosexual and trans people through reparative therapy. "Born this way" arguments are often used in current struggles for social recognition and legal rights for trans and LGB people; while socialization theories have been mobilized in breaking down gendered occupational restrictions on women and to legitimate nonbinary gender positions.

Rather than an a priori rejection of biological research as reactionary, I pose a more difficult task—to analyze both developmental theories in a way that maintains credibility with biological and socialization researchers. As does Kessler (2007), I argue that central to an effective social constructionist analysis is critiquing *both* socialization and biological research that start by assuming that female and male are the only available categories. Developing an approach that integrates research across disciplines and methodologies into a biopsychosocial model of gender development is therefore essential. As I have argued elsewhere, engaging with biological explanation and incorporating it into a broader social framework can make an important contribution to feminist and trans activism and theory (Lane 2009).

I argue that an appropriate framework for analyzing research into what causes people to be trans is a feminist sociology of science about trans. First, scientific evidence is strongly deployed in social and political struggles around trans; struggles over the credibility of knowledge about etiology are integral to struggles over power between and within disciplines, professions, and activism. Secondly, this evidence is mobilized in a particular way, which has both similarities and differences with struggles around sex and gender more generally, sexual orientation, and health issues concerning HIV-AIDS. Thirdly, the relation between sex and gender is posed in a very particular way for trans people. We need a detailed sociological analysis of the processes of scientific knowledge production, which is informed by a critique of gendered power relations.

In doctoral research (Lane 2011), I sought frameworks that have been productively applied in similar fields. Studies on the sociology of trans by researchers such as Richard Ekins and Dave King (1999), Suzanne Kessler and Wendy McKenna (2000), Myra Hird (2002), and Surya Monro (2007) engage with a range of trans people's experiences. However, their discussion about etiology is usually quite limited, with its focus on how trans people use biological explanation in their personal interactions. A body of research using a framework of feminist sociology of science about sex and gender (or feminist science studies) by researchers such as Donna Haraway (1991: 186–87), Steven Epstein (1996: 3), and Anne Fausto-Sterling (2000) cover similar bodies of research but treat trans experience as illustrative material for broader questions about sex and gender. These fields are closely connected with two others—general sociology of science and feminist theorization of embodiment and the sex/gender relation. In extending analysis beyond the production of knowledge into its contestation and mobilization, I wove together theoretical frameworks from sociology of psychiatry, health, and social movements into a feminist sociology of science about trans.

This framework can combine a close analysis of the empirical data in the relevant scientific disciplines with a sociological critique of the power relations that shape the institutional structures, theoretical paradigms, and technical practices of science (Spanier 2001: 262–63; Fujimura 2006). This is complemented by a sociological understanding of how knowledge is developed within and contested between disciplines. Social relations of power shape and are shaped by struggles to challenge and defend the historically established dominance of medicine and psychiatry over trans health care against their professional rivals and their clients. These struggles over power and knowledge do not stay neatly within the boundaries of academic and scientific literature—trans people, their allies, and enemies mobilize scientific knowledge for social and political ends. Attending to the politics of knowledge making requires a focus on examining the processes by which scientific knowledge is produced around trans. My approach is to "study up" (Harding 2004: 30) the people researching trans, rather than to "study down" the marginalized group of trans people.

The field of trans etiology is plagued by dichotomous thought, beginning with assumptions about the female/male distinction in sex-difference research and extending into other forms of knowledge and activism. All human knowledge—biological and social—is socially produced and culturally accepted as valid within an intricate web of government, corporate, academic, and disciplinary institutions. I argue that the historical development of knowledge about trans has produced multiple, nested dichotomies that hinder research and interdisciplinary communication—female/male, pathological/normal, trans/cisgender, transgender/transsexual, and subverting/maintaining gender conformity. Knowledge constructed along such lines often leads to blind alleys. In research, unwarranted and incommensurable assumptions are built into research frameworks. In activism, political unity is fractured.

In a broad social context, female versus male is often posed as a fundamental dichotomy. For conservative religious or biological determinist approaches, all exceptions are monstrous errors that go against God's law or nature's design. Much sexual-difference feminism strongly polices the boundaries of the category "woman" (Raymond 1979; Gatens [1983] 1991), while in many gender-based feminist, queer, and trans studies approaches, subverting the female/male dichotomy is the central project. Fausto-Sterling (2000) sought to undermine dualist divisions in knowledge construction around sex, gender, and sexuality through mobilizing neural connectionism and development systems theory. Beginning with the fundamental assumption in most biological research of a female/male division, she examined how gender/sex, constructed/real, and nurture/nature are dichotomized (1–29). By viewing the female/male dichotomy as other than a given biological and/or social reality, the question resolves to how knowledge is constructed around this division. This varies across disciplines, with social scientists typically searching for social explanation from a starting assumption of female/male similarity. They seek to explain how the mutable, socially constructed sex and gender categories have been historically invented. By contrast, physical science and biomedical researchers into sex, gender, and trans typically search for biological causation from a starting assumption of the existence of female/male dimorphism. They seek to discover fixed, essential, ahistorical characteristics that underlie human behavior. These contrasting assumptions and goals shape what data are seen as important and what are discarded as irrelevant or anomalous, restricting in advance the range of what can be discerned and the possibilities for interdisciplinary communication and collaboration.

Divisions around the basis for rights claims similarly restrict trans activism when a dichotomy is made between transsexual and transgender. Such arguments embed differing approaches to female/male distinctions. Some "transsexual separatist" (Davidson 2007: 63) activism maintains a female/male dichotomy, but this dichotomy is located in brain sex rather than bodily sex—privileging transsexualism as an immutable neurological intersex condition versus transgender as social gender play. Some radical transgender activism seeks to dispense with the dichotomous female/male distinction altogether—privileging transgender as subversive gender transgression versus transsexuality as essentialist gender conformity (Rubin 1998; Namaste 2000; Prosser 1998). I argue for an understanding of the nature/culture relation that aims to shift debate concerning bodies as authentic and real versus constructed and mutable, as such debate establishes a false dichotomy that may be overcome by reappraising scientific understandings of sex/gender.

Little social constructionist and poststructuralist analysis offers any detailed engagement with biological, bodily materialities and thus cannot integrate them into their approach. Much feminist and trans theory that has conflated social constructionist analysis of gender with socialization theory rejects biological arguments around gender development as essentialist and thus as necessarily reactionary. Feminist theorists and biologists such as Haraway (1991), Elizabeth Grosz (2005), Hird (2004), Elizabeth Wilson (2004), Spanier (1995), and Fausto-Sterling (2000) have not always been trans positive: for example, see Grosz (1994: 207). However, they provide conceptual strategies that undermine dualist conceptions of nature/culture and real/constructed. Engaging with new materialist biology, with its emphasis on nonlinearity, contingency, diversity, and open-endedness allows an understanding of gender development as an intertwined biological and social process of transformation. This opens the way to understanding trans differently—seeing *all* gender variance as a healthy part of human variation, not as pathology or disorder. In developing such an understanding, the views of trans biologists Joan Roughgarden (2004) and Julia Serano (2007) and sociologist Aaron Devor (1997) seem broadly compatible with those of trans-friendly sexologist Milton Diamond (2006). These approaches indicate the interaction of the biological and the social in producing gender variance as diversity.

Implementing a feminist sociology framework that draws on science studies necessitates a detailed engagement with the relevant biological literature, contextualized by a critique of the social power and positioning of the researchers, clinicians, and trans people. This framework works at the intersection of the biological and the social, both in disciplinary terms and in theorizing the processes of gender development through a biopsychosocial model.

Such a biopsychosocial approach to general medicine is well developed and is accepted by significant parts of the medical professions. However, the politics of knowledge production and deployment around trans obstructs a similar implementation, despite its conceptual and political merit. I argue for reading biological research on trans as demonstrating a drive to alter the sexed body that has some neurological correlates—which are not dichotomous but diverse. This reading can contribute to developing a trans political movement as an alliance for social and legal recognition for all gender-variant people, and assist struggles to alter clinical practice and achieve legal and social recognition and rights for trans people through repositioning trans as healthy variation rather than pathological disorder.

Riki Lane is a research fellow at Monash University in Melbourne, Australia, researching primary health-care research, and a research/project worker at Monash Health's Gender Dysphoria Clinic. Doctoral and subsequent work has investigated the social and political implications of the "brain-sex" theory of trans, and the shifting paradigms in trans health care.

Note

1.   In this article, I generally use *transgender* for an identity that disrupts male and female categories, *transsexual* for an identity of crossing to the "other" gender position, and *trans* as an umbrella term. These terms are often disputed and used differently.

References

Birke, Lynda I. A. 2000. *Feminism and the Biological Body*. New Brunswick, NJ: Rutgers University Press.

Burkett, Elinor. 2015. "What Makes a Woman?" *New York Times*, June 6.

Davidson, Megan. 2007. "Seeking Refuge under the Umbrella: Inclusion, Exclusion, and Organizing within the Category Transgender." *Sexuality Research and Social Policy* 4, no. 4: 60–80.

Devor, Holly. 1997. *FTM: Female-to-Male Transsexuals in Society*. Bloomington: Indiana University Press.

Diamond, Milton. 2006. "Biased-Interaction Theory of Psychosexual Development: 'How Does One Know If One Is Male or Female?'" *Sex Roles* 55, nos. 9–10: 589–600.

Ekins, Richard, and Dave King. 1999. "Towards a Sociology of Transgendered Bodies." *Sociological Review* 47, no. 3: 580–602.

Epstein, Steven. 1996. *Impure Science: Aids, Activism, and the Politics of Knowledge, Medicine, and Society*. Berkeley: University of California Press.

Fausto-Sterling, Anne. 2000. *Sexing the Body: Gender Politics and the Construction of Sexuality*. New York: Basic Books.

Fujimura, Joan H. 2006. "Sex Genes: A Critical Sociomaterial Approach to the Politics and Molecular Genetics of Sex Determination." *Signs* 32, no. 1: 49–82.

Gatens, Moira. (1983) 1991. "A Critique of the Sex/Gender Distinction." In *A Reader in Feminist Knowledge*, edited by Sneja Gunew, 139–57. London: Routledge. First published in *Beyond Marxism: Interventions after Marx*, edited by Judith Allen and Paul Patton, 143–60. Leichhardt, Australia: Intervention Publication. Citations refer to the Routledge edition.

Grosz, Elizabeth A. 1994. *Volatile Bodies: Toward a Corporeal Feminism*. St. Leonards, Australia: Allen and Unwin.

———. 2005. *Time Travels: Feminism, Nature, Power*. Crows Nest, Australia: Allen and Unwin.

Haraway, Donna Jeanne. 1991. *Simians, Cyborgs, and Women: The Reinvention of Nature*. London: Free Association.

Harding, Sandra. 2004. "A Socially Relevant Philosophy of Science? Resources from Standpoint Theory's Controversiality." *Hypatia* 19, no. 1: 25–47.

Hird, Myra J. 2002. "For a Sociology of Transsexualism." *Sociology* 36, no. 3: 577–95.

———. 2004. *Sex, Gender, and Science*. New York: Palgrave Macmillan.

Kessler, Suzanne J. 2007. Author interview, Purchase, NY, September 10.

Kessler, Suzanne J., and Wendy McKenna. 2000. "Who Put the 'Trans' in Transgender? Gender Theory and Everyday Life." *International Journal of Transgenderism* 4, no. 3: 223–36.

Lane, Riki. 2009. "Trans as Bodily Becoming: Rethinking the Biological as Diversity, Not Dichotomy." *Hypatia* 24, no. 3: 136–57.

———. 2011. *Trans, Science, and Society: The Politics of Knowledge of the Brain Sex Theory of Trans.* PhD diss., La Trobe University, Melbourne.

McKenna, Wendy, and Suzanne J. Kessler. 2000. "Retrospective Response." *Feminism and Psychology* 10, no. 1: 66–72.

Monro, Surya 2007. "Transmuting Gender Binaries: The Theoretical Challenge." *Sociological Research Online* 12, no. 1. www.socresonline.org.uk/12/1/monro/monro.pdf.

Namaste, Viviane K. 2000. *Invisible Lives: The Erasure of Transsexual and Transgendered People.* Chicago: University of Chicago Press.

Prosser, Jay. 1998. *Second Skins: The Body Narratives of Transsexuality, Gender, and Culture.* New York: Columbia University Press.

Raymond, Janice G. 1979. *The Transsexual Empire: The Making of the She-Male.* Boston: Beacon.

Roughgarden, Joan. 2004. *Evolution's Rainbow: Diversity, Gender, and Sexuality in Nature and People.* Berkeley: University of California Press.

Rubin, Henry S. 1998. "Phenomenology as Method in Trans Studies." *GLQ* 4, no. 2: 263–81.

Serano, Julia. 2007. *Whipping Girl: A Transsexual Woman on Sexism and the Scapegoating of Femininity.* Emeryville, CA: Seal.

Spanier, Bonnie. 1995. *Im/Partial Science: Gender Ideology in Molecular Biology, Race, Gender, and Science.* Bloomington: Indiana University Press.

———. 2001. "'Your Silence Will Not Protect You': Feminist Science Studies, Breast Cancer, and Activism." In *Feminist Science Studies: A New Generation,* edited by Maralee Mayberry, Banu Subramaniam, and Lisa H. Weasel, 258–74. New York: Routledge.

Wilson, Elizabeth A. 2004. *Psychosomatic: Feminism and the Neurological Body.* Durham, NC: Duke University Press.

Conditions of Critique
Responding to Indigenous Resurgence within Gender Studies

SCOTT L. MORGENSEN

Abstract Indigenous critics are interrogating the violences of modernity as conditions for under-standing or debating gender, alongside critical works in trans studies and in queer-of-color, queer diaspora, and women-of-color feminist theories. This essay asks how two-spirit, queer indigenous, and indigenous feminist critiques call scholars in gender studies to ensure that discussions of gender respond to indigenous decolonization and its relationships with antiracist and anticolonial projects. In particular, two-spirit, queer indigenous, and indigenous feminist theories present resurgence as a means to challenge and transform colonial authority. The centering of indigenous epistemologies within resurgence work questions who defines language or the knowable within colonial situations. This essay asks how responding to indigenous resurgence can help to challenge and transform the racial and colonial violences that condition conversations about gender, including those addressing trans and feminist relationships.

Keywords indigenous, resurgence, epistemology, gender, whiteness

The categorical distinctions and joinings invoked by *trans/feminism* lead me to ask how racial and colonial power condition this term and the discussions that it invites. Scholars in critical trans studies and at its intersections with queer studies demonstrate that gender is constituted by such interlocking structures as necropower (Snorton and Haritaworn 2013), antiblackness (Bassichis and Spade 2014), empire (Shakhsari 2014), the prison-industrial complex (Stanley and Smith 2015), and these and other formations within law (Spade 2011). They reject the invocation of racialized bodies to diversify white gendered knowledge, and they expose the violence of multicultural inclusion from the disruptive stakes of trans people of color. Alongside critical works in trans studies and in queer-of-color, queer diaspora, and women-of-color feminist theories, indigenous critics are interrogating the violences of modernity as conditions for understanding or debating gender. In answer to these and related works, I ask how conversations

TSQ: Transgender Studies Quarterly * Volume 3, Numbers 1–2 * May 2016
DOI 10.1215/23289252-3334379   © 2016 Duke University Press

about trans and feminism articulate epistemologies of whiteness amidst ongoing racial and colonial power. Specifically, I address in this essay how two-spirit, queer indigenous, and indigenous feminist critiques press me—a white settler practicing gender studies in a colonial academy—to ensure that my discussions of gender respond to indigenous decolonization and its relationships with antiracist and anticolonial projects. I take especial interest here in the ways that the centering of indigenous epistemologies in two-spirit, queer indigenous, and indigenous feminist critiques places in question who defines language and the knowable within colonial situations.

When I consider the distinctions and links named by *trans/feminism*, I recall how late twentieth-century academic and activist feminisms in the United States first taught me to question how race and nation structure feminist debates on transgender. Writing about that time, Emi Koyama argued that in a white supremacist society like the United States, white women's desires for the unmarked sameness of whiteness directly inform antitrans sentiment in Western feminism (Koyama 2006). Following her insights, scholars and activists could ask if trans responses to antitrans feminism ever left its racial form intact, or even repeated it if trans or allied people responded by arguing for trans inclusion in whiteness or empire, as Salvador Vidal-Ortiz recently illuminated. (Vidal-Ortiz 2014). I recall being asked during the 1990s, alongside other white cis queer feminists, to align with white trans feminists in challenging antitrans politics within feminism. Showing up for this request was promoted as a way to position us as supporters of trans belonging in feminist and queer academic and activist spaces. But while such responses could appear to have strengthened alliances, in fact they placed one alignment of white people in contest with another over the boundaries of feminism, a project known to be structured by normative whiteness. Feminists of color and indigenous feminists already interrogated white feminism while grounded in feminist anticolonialisms and antiracisms that they sustained elsewhere on distinct terms. Koyama argued that even when discussions of trans and feminism did not center the work of feminists of color, challenging whiteness is precisely what feminism *and* transfeminism do when they work in the legacies of women-of-color feminism or other gendered interrogations of race, colonization, and empire, as in leading work in trans studies today. From these histories, I learned to notice whenever discussions of trans and race, or of race and trans/feminist relationships, remain in the background or are absent and to be responsive to trans interventions that foreground antiracist and anticolonial work. The need for such interventions remains fresh, as I experienced recently while redesigning an introductory gender studies course. While many recent sources center two-spirit and trans/queer-of-color critiques, a plethora of published and online commentary on trans and feminism still makes no mention of race or nation as conditions of their debates. As scholars of trans, race, and nation already show, delinking trans/queer-of-color and two-spirit critiques from gender politics normalizes white trans and feminist subjects and blocks interrogating the racial and colonial violences that condition feminist and trans categories, trans relationships to feminism, and gender itself.

In answer to the decolonial work of two-spirit and queer/trans-of-color activists and scholars, my scholarship aimed to explain how colonial desires for indigeneity helped to establish the white settler as the normative subject of liberation in US and Canadian LGBT politics. I learned that in the twentieth century, when two-spirit critics challenged settler whiteness, they specifically interrupted colonial systems of categorization. Indigenous people challenged violence by discarding colonial discourses and then deploying a counterpoint term—*two-spirit*—that resists translation into Western sexuality or gender categories. I also learned that when activists chose to identify as feminist, lesbian, gay, bisexual, or trans on indigenous terms, they refused to singularly belong to those sexuality and gender categories and thus interrupted colonial epistemic authority. Evan Towle and Lynn Morgan noted these anticolonial qualities in their critique of appropriations of indigenous knowledge by Western scholars and activists who advocate a global trans politics (Towle and Morgan 2002). Extending from Towle and Morgan's intervention, I note that the terms *two-spirit, queer indigenous,* and *indigenous feminist* also resist appropriation when they refuse to be disentangled from indigenous assertions of relationality and inhabitance. Indigenist categories like these expose the geopolitics of colonial knowledge—possibly including feminist, queer, or trans knowledge—because they reassert indigenous epistemologies within work for decolonization: a practice that indigenous theorists have theorized as resurgence (Alfred and Corntassel 2005; L. Simpson 2011). Scholars of two-spirit communities in indigenous studies also examine how indigenous people confront the limits of the term *two-spirit,* if it appears to reference pan-tribal before national ties, or urban more than rural or reserve experiences, among other qualities (Gilley 2006; D. Wesley 2015). Yet even as indigenous people discuss these matters, two-spirit and other indigenist categories still interrupt colonial translation, just as they make their interlocutors politically responsive to indigenous epistemologies and to their governmental assertions of relational inhabitance.

I learned how two-spirit resurgence informs trans studies through the signal contribution of Saylesh Wesley (Stó:lō) to the first volume of *TSQ* (S. Wesley 2014). The story Wesley tells in her essay portrays and enacts the decolonization of Stó:lō gendered knowledge and peoplehood. Wesley's story is framed around her decision to ask her grandmother to help name her place as a trans woman within Stó:lō language and social life. She makes this request based on her responsibilities within matrilineal Stó:lō society to her grandmother, who is a renowned traditional weaver and basket maker. Her request also reflects her efforts to deepen their familial relationship, after many years of having sought to help her grandmother unlearn transphobic and homophobic beliefs that she traces to her grandmother's colonial education in residential schools. After receiving the request, Wesley's grandmother gifts to her the Stó:lō term *sts'iyóye smestíyexw slhá:li*. Translated into English as "twin-spirited woman," this term reflects the meaning of the category "two-spirit" that Wesley previously shared with her grandmother; yet it announces a gendered status that is Stó:lō specific. During her weaving apprenticeship under her grandmother, Wesley accepted an invitation from a Tsleil-Waututh (Burrard First Nation) family to "'open the floor' for the memorial gathering of their late two-spirited son" (S. Wesley 2014: 348). She wove a cedar bark cape under her grandmother's mentorship to wear during her ceremonial dance. She makes the self-observation that she "needed to dance for more than just this memorial—for five hundred-plus years of two-spirited ancestors and their deleted identities" (348).

Through her stories, Wesley illuminates the many ways that the name *sts'iyóye smestíyexw slhá:li* does much more than translate *two-spirit* into Stó:lō language. As a term of identity within Stó:lō relationships, *sts'iyóye smestíyexw slhá:li* reimagines traditional knowledge and roles, transmits them through the instruction of elders, manifests them within transnational relationships among indigenous peoples, and links gendered familial ties to resurgence and decolonization. In Wesley's exchange with her grandmother—offering indigenous knowledge in the form of the term *two-spirit*, then receiving *sts'iyóye smestíyexw slhá:li*—kinship and relationality set the context for resurgence among Stó:lō and other indigenous peoples. In these ways, *sts'iyóye smestíyexw slhá:li* disturbs Western desires to reduce its meaning to the English or Latin term *trans*. This follows not only from the term being named in Stó:lō language. The resistance of *sts'iyóye smestíyexw slhá:li* to Western translations displays Stó:lō relationality and resurgence pushing back against colonial knowledges that would reduce or constrain what indigenous knowledges might mean. *Sts'iyóye smestíyexw slhá:li* communicates landed and collective resurgence when spoken by Stó:lō or other indigenous people: resonances that cannot be ignored once nonindigenous people interact with the term and its epistemic and political implications.

I offer this reading of Saylesh Wesley's essay to highlight how, in its contribution to trans studies, the essay resonates with two-spirit, queer indigenous, and indigenous feminist theories that center resurgence as a means to challenge and transform colonial authority. For instance, indigenous feminist scholars broadly argue that colonial gender violence rests at the heart of the European colonization of indigenous peoples, and notably in the gendered and racial reordering of indigenous societies by colonial systems of categorization (Anderson

2000; Denetdale 2009; Kauanui 2008; Miranda 2010; A. Simpson 2014). In Canada, scholars examine how the 1876 Indian Act interrupted indigenous governance by imposing patrilineal membership and patriarchal authority within law, which exiled out-married indigenous women and their descendants and disturbed women's authority over land and treaty making (Lawrence 2004; McAdam 2014). Deborah Miranda (Costanoan Esselen) argues that colonial gender violence and conformity to colonial rule accrete around a practice of gendercide, in which Europeans sought to eliminate all variance from heteropatriarchal gender systems. Miranda explains that during the Spanish colonization of California, gendercide targeted not only those subjects who today might be thought of as two-spirit but also the relationships linking them with all members of society and, more deeply, the epistemologies of relationality and shared governance that supported relationship. For Miranda (2010: 253), the "extermination of the *joyas*" models a key method in the European subordination of indigenous peoples as a racialized caste under colonial rule. Building from theories of colonial gender violence, indigenous feminist and two-spirit activists today argue for rejecting heteropatriarchy and for honoring indigenous women and two-spirit people within resurgence work. In the words of Sarah Hunt (Kwagiulth), "as we reinstate the roles of women and two-spirit people in systems of Indigenous governance and law, ending gendered violence can be understood as integral to self-determination" (Hunt 2014b: 193).

Challenges to colonial gender violence and to its embedding in indigenous self-rule mobilize many contemporary indigenous movements. In Canada, movements addressing missing and murdered indigenous women or #MMIW pursue a number of interrelated goals. They educate about the colonial transformation of gender in indigenous nations, uphold indigenous women's leadership, seek responses to sexual assault that "do not involve state police and the state legal system," in the words of Leanne Simpson (Michi Saagig Nishnaabe), and (as Hunt argues) seek to implement indigenous laws that oppose violently heteropatriarchal rule (L. Simpson 2014b; Hunt 2014a; see also Deer 2009; Nason 2014). Such themes inform the Idle No More movement, in which women have acted as leaders in defending traditional indigenous territories and governance. From the explicitly grassroots organizing invited by the four women cofounders, to the ceremonial fast of Attawapiskat Chief Theresa Spence (Ogichidaakwe Spence, for Leanne Simpson), the actions gathered around Idle No More announced forms of indigenous peoplehood and governance that exceed the state-sanctioned order bequeathed by what Glen Coulthard (Yellowknives Dene) calls the "colonial politics of recognition" (Coulthard 2014; Kino-nda-niimi Collective 2014; L. Simpson 2014a). Indigenous activists and scholars argue that two-spirit organizing resonates with such movements when it seeks to transform heteropatriarchy as part of indigenous resurgence. Dana Wesley (Cree) argues that participating in resurgence is a deep desire among urban two-spirit youth in Toronto: notably, in their wish to connect with kin and elders who can teach nation-specific two-spirit roles or responsibilities (D. Wesley 2015). Wesley also calls on indigenous movements like Idle No More to ask whether their acknowledgments of two-spirit people among those whom they represent generate two-spirit leadership, stating, "There have to be serious efforts made to foster relationships between Two-Spirit people and wider Indigenous communities. . . . Creating real connections with Two-Spirit people means asking them what matters to them in relation to nation building" (D. Wesley 2015: 101). Wesley discusses the explicit commitments to decolonization within the projects of the Toronto-based Native Youth Sexual Health Network, which include efforts to forge ties between two-spirit youth and indigenous communities that can support resurgence. In modes of activism such as these, indigenous people critically address gender in collective life, landed inhabitance, and governance, and all as part of decolonizing indigenous peoplehood and the colonial legal, economic, political, and cultural systems that still surround them.

When I consider how discussions of trans/feminist relationships might articulate indigenous feminist and two-spirit scholarship or activism, I do so as a white person who is attempting to respond to the leadership of indigenous and racialized people in work to decolonize knowledge and society. I am not a participant in indigenous discussions about trans and feminist relationships, and my essay does not portray them. Rather, by citing indigenous writers who address gender in relation to resurgence and decolonization, I indicate my responsibility to their work when I address gender within gender studies. Among the questions their work leads me to ask are these: What might indigenous resurgence request of discussions in the United States or Canada about trans and feminist relationships (past or present; actual or potential)? How might what gets said about trans or feminism shift once it addresses some of the contexts of indigenous resurgence, such as colonization, geopolitics, white supremacy, racialization, antiracism, anticolonialism, or indigenous epistemologies, peoplehood, governance, or decolonization? Are these questions intensified if trans and feminist relationships get discussed in spaces that are materially colonial toward indigenous peoples: that is, in spaces that are shaped by forms of white-supremacist occupation or by the universalization and naturalization of Western knowledge and law? And given that indigenous resurgence challenges the coloniality of white supremacy, in what ways does it or might it articulate efforts by black people or other racialized peoples to challenge antiblackness, empire, global capitalism, and all forms of colonization; and how might gender inform such work? (Byrd 2011; King 2013; Walia 2012). As noted, such questions about the conditions of trans and feminist critiques already arise in long-standing forms of antiracist and anticolonial trans, queer, and two-spirit activism, and in critical works in trans and queer studies that emerge from or address such work.

Responding to these projects, then, I approach trans/feminist discussions within gender studies by attending to how they are conditioned by racial and colonial violence, and how they potentially or directly address these violences. Doing so responsibly orients such discussions toward antiracism and anticolonialism; but my review of writing on indigenous resurgence also meant to invoke another implication. Indigenous resurgence epistemologically undercuts the imperial power of universal gender discourses, which become geopolitically settler-colonial when they naturalize Western thought on indigenous lands as evidence of their own universality. Thus, as a political and epistemic act, resurgence exposes and undercuts gendered claims that would avoid examining their relationship to colonization or decolonization. Crucially, indigenous resurgence is not a minoritizing politics: it challenges the colonial force that consigns indigeneity to a "minority" status within settler states and that establishes Western knowledge as a universal frame for producing modern subjects. In kind, questioning the epistemic grounds of modern subjectivity also informs queer-of-color and queer diaspora critiques, which disrupt colonial/imperial whiteness and its efforts to particularize, manage, or evict queered diasporic and racialized peoples and politics (Eng 2011; Manalansan 2003; Reddy 2011; Rodriguez 2003). Chela Sandoval, Roderick Ferguson, and Grace Hong also explain how women-of-color feminist theories and movements disrupt epistemologies and methodologies of globalization and modernity and inspire racialized and diasporic queer critiques (Ferguson 2004; Hong 2006; Sandoval 2000). Such ties animate trans studies and its engagements with queer studies, as when Jin Haritaworn, Adi Kuntsman, and Silvia Posocco investigate queer as a necropolitical status, or when Marcia Ochoa interprets how Venezuelan *transformistas* survive racial and colonial violence through critical negotiations of national and transnational power (Haritaworn, Kuntsman, and Posocco 2014; Ochoa 2014). I read these intellectual genealogies as being resonant with two-spirit and indigenous feminist thought when resurgence names the political conditions of colonial and racial power that structure categorization. The power exerted by gender categories may not be resolved in those categories' own terms if they derive from a political field defined by racial and colonial violence. Changing terms may be an appropriate tactic; or, as Dipesh Chakrabarty indicates, geopolitically provincializing terms may destabilize their erstwhile universal reach (Chakrabarty 2000). Indigenous resurgence pursues such questions by taking them up in relation to the politics of indigenous decolonization, which participates in disrupting the conditions and shifting the grounds on which we might define or discuss gender.

Scott L. Morgensen is associate professor in the Department of Gender Studies at Queen's University. He is the author of *Spaces between Us: Queer Settler Colonialism and Indigenous Decolonization* (2011). With Leela Viswanathan he is coeditor of the *Journal of Critical Race Inquiry*.

Acknowledgments

For reading and responding to portions of earlier drafts I thank Saylesh Wesley and J. Kehaulani Kauanui, as well as the anonymous reviewers for *TSQ: Transgender Studies Quarterly*. I am solely responsible for all content. I thank the *TSQ* editors for their invitation to contribute to this special issue.

References

Alfred, Taiaiake, and Jeff Corntassel. 2005. "Being Indigenous: Resurgences against Contemporary Colonialism." *Government and Opposition* 40, no. 4: 597–614.

Anderson, Kim. 2000. *A Recognition of Being: Reconstructing Native Womanhood*. Toronto: Sumach.

Bassichis, Morgan, and Dean Spade. 2014. "Queer Politics and Anti-Blackness." In *Queer Necropolitics*, edited by Jinthana Haritaworn, Adi Kuntsman, and Silvia Posocco, 191–210. New York: Routledge.

Byrd, Jodi. 2011. *The Transit of Empire: Indigenous Critiques of Colonialism*. Minneapolis: University of Minnesota Press.

Chakrabarty, Dipesh. 2000. *Provincializing Europe: Postcolonial Thought and Historical Difference*. Princeton, NJ: Princeton University Press.

Coulthard, Glen. 2014. *Red Skin, White Masks: Challenging the Colonial Politics of Recognition*. Minneapolis: University of Minnesota Press.

Deer, Sarah. 2009. "Decolonizing Rape Law: A Native Feminist Synthesis of Safety and Sovereignty." *Wicazo-Sa Review* 24, no. 2: 149–67.

Denetdale, Jennifer. 2009. "Securing Navajo National Boundaries: War, Patriotism, Tradition, and the Diné Marriage Act of 2005." *Wicazo-Sa Review* 24, no. 2: 131–48.

Eng, David. 2011. *The Feeling of Kinship: Queer Liberalism and the Racialization of Intimacy*. Durham, NC: Duke University Press.

Ferguson, Roderick. 2004. *Aberrations in Black: Towards a Queer of Color Critique*. Minneapolis: University of Minnesota Press.

Gilley, Brian Joseph. 2006. *Becoming Two-Spirit: Gay Identity and Social Acceptance in Indian Country*. Lincoln: University of Nebraska Press.

Haritaworn, Jin, Adi Kuntsman, and Silvia Posocco. 2014. Introduction to *Queer Necropolitics*, edited by Jinthana Haritaworn, Adi Kuntsman, and Silvia Posocco, 1–27. New York: Routledge.

Hong, Grace. 2006. *The Ruptures of American Capital: Women of Color Feminism and the Culture of Immigrant Labor*. Minneapolis: University of Minnesota Press.

Hunt, Sarah. 2014a. "I Am Accountable to Loretta Saunders." Indigenous Nationhood Movement. Nations Rising, March 3. www.nationsrising.org/i-am-accountable-to-loretta-saunders/.

———. 2014b. "More than a Poster Campaign: Redefining Colonial Violence." In *The Winter We Danced: Voices from the Past, the Future, and the Idle No More Movement*, edited by the Kino-nda-niimi Collective, 190–93. Winnipeg: ARP Books.

Kauanui, J. Kēhaulani. 2008. *Hawaiian Blood: Colonialism and the Politics of Sovereignty and Indigeneity*. Durham, NC: Duke University Press.

King, Tiffany Lethabo. 2013. *In the Clearing: Black Female Bodies, Space, and Settler-Colonial Landscapes*. PhD diss., University of Maryland, College Park.

Kino-nda-niimi Collective. 2014. "Idle No More: The Winter We Danced." In *The Winter We Danced: Voices from the Past, the Future, and the Idle No More Movement*, edited by the Kino-nda-niimi Collective, 21–26. Winnipeg: ARP Books.

Koyama, Emi. 2006. "Whose Feminism Is It Anyway? The Unspoken Racism of the Trans Inclusion Debate." In *The Transgender Studies Reader*, edited by Susan Stryker and Stephen Whittle, 698–705. New York: Routledge.

Lawrence, Bonita. 2004. *"Real" Indians and Others: Mixed-Blood Urban Native Peoples and Indigenous Nationhood*. Lincoln: University of Nebraska Press.

Manalansan, Martin. 2003. *Global Divas: Filipino Gay Men in the Diaspora*. Durham, NC: Duke University Press.

McAdam, Sylvia. 2014. *Nationhood Interrupted: Revitalizing* Nêhiyaw *Legal Systems*. Saskatoon, SK: Purich.

Miranda, Deborah. 2010. "Extermination of the *Joyas*: Gendercide in Spanish California." *GLQ* 16, nos. 1–2: 253–84.

Nason, Dory. 2014. "We Hold Our Hands Up: Indigenous Women's Love and Resistance." In *The Winter We Danced: Voices from the Past, the Future, and the Idle No More Movement*, edited by the Kino-nda-niimi Collective, 186–90. Winnipeg: ARP Books.

Ochoa, Marcia. 2014. *Queen for a Day: Transformistas, Beauty Queens, and the Performance of Femininity in Venezuela*. Durham, NC: Duke University Press.

Reddy, Chandan. 2011. *Freedom with Violence: Race, Sexuality, and the U.S. State*. Durham, NC: Duke University Press.

Rodriguez, Juana Maria. 2003. *Queer Latinidad: Identity Practices, Discursive Spaces*. New York: New York University Press.

Sandoval, Chela. 2000. *Methodology of the Oppressed*. Minneapolis: University of Minnesota Press.

Shakhsari, Sima. 2014. "Killing Me Softly with Your Rights: Queer Death and the Politics of Rightful Killing." In *Queer Necropolitics*, edited by Jinthana Haritaworn, Adi Kuntsman, and Silvia Posocco, 93–110. New York: Routledge.

Simpson, Audra. 2014. *Mohawk Interruptus: Political Life across the Borders of Settler States*. Durham, NC: Duke University Press.

Simpson, Leanne. 2011. *Dancing on Our Turtle's Back: Stories of Nishnaabeg Re-creation, Resurgence, and a New Emergence*. Winnipeg, MB: Arbeiter Ring.

———. 2014a. "Fish Broth and Fasting." In *The Winter We Danced: Voices from the Past, the Future, and the Idle No More Movement*. edited by the Kino-nda-niimi Collective, 154–57. Winnipeg, MB: ARP Books.

———. 2014b. "Not Murdered and Not Missing: Rebelling against Colonial Gender Violence." Indigenous Nationhood Movement. Nations Rising, March 5. www.nationsrising.org /not-murdered-and-not-missing/.

Snorton, C. Riley, and Jin Haritaworn. 2013. "Trans Necropolitics: A Transnational Reflection on Violence, Death, and the Trans of Color Afterlife." In *The Transgender Studies Reader 2*, edited by Susan Stryker and Aren Z. Aizura, 66–76. New York: Routledge.

Spade, Dean. 2011. *Normal Life: Administrative Violence, Critical Trans Politics, and the Limits of Law*. Boston: South End.

Stanley, Eric A., and Nat Smith. 2015. *Captive Genders: Trans Embodiment and the Prison Industrial Complex.* 2nd ed. Oakland, CA: AK.

Towle, Evan, and Lynn Morgan. 2002. "Romancing the Transgender Native: Rethinking the Use of the 'Third Gender' Concept." *GLQ* 8, no. 4: 469–97.

Vidal-Ortiz, Salvador. 2014. "Whiteness." *TSQ* 1, nos. 1–2: 264–66.

Walia, Harsha. 2012. "Decolonizing Together: Moving beyond a Politics of Solidarity toward a Practice of Decolonization." *Briarpatch Magazine*, January 1. www.briarpatchmagazine .com/articles/view/decolonizing-together.

Wesley, Dana. 2015. "Reimagining Two-Spirit Community: Centering Narratives by Urban Two-Spirit Youth." MA diss., Queen's University.

Wesley, Saylesh. 2014. "Twin-Spirited Woman: Sts'iyóye smestíyexw slhá:li." *TSQ* 1, no. 3: 338–51.

Discussing Transnormativities through Transfeminism

Fifth Note

RUIN

Abstract This essay explores four aspects of transnormativities through transfeminism. In South Korea, transnormativity is a key issue in transgenderism. However, it has been seriously marginalized in discussions about transgender. Furthermore, mass media, nontrans people, and nontrans social systems, transgender communities, and nontransfeminist scholars re/produce and re/enforce transnormativity by citing hegemonic gender norms. In the same way, they re/enforce and re/produce the hegemonic gender norms by citing transnormativity. In this essay, the author argues that transnormativities include the elimination of temporality, excluding the ways that may threaten the norms, naturalizing the myth that there is natural gender without any instability, and translation without thinking the hierarchy of language.

Keywords transnormativity, transfeminism, translation, hegemonic gender norms

The March 2001 public broadcast debut of Harisu, a transgender singer, brought about an epistemic shift in South Korea (henceforth, Korea). Treating this as the first time that a transgender person had ever appeared in Korea, the mass media sensationalized Harisu as "more beautiful than a woman," and, fifteen years later, news about her life still appears in the popular media. Of course, news about sex change and cross-dressing has consistently appeared in Korean mass media since the 1920s. After 1945, following three years of de facto US rule and a pervasive US political and cultural influence that continues to this day, Korean media ran the story of Christine Jorgensen as well as other sex-change news from overseas. In the 1980s, some books published interviews with MTFs/transwomen in Korea. In 1992, MTFs/transwomen were featured on the front cover of a major magazine (*Sisa Journal* 1992) and were discussed in public broadcasts. Even though trans people were constantly appearing in the Korean media under a variety of categories and labels, often garnering considerable attention, all such instances

TSQ: Transgender Studies Quarterly ★ Volume 3, Numbers 1–2 ★ May 2016 **202**
DOI 10.1215/23289252-3334391 © 2016 Duke University Press

were treated as isolated and novel events, as if each represented the first time trans issues had ever been publicly discussed. In this respect, Harisu is quite special. She did not appear and then disappear as an isolated case; rather, she has been offered as a kind of continual shock, remaining highly visible and oft discussed.

In Korea, the idea of a binary, essentialist gender system is hegemonic. Harisu's debut publicly displayed the fact that sex and gender can indeed change, and because of this, many nontrans people began to acknowledge the mutability of sex and gender. But the expression "more beautiful than a woman" deployed by the media generated all sorts of trouble. Harisu and other MTFs/transwomen were represented as epitomizing dominant female gender norms and ideals, and transgender people in general were represented as diligently enacting hegemonic gender norms. The more the expression "more beautiful than a woman" was absorbed into the culture, the more trans people's lives were regulated and defined according to those norms. This is why debates on transnormativity have become so important in Korea today.

In this essay, I theorize four features of transnormativities through a transfeminist investigation: (1) the erasure of lived temporalities, (2) the exclusion of threats to the normative order, (3) the presumption of a stable gender binary, and (4) the invisibility of cultural and linguistic hegemonies in matters of translation and theory production. In doing so, I discuss the impact of Harisu's debut on mainstream "knowledge" about trans people, on dominant norms and narrative within trans communities, and on nontrans-feminist attitudes about trans people. I conclude by exploring the ways in which cultural and language power differentials can marginalize non-US/European theorizing by representing it as a mere "field report" from an exotic location.

The Erasure of Lived Temporalities
Following Harisu's debut, transgender has been explored in many documentaries and other programs. Most of these works frame transgender people within a normalizing narrative. Consider, for example, the easily imagined story of an MTF/transwoman who grew up thinking she was a woman even as a little child, who hated her own penis, who had conflicts with her own body, who went through difficult times, who wishes to live as a normal woman, and so therefore now seeks the required medical treatment. This is the typical narrative about transgender that is continually perpetuated by the media. This transnormative narrative is designed for consumption by nontrans people in order to facilitate their understanding of trans people, to set their expectations of them, and to structure interactions with them. Thus, even before actually meeting a trans person, nontrans people already "know" all about trans people. Despite the fact that when somebody says, "I am a transgender person," one still knows next to nothing about the person, nontrans

people are already confident that they know everything about that person. This "exhaustive knowledge" (that is, in fact, vacuous) yields the first feature of transnormativity in Korea—namely, the erasure of the lived temporality of particular trans lives.

The confidence that one already knows everything about transgender people forecloses any efforts to find out more, or to actually get to know a trans person. Most academic articles on transgender in Korea merely reaffirm the transnormative narrative, hence contributing to the reproduction of the norms. Such representations trap transgender people in a static image, erasing the details of complex lives that change over time. Without the concreteness of the actual person, trans people become beings without a social context, trapped within the gender role set by society. Such transnormative narratives come to effectively constitute the nature of transgender.

The "radical naturalization of Time (i.e., its radical dehistorization)" works to re/produce others within the (neo-)colonial order (Fabian [1983] 2002: 16–17); thus, the elimination of the actual lived temporality of transgender people within such an order becomes a normativizing practice that transforms beings not constrained by gender binary categories into beings understood through a normative and othering ordering. In routinely depicting trans people before Harisu as novel and unfamiliar in each and every instance, in describing them as being essentially foreign to the normative order of society, the media were each and every time erasing their lived temporalities while depicting them according to the hegemonic gender norms, thereby producing transnormativity as a result. A crucial task for transfeminism, as it thinks through the problems of transnormativity, is to explore the local temporalities of lived transgender lives, and to trouble and disrupt normativizing and hegemonic temporalities.

The Exclusion of Threats to the Normative Order

Sadly, and unsurprisingly, transnormative narratives also circulate within and help to structure transgender communities themselves. Most transgender communities in Korea formed around online homepages since the 1990s. Most of the information provided by these sites (e.g., Network for TransSexual, www.net4ts .com) concerns medical treatment. Almost all the comments in the forums are premised upon life histories derived from the transnormative narrative, thus positioning medical treatment as an essential step for life to move forward. Trans persons who do not desire medical treatment frequently have their very identities as trans called into question. While the view does exist that medical treatment is not definitive of trans experiences, it is hardly common. Consequently, those who do not fit into these communities, those who feel they cannot honestly or comfortably share their actual life stories often leave, sometimes joining genderqueer communities that critique the more transnormative transgender communities. This exclusion of threats to the normative order, even within trans communities themselves, constitutes the second feature of transnormativity.

Some caution is required in raising concerns about those trans people who eagerly embody hegemonic gender norms, given that conformity to norms arises from striving to survive in a trans-negative society; to simplistically criticize trans people as conformist is to ignore the hostile social context in which trans people live (Bettcher 2006). Moreover, transgender people enacting hegemonic gender norms can also sometimes challenge the gender binary system: if a MTF/trans-woman can pass for a nontrans woman, how can a nontrans woman be confirmed as a nontrans woman? The very ability to successfully cite the norm from a position of difference undermines the basis of naturalized privilege that nontrans people exercise over trans people. Yet, because the attempt to enact hegemonic gender norms in striving to survive is itself the enactment of the dominant norm within the community, critique is nonetheless necessary—and it does in fact currently take place both within and among the various trans and genderqueer communities.

Transnormativity is, to build upon Susan Stryker's (re)formulation of homonormativity, more than policing the gender practices of individual trans persons and re/producing a fittingly heteronormative lifestyle in the neoliberal era; it is more than the mere disqualification of any act on the part of a trans person that threatens the normative order (2008: 155). Transnormativity both naturalizes discordant lives within hegemonic gender norms and at the same time excludes lifestyles, gender practices, and voices of any trans person who does not adhere to the norms, thereby containing or eliminating ways of being and living that threaten the norms. Insofar as the reproduction of the hegemonic gender norms concerns trans and nontrans people alike, transnormativity should be viewed as an important issue for all feminists, whether or not they are trans.

The Presumption of a Stable Gender Binary

What is the relationship between transgender and nontrans feminism in Korea? Harisu's successful debut created a rather complex situation. In the first several years following Harisu's debut, a few nontrans feminists publicly attacked trans people in some publications, accusing them of reinforcing sexist norms of femininity, and thereby helping to perpetuate the gender discrimination that nontrans women experience (J. N. Kim 2001; Lee 2001). They represented MTFs/transwomen as the materialization of a (heterosexual) male sexual fantasy, concluding that while they may be called "women," they are, in fact, nothing more than artificial constructs (Lee 2001: 103–7). Numerous nontrans feminists, however, chose to stay silent regarding this issue, rather than publicly speaking up, while nevertheless privately criticizing transgender people for reinforcing gender stereotypes. In the first few years after Harisu's mass-media debut, trans people were almost universally viewed by nontrans feminists as helping to foster female oppression, rather than challenging the distinction between sex and gender.

This strong initial nontrans-feminist opposition to trans people eventually began to wane. When, in 2006, the Supreme Court decided to allow legal gender changes for the first time in Korea, and a transgender rights organization was established, many nontrans-feminist organizations expressed their support. By this time, many nontrans feminists had begun to construe MTFs/transwomen as a social and sexual minority who had to be supported in keeping with a comprehensive human rights perspective, even if they still seemed difficult to relate to. There was no notable event or single turning point between 2001 and 2006 that precipitated this change in attitude; rather, as a discourse of universal human rights increasingly came to frame the conversation, many commentators became concerned about appearing to be "politically incorrect" and thus became more reluctant to denounce "minorities." Nontrans feminists still understood gender and gender oppression from their own experience, and they considered the critique of gender to properly be their purview and theirs alone, while relegating transgender experiences and ways of life to being "particular sexual practices" such as cross-dressing or fantasies of changing sex (Stryker 2008: 148).

In the aftermath of Harisu's celebrity, even as feminists began cautiously to embrace trans issues in the name of human rights, the binary concept of gender endorsed by nontrans feminists remained unchallenged. One might even say that the opportunity to place blame on transgender people for reinforcing gender stereotypes allowed nontrans feminists to remain ignorant of their own stubborn reluctance to recognize the oppressive nature of the gender binary system itself, as well as of their own reliance upon it. This presumption of a stable gender binary is the third feature of transnormativity, and it provides a way to understand the noninclusion of transgender and queer theories in feminist studies.

In the introduction to *Transfeminist Perspectives in and beyond Transgender and Gender Studies*, Anne Enke notes that transgender studies still occurs at the margins of women's and gender studies in the United States (2012: 2). As a trans studies scholar in Korea, I agree with Enke's statement, yet I am also troubled by it because, rather than being marginal within women's and gender studies, in Korea, transgender research—or even queer research—is virtually nonexistent. For there to be such research in women's studies, one must first justify how it relates to feminism. One Korean feminist scholar even stated, in an interview with Judith Butler, that queer is an inappropriate topic within Korean gender studies (H. S. Kim 2008). While not opposing them outright, most nontrans/nonqueer Korean feminists treat queer and transgender topics as being merely private and trivial personal interests, rather than being significant to the very formulation of gender. One would be lucky to find even a single course on queer theory offered in any Korean graduate program. And while MA theses on queer issues do stream out from women's studies programs, this is not because women's studies is actively receptive to queer research. On the contrary, it is simply the only discipline that can even begin to accommodate such work. In such an academic climate, then, it is easy to understand why transgender is scarcely even recognized by nontrans-feminist academics.

That transgender is not considered important by nontrans feminists shows the extent to which they understand transgender through a transnormative narrative. The common view that trans people are "born that way" and are therefore biologically different from nontrans people only reinforces the gender binary. This is, again, the third feature of transnormativity. It involves defining gender in terms of a binary system and categorizing those who do not fall within the hegemonic gender categories and norms as marginal to it, thereby deeming them ineligible for serious consideration in the disciplines of women's or gender studies. Several problems thus ensue.

First, the gender normativity of trans people becomes self-defeating—the very norms that such trans people strive to enact are precisely those norms that disqualify them as normative subjects. Consequently, our self-understanding as trans people is not derived from our own interpretation of our own existence; it depends, rather, on the interpretations of others. Our very existence thereby becomes a contradiction. We see this contradiction acted out within nontrans feminisms: drawing as they do upon transnormative discourses, transgender people are simultaneously defined as both enacting and reinforcing norms while at the same time being placed outside the norms. Such approaches reproduce the normativizing myth that there is an inborn and natural gender, a gender without any trouble in it, and that nontrans people embody this gender with no instability. While it is impossible for norms to be perfectly enacted by anyone, by differentiating nontransgender and transgender people on the basis of transnormativity, nontrans feminism makes nontrans women out to be wholly normative and nontransgressive.

The Invisibility of Cultural and Linguistic Hegemonies

Now, to be sure, it is not as if currently there are no works in Korea that seek to restructure the concept of gender within feminism or to study transfeminism. In my own previous works, I have argued that assigning an individual at birth to a binary gender through cultural practices and then nonconsensually forcing gender roles upon that individual is a form of gender violence (Ruin 2008, 2014). In doing so, I sought to find ways to connect transgender and nontrans feminism, thereby promoting the possibility of transfeminism. Ji Hye Kim, the most accomplished queer scholar in Korea, rewrote the history of queer in Korea, pointing out that gender practices in Korea are by no means based on a gender binary (2010). By discussing the tensions and overlaps of nontrans feminism, lesbian/queer theory, and transgenderism, J. H. Kim aims to expand Korean nontrans feminism in queer and trans directions (2011, 2012). Finally, disability researchers, queer researchers, and trans-genderqueer researchers have been working together for many years to generate trans-disability-queer theory in a feminist context.

These transfeminist discussions, however, are still so nascent that they do not even begin to approach the status of "marginality" that Enke laments in the US academy. I felt quite conflicted when I read such statements. On the one hand, because Korea has been heavily influenced by the United States since the 1940s, as a scholar in Korea I benefit a great deal from the ongoing discussions of transgender and transfeminist studies in the United States. And I see how transgender studies can still be considered marginal to gender studies there. On the other hand, the scope and meaning of *marginal* can be defined differently, in different contexts. Even in writing this, I became unsettled and felt distressed because I found myself highlighting more of the negative aspect of trans-feminist studies in Korea, in contrast to it being better elsewhere.

Given the global hierarchy between the United States/Europe and the rest of the world, many postcolonial scholars have raised the legitimate concern that research on the global South and East merely provides data, while the United States and Europe provide the theory for understanding and interpreting what that data means. And even as such asymmetrical power relations remain in place, they now also involve theory from non-US/European nations being treated as mere data or being relegated to the status of the exotic or the marked. While internal critique within places such as Korea may aim to articulate positive possibilities, the negative conditions being critiqued can make a stronger impression in the United States and Europe than the theoretical and political articulation of emergent positive possibilities, thus transforming internal critique into a "pitiful situation" that legitimizes the critical intervention of an external perspective. Through the naturalizing operation of hegemonic temporalities, and the erasure of local cultural temporalities, theorizing from non-US/European places far too easily can be understood as only a "report from the field," as the presentation of data. In this essay, I am aiming to *theorize* transnormativities, and to do so I draw on transgender phenomena within Korea. But because of the "othered" nature of the phenomenon upon which I draw, as well as the geopolitical and cultural location from which I theorize, my theorizing itself risks being represented as a mere field report on the pitiful situation of trans people, and of trans theorizing, in Korea.

My goal here is not to criticize Enke's use of the term *marginal*. Indeed, I learned much from Enke's book and feel a bit apologetic about referring to Enke so many times regarding this one particular point. My goal, rather, is to speak about the language of US English, the hegemonic global power of the United States, and the politics of translation. I wrote this in Korean, and then with the help of others, translated it into US English, after which it received a further layer of editing and translation from the editors of *TSQ: Transgender Studies Quarterly*. So, even as I was writing this, I constantly worried about how this discussion from Korea would be understood, and how this would be translated into US English. As one who has become un/familiar with globally hegemonic US English, it is quite difficult for me to speculate about how this short article will be translated and understood.

It is a principle of good writing that in order for the reader to participate in the author's discussion, the writer must do the important work of explaining the context of the argument. Given the necessity of using language to express our thoughts, and given as well the power hierarchies that shape the international politics of knowledge production, the experience of "explaining context" takes on quite a different dimension for those who are marginalized within the global dominance of US English and a US/European perspective. A person born in the United States, especially a white person using English as their own mother tongue, does not necessarily feel the need to explain their own cultural context or to recount the history of the United States. They can lay out their discussion without feeling the need to explain the circumstances that make their discussion salient. Despite this, such writing circulates globally, and non-Americans must use additional labor to "understand" that writing. But to write in US English about debates within a Korean context, to readers who know nothing of Korean history, language, and culture, is an entirely different task. I must continually explain the Korean cultural context, as if writing a field report. Sadly, even in the act of writing this, I feel myself becoming marginal within my own writing.

In this essay, I have explored the features of transnormativities in Korea and discussed the impact of Harisu on Korean society. When I first mentioned Harisu, I was very tempted to compare her with Christine Jorgensen. To US readers who don't know of Korean contexts, Jorgensen could be a good example for understanding the effects caused by Harisu. In the academic world, it is very common to use cases of the United States as examples to explain cases of other countries. For example, many non-US academics and activists cite the Stonewall riots to describe their own LGBT/queer movements (e.g., Espino 2015; Leilei 2015). Many of them describe the Stonewall riots as a touchstone of their movement, as if Stonewall were the mythical origin of all LGBT/queer movements around the world. The hegemonic global power of the United States and US English makes US history and cases the normative standard for explaining something that occurred in quite different social, cultural, and linguistic contexts. So, I didn't compare Harisu to Jorgensen. The two appeared in very different social and historical situations; moreover, I do not want to make US history the standard. Should the United States be a norm in transfeminist studies? I'd rather write a simple field report than write an academic article that cites the United States as the universal criteria.

I wish, therefore, to theorize yet another feature of transnormativity. Transnormativity can also be found in works that describe transgender as an umbrella category capable of encompassing all forms of gender variance or as a universal experience observable in all cultures, without thinking at the same time about the hierarchies of language or knowledge that exist between nations, and about the problems caused by these power differentials when trying to translate from one cultural context to another. In light of this, transfeminism must also critically investigate the power differentials inherent in the use of different languages, it must be attentive to the politics of translation, and it must always question and challenge the operations of transnormativity in those processes. This is what is now happening in Korea and, delightfully, seems to be where *TSQ* is headed as well.

Ruin is the director of the Institute for Trans/Gender/Queer and main archivist of the Korea Queer Archive. Zher current research is concerned with the tension and overlap between violation, offenders with disability, and transgender offenders. Also, zher dissertation project focuses on the transgendering of modern Korean history.

Acknowledgments

I would like to express my sincere appreciation to Susan Stryker, who recommended me to write this; Stryker and Talia Mae Bettcher, who proofread this article with devoted care; and Eunhae Cho, who helped me through numerous debates.

References

Bettcher, Talia Mae. 2006. "Appearance, Reality, and Gender Deception: Reflections on Transphobic Violence and the Politics of Pretence." In *Violence, Victims, and Justifications: Philosophical Approaches*, edited by Felix Ó. Murchadha, 175–200. Bern, Switzerland: Peter Lang AG.

Enke, Anne. 2012. "Introduction: Transfeminist Perspectives." In *Transfeminist Perspectives in and beyond Transgender and Gender Studies*, edited by Anne Enke, 1–15. Philadelphia: Temple University Press.

Espino, Patrick. 2015. "History, Struggle, and Visibility of LGBT Movement in the Philippines." Paper presented at the 2015 Asia Conference on LGBT of the Sixteenth Korea Queer Festival Organizing Committee, Seoul, May 9.

Fabian, Johannes. (1983) 2002. *Time and the Other: How Anthropology Makes Its Object.* New York: Columbia University Press.

Kim, Hye Sook. 2008. "Judith Butler: Interview with Seven World-Famous Philosophers." *Joong-Ang ilbo (Joong Ang Daily)*, January 31. article.joins.com/news/article/article.asp?total_id =3028512.

Kim, Jeong Nan. 2001. "Harisu, Artificial Woman." In *The Return of the Languages*, edited by Jeong Nan Kim, 120–23. Seoul: Kaema.

Kim, Ji Hye. 2010. "A Study on Intimacy between Women in 1950's Female Gukgeuk Community." *Journal of Korean Women's Studies* 26, no. 1: 97–126.

———. 2011. "The Tension and Overlap between Feminism, Lesbian/Queer Theory, and Transgenderism." *Feminist Studies in English Literature* 19, no. 2: 53–77.

———. 2012. "A Reconsideration of Feminist Gender Theory and Politics, Focusing on the Controversies Surrounding Female/Trans Masculinities." *Feminist Studies in English Literature* 20, no. 2: 63–92.

Lee, Kyung. 2001. "Reading the Code of International Dateline: Take Care of Harisu." *Theoria: A Journal of Feminist Theories and Practices*, no. 5: 101–13.

Leilei, Li. 2015. "Past, Present, and Prospects of China's LGBT Project." Paper presented at the 2015 Asia Conference on LGBT of 16th Korea Queer Festival Organizing Committee, Seoul, May 9.

Ruin. 2008. "Studies on Multi-complexities of Gender Categories." MA diss., Sogang University.

———. 2014. "Gender, Recognition, and Gendering the Body/Gendering Violence: Fourth Notes for Trans(Gender) Feminism." *Women's Studies Review* 30, no. 1: 199–233.

Sisa Journal: Weekly Magazine. 1992. "Gay in Korea: Women Who Were Born as Men." Special issue, July 30.

Stryker, Susan. 2008. "Transgender History, Homonormativity, and Disciplinary." *Radical History Review*, no. 100: 145–57.

Looking Back on
"Queering the Center"

NAOMI SCHEMAN

Abstract The essay is a retrospective reflection on "Queering the Center by Centering the Queer: Reflections on Transsexuals and Secular Jews," which critically explored the structures of normative intelligibility through a comparison of experiences of unintelligibility. Twenty years later, extraordinary progress has been made in rendering transsexual lives intelligible, in part by replacing invisibly professionally managed transformations with openly lived journeys. But core conceptual dichotomies that problematically set the terms of intelligibility remain entrenched—in particular, between determined facticity and ungrounded freedom—leading to some trans women's arguing that there is some core meaning of *woman* that as a matter of fact includes them, and others' defiantly claiming the right to self-identify as women freed from any shared social understanding of what that means. The essay suggests that there is more political hope in arguing against currently normative understandings of gender while struggling to find plural, often contentious, but interrelated, coalitional understandings that do justice to the wide range of gender's discontents.
Keywords transsexual, secular Judaism, queering the center

About ten years ago, I was asked to meet with a Queering Theory class taught by a PhD student in the University of Minnesota's Department of Gender, Women, and Sexuality Studies to discuss my essay "Queering the Center by Centering the Queer: Reflections on Transsexuals and Secular Jews" (Scheman 1997; hereafter, "Q the C"). In "Q the C" I discuss the role others play in making an individual's life intelligible, both in moment-by-moment acknowledgment and in the sharing of memories and the shaping of a narrative. The normative unintelligibility of a transsexual life story was, I argued, not remedied by the tightly controlled procedures that facilitated a shift of socially recognized gender at the cost of the denial of a continuous narrative. I explored the cruel demands of narrative rupture, and the loss of the past, exacted as the price of a livable present and future, and I argued for recognizing the unjust politics of intelligibility that made such demands in an attempt to preserve the comfortable ignorance of the normatively gendered.[1]

TSQ: Transgender Studies Quarterly * Volume 3, Numbers 1–2 * May 2016
DOI 10.1215/23289252-3334403 © 2016 Duke University Press

A student in the class asked a question, and although I don't recall just what it was, I do remember that it was clear from the conversation that followed that we were talking at cross-purposes. The instructor realized what was happening: what I had taken as a space of abjection, of exclusion from social intelligibility and of conditional admission into intelligibility at a cruelly exorbitant cost, was for the student rather a space of beckoning transgressive possibility, of escape from constraining gender normativity into a shared space of fluidity and exciting new ways of being human. I want to revisit some of the central ideas in that essay in light of the changes in (some parts of) the world highlighted by my exchange with the student.

My essay actually looked forward to some of those changes, even as it urged caution about just who is likely to be able to take advantage of them, for whom the spaces of transgressive possibility will genuinely be open; but it is certainly true that—along with many others—I was astonished by the speed with which, at least in some worlds, narratives of clandestine med-psych management of gender reassignment were being displaced by openly transsexual life stories and by diverse embodiments of gender queerness. Serendipitously, as I was thinking about writing the present essay, I had a conversation with a graduate student in Beijing that helped me to think about what has been happening.

I was in Beijing to give a series of lectures on Ludwig Wittgenstein and contemporary philosophy, arguing that his most important influence is on work in feminist, queer, critical-race, postcolonial, and disability theory, especially in helping to break the grip of some of the core pictures of European modernity. One of those pictures is that without absolute foundations that determine truth and falsehood, rightness and wrongness we are left adrift: there is no meaningful space between the determined and the arbitrary (if God is dead, then everything is permitted; if there is no absolute objectivity, then we can't talk about truth or reality). This picture is equally shared by many who lament and many who celebrate the loss of foundations; and I was arguing that part of Wittgenstein's legacy is to help inspire the work of those who reject that picture, who are working on mapping that supposedly empty space between the determined and the arbitrary.

Fan Zhao, the graduate student in Beijing, told me about a frequently cited quote from the early twentieth-century left-wing writer Lu Xun: "Hope cannot be said to exist, nor can it be said not to exist. It is just like paths across the earth. For actually the earth had no paths to begin with, but when many people pass one way, a path is made."[2] Lu Xun was making a point about hope, and paths were a useful way of making that point: it is presumably obvious that there are no paths prior to their being trodden, but they are no less real for that, and those who would lament pathlessness ought rather to start walking. But Fan Zhao told me this story not to make a point about hope but to note that the point about paths is interesting in its own right, and that is what led me to think about how to characterize what had happened between when I wrote "Queering the Center" and when I was befuddled by the classroom discussion of it.

The situation as I described it in that essay was one in which some people were unable to live as the people they knew themselves to be in the social spaces in which they found themselves; and relatively powerful people offered them a plane ride to another, habitable place. The plane rides were expensive, and they were plane rides, meaning that you started out in one place and ended up in another without being in any place in between; and the journey was out of your hands, the route set by others; and no matter how desirable you might think the final destination, there weren't a whole lot of choices. What happened in the following years was that some very courageous, very imaginative people started laying down paths; and the difference between a path and a plane ride is all the difference in the world.

As a path goes from here to there, those who traverse it may well find themselves paying attention to where they are in the journey—opening up the possibility that there are not just the places of the journey's origin and its destination, but an unlimited number of places in between—places where one might stop for a while or return to, places where people might even live. And, as Lu Xun reminds us, a path is a path only when enough people walk it, when we have fellow travelers, those who are on a similar journey or who accompany us on ours: a path is a social construction, not an individual accomplishment. Not only is a path not an airplane route, it is also not a road: decided on by those in power, plotted in advance, built in one fell swoop. A path may start with individual bravado, but it becomes real through solidarity. Its route is neither determined nor arbitrary, and there may well be multiple paths from here to there (responding to the calls of the easiest, most direct, or most scenic route), as well as newly discovered, unexpected "theres," different destinations. And unlike the passage of airplanes, paths, though technologically modest, literally change the face of the earth. As Wittgenstein puts it, "this is what we do" (our forms of life), and as enough of us do it differently, lay down alternative paths, what we do— what we find intelligible—changes. Importantly, it changes not just for those who may be following that path: we all live on the earth, and when its face changes, it potentially changes for all those who inhabit it. Although the implications of the change have a lot to do with the closeness of our lives to the lives of those forging new paths, we can't predict in advance the extent of the shifts in the earth's physiognomy. (As many have pointed out, for example, it's not true that straight people's marriages will remain unaffected by the legal reality and social acceptance of same-sex marriages.)

Meaning, like a path, is something we make, not something we find; and my remarking above on the courage and imagination of path breakers reminded me of a point Marilyn Frye made in 1983: "There probably is really no distinction, in the end, between imagination and courage. We can't imagine what we can't face, and we can't face what we can't imagine. To break out of the structures of the arrogant eye we have to dare to rely on ourselves to make meaning and we have to imagine ourselves beings capable of that: capable of weaving the web of meaning which will hold us in some kind of intelligibility" (80).

Frye goes on from this point in a way that is especially fitting for reflecting on the complex, often deeply contentious relationships among diverse feminist and trans theories and theorists. She notes that "the making of meaning is social and requires a certain community of perception. We also are individually timid and want 'support.' So it is only against a background of an imagined community of ultimate harmony and perfect agreement that we dare to think it possible to make meaning." But, she goes on:

> This brings us into an arrogance of our own, for we make it a prerequisite for our construction of meaning that other women be what we need them to be to constitute the harmonious community of agreement we require. . . . Meaning is indeed something that arises among two or more individuals and requires some degree of agreement in perception and values. (It also tends to generate the required community and the necessary degree of agreement.) The community required for meaning, however, is precisely *not* a homogeneous herd, for without difference there is no meaning. Meaning is a system of connections and distinctions among different and distinguishable things. The hypothetical homogeneous community which we imagine we need *could* not be the community in which we can make ourselves intelligible, im-mediately, to and for ourselves. (80–81)

I left open at the end of "Q the C" what should become of how gender is theorized: not just because I didn't know, but because it wasn't for me to say. Understandings of gender would—and will—have to emerge from social and political struggles involving, contentiously, all those who are, differently, marginalized, subordinated, violated, and harmed by dominant worlds of gender intelligibility, including, though not privileging, cis-women like me. In the nearly twenty years since I wrote that essay, those struggles have continued, but they have too often been waged as though one or another side needs to win, with an insistence that what should emerge is a single, unitary, clear, and precise definition of what it is to be a woman.

Part of the reason for that insistence, I want to suggest, are the demands made by a bad metaphysics—specifically, another, closely related dichotomy at the heart of European modernity, that between facticity and freedom, between determination by a scientifically discernible inner nature and purely autonomous individual free choice. I suggest that we can see the problems with the facticity-versus-freedom dichotomy by looking at the two neologisms I introduced in "Q the C": *perinatally pinked* and *christianormativity*. I suggested *perinatally pinked* to help clarify conflicting understandings of and interests in the identity *woman*. To be perinatally pinked is to have been labeled as female around the time of one's birth. The term arguably captures much of what many lesbian separatists and radical feminists have in mind in emphasizing the need for spaces in which to heal from the damage inflicted by such labeling, which is seen as inherently stigmatizing and subordinating, and to create new ways of being women; and it's not tendentious to note that it does not apply to trans women. But while the clarity and precision of the term might help in understanding what matters most when some feminists think about what it means to be a woman, I knew full well at the time (however much the analytic philosopher in me was tempted otherwise) that it is not only the prissy silliness of the term that unfits it as a term of identity: clarity and precision are not what we need in the terms by which we identify ourselves and each other. To think that they are is to regard the messiness, the conflict, the vagueness, the shifting slipperiness of the terms we actually use and the practices that underwrite them as regrettable, remediable accidents.

The temptation to think this way—either by coining new terms or by struggling over the "proper" definition of the ones we have—is widespread. Resisting that temptation is central to the arguments I was making in "Q the C," and I want to expand on the thought that what I called "christianormativity" (in particular, as central to shaping European modernity) is behind that temptation. Christianormativity is part of a cluster of nodes of privilege that characterize European modernity, privilege that proclaims itself universal and generically human, thereby writing out of full humanity those who are deemed unable or ruled ineligible to conform to its norms. Those who are taken to conform are self-legitimating, self-defining individuals, vested with the authority of naming themselves, with the privileged access to their own inner selves that philosophers take "us" all to have. This presumed authority over one's self is, as María Lugones (2003) has argued, an illusion, as it is undergirded and made intelligible by networks of social support that are normatively invisible. But its illusoriness doesn't diminish its power. Such full persons are complemented by a world of knowable objects (including the large majority of the world's population who are not-quite-persons) that are what they are because of their supposedly scientifically discoverable inner natures.[3]

This dichotomy continues to shape much current debate and to constrain emerging paths with an unstable oscillation between what I called "privileged access voluntarism" and "expert essentialism." Since the publication of "Q the C," it seems to me that both the expert essentialist and the privileged access voluntarist responses have actually intensified, especially in popular and social media: we have a proliferation of purported explanations of transsexuality meant to ground claims by transsexual people to a presumptively scientifically explicable truth about their gender identity, along with a growing movement to recognize people's right to the bare and incorrigible assertion of gender identity, not accessible to or in need of any justification or confirmation.[4]

Claims of having been "born that way," backed up by (scientifically questionable) appeals to neuroscience or endocrinology or genetics, are under-standable given the typically unarticulated and unquestioned assumption that some forms of identity require explanation, along with the also typically unar-ticulated and unquestioned constraints on what makes an explanation (or an identity) intelligible and acceptable. It is also understandable that, in the face of such a demand, some people will refuse, relying instead on the other (equally problematic) intelligibility schema—namely, bare self-assertion, whether framed as the right to identify as one sees fit or as privileged, incorrigible access to the truth about oneself, in either case accountable to no one. Discussion of non-normative gender identity—like discussion of so many other areas of human identity and behavior—tends to swing between the individualistically volunta-ristic and the reductively causal explanatory, either attempting with bravado to stake a claim to self-determination or accepting one's own objectification in the hope of being at least intelligible and, hopefully, unblameworthy.

The student's question in the class ten years ago was coming from a "beyond the binary" world of transgender theory, activism, and daily life, a world that rejects the demand of unequivocal gender attribution in favor of ungroun-ded, unbounded, and nonbinding nonidentities. Especially in its most extreme, theory-driven forms, this world can resist any socially grounded norms of intel-ligibility whatsoever, running into the sorts of problems I discuss in "Q the C" related to Wittgensteinian considerations about the sociality of meaning. But as Talia Bettcher has argued (2014), when such understandings of gender (even in more plausible, less extreme forms) become (paradoxically) normative, they render illegitimate or at least politically retrograde the lives of trans women and men who identify as women or men, for whom binary gender helps rather than hinders their efforts to be themselves. In a series of essays, Bettcher (including 2009, 2014, 2015) has been articulating an account of gender identity that takes seriously the many, very different worlds of sense inhabited by transsexual men and women, by variously transgender people, as well as by intersex people and cis-women—beginning, as many standpoint theorists would urge, with those whose identities make them maximally vulnerable to intersecting axes of subordination and marginalization.[5] At the heart of her account is the notion of "moral geni-talia," the genitals that one is presumed to have been born with, hence to have a right to, and that one's gender presentation is supposed to euphemistically refer to, while norms of privacy shield them from public visibility. In very different ways, the presumptions, supposings, and demands associated with moral genitalia shape the worlds in which we all live, the vulnerabilities to which we are exposed, and, consequently, the forms of resistance we engage in and the resistant worlds of sense we create.[6] For Bettcher—and I think this is one of the greatest strengths of her account—it is the differences, even the struggles and conflicts, that give hope for a genuinely inclusive politics, including the rejection of the demand for a unitary definition of *woman*, not because we do not need—or should positively reject—shared sense making, but because we should recognize our collective, often contentious, agency in making sense and our complex relationships to others who are making it alongside us, in adjacent, interacting worlds.

As Aren Aizura argues, "ambivalence and ambiguity are part and parcel of political resistance. If the discursive production of an identity category is also a technique of regulatory power (no matter whether the category is deployed in medico-legal discourse or subculture), 'perhaps only by risking the *incoherence* of identity is connection possible' (Butler 1997: 149). I take this to imply a strategy which takes advantage of contradictory tensions within recognition and turns it into a political practice" (Aizura 2006: 303). The political hope Aizura and Bettcher find in this recognition—of a transformed and transformative feminism—is, I think, in line with the spirit of "Q the C": rather than trans women's arguing that there is some core meaning of *woman* that as a matter of fact includes them, or defiantly claiming the right to self-identify as women freed from any shared social understanding of what that means, there is more political hope in arguing against the currently normative understandings of gender (understandings that—of course for different reasons—cis-female feminists deplore) and struggling to find plural but interrelated coalitional understandings that do justice to the wide range of gender's discontents.

Naomi Scheman is a professor of philosophy and of gender, women, and sexuality studies at the University of Minnesota. Her essays have been collected in two volumes, *Engenderings: Constructions of Knowledge, Authority, and Privilege* (1993) and *Shifting Ground: Knowledge and Reality, Transgression and Trustworthiness* (2011).

Notes

1. I drew especially heavily on Stryker 1994. Stryker was describing what I am calling the "airplane journey"; in so doing, of course, she was also defiantly violating its terms and conditions.

2. The aphorism is easily found on the Internet, in multiple translated versions, though I could discover no citational information beyond the date: 1921. The version Fan Zhao gave me translated what is here *paths* as *roads*, which, as I note below, doesn't actually capture the meaning.

3. Some readers will note the relevance here of Jean-Paul Sartre's distinction between being-for-itself and being-in-itself, and hence of Simone de Beauvoir's argument that what Sartre took to be a generically human predicament is in actuality a socially fixed stratification.

4. I do not mean to be including in this critique Talia Bettcher's arguments (2009) for first-person authority about gender identity. Those arguments do not presume first-person authority over the *meaning* of the claim to be a woman or a man, nor are such claims altogether immune from critique. Bettcher's arguments are subtle and, I think, persuasive; and I would place them in the middle ground I am trying to map.

5. In Scheman 2014 I argue for thinking of vulnerability as a standpoint: to be vulnerable is to be in a better position to come to know, and privileged invulnerability promotes ignorance.

6. Like me, Bettcher is inspired by María Lugones's conception of worlds of sense and draws on the theorizing in Lugones 2003.

References

Aizura, Aren Z. 2006. "Of Borders and Homes: The Imaginary Community of (Trans)Sexual Citizenship." *Inter-Asia Cultural Studies* 7, no. 2: 289–309.

Bettcher, Talia Mae. 2009. "Trans Identities and First-Person Authority." In *You've Changed: Sex Reassignment and Personal Identity*, edited by Laurie Shrage, 98–120. New York: Oxford University Press.

———. 2014. "Trapped in the Wrong Theory: Rethinking Trans Oppression and Resistance." *Signs* 39, no. 2: 43–65.

———. 2015. "Intersexuality, Transgender, and Transsexuality." April. In *The Oxford Handbook of Feminist Theory*, edited by Lisa Disch and Mary Hawkesworth. www.oxfordhandbooks .com/view/10.1093/oxfordhb/9780199328581.001.0001/oxfordhb-9780199328581-e-21.

Butler, Judith. 1997. *The Psychic Life of Power: Theories in Subjection*. Stanford, CA: Stanford University Press.

Frye, Marilyn. 1983. "In and out of Harm's Way: Arrogance and Love." In *The Politics of Reality: Essays in Feminist Theory*, 52–83. Trumansburg, NY: Crossing Press.

Lugones, María. 2003. *Pilgrimages/Peregrinajes: Theorizing Coalition against Multiple Oppressions*. Lanham, MD: Rowman and Littlefield.

Scheman, Naomi. 1997. "Queering the Center by Centering the Queer: Reflections on Transsexuals and Secular Jews." In *Feminists Rethink the Self*, edited by Diana Tietjens Meyers, 124–62. Boulder, CO: Westview. Reprinted in Scheman, Naomi. 2011. *Shifting Ground: Knowledge and Reality, Transgression and Trustworthiness*. New York: Oxford University Press.

———. 2014. "Empowering Canaries: Sustainability, Vulnerability, and the Ethics of Epistemology." *International Journal of Feminist Approaches to Bioethics* 7, no. 1: 169–91.

Stryker, Susan. 1994. "My Words to Victor Frankenstein above the Village of Chamonix: Performing Transgender Rage." *GLQ* 1, no. 3: 237–54.

Transfeminism and Decolonial Thought

The Contribution of Brazilian Travestis

JOSELI MARIA SILVA and MARCIO JOSE ORNAT

Translated by SEAN STROUD

Abstract This article discusses the expansion of the concept of transfeminism in Brazil and the relationship of that concept to the political practices of the social movements of *travestis* and transsexuals. This concept is still in the initial phase of acceptance within the academic sphere in Brazil, and it does not, as yet, form part of the struggle for the rights of *travestis* and transsexuals, who are still stigmatized and excluded by society in general. This article argues that the future of transfeminism in Brazil depends on the development of a decolonialist approach, which represents the opportunity to develop a strategy with which to overcome the notion of the primacy of scientific knowledge over those who suffer the effects of epistemic violence. This approach incorporates concepts produced through the daily struggles of those who suffer the stigma of inferiority and dehumanization.

Keywords transfeminism, decolonial thought, Brazilian *travestis*

W hen asked what she thought about the idea of transfeminism as a contemporary political movement for the achievement of the social rights of *travestis* in Brazil,[1] Diamante—a *travesti*, sex worker, and remarkable activist of long standing—replied, "Is that something to eat or to drink?" followed by a hearty laugh.[2] Diamante has been a regular participant in the National Meetings of *Travestis* and Transsexuals Working in the Fight against AIDS (Encontros Nacionais de Travestis e Transexuais que atuam na Luta contra AIDS, ENTLAIDS).[3] At annual meetings for more than twenty years, this group has demanded that the Brazilian government recognize the rights of its members, and it denounced the violation of the rights of *travesti* and transsexual citizens. Another organization, the National Group of *Travestis*, Transsexuals, and Transgenders (Articulação Nacional de Travestis, Transexuais e Transgêneros, ANTRA)

TSQ: Transgender Studies Quarterly ∗ Volume 3, Numbers 1–2 ∗ May 2016
DOI 10.1215/23289252-3334415 © 2016 Duke University Press

was founded in 2000 in Porto Alegre, to work toward a unified national policy between various NGOs (nongovernmental organizations) that are scattered throughout Brazil.[4]

Diamante's ironic response expresses the extremely limited knowledge about transfeminism that exists among Brazilian *travesti* and female transsexual activists;[5] however, this concept is slowly becoming a feature of the academic field of gender and sexuality studies. In 2013, the largest and most traditional meeting on gender and feminism in Brazil featured the first debates on the subject, entitled "Transgender Feminism or Transfeminism," as well as a roundtable entitled "Transfeminisms in Brazil."[6] In 2013, the First International Seminar on Deconstructing Gender was launched at the Federal University of Rio Grande do Norte in the city of Natal; its central theme was "Subjectivity, Citizenship, and Transfeminism." The first Brazilian book on the subject was published in 2014 under the title *Transfeminism: Theories and Practices* (*Transfeminismo: Teorias e práticas*), edited by Jacqueline Gomes de Jesus and others.

An analysis of the very limited number of books about this issue published in Brazil demonstrates that the theoretical framework of transfeminism that is being developed in the Brazilian academic field is anglophone (with particular emphasis on works by Butler 1990, 1993; Koyama 2001; and Stone 1991). The anglophone hegemony that exists in relation to studies of sexuality has resulted in a situation in which the categories and concepts that have been created in Anglo-American regions of the world are considered to be universal and adaptable to any reality. The different positions of power that exist between different knowledges create hierarchies that make up the geopolitics of knowledge. As a result, epistemic violence is inflicted upon researchers from the global South (who are considered to be merely reproducers of theories from the global North). But above all, this epistemic violence harms the vulnerable and stigmatized population of *travestis* and female Brazilian transsexuals who, in a globalized world, increasingly have access to the knowledge produced in the academic fields of the global North.[7]

Brazilian transfeminist perspectives are enthusiastic, optimistic, supportive, and inclusive. The individuals who carry the banner of transfeminism define themselves as belonging to a scientific as well as political tendency that is fighting to dismantle the existing links between gender and biology, and to introduce into the debate the idea of intersectional oppressions, notably, class and race. In this sense, transfeminism is a powerful, creative intervention into our ways of being in the world, in that it goes beyond binarism and the essentialism of identities. However, as Jaqueline Gomes de Jesus et al. (2014: 6) point out:

> Transfeminism is undergoing a process of construction: it is a frontier literature. It has only been developed in Brazil during the last five years and for this reason its

theoretical and ethical horizons are still being delineated. Transfeminism does not exist in isolation; it needs skilled people to handle it. These sorts of skills are developed with practice, by learning through daily suffering or through the recognition of harsh realities. Transfeminism is not only learned through reading about it, the words have to pulse in the veins of the reader.

The challenge for transfeminism in Brazil—to try to break down the walls of the elitist Brazilian academy[8]—means that it will have to engage with the knowledges that are constructed from the hard daily lives of *travestis* and female transsexuals, which are marked by extreme social and economic exclusion. These are the groups that are most vulnerable to violent and untimely death within the Brazilian LGBT community.

The introduction of transfeminism into the Brazilian academy has the latent potential to break with the modern European epistemic tradition, which ranks its own knowledge as being superior to the various knowledges of vulnerable social groups. Science serves to name and categorize reality, and in this way it produces a logic that ends up being shared, even by groups that are violated by scientific discourse (Fanon [1952] 1967). Therefore, understanding how *travestis* and female Brazilian transsexuals have constructed their identities amid political struggle is of fundamental importance in establishing a path that can lead toward liberation. From this perspective, we would cite the importance of the knowledge possessed by the *travestis* Diamante, Pérola, and Rubi, who in 2013, through the auspices of ENTLAIDS, analyzed the categories of identity that have provoked much controversy within the *travesti* and transsexual movement in Brazil.

Brazilian *travestis* established a specific movement of their own within the broader Brazilian LGBT movement, despite the stigmatization they suffered within that very movement. The issue of how to linguistically refer to themselves was the subject of numerous discussions in group meetings. During the last few years, a growing number of people in these meetings have begun to self-identify as transgender, often expressing this self-identification by saying something to the effect of, "Before I thought I was a *travesti*, but now I think I'm transsexual." These positionings confirm the idea that processes connected with identity are relational and are spatio-temporally situated.

The spread of public discussions of transsexuality in Brazilian society, as well as increased access to medical techniques, have increased tensions in the relationships between *travestis* and female transsexuals.[9] The possibility of accessing a transsexual identity, predicated as it is on medical and legal procedures, has only recently become a reality for Brazilian *travestis*.[10] This has led to a diversification of identity claims, and it has exacerbated tensions within and between the two groups.

The fluidity of identity, which is common to all human beings, has been the object of paradoxical interpretations by *travestis*. Their discourses simultaneously combine the potential of gender subversion and the internalization of medical discourse. Pérola, for example, denies the existence of essential identities but at the same time offers definitions that distinguish *travestis* and female transsexuals based on the relationship that these people may have with their genitalia:

> I think that it is absurd to put labels on people to know who they are. I use the term *travesti* to define myself, and to me that is a political issue. I could also define myself as a transsexual, but I prefer to be a *travesti* and that is a question of militancy because the stigma associated with the word *travesti* is much greater than the stigma associated with being called a transsexual. The social weight of condemnation for *travestis* is much heavier than it is for transsexuals. Look, if I say I'm transsexual, society says "poor thing" because they think that I'm sick and that I did not choose this path! No, I don't want that! I am a *travesti* and for me this is a political position. For me there is no difference in being a *travesti* or a transsexual but speaking technically I am a *travesti* because a transsexual has trouble accepting the body they have, and I don't have any problem about having a penis. But I can see that being a transsexual is easier because you are forgiven by society; you are putting yourself forward to be corrected. That is not being a *travesti*! Being a *travesti* means contradicting everything, fighting, and being what you are without anyone else's approval!

For Rubi, another militant *travesti*, the rise of transgender subjectivity in Brazil is loosely linked to an attempt by some people to overcome the fact that the word *travesti* is linked by many with prostitution, violence, poverty, and disease. According to Rubi, "an aversion to one's biological body, specifically the genitals, cannot be the only element that differentiates a *travesti* from a transsexual." Diamante also questions the boundaries between *travestis* and female transsexuals: "There are people who say that they are transsexual just so that they won't be like us *travestis*. But I have caught several of them masturbating (laughs). So what's this story about disliking their penis? They don't take pleasure from it? For me, that's a joke!"

Travesti discourses provoke questions about the limits of identity and the impossibility of defining boundaries between Brazilian *travestis* and female transsexuals. However, there is still a tendency to refer to medical concepts when defining *travestis* and female transsexuals, even within those groups themselves. It is important to note that while the depathologization of transsexuality is central to academic transfeminist discussions, this topic is not a priority in the political meetings of *travestis* and transsexuals. There is a certain fear on their part that the depathologization process might jeopardize their inclusion in the National Health System in Brazil.

At the ENTLAIDS conference in Brazil in September 2013, a new controversy surrounding the use of the term *travesti* occurred. One of the working groups proposed by the organizers of the event was intended to discuss demands that the Portuguese-language dictionary contain a definition of the word *travesti* that was considered appropriate for use by *travestis* themselves. The female transsexual group present at the meeting proposed to delete the word *travesti* from the dictionary because there was a consensus among both female transsexuals and *travestis* that the word did not express the experience of *travestis*.[11] According to one of the discussions that followed, "being a *travesti* entails living twenty-four hours a day as a female, including performing bodily changes using hormones and the injection of industrial silicone."[12] They also suggested that *travesti* experience could be adequately expressed through the dictionary definition of *transsexual*.[13] Addressing herself to the female transsexuals who were present at the meeting, Rubi argued against this proposal, saying:

> All of you forget that when the LGBT movement was created in Brazil, while gays were protected in their homes, it was the *travestis* who were being beaten up in the streets by police and clients. You forget that it was the *travestis* who fought for citizenship in Brazil. You forget that it was us who literally got punched in the face. I have been beaten up a lot during my life as a *travesti* and I never wanted to hide behind a term as you want to hide [referring to the use of the term *transsexual*]. . . . If we erase the word *travesti* from the dictionary we will delete our history. What we have to do is change the meaning of the word, which is not consistent with the reality of *travestis*. I'm not a transsexual, I'm a *travesti*! I will never have a sex change! This will die when I do! [making a gesture to show her penis].[14]

Brazilian *travestis* are historically and politically situated individuals who construct their subjectivities by assigning meanings to themselves and to others. They share life stories that are characterized by exclusion by their families as well as schools and health and legal institutions. But above all, to identify as *travesti* means to struggle against and resist gender norms, through epistemic disobedience, using one's own body as a battleground for the achievement of social recognition. The internal disputes concerning *travesti* and female transsexual identities within the relevant social movements in Brazil are constructed from the starting point of simultaneous and paradoxical transgression against, and obedience to, the social order of gender. The challenges facing Brazilian transfeminism are the need to recognize the knowledge produced by *travestis* and transsexuals themselves, as well as the need to overcome the power of Anglo-American enunciation and to take into consideration the cultural differences that shape Brazilian sexual identities. Perhaps, as we conclude, we can answer the question posed by Diamante used to open this discussion. After all, it matters little whether transfeminism is for eating or drinking. What really matters is that for transfeminism to be materially engaged with the conditions of life in the Brazilian context, it must incorporate the everyday experiences of Brazilian *travestis* and female transsexuals. If it can do so, let transfeminism be the food that strengthens us in order to invent worlds that are possible, and that go beyond the current destructive order of gender.

Joseli Maria Silva is a professor of geography at the State University of Ponta Grossa. She is chief editor of the *Revista Latino-Americana de geografia e gênero* (*Latin American Journal of Geography and Gender*). She is also a member of Renascer (Reborn), an NGO that works in support of citizenship and the human rights of LGBT groups.

Marcio Jose Ornat is a professor of geography at the State University of Ponta Grossa and vice coordinator of the Group of Territorial Studies at the same university. He is a member of Renascer (Reborn), an NGO that works in support of citizenship and the human rights of LGBT groups.

Acknowledgments
We would like to thank Susan Stryker for her generosity as the editor in supporting us to overcome our English-language limitation. Thank you in particular to Sean Stroud by providing the whole translation.

Notes
1.   In Brazilian society, the word *travesti* does not have the same meaning as *transvestite*. *Travestis* are people who are designated male at birth but live according to the female gender. They perform a series of bodily changes but generally reject sex-reassignment surgery.
2.   All the names used in this article are fictitious. Quotations come from interviews conducted in September and December 2013 in Curitiba, Brazil, and March 2015 in Ponta Grossa, Brazil.
3.   The history of the organization of *travestis* and female transsexuals is linked to meetings of groups campaigning against the spread of AIDS throughout Brazil during the 1980s. The first official meeting occurred in Rio de Janeiro in 1993, and since then there have been annual meetings that have discussed various issues and demands. Peres (2015) points out that in 2004, during the eleventh meeting of the group in Campo Grande, in the state of Mato Grosso do Sul, the acronym that had hitherto been ENTLAIDS (National Meeting of *Travestis* and Liberated in the Fight against AIDS, Encontro Nacional de Travestis e Liberados na Luta contra a AIDS) became ENTRAIDS (National

Meeting of *Travestis* and Transsexuals in the Fight against AIDS, Encontro Nacional de Travestis e Transexuais na Luta contra AIDS). This name change brought a greater specificity to subsequent meetings, including the participation of *travestis* and transsexuals. Despite the modification of the official acronym, today the meetings are still known as ENTLAIDS, and this is the acronym that will be adopted in this text. It is important to point out that the term *transsexual* refers overwhelmingly to female transsexuals. An organization of male transsexuals was founded in 2012 with the creation of the Association of Trans Men (Associação Brasileira de Homens Trans, ABHT), and in 2013 the Brazilian Institute of Transmasculinity (Instituto Brasileiro de Transmasculinidade, IBRAT) was founded.

4. In 2013, ANTRA revealed that it had 105 affiliated organizations.

5. When we use the term *female transsexual,* we mean someone who was assigned male at birth and who seeks to be legally and socially recognized as a woman, based on medical procedures to transform their bodies, including genital transformation surgeries. In Brazil, a "female transsexual" is what is now often called a "transsexual woman" in the United States; it does not refer to a person assigned female at birth who pursues medicalized masculinization procedures.

6. The debates took place between the following participants: Jaqueline Gomes de Jesus, Paula Sandrine Machado, and Ana Paula Vencato, all of whom are cisgender women, at the International Seminar "Doing Gender 10"—Current Challenges of Feminisms (Seminário Internacional Fazendo Gênero 10—Desafios Atuais dos Feminismos).

7. For more on the decolonial perspective, see Mignolo 2000, 2009, and Quijano 2000.

8. Because of the process of exclusion that *travestis* experience in schools, few of them are able to have access to further education, let alone work in the faculty of a university.

9. Almost all the transsexuals who participated at ENTLAIDS in 2013 were female.

10. In 1997, the Federal Council of Medicine in Brazil regulated experimental sex-change surgery, but only in university hospitals. In 2008, the Brazilian government officially recognized sex-reassignment surgery, which is now carried out by the National Health System. Transsexualism is cataloged in the International Disease Registry (Cadastro Internacional de Doenças, CID) as a disease for which the only prophylaxis is sex-change surgery.

11. The word *travesti* is defined in Portuguese-language dictionaries as "people who occasionally dress in clothing of the opposite sex as a fetish" (*Michaelis Moderno Dicionário da Língua Portuguesa* [Online], s.v. "travesti," accessed September 10, 2014, michaelis.uol.com.br/moderno/portugues/index.php.

12. The techniques of bodily transformation of *travestis* are carried out clandestinely and are deemed to be illegal under Brazilian law.

13. According to the group that made this proposal, the dictionary definition of *transsexual* is "a person (usually male) who wants to belong to the opposite sex and who even wears clothes of the opposite sex or who undergoes sex-change surgery." Thus, the only difference between *travestis* and transsexuals was in relation to their genitals. According to the debate, *travestis* do not consider that having a penis is problematic, but transsexuals are repulsed by it.

14. As a *travesti,* Ruby self-identifies with the female gender.

References

Butler, Judith. 1990. *Gender Trouble: Feminism and the Subversion of Identity.* London: Routledge.
———. 1993. *Bodies That Matter: On the Discursive Limits of "Sex."* London: Routledge.

Fanon, Frantz. (1952) 1967. *Black Skin, White Masks*. Translated by Charles Lum Karkmann. New York: Grove.

Jesus, Jaqueline Gomes de, et al. 2014. *Transfeminismo: Teorias e práticas (Transfeminism: Theories and Practices)*. Rio de Janeiro: Metanoia.

Koyama, Emi. 2001. "The Transfeminist Manifesto." Eminism.org. www.eminism.org/readings /pdf-rdg/tfmanifesto.pdf (accessed June 10, 2014).

Mignolo, Walter. 2000. *Local Histories/Global Designs: Coloniality, Subaltern Knowledges, and Border Thinking*. Princeton, NJ: Princeton University Press.

———. 2009. "Epistemic Disobedience, Independent Thought, and De-colonial Freedom." *Theory, Culture, and Society* 26, nos. 7–8: 1–23. doi:10.1177/0263276409349275.

Peres, Wiliam Siqueira. 2015. *Travestis brasileiras: Dos estigmas à cidadania (Brazilian Travestis: From Stigma to Citizenship)*. Curitiba, Brazil: Juruá.

Quijano, Anibal. 2000. "Coloniality of Power, Eurocentrism, and Latin America." *Neplanta: Views from South* 1, no. 3: 533–80.

Stone, Sandy. 1991. "The *Empire* Strikes Back: A Posttranssexual Manifesto." In *Body Guards: The Cultural Politics of Gender Ambiguity*, edited by Julia Epstein and Kristina Straub, 280–304. New York: Routledge.

Trans*feminist Intersections

REESE SIMPKINS

Abstract The author argues that trans* materialities are part of a trans*feminist politics of becoming-intersectional, which emphasizes the movement underlying identificatory processes. Articulating trans* as a dynamic movement of becoming-intersectional undermines both the normative construction of bounded categories and the identities that emerge from these processes, thereby allying trans*, feminist, and intersectional politics. Moreover, conceptualizing politics in this manner foregrounds the "categorical miscegenation" of both intersectional theorizing and trans* scholarship, and it contributes to ongoing conversations in both bodies of scholarship that are concerned with the ways in which categories operate politically. By highlighting the political stakes in the materialization of matter and the concomitant production of categories and identifications, a trans*feminist politics of becoming-intersectional foregrounds process over positionality and takes place at a fundamental level—at the level of materiality, where the ways in which matter materializes resonates politically.
Keywords trans*, feminism, intersectionality, becoming, materiality

> Race and ethnicity are . . . coterminous with sexuality, just as sexuality is impli-
> cated in race and ethnicity. To that extent, any analytical effort to keep these
> categories apart from one another may turn out to be counterproductive, for it is
> their categorical enmeshment—their categorical miscegenation, so to speak—
> that needs to be foregrounded.
> —Rey Chow, *The Protestant Ethnic and the Spirit of Capitalism*

I head this article with the above quotation from Rey Chow because I am interested in crafting a trans* politics of "becoming-intersectional" that can be directed toward identification and subjectivity but that contains at its core a dynamic understanding of matter's complexity—a complexity that operates with intersectionality's logic of "categorical miscegenation." As I argue in greater detail below, intersectionality's onto-epistem-ological framework is based on a complex multiplicity that works to undo normative categorizations and promotes the

TSQ: Transgender Studies Quarterly * Volume 3, Numbers 1–2 * May 2016
DOI 10.1215/23289252-3334427 © 2016 Duke University Press

mutual imbrication of categories, or what Chow refers to as "categorical miscegenation." In this context, I argue that trans*feminist politics takes place at the ontogenetic level of materiality.

My work on this project is born of an interest in antiracist, feminist, and trans* scholarships, and of the relationship between these bodies of knowledge, the theories they produce, and the possibilities for identification and social justice. Specifically, I am concerned with the way contemporary discussions of "transgender issues in the classroom, mass media, and everyday conversations separate out transphobia, heterosexism, and misogyny from racism, ethnocentrism, and Eurocentrism" (Juang 2006: 243). By separating out trans* from other axes of oppression, trans* gets marked as a form of sex/gender difference separate from class, race, nationality, ethnicity, and so forth. Without both attending to a broader understanding of the mutual construction of categories and excavating the impetus to keep these categories separate, trans* produces its own set of normative boundaries. As such, I take seriously the work in trans* studies that highlights the ways in which trans* politics privileges those who are able to approximate heteronormative, white, middle-class, able-bodied citizenship norms (Aizura 2006; Bhanji 2012; Lamble 2008).

With these considerations in mind, I aim to articulate an intersectional trans*feminist politics that is based on process and movement. Conceptualizing politics in this manner foregrounds the categorical miscegenation of both intersectional and trans* theorizing and contributes to ongoing conversations in both bodies of scholarship that are concerned with the ways in which categories operate politically. I argue that trans* materialities are part of a trans*feminist politics of becoming-intersectional, which emphasizes the movement underlying identificatory processes. Articulating trans* as a dynamic movement of becoming-intersectional undermines both the normative construction of bounded categories and the identities that emerge from these processes, thereby allying trans*, feminist, and intersectional politics. By highlighting the political stakes in the materialization of matter and the concomitant production of categories and identifications, a trans*feminist politics of becoming-intersectional foregrounds process over positionality and takes place at a fundamental level—at the level of materiality, where the ways in which matter materializes resonate politically.

My argument has three sections. I begin by discussing the addition of the asterisk to *trans** in contemporary trans* scholarship, which I argue opens up an affective dimension of trans* embodiment. Next, I address the relationship between trans* materialities and intersectionality by engaging intersectionality at the level of onto-epistem-ological production. I conclude by articulating a trans*feminist politics of becoming-intersectional that extends from becoming to identification.

Trans*ing Embodiment

In terms of Anglo–North American scholarship, the first appended punctuation to *trans** occurred in a coedited article by Susan Stryker, Paisley Currah, and Lisa Jean Moore, who argue that their "use of a hyphen" delinks *trans-* from transgender and identity, thereby allowing the authors to attend to the "vital and more generally relevant critical/political questions . . . compacted within the theoretical articulations and lived social realities of 'transgender' embodiments, subjectivities, and communities" (2008: 12). In particular, they link the appended punctuation to "categorical crossings, leakages, and slips of all sorts," including those based on "-gender, -national, -racial, -generational, -genic, -species" (11). Moreover, Finn Enke's discussion of the hyphen/asterisk argues that the appended punctuation "force[s] us to know *trans* as modification and motion across time and space" (2012: 7–8). Finally, in the introduction to the "Tranimalities" issue of *TSQ: Transgender Studies Quarterly*, Eva Hayward and Jami Weinstein suggest that the asterisk "is both an intensification and a placeholder, both an absence and site of radical proliferation," which they link to the "textures of spacetime" and the "moving mattering" of *trans** (Hayward and Weinstein 2015: 198, 199). These statements not only suggest that the asterisk fosters connections that emphasize the categorical miscegenation to which I refer above, they also suggest that the asterisk produces *trans** as a force of material movement. As I show below, one of the connections made possible by the asterisk is the creation of new tools through which to articulate the materiality of embodiment. Thus, *trans** scholarship, like that of Stryker and Hayward, emphasizes the entanglement of spatial relations and *trans** embodiments, while at the same time highlighting the ways that affect works to undo identitarian conceptualizations of *trans**.

Stryker's discussion in "Dungeon Intimacies" suggests that *trans** identifications and embodiments are premised on the affective incorporation of space. She argues that her practice of "transsexual sadomasochism in dungeon space enacts a *poesis* (an act of artistic creation) that collapses the boundary between the embodied self, its world, and others" (Stryker 2008: 39). Here, she conceptualizes transsexual body modification as "the means through which [she] grasped a virtuality manifested in dungeon space and gave it a materiality capable of extending its effects beyond the dungeon walls" (43). In other words, Stryker's S/M practices in the dungeon congeal a virtual identity, the materiality of which is extended beyond the walls of the dungeon. Trans* identifications and the associated sexed/gendered self are the affective extension of space that allow the embodiment of a particular sensory beyond the space in which they originate.

To speak of embodiment as the affective incorporation of space is a significant shift from normative conceptualizations of embodiment, generally, and trans* embodiment, particularly, in which trans* sex operates as a movement of ongoing spatiality, embodied and extended through space-time. In this context, trans* sex operates according to Eva Hayward's conceptualization of "transposition." As Hayward explains, transpositions are "the spatial-sensual-temporal processes that mark . . . trans-sex transitions" (2010: 237). These transpositions extend the framework of transition to incorporate a multiplicity of affective resonances beyond the standard conceptualization of transition in terms of sex/gender difference and identification, in which some trans* bodies transition from one sex to another. Instead, Hayward situates her transposition within an affective geography of San Francisco's Tenderloin District, where her transposition is enabled through the social space in which her transition and the associated body modifications take place. This affective movement extends embodiment beyond the normative boundaries of "the body" by incorporating a larger affective geography of social space.

Because affect forges connections between organisms and their milieu, affective processes of becoming produce porous embodiments (Crawford 2008). The dimension of affect is a dimension of becoming, a dimension of relationality and connection that erodes the borders and boundaries on which subjectivities and identifications are established. One way trans* people "make sense of" the affective dimension is as a disjuncture between embodied sensations and the discursive materiality of sex/gender norms. At some point, for trans* people there is a disjuncture between the "truth" of their sexed/gendered embodiment and the way they conceptualize themselves. Trans* identifications emerge not from "biological" evidence, bodily appearance, or impressed/socialized sex/gender norms but from a disjuncture between an embodied sensation/feeling and the biological "truth" of their sex/gender. The radically open becoming-body "experiences" sensation in a different register than normative understandings of materiality and embodiment allow.

Becoming-Intersectional

The challenge trans* embodiments pose for normative constructions of "the body" as container is mirrored in feminist work on intersectionality, as both sets of scholarship point to ways in which bodies extend beyond normative categorical frameworks. Ange-Marie Hancock (2007) makes clear that the tendency to use preformed understandings of categories and the relations between and within those categories undercuts one of the key concerns of intersectionality. Indeed, Kimberlé Crenshaw's (1989) original positing of intersectionality suggests that categories are mutually implicated. Thus, trans* feminism must account for the significant challenge that intersectionality as an epistemological method brings to hegemonic ontological frameworks.

One way of prizing apart the link between intersectionality and the reliance on stable identities is by complexifying the way in which categories are understood, in which labeling and categorizing are never self-evident, but are relational processes (Walby, Armstrong, and Strid 2012). Instead of directly locating the subjects/selves who inhabit specific identities in relation to power, intersectionality as a method actually requires an onto-epistem-ological framework that can incorporate the dynamic variation of matter—a framework that understands matter both as context specific and as an overarching systemic whole that cannot simply be taken apart and put back together. In a trans* context, this means that discussing trans* as separate from "other" categories fundamentally misconstrues the operation of power and paints a simplistic picture of identification. Trans* people do not simply express nonnormative sex/gender identifications; these identifications take place within the context of racialization, class, ethnicity, and citizenship concerns, among other things (Juang 2006; Lamble 2008). Trans*feminist theory and politics, then, must contain a dynamic understanding of identificatory processes that works through the complex terrain of category mixing.

This dynamism is apparent in Crenshaw's original formulation of intersectionality, which likens discrimination to the flow of "traffic through an intersection. . . . If an accident happens in an intersection, it can be caused by cars traveling from any number of directions and, sometimes, from all of them" (Crenshaw 1989: 149). Based on social conditions, discriminatory power differentials enable certain traffic movements, while disabling other movements. Because much of the work on intersectionality has focused more on which traffic flows are permitted and which are not, or in other words, which identities are privileged and which are not, intersectional analyses often engage in a positional analysis, whereby social location becomes highly significant. However, while identity and the differential operation of categories play a significant role in determining the subject's location in relation to privilege and oppression, Crenshaw's example lends itself just as easily to a reading of dynamic movement. As Jasbir Puar (2011) states, "Crenshaw indicates . . . [that] identification is a process; identity is an encounter, an event, an accident. In fact, identities are multi-causal, multi-directional, liminal; traces aren't always self-evident. In this 'becoming of intersectionality,' there is emphasis on motion rather than gridlock; on how the halting of motion produces the demand to locate." The "becoming of intersectionality," thus, points toward normative categorical ontologies as those which halt movement and require identification.

Process, Becoming, and the Myth of Mobility

According to the logic of identity, trans* is a highly regulated space. Understood thusly, trans* people are subject to the demands of various discursive regimes, including those regimes associated with what are now familiar intersectional categories. In contrast, by emphasizing the force of becoming, both trans* and intersectionality are delinked from their basis in identity and are reconceptualized as movement, as the force of becoming. Rather than referring to the stability of identity, categorical positionings are processes through which bodies are marked as other. A trans*feminist politics of becoming-intersectional takes place at this onto-epistem-ological level, at the level in which normative categorical relations operate. This politics of becoming-intersectional incorporates both identity-based politics, as well as the more fundamental, highly contextual politics of becoming. The point is *not* to see identification in normative categorical terms—categories are not discrete, nor are they mutually exclusive.

As such, politics is not stable, and political strategies must be similarly flexible, forging what may seem like disparate connections. No longer do political strategies pin identities to a social grid (Massumi 2002) and produce certain bodies as absolutely marginalized or privileged; instead, there is a shifting set of contexts through which marginalization and privilege are produced—no body can take the position of "most marginal," and there are no "pure" subject positions. Rather, the sets of forces that produce marginalization and privilege, as well as the identities, identifications, and subjectivities that inhabit spaces of marginalization and privilege, are understood as events.

Indexing ongoing material dynamism into the onto-epistem-ological formulations of identification allows for the dynamic play of material forces that join and recombine in different ways every time an event occurs. A trans*feminist politics of becoming is based on this dynamic materiality in which identities, identifications, and subjectivities are produced anew every time they are (re) articulated. The proliferation of events and forces hinges on the deployment of multiplicitous identifications that have no pivot, no central core—the point, to paraphrase Gilles Deleuze and Félix Guattari (1987), is not to refuse to say "I/identify" but to create conditions in which it no longer matters whether one says "I/identifies." This is a trans*feminist politics of becoming-intersectional that politicizes materiality and challenges the normative construction of categories by engaging intersectionality's categorical miscegenation at the onto-epistem-ological level.

---

reese simpkins is a visiting scholar in sexuality studies at York University. His research project, "Trans* Autopoiesis: Material Embodiment and the Production of Space/Time," is housed at York University's Centre for Feminist Research. His work focuses on posthumanism, trans* theory, and science studies.

References

Aizura, Aren Z. 2006. "Of Borders and Homes: The Imaginary Community of (Trans)sexual Citizenship." *Inter-Asia Cultural Studies* 7, no. 2: 289–309.

Bhanji, Nael. 2012. "Trans/criptions: Homing Desires, (Trans)sexual Citizenship, and Racialized Bodies." In *Transgender Migrations: The Bodies, Borders, and Politics of Transition*, edited by Trystan Cotten, 157–75. New York: Routledge.

Chow, Rey. 2002. *The Protestant Ethnic and the Spirit of Capitalism*. New York: Columbia University Press.

Crawford, Lucas Cassidy. 2008. "Transgender without Organs? Mobilizing a Geo-Affective Theory of Gender Modification." *WSQ* 36, no. 3: 127–43.

Crenshaw, Kimberlé. 1989. "Demarginalizing the Intersection of Race and Sex: A Black Feminist Critique of Antidiscrimination Doctrine, Feminist Theory, and Antiracist Politics." *University of Chicago Legal Forum* 140: 139–67.

Deleuze, Gilles, and Félix Guattari. 1987. *A Thousand Plateaus: Capitalism and Schizophrenia*. Minneapolis: University of Minnesota Press.

Enke, Anne. 2012. "Introduction: Transfeminist Perspectives." In *Transfeminist Perspectives in and beyond Transgender and Gender Studies*, edited by Anne Enke, 1–15. Philadelphia: Temple University Press.

Hancock, Ange-Marie. 2007. "When Multiplication Doesn't Equal Quick Addition: Examining Intersectionality as a Research Paradigm." *Perspectives on Politics* 5, no. 1: 63–79.

Hayward, Eva. 2010. "Spider Sex City." *Women and Performance: A Journal of Feminist Theory* 20, no. 3: 225–51.

Hayward, Eva, and Jami Weinstein. 2015. "Introduction: Tranimalities in the Age of Trans* Life." *TSQ* 2, no. 2: 195–208.

Juang, Richard M. 2006. "Transgendering the Politics of Recognition." In *Transgender Rights*, edited by Paisley Currah, Richard M. Juang, and Shannon Minter, 242–61. Minneapolis: University of Minnesota Press.

Lamble, Sarah. 2008. "Retelling Racialized Violence, Remaking White Innocence: The Politics of Interlocking Oppression in Transgender Day of Remembrance." *Sexuality Research and Social Policy* 5, no. 1: 24–42.

Massumi, Brian. 2002. *Parables for the Virtual: Movement, Affect, Sensation*. Post-contemporary Interventions. Durham, NC: Duke University Press.

Puar, Jasbir K. 2011. "'I Would Rather Be a Cyborg than a Goddess': Intersectionality, Assemblage, and Affective Politics." *Transversal—EIPCP Multilingual Webjournal*, January. eipcp.net /transversal/0811/puar/en.

Stryker, Susan. 2008. "Dungeon Intimacies: The Poetics of Transsexual Sadomasochism." *Parallax* 14, no. 1: 36–47.

Stryker, Susan, Paisley Currah, and Lisa Jean Moore. 2008. "Introduction: Trans-, Trans, or Transgender?" *WSQ* 36, no. 3: 11–22.

Walby, Sylvia, Jo Armstrong, and Sofia Strid. 2012. "Intersectionality: Multiple Inequalities in Social Theory." *Sociology* 46, no. 2: 224–40.

Broadening the Gendered *Polis*

Italian Feminist and Transsexual Movements, 1979–1982

STEFANIA VOLI

Abstract In the late 1970s to the early 1980s, the Italian transsexual movement began gaining visibility in the public sphere, also making use of the feminist political lexicon. This contamination emerged in the life stories of some trans pioneers, who consider feminism a fundamental element of their political and individual trajectory of subjectivation. In contrast, historiographical reconstructions of Italian feminist movements as well as feminists' accounts never mention the transsexual movement. During battles for the right to change one's gender, transsexuals were supported by only a few feminist members of Left parties. The article analyzes the reasons that prevented Italian feminist and transsexual movements from establishing an open alliance against the patriarchal system deeply rooted in the Italian society of the time.

Keywords 1970s–1980s Italian transsexual movement, Italian feminist movements, contemporary Italian history

This article aims to deepen our understanding of the relationship between feminist and transsexual movements in Italy during the 1970s and 1980s, which at a superficial level do not seem to share much common ground. The most useful concept for transversally connecting transsexuality and feminism is gender, by which we mean, to follow Joan Scott's (1986) definition, a primary field within which or by means of which power is articulated. Transsexual experience reveals this dimension of gender's fundamental potentiality: it makes visible the means by which gender internally expresses power relations within a category as well as across categories, while also pointing to the possibility of moving beyond this category and the binarism that constructs it. Central to this understanding, and to the discussions that can be developed from it, is the point Angela Davis raises in one of her recently published "difficult dialogues": "Now that we have begun to challenge the binary assumptions behind gender, we can [challenge] hierarchies of gender as well. Where, for example, does a transgender woman figure into the hierarchy?" (Davis 2012: 191). Davis's statement finds direct expression in concrete

TSQ: Transgender Studies Quarterly * Volume 3, Numbers 1–2 * May 2016   **235**
DOI 10.1215/23289252-3334439   © 2016 Duke University Press

historical experience if we look at the transsexual movement in relation to the history of feminism in the Italian context at the turn of the 1970s and 1980s: within the women's movement, the central question at the time was, in fact, the question of power, and within this question is the means of analyzing the (missed) relationship between feminism and the transsexual movement, particularly with transsexual women.[1]

Locating the Transsexual Movement in History

It is useful to begin with a brief discussion of the histories of feminist and transsexual movements in Italy between 1979 and 1982. Despite there being a significant amount of published biographical material about transsexual people (just to cite the most known: Cecconi 1976; Marcasciano 2002, 2006, 2007, 2015), a substantial collection of various kinds of primary-source documents regarding transsexual experience (albeit not yet effectively collected, organized, and analyzed as a whole),[2] and a few recent works of historical scholarship (Schettini 2011), the transsexual movement's history in contemporary Italy has yet to be comprehensively reconstructed. It is possible that the difficulty of historicizing Italian transsexual experience is due to historians' general resistance to approaching themes that reveal, beneath the surface of seemingly straightforward political history, intense and intimate intersections of sexuality and power that complicate the conventional separation of public and private spheres (Asquer 2012: 8).

Transsexuality began to gain public visibility in Italy in the 1950s and 1960s; though at first characterized as a marginal and private matter, by the end of the 1960s there emerged a nascent transgender community, and by the early 1970s, it became a subject of political and social concern (Marcasciano 2015; Arietti et al. 2010). Several events in the late 1960s and throughout the 1970s accelerated the process of making transsexuality a public issue around the Western world, the most famous of which was the 1969 Stonewall riots in New York. Stonewall was preceded, however, by a growing wave of radical protest against the oppression of GLBT people: in 1966 a group of transgender and transsexual women, gays, and prostitutes rebelled against their repeated harassment by police at Compton's Cafeteria in San Francisco (Stryker 2008: 58). In 1967, in Italy, Romano Lecconi became the first Italian citizen to publicly announce a decision to undergo sex-reassignment surgery (in Geneva, Switzerland) and was subsequently sentenced to confinement in a small town in southern Italy on the basis of being considered a morally and socially dangerous person.[3] In 1972, the Court of Lucca legally recognized "La Romanina," as she was popularly known, in her new gender as Romina Cecconi (Cecconi 1976).

In 1970, a group of transsexuals in Rome, tired of the abuses of law enforcement, protested by getting themselves arrested en masse. In the small northern city of San Remo in 1972, members of various European homosexual associations gathered publicly for the first time in Italy to disrupt the International Congress on Sexual Deviancy organized by the Italian Center for Sexology, which supported conversion therapy. Among the associations present was an important future ally in the battle for the rights of transgender people, the newly formed group known as FUORI! (in Italian, an acronym for Fronte Unitario Omosessuale Rivoluzionario Italiano, the United Italian Homosexual Revolutionary Front). And in 1977, the Turin publisher Einaudi released Mario Mieli's work, *Elementi di critica omosessuale* (in 1980 translated into English: *Homosexuality and Liberation: Elements of a Gay Critique*), still a touchstone of GLBTQ political culture in Italy today.

As even this short time line shows, it is not possible to discuss the Italian transsexual movement without discussing the broader political, social, and cultural environment that gave rise to other protest movements of the 1960s and 1970s. The social actors who took part in these movements experienced firsthand the exhilaration of self-discovery, and they gained the ability to claim rights and desires for themselves as well as for their groups. They rejected all forms of institutional authority, freed themselves from repressive customary forms of sexual behavior, challenged the traditional division of gender roles, and grasped the possibility of transforming individual needs through collective action (Lumley 1990; Della Porta 1996).

The transsexual movement in the late 1970s was the last of this wave of social and political movements to emerge in Italy. In 1979, in a public swimming pool in Milan, a group of transsexuals—not recognized as such by the state, and recognized even less as women—staged a protest by wearing only men's swim trunks, thereby exposing their bare breasts. Their aim was to dramatize the contradictory nature of their situation while at the same time asserting ownership over their own bodies and gender expression (Marcasciano 2006: 42). This simple action ignited a clamorous protest and provoked the curiosity of the national media. It both catapulted transsexual issues into public conversation and inspired a large number of transsexuals to publicly fight for their rights. From that moment, transsexual activist groups began to blossom in many Italian cities, protesting against the discrimination that they endured and advocating for a law to allow them to change their sex and name in accordance with their chosen gender identity.

That same year, as part of the wave of new mobilization, the Italian Transsexual Movement (Movimento Italiano Transessuale [MIT]) was born (and formally founded in 1981).[4] In February 1980, Franco De Cataldo, a Radical Party member of Parliament, sponsored a bill allowing transsexual women to legally change their names, which was supported by FUORI! as well as the Italian

Communist Party (PCI). On October 1980, MIT held its first national demonstration in Rome to urge immediate discussion of the bill. In the same year, a group of transsexuals representing MIT met in Strasbourg with other radicals to proclaim "liberté, egalite, transexualitè" (*La Nazione* 1980).

In January 1981, the First National Transsexual Congress took place in Milan, involving all the major transsexual groups from Milan, Florence, Turin, Bologna, Genoa, and Rome, with the intent of bringing "transsexuals, lesbians, homosexuals, and heterosexuals all together in a free and non-violent society" (MIT 1981). The stated objectives of the congress included freeing transsexuality from the exclusive purview of the mass media and the medical establishment and promoting greater awareness of transsexual perspectives among the public in order to facilitate broader rights for trans people. Between March and November of 1981, at least four more national demonstrations were convened to seek approval for De Cataldo's law. One of the transsexual protest slogans reported by the leading conservative newspaper *La Stampa* (*The Press*) was "*Vogliamo essere definite donne!*" (We want to be defined as women!; *La Stampa* 1981b). Police responded with force to the last of these demonstrations in front of the senate, injuring three protestors and taking many others into custody (*La Stampa* 1981a).

The Second National Congress of the Italian Transsexual Movement took place in Milan in January 1982, billed as an opportunity to reflect on the struggles of the past three years but also as a chance to envision the movement's future prospects in light of the political realities of the times. Finally, on April 14, 1982, after two years of protests and six months of parliamentary debate, the Italian parliament approved Law 164: Rules Concerning the Rectification of Sex-Attribution. The law made it possible for transsexuals to proceed with the surgical adjustment of sex characteristics and change of registered name. Considered flawed by many stakeholders, who saw it as a compromise between various political forces, the law still represented the success of a major civil rights battle, as well as a turning point in the history of law and morals of our country (Arietti et al. 2010): as a pioneering legal step, it was only the second such law in Western Europe, after Germany (1980). The law did in fact seem to recognize the possibility of a variation—until then considered no more than an error of nature—in the rigid binary social classification of the sexes.[5]

"Donna io, donna tu, femminista vieni giù!"

For feminist groups, the years 1979–82 similarly mark a period of profound transformation. After a period of great mobilization and public visibility, at the end of the 1970s Italian feminist movements were characterized by small groups and collectives that, though small, nevertheless succeeded in setting in motion far-reaching and widespread changes that affected political practices at both the individual and collective levels, leading to the creation of innumerable autonomous feminist centers, libraries, bookstores, cafés, and women's shelters (Calabrò and Grasso 2004). The 1980s ushered in a new phase of Italian feminist history (also known as "*femminismo diffuso*," that is, widespread feminism), during which differences between women became the main issue and, not uncommonly, the source of many conflicts.

Of particular importance at the outset of the new decade was the so-called difference/differences debate over whether women's oppression should best be understood as the consequence of a totalizing binary hierarchy within which women are subjugated by patriarchy, or whether women's oppression needed to be understood instead within a matrix of other oppressions, as one intersecting vector of oppression among many others (Guerra 2008). This debate, already present in many internal disputes within Italian feminist groups as well as in tensions between Italian feminist movements and other transversally related movements, was amplified and intensified by significant theoretical and political tensions—primarily coming from the United States, between white and black feminists, between liberal Western feminists and transnational feminists, and between lesbians and heterosexual women—that radically challenged the capacity of the category "woman" to represent *all* women, free from internal hierarchies of power (Miletti and Passerini 2007). Given this, I would argue that the intersection of feminist movements with the transsexual movement reveals two experiences that have simultaneously existed in Italy but rarely converged.

For example, on the occasion of the First National Congress of the Italian Transsexual Movement, a journalist covering the event noted friction, "subterranean but real," between transsexuals and feminists, exemplified by an anonymous remark, "You transsexuals exalt the worst aspect of women as objects, of the woman as a doll subjected to male dictatorship" (*Nuova scienza* 1981). In other words, transsexuals were accused of reviving a model of femininity against which feminists had fought—a theoretical position that generated a common narrative widespread among many radical feminisms of this period, both within and outside Italy. The slogan chanted by transsexual women at the March 1981 protest, reported in another newspaper, *Paese sera*, however, offers perhaps the best example of the untapped potential relationship between feminist and transsexual movements: "Donna io, donna tu, femminista vieni giù!" (roughly, I'm a woman; you're a woman—feminists, come and join us!). It was "an invitation," as the journalist observed, "to join efforts in a battle that, for those who have been women and those who have become women, has many common denominators" (*Paese sera* 1981).

During the Second Congress of the Italian Transsexual Movement, there were numerous references to the battlegrounds of the feminist movements: divorce, abortion, self-determination, and sexual liberation. Furthermore, Enzo Francone of FUORI! described the transsexual movement as "the tip of the struggle for sexual liberation," since, in his opinion, "trans women stir the biggest, most deeply hidden, most uncomfortable taboos" (Francone 1982). Party politicians speaking at the congress, including the communist senator Giglia Tedesco Tatò (1982) and the radical deputy of the chamber Adele Faccio (1982), extensively dwelt on the importance of breaking with widespread sexual taboos in order to advance transsexuals' rights. Tatò stressed the potential of the feminist slogan "Woman is beautiful" to include transsexuals and asserted that transsexuals were engaged in a "battle for all women" because "the battle for the emancipation and liberation of women passes through the transsexual battle" (Tatò). Faccio invited the organizers to "remember that we have to rely on women; they are the ones who best recognize difference because they have had to live differently as women" (Faccio 1982). Luciano Violante of the Italian Communist Party told transsexuals, "Yours is a civil right to sexual identity. This battle is not only for you but for everyone; it's like the battle of the women's movement, which was not only for women, but served to correct the total balance of power" (Violante 1982).

Life stories can bring to light connections between the transsexual and feminist movements that are just barely made visible by public pronouncements. One early transsexual activist has noted that she felt "first—first of all—feminist," recalling that she "dressed as a feminist during the years of protest" and adding, "If I had not first been feminist, I would never be as I am" (Marcasciano 2002: 38). Similarly, Italian trans activism pioneer Porpora Marcasciano (from 2010 also president of MIT) has stated, "I've always enjoyed taking part in women's issues, but I've always tip-toed in among the feminists, out of respect, out of modesty, but also out of fear! Many trans people are seeking a passport, a tourist visa, or a residence permit for feminist territory . . . because the transsexual or transgender territory lies alongside, very close to it" (Marcasciano 2006: 38).

What Kind of Difference? Nodes for Future Research

The renowned Italian feminist historian Anna Rossi-Doria, in her elucidation of the internal conflicts within feminism, has observed, "Perhaps when our differences turned out to be too harsh, we chose, more or less consciously, the ancient weapon of silence" (Rossi-Doria 2007: 257). If this silence figures prominently in the effort to build a relationship between feminist and transsexual movements now, the current emptiness of that relationship attests to the presence of an additional nexus of power, not yet disentangled nor even adequately analyzed in Italian feminisms. Generally speaking, feminist "difference theory" (Diotima 1987) has played an important role in the creation of an obfuscating hegemony that operates against all women and feminists perceived as other, a "hegemony that shifted the reality of bodies and experience onto the level of the symbolic order, taking a practice that had proved able to withstand the contradictions, paradoxes and dark confusion of the sexes and putting it aside to the point of disappearance" (Melandri 2000: 7).

For the preeminent French feminist philosopher of difference, Luce Irigaray, women lack a proper concept of themselves and the world, which can be remedied only by acquiring a cognitive tool based on the female body, a place as much physical as it is symbolic (Irigaray 1984). The recognition of difference, based on the morphology of the female body as an absolute ontological value, has meant that any divergence from phallocentrism unable (or unwilling) to fall within this territory has paid the price of a loss of intelligibility (Butler 1990). The ensuing normativity of sexual and gender identity developed not only along the axis of male-female relationships but also—and perhaps especially—within womanhood, in which relations of power legitimized that which was similar to internal norms and penalized that which appeared as other. In other words, feminist difference theory has taken those who have not wanted to (or could not) conform to the binary division of sexes and bodies and confined them to the margins of citizenship, in the sense of citizenship as a politically legitimated mutual recognition of variously embodied experiences. In the specific case of the relationship between feminist movements and trans movements, the recognition of difference has meant that individuals historically located on the margins of public space as women have taken on a specific role: they have transformed themselves into agents of surveillance who act to prevent any identities that transgress the dominant norms from crossing this border, and they reject—physically and by force if necessary—the individuals who embody such identities (Marcasciano 2007: 169).

Ideally, through research into and experimentation with many possible gender identities, the concept of gender as a category of analysis would unsettle the attraction biology had for many feminists. Although foundational work on gender theory had already been undertaken by Gayle Rubin in the 1970s (Rubin 1975), the concept of gender was not widely disseminated in Italian feminism until the second half of the 1980s, primarily through the work of Joan Scott (1986), who helped launch a broader discussion of the relationship between sex and gender and the utility of gender as an analytical category. We thus arrive at the 1990s, when Judith Butler's *Gender Trouble: Feminism and the Subversion of Identity* (1990) paved the way for gender theory to take a radically antinormative direction, followed by queer and transgender studies. Within this new theoretical landscape, it was finally possible to recognize the ability of the transgender issue to challenge the universal sufficiency of the category "woman," thereby promoting new analyses, new strategies, and new practices for combatting every kind of gender discrimination. The words and deeds of trans women displayed a desire to build other differences, not as imitation or caricature of the feminine but as an embodied experience of different otherness that, among other things, could have broken (and still can break) new ground for feminist practices.

This potential contribution is nowhere more critical than in the area of embodied citizenship: women have been excluded from full citizenship on the basis of their supposed lacks and shortcomings (physical, biological, and sexual), while for transsexual individuals exclusion is justified by their excess (physically, and of life experiences); in both cases, however, the price was (and is) invisibility and lack of recognition or legitimacy in the public sphere and, thus, in History itself. Movements of women and transsexuals alike have focused on sharing, reappropriating, and politicizing their experiences of embodiment and sexuality (not to mention health and medicalization). Both have made of the body a field of research for building theories, practices, and claims: not being able to build links between these two experiences represents a missed opportunity to reflect on embodied and gendered citizenship in a new way.

For example, in many ways, the transgender political movement's focus on its relation with the "medical establishment" is more similar to the feminist struggle for reproductive freedom than it is to gay liberation. Transgender people, like women who want to terminate a pregnancy or gain access to contraception, demand the right to free, legal, competent, and respectful medical services for a nonpathological need that is nonetheless often highly socially stigmatized, a need that is intensely intimate and may be an emotionally painful path toward liberation and the awareness of how to live one's own body freely (Stryker 2008: 87).

In conclusion, I would argue that, no less than feminism, transsexual experience actually offers an opportunity to expand the histories and theories of law, (bio)power, bodies, sexuality, citizenship, self-determination and gender. In the words of the trans activist and scholar Stephen Whittle, "A system of values where gender loses some of its power of oppression, in which distinct and different voices are not only heard, but listened to, is hence a better system of values. This is what we, who are trans, can get from such a system, but also—and perhaps more importantly—something that we can give back" (Whittle 2006: 202).

Stefania Voli has a Phd in gender identities in modern and contemporary history. Since 2012, she has been working on the relationship between transgender bodies and citizenship in contemporary Italian society as a PhD candidate in sociology and social research at the University of Milan-Bicocca, Italy. She is an MIT (Transgender Identity Movement) activist and volunteer coworker.

Acknowledgments

This article was originally published in Italian as Stefania Voli, "Allargare la polis dei generi. Movimenti femministi e movimento transessuale tra anni Settanta e Ottanta in Italia: silenzi, azioni e omissioni. Una questione storiografica da aprire," in *Genere e storia: percorsi*, edited by Cesarina Casanova and Lagioia Vincenzo (Bologna: Bononia University Press), 257–76.

Notes

1.   During the campaign for Law 164/1982, transsexual women were the only visible protagonists on the public stage. Even in trans women's public speeches, the issue of sex (and name) changes were always approached in feminine terms. The experience of FtM trans people, less recognizable (in aesthetic and political terms) due to FtMs' ease of "passing" as men, has created different experiences of discrimination, creating a different political path that was not embodied in more obvious political actors until the 1990s (Stryker 2008: 71).

2.   I refer in particular to the Documentation Center of MIT (Transsexual Identity Movement) in Bologna.

3.   In Italy, before the approval of Law 164/1982, it was illegal to change one's sex. Transvestitism was governed by the Criminal Code as illicit concealment (Art. 85); alternatively, trans people were considered "habitual offenders" (Art. 1) and, if judged "potentially dangerous to public safety or the national order" (1931 Fascist Public Safety Laws, Royal Decree no. 733), the law could be enforced to the extent of confinement or special surveillance. Subsequently (pursuant to Law 1423/1956 "Preventive Measures against Those Threatening Security and Public Morals"), transsexuals were likely to be subjected to warnings, preventive measures, confinement, and the confiscation of their identity documents and driving licenses.

4.   Due to disagreements with the former association MIT (Italian Transsexual Movement) established in 1979, MIT (Transsexual Identity Movement) was born in 1988, in Bologna, and is still the main trans association in Italy.

5.   In fact, to this day, Law 164/1982 remains the only law concerning GLBTIQ rights in Italy. Several initiatives are currently under way to promote changes in Law 164, in particular, to make it possible to change personal data without the requirement of surgery to remove sexual characteristics and thus sterilization (surgery is not specifically imposed by the law, but rather judges have interpreted the law thus far to require it). Activists are promoting the use of Italian court rulings to attain sex and name changes even without surgery. In line with these requests, the most important change has occurred very recently: with Judgment no. 221 (dated November 5, 2015) the Constitutional Court ruled that law 164/1982 does not require any surgery as a prerequisite for rectification registry. This decision puts an end to obligatory surgery as a requirement for gender reassignment, as set forth by the majority of Italian courts since 1982. See also MIT's campaign, "Another Gender Is Possible" (MIT 2014) and details on Bill no. 405, "Rules on the Modification of the Attribution of Sex," which is awaiting discussion in the Italian senate.

References

Arietti, Laurella, et al. 2010. *Elementi di critica trans (Elements for a Trans Critique)*. Rome: Manifestolibri.

Asquer, Enrica. 2012. Introduction to "Culture della sessualità: Identità, esperienze, contesti" ("Cultures of Sexuality: Identities, Experiences, Backgrounds"), edited by Enrica Asquer, special issue, *Genesis* 11, nos. 1–2: 7–17.

Butler, Judith 1990. *Gender Trouble: Feminism and the Subversion of Identity.* New York: Routledge.

Calabrò, Anna Rita, and Laura Grasso. 2004. *Dal movimento femminista al femminismo diffuso: Storie e percorsi a Milano dagli anni '60 agli anni '80 (From Feminist Movement to Widespread Feminism: Histories and Paths in Milan, from the 1960s to 1980s).* Milan: Franco Angeli.

Cecconi, Romina. 1976. *Io, la "Romanina": Perché sono diventato donna ("Romanina" It's Me: Why I Became a Woman).* Florence: Vallecchi.

Davis, Angela. 2012. *The Meaning of Freedom: And Other Difficult Dialogues.* San Francisco: City Lights Open Media.

Della Porta, Donatella. 1996. *Movimenti collettivi e sistema politico in Italia 1960–1995 (Collective Movements and Political System in Italy 1960–1995).* Rome: Laterza.

Diotima. 1987. *Il pensiero della differenza sessuale (Sexual Difference Theory).* Milan: La Tartaruga.

Faccio, Adele. 1982. Speech presented at the Second MIT National Congress, Milan, January. www .radioradicale.it/scheda/2706/2719-ii-congresso-nazionale-del-movimento-italiano -transessuali.

Francone, Enzo. 1982. Speech presented at the Second MIT National Congress, Milan, January. www.radioradicale.it/scheda/2706/2719-ii-congresso-nazionale-del-movimento-italiano -transessuali.

Guerra, Elda. 2008. *Storia e cultura politica delle donne (Women's History and Political Culture).* Bologna: Archetipolibri.

Irigaray, Luce. 1984. *Éthique de la différence sexuelle (Ethics of Sexual Difference).* Paris: Éditions de Minuit.

Lumley, Robert. 1990. *States of Emergency: Cultures of Revolt in Italy, 1968–78.* London: Verso.

Marcasciano, Porpora. 2002. *Tra le rose e le viole: La storia e le storie di travestiti e transessuali (Transvestites and Transsexuals' History and Stories).* Rome: Manifestolibri.

———. 2006. "Trans, donne e femministe: Coscienze divergenti e/o sincroniche" ("Trans, Women, and Feminists: Divergent and/or Synchronic Forms of Consciousness"). In *Altri femminismi: Corpi culture lavoro (Other Feminisms: Bodies, Cultures, Work),* edited by Teresa Bertilotti et al., 37–54. Rome: Manifestolibri.

———. 2007. *Antologaia: Sesso genere e cultura degli anni '70 (Anthologay: Sex, Gender and Culture in the 1970s).* Milan: Il dito e la Luna.

———. 2015. *Antologaia: Vivere sognando e non sognando di vivere. I miei anni Settanta (Anthologay: To Live Dreaming and Not Dreaming of Living).* Milan: Edizioni Alegre.

Melandri, Lea. 2000. *Una visceralità indicibile: La pratica dell'inconscio nel movimento delle donne degli anni Settanta (Unspeakable Viscerality: "Unconscious Practice" in the Women's Movement in the 1970s).* Milan: Franco Angeli.

Mieli, Mario. 1977. *Elementi di critica omosessuale (Homosexuality and Liberation: Elements of a Gay Critique).* Milan: Feltrinelli. 1980: London: Gay Men's Press.

Miletti, Nerina, and Passerini, Luisa, eds. 2007. *Fuori della norma: Storie lesbiche nell'Italia della prima metà del Novecento (Outside the Norm: Lesbian Stories in the Early Italian 20th Century).* Turin: Rosenberg and Sellier.

MIT (Movimento Italiano Transessuale). 1981. "First National Congress of MIT, Milan 24–25 January. Transsexuals, lesbians, gays, heterosexuals, all together for a libertarian and non-violent society" (original leaflet preserved at the MIT Documentation Center, Bologna).

————. 2014. "Un altro genere è possibile" ("Another Gender Is Possible"). Social media campaign. www.facebook.com/Un-Altro-Genere-%C3%A8-Possibile-705757922817025/ (accessed November 11, 2015).

La Nazione (The Nation). 1980. November 20.

Nuova scienza (New Science). 1981. "The Transsexual." March 3.

Paese sera. 1981. "Transsexuals Are Calling for a Recognition Law." March 11.

Rossi-Doria, Anna. 2007. *Dare forma al silenzio: Scritti di storia politica delle donne (Shaping Silence: Writings in Women's Political History)*. Rome: Viella.

Rubin, Gayle. 1975. "The Traffic in Women: Notes on the 'Political Economy' of Sex." In *Toward an Anthropology of Women*, edited by Rayna Reiter. New York: Monthly Review Press.

Schettini, Laura. 2011. *Il gioco delle parti: Travestimenti e paure sociali tra Otto e Novecento.* Florence: Le Monnier.

Scott, Joan W. 1986. "Gender: A Useful Category of Historical Analysis." *American Historical Review* 91, no. 5: 1053–75.

La Stampa (The Press). 1981a. "Police Rush Transsexuals in Front of the Senate." November 12.

————. 1981b. "Sit-In of Transsexuals in Rome: 'We Want to Be Defined as Women.'" March 11.

Stryker, Susan. 2008. *Transgender History*. Berkeley, CA: Seal.

Tatò Tedesco, Giglia. 1982 Speech presented at the Second MIT National Congress, Milan, January. www.radioradicale.it/scheda/2706/2719-ii-congresso-nazionale-del-movimento-italiano -transessuali.

"Transsexual: Law 164/1982 Approved." Press conference sound recording. www.radioradicale.it /scheda/3021/3034-transessuali-approvata-la-legge-legge-n-1641982.

Violante, Luciano. 1982. Speech presented at the Second MIT National Congress, Milan, January. www.radioradicale.it/scheda/2706/2719-ii-congresso-nazionale-del-movimento-italiano -transessuali.

Whittle, Stephen. 2006. "Where Did We Go Wrong? Feminism and Trans Theory: Two Teams on the Same Side?" In *The Transgender Studies Reader*, edited by Susan Stryker and Stephen Whittle, 194–202. New York: Routledge.

The Woman Question

LORI WATSON

Abstract The author was inspired to write this article in light of the ongoing and recent claims by some radical feminists that trans women are not women. This is much more than a debate among differing theoretical positions. Women have been threatened, both trans* and cis women. The vitriol on both sides is alarming and undermining of the feminism we all share. Rather than write an academic, philosophical treatise on the meaning of "woman," the author wrote this from her first-person experience, as someone who was "born female" and identifies as a woman but is often socially read as trans* (a trans man). The author aims to articulate a radical feminist understanding of women that shows trans women are women in concrete, personal terms.
Keywords feminism, woman, trans*, hierarchy

The dispute between some self-identified feminists and trans persons, trans women especially, and trans-supporting feminists has erupted into a full-scale ideological war. Once at the level of conflict, officially undeclared, we have moved into the territory of "you are either with us or against us," with real threats against real people—from both sides.[1] Trans women clearly feel that their existence—and this is not a metaphor—is at stake.[2] Among those feminists who publicly defend exclusion of trans women from the category "woman," some feel that women's ability for self-definition is threatened by trans women's claim to "womanhood."[3] All of us invested in feminism, and as such in women, have a stake in this conflagration. With that in mind, I offer the following in the style of an open letter to those who do not think trans women are women.

Let me start by stating up front, I believe trans women are women.[4] I reject a feminism that excludes trans women. There were times in my past when I could not, or would not, have written those two sentences. One might say I have evolved on this issue. I am thankful for that. In what follows, I want to share a collection of thoughts and experiences that led me here, hoping that I might convince some to rethink their position. This is not a systematic argument addressing every objection that could be made or has been made on the subject.

TSQ: Transgender Studies Quarterly * Volume 3, Numbers 1–2 * May 2016
DOI 10.1215/23289252-3334451   © 2016 Duke University Press

My evolution starts from two facts. First, I know and care about some trans women (and trans men, too). I listened to them. Their experiences, their reality, their sometimes sense of despair and anger, their humanity is foundational for me. They own their experience, their lives; their right to live in the world is unquestionable. Starting from a position of trying to understand someone else's reality, the phenomenology of their existence, is something we should all do, whether concerning trans women or anyone else. Individual and collective empathy is too often untapped. Second, more often than not, I am identified by others, who do not know me, as a man; I would conjecture that in everyday interactions with strangers, I am taken to be a man over 90 percent of the time. This identification started happening regularly about sixteen years ago when I cut my hair very short. (I had always dressed in "men's clothing" since my teenage years. Add to this that I am nearly six feet tall and have broad shoulders and a "healthy" frame. This is the body I was given.) In fact, others so routinely identify me as a man that I am often caught off guard and surprised if someone correctly identifies me as a woman. These experiences have changed me; they are, now, a defining feature of my life. Perhaps having experienced my gender/sex so uniformly and routinely confused has allowed me to "see" things, to understand the experience of living in a world in which your body is interpreted one way and your authentic self entirely rejects that other imposed identification. I am not a man. I do not identify as a man. I don't want to be a man, trans or otherwise.[5] I am a woman, but the overwhelming majority of humankind, men and women alike, does not yet recognize my womanhood as a way of being one.

Following up that thought, living in the world as it is, I have to fight for recognition as a woman on a daily basis. My choices are to correct people when they call me "sir" or assume I am a man, or let it go, which often means functioning socially as a man. Let me paint a brief picture of what this looks like. Doing something as basic as going to the bathroom, anywhere that is public, is a nightmare. Few places have "unisex" bathrooms. So here are my choices: go into the women's bathroom and face public shouting, alarm, ridicule, and confrontation. Or go into the men's bathroom, look down at the floor, walk quickly into a stall, and hope no one pays any attention to me but face the serious fear that they might. Mostly, I choose the men's. However, at work I can't make that choice. I can't imagine running into my male colleagues, who know I am a woman, in there. So it's the women's. But, not everyone in the bathroom at a given time knows me or knows that I work there or knows that I am a woman. I have to time my bathroom breaks for when I think no one is in there or likely to be in there. I haven't always succeeded.

One day, while using the women's restroom, on the same hallway as my office, the custodian confronted me. She was entering the bathroom to clean it. I was washing my hands. She opened the door and held it open, three other women were attempting to enter the bathroom at the same time. She said, "WHAT are YOU DOING?" I replied, "Washing my hands?" She said, "No, WHAT are YOU DOING in HERE?" I was frozen. By now, several of my colleagues and unknown students were standing in the hallway observing the commotion, and all this was happening within earshot of the department office. The door to the bathroom was still being held open. She rephrased the question: "WHAT ARE YOU DOING IN THE WOMEN'S BATHROOM!?" I said, "I am a woman." She just stared at me with complete confusion. I walked out. There was laughter. I didn't look back to see who or how many were laughing. Under the circumstances, I can understand why this woman was alarmed and confused. She sincerely believed I was a man in the woman's bathroom. Although, it sure would be nice if she and others like her would grant that people like me know which bathroom we are in and have a good reason for being in there. My saying the words "I am a woman" never occurred to her, and she could barely process them in the moment. Now, imagine confronting this EVERY. SINGLE. DAY. in dozens and dozens of ways and interactions (noting that many of you reading this won't have to "imagine" it at all). Imagine standing over the coffin of your dead grandfather's body, while the funeral director turns to your father and says, "This must be your son, I have heard so much about," and all your father can say in response is a quiet "no, this is my daughter." Imagine going to the emergency room for what you believe to be an ovarian cyst, and the physicians and nurses are so baffled they ask you your name and repeatedly check your chart for your sex identification and then ask to see your driver's license, something you've already given at check-in, to triple confirm, one presumes, that you aren't delusional. I could go on. I have hundreds of such stories. All this because your body is socially interpreted as masculine, yet you identify as a woman. These are my stories, and I was born female and assigned to the female sex, and I identify as a woman.

I didn't make this world and its social meanings. My power to transform them as an individual is negligible, if it exists at all. Yet, I have to live in this world. I am trying to live a gender—to the extent that doing so is required for being socially intelligible—and obviously have a body, and these two things are regarded as incongruent from the dominant point of view. In this way, I share a social space with trans persons. I assume my feminist sisters would reject the suggestion that I should be forced to transition my sex or identity to conform to a world that doesn't, on the whole, recognize my existence as a woman (though few, there are some safe spaces). Yet, in refusing to acknowledge trans women as women, this is, in effect, what such feminists are asking of trans women. What follows from the refusal of recognition may not be precisely clear as to what such feminists think trans women should do or how they should live. But insofar as claims that position trans women as "men impersonating women" are uttered, and they are, it seems to me they are saying: live your life as a socially recognized man, make your body and gender conform, insofar as you "can't" change your body (essentialism?), change your gender or gender presentation. Or maybe they think, "Go ahead and be as 'feminine' as you like, but do it with a male-identified body, and don't claim to be a woman."

Setting aside the presumptuousness of telling someone else how to live in their body, this seems to me to situate trans women as uniquely bearing the responsibility of confronting the false sex dualism and binary gender hierarchy we all live in. Perhaps underlying the refusal to recognize trans women as women is the belief that true liberation from sex-role oppression and gender hierarchy requires that we create a world in which sex roles disappear, in which gender is nonexistent or so completely fluid as to effectively be a noncategory.[6] Well, we don't live in that world, and are unlikely to. Why should trans women, as individuals, bear a special burden in getting us closer to it? Most women (including radical feminist women) live a gender that is socially recognized as in the category "woman"; that is, they conform to certain gender stereotypes of femininity. They are living and existing, with a gender and sex, in the world as it is now, not as it might be in "the ideal world." By keeping their sex and gender, body and identity and self-presentation, coincident, don't they further conventional sex-role notions that gender is biologically natural? Doesn't this similarly position them in their own critique as they position trans women? The criticism of trans women as failing to act in ways that are consistent with an ideal of liberation from sex and gender is a little like criticizing any of us for making a decent living under capitalism, or investing our retirement funds in the stock market, if the aim of liberation is the destruction of capitalism as a social, political, and economic system. Even Karl Marx had to eat in the here and now.

The central claim many offer for excluding trans women from the category "women" is that trans women were not socialized to womanhood since birth and so lack the necessary lived experience, material reality, on which to base a claim to womanness.[7] I fully acknowledge that there is a material reality to being a woman in this world. But I see two problems with this position. First, in offering this standard of womanhood, I think many are saying, in effect, "Trans women are not women *like me*." But the material reality of women is not uniform. Intersectional analyses of gender teach that women's experience of womanhood is importantly varied across other categories, especially across other hierarchies—including race, class, religion, sexuality, geopolitical location, able bodiedness, and age, to name a few. If we explore the points of overlap and departure among all these categories of women, we do find commonality, for example, as subordinated on the basis of sex, as subject to sexual harassment, sexual violence, and gender-based violence because of one's sex. However, women's vulnerability to such subordination is not identical; it varies along with other inequalities.

Second, and relatedly, asking how trans women stand solely in relation to women, typically seen as such, asks the wrong question. The crucial question is: How do trans women stand in relation to men, to the forms of male power that function to subordinate women on the basis of sex? Are trans women subordinated on the basis of their sex? Are they subordinated on the basis of their place in the sex/gender hierarchy?[8] That is the central question, not how or who they were born as. Trans women are routinely denied employment on the basis of their sex. Denied health care on the basis of their sex. Forced into prostitution for survival on the basis of their sex. Denied access to housing on the basis of their sex. Violently attacked, and all too frequently murdered, on the basis of their sex. Much of this occurs because they are not seen to fit adequately the sex-role stereotypes of either femininity or masculinity. If subordination on the basis of one's sex is central to the social and political meaning of "woman," and it is, then what can possibly be the response to denying that trans women are precisely in this position? That they were born with a penis? I thought we were past biological essentialism, at least since Simone de Beauvoir.

This is only half the story, though. Not only must women have been born women (assigned to the category "female" at birth), they must also presently identify as women, according to some versions of the claim that trans women are not women. Trans women are missing the first necessary condition, it is said. I suppose this means that trans men are men, since they lack the second necessary condition. However, Sheila Jeffreys refuses to recognize trans men as men, routinely referring to them as "women" and "female-bodied persons" (2014: 101–22). There is an essentialism here. Putting this together, at least one frequently defended version of the standard for "woman" is "original" identification by others, as such that begins a process of socialization to femininity—as dominantly practiced and enforced—plus present subjective identification as such. I take it that this is what the phrase "woman born woman" expresses. This view further suggests that such women are uniquely positioned to advocate for the political emancipation of women as a class. If so, what should we make of all the women-born-women that don't? Do those who embrace male dominance fail to interrogate it, reenact its imperatives, and relish in the kinds of power doing so provides them? This question is especially acute when contrasted with a group of persons to have actively, and at enormous personal costs, rejected maleness, masculinity, and everything it represents. They do not want to be men in this world. They refuse. If I am choosing who "my people" are, the choice seems obvious.

Now to the topic of masculine/male privilege: some argue that insofar as trans women grew up male identified, they have a social history that includes being conferred male privilege, and this experience and the psychology constructed upon it cannot be undone. This implies either they carry the legacy of having been conferred male privilege and this is sufficient to exclude them from the category "woman" or, having once been socialized to privilege, they can never develop the psyche of a "woman"—as if there were one such thing. These are empirical claims; one might rightly demand some evidence here. I haven't seen any, other than the claims on blogs that individual trans women have acted rudely or entitled in some way that is interpreted as being a product of male privilege.[9] As such, all we may be dealing with here is a hasty generalization possibly premised upon confirmation biases. But no doubt plenty of people can be jerks, and being trans* doesn't immunize a person from any of the behaviors that we all as humans display at one time or another. Though, in any individual case of criticizing someone for being an ass, especially marginalized persons who are routinely dismissed as mentally ill, deviant, devious, deluded, and so on, a heavy dose of caution is in order.

The deeper question here is the plausibility of claiming once male privileged always male privileged. As with the category "woman," the category "man" is varied across all kinds of differences and hierarchies. And so, generalizations often work to dismiss, exclude, or erase the experiences of some. However, socialization to masculinity is itself about socially demonstrating one's ability to dominate—women and those men "lower" in the hierarchy. It's quite plausible to think that many trans women's experiences of socialization to social masculinity was an uncomfortable and unhappy experience—an experience they reject and rejected. Even more, many trans women are not identifiable as trans, and haven't been for some time. (In point of fact, a trans woman friend of mine has escorted me to the women's bathroom, at my request, because I knew no one would question her right to be there, and in that way she served to confirm that I had a right to be there. Another woman walking with you into a women's bathroom is one way to avoid a confrontation.) In this respect, they experience male privilege like the rest of us do, as an exertion of power over us. If trans women are socially identified as trans, privilege preceded by any adjective is not a word that comes to mind in describing their experience. That one could claim that trans women have male privilege in any traditional sense belies any serious knowledge of what trans women's lives are actually like. Even more curious is the seemingly broader claim underlying the position here: the denial that those socialized to masculinity could ever give up or lose male privilege. Isn't eliminating male privilege one of the goals of radical feminism?

A final thought: feminism, as I understand it, is the theory and practice of dismantling male power, gender hierarchy, and women's subordinate position as structurally and institutionally manifest. This requires a women's movement, a political movement. This we all know. This movement can't occur while marginalizing, refusing to recognize, and denying the existence of our trans sisters. Recognizing our differences as women has always been at the center of feminism done right. Not all women are women like me or like you, and restricting the category of "woman" in this way keeps us all from further building the movement we so desperately need.

Lori Watson is associate professor of philosophy at the University of San Diego. She works on feminism, political philosophy, philosophy of law, and the intersection of all three. She has published on pornography, prostitution, feminist theory, and political liberalism. She is presently working on a monograph, with Dr. Christie Hartley, called *Feminist Political Liberalism*.

Acknowledgments
Thanks to Catharine MacKinnon, John Stoltenberg, Rachel McKinnon, and Christie Hartley for reading various drafts of this article.

Notes

1. A lot of this discourse has occurred on blogs and social media. There are clear, documented cases of threats to some feminists of violence, including rape, by alleged trans women (I say "alleged" because I can't know for sure the identity of the persons making the threats). There are also cases of "outing" trans women by some feminists, including revealing their addresses, places of employment, and other information, as well as public ridiculing of their bodies. An especially cruel example is a prominent antitrans feminist holding a paper shaped like a human body that reads "sorry about your dick," with an arrow pointing to the "genital" area of the paper doll.

2. The attempted suicide rate and suicide rate among trans persons and gender-non-conforming persons is disproportionately high, approaching 50 percent for some subgroups within these categories (younger persons, homeless persons, and unemployed persons being especially vulnerable). See Haas, Rodgers, and Herman 2014.

3. The term *TERF* (trans exclusionary radical feminists) is often used to describe these feminists. I avoid this term because I want to address those who disagree with me on terms that will allow for open and honest listening, and labeling, as such, often shuts down those pathways.

4. This does not mean I endorse any view that situates trans* persons as biologically determined. One prominent biological explanation of trans women is that they have "female brains" but male-identified bodies. The science simply does not support this claim. Moreover, it relies on a gender essentialism that is deeply problematic and false. It's perfectly consistent to think that sex/gender is socially constructed and that trans women are women. For discussion of the brain science, see Fine 2010 and Jordan-Young 2010.

5. Nothing in what follows aims to speak for trans* persons. I have never had the feeling that "I am a man" in any sense. Hence, my experience differs from trans* persons' experiences in crucial ways.

6. Andrea Dworkin imagines such an ideal in her early work *Woman Hating* (1974). However, and this is critical, she says the following regarding "transsexual women": Under

conditions in which the male-female binary is presumed to be natural and unalterable, "every transsexual is in a state of primary emergency as a transsexual. . . . Every transsexual has the right to survival on his/her own terms. That means every transsexual is entitled to a sex-change operation, and it should be provided by the community as one of its functions. . . . By changing our premises about men and women, role-playing, and polarity, the social situation of transsexuals will be transformed, and transsexuals will be integrated into community, no longer persecuted and despised" (186). She goes on hypothesize that, under a different kind of community, one built around "androgynous identity," transsexuality as we now know it may not exist because we will have expanded the range of possible identities and, in effect, have new ways of being. Whether one accepts or rejects the last claim, the first two are astonishing for the fact that they were written in 1974 and that Andrea Dworkin is a radical feminist heroine, if there ever was one. For an essay by John Stoltenberg, Andrea's life partner, reflecting on Andrea's view on trans persons, see Stoltenberg 2014. For an interview with Catharine MacKinnon on trans women, see Williams 2015.

7.   Janice Raymond makes this point, as does Sheila Jeffreys. Jeffreys approvingly quotes Raymond, saying, "We know that we are women who are born with female chromosomes and anatomy, and that whether or not we were socialized to be so-called normal women, patriarchy as treated and will treat us like women. Transsexuals have not had this same history. . . . Surgery may confer the artifacts of outward and inward female organs but it cannot confer the history of being born a woman in this society" (Jeffreys 2014: 6).

8.   For some relevant data, see Grant et al. 2011.

9.   For an analysis of the way that trans women face stereotype threat, see McKinnon 2014.

References

Dworkin, Andrea. 1974. *Woman Hating*. New York: E. P. Dutton.

Fine, Cordelia. 2010. *Delusions of Gender*. New York: W. W. Norton.

Grant, Jaime M., et al. 2011. *Injustice at Every Turn: A Report of the National Transgender Discrimination Survey*. National Center for Transgender Equality and National Gay and Lesbian Taskforce. www.thetaskforce.org/static_html/downloads/reports/reports/ntds_full.pdf.

Haas, Ann P., Philip L. Rodgers, and Jody L. Herman. 2014. *Suicide Attempts among Transgender and Gender Non-Conforming Adults: Findings of the National Transgender Discrimination Survey*. American Foundation for Suicide Prevention and Williams Institute, January. williamsinstitute.law.ucla.edu/wp-content/uploads/AFSP-Williams-Suicide-Report-Final.pdf.

Jeffreys, Sheila. 2014. *Gender Hurts: A Feminist Analysis of the Politics of Transgenderism*. New York: Routledge.

Jordan-Young, Rebecca M. 2010. *Brain Storm*. Cambridge, MA: Harvard University Press.

McKinnon. Rachel. 2014. "Stereotype Threat and Attributional Ambiguity for Trans Women." *Hypatia* 29, no. 4: 857–72.

Stoltenberg, John. 2014. "#Genderweek: Andrea Was Not Transphobic." *Feminist Times*, April (article amended April 28). www.feministtimes.com/%E2%80%AA%E2%80%8Egenderweek-andrea-was-not-transphobic/.

Williams, Cristan. 2015. "Sex, Gender, and Sexuality: The TransAdvocate Interviews Catharine A. MacKinnon." *TransAdvocate*, April 7. www.transadvocate.com/sex-gender-and-sexuality-the-transadvocate-interviews-catharine-a-mackinnon_n_15037.htm.

Radical Inclusion

Recounting the Trans Inclusive History of Radical Feminism

CRISTAN WILLIAMS

Abstract This article reviews the ways in which radical feminism has been and continues to be trans inclusive. Trans inclusive radical feminist opinion leaders, groups, and events are reviewed and contrasted against a popular media narrative that asserts that radical feminism takes issue with trans people. Reviewed are historical instances in which radical feminists braved violence to ensure their feminism was trans inclusive.
Keywords feminism, radical feminism, TERF

I n this article, I will review some of the ways in which the inclusion and support of trans people by radical feminists has been hidden from trans and feminist discourse, thereby creating the perception that radical feminism isn't supportive of trans people. John Stoltenberg, a radical feminist author and long-term partner of the pioneering radical feminist opinion leader Andrea Dworkin, wrote (pers. comm., February 13, 2015), "The notion that truly revolutionary radical feminism is trans-inclusive is a no brainer. I honestly do not understand how or why a strain of radical feminism has emerged that favors a biology-based/sex-essentialist theory of 'sex caste' over the theory of 'sex class' as set forth in the work of [Monique] Wittig, Andrea [Dworkin], and [Catharine] MacKinnon. Can radical feminism be 'reclaimed' so that its trans-inclusivity—which is inherent—is made apparent? I hope so." It is to this hope that I wish to draw attention to in this article.

To this end, I will utilize the feminist term *trans exclusionary radical feminist* (TERF) to distinguish the "biology-based/sex-essentialist" ideology Stoltenberg identified as being different from the analysis of the radical feminist opinion leaders he explicitly noted. In 2008, an online feminist community popularized *TERF* as a way of making a distinction between these two types of feminism. While this lexical distinction is useful, online TERF activists sometimes

TSQ: Transgender Studies Quarterly ★ Volume 3, Numbers 1–2 ★ May 2016
DOI 10.1215/23289252-3334463 © 2016 Duke University Press

assert this term to be a slur, since some Internet users have used it in derogatory ways. Internet conflicts aside, I use this term in a manner consistent with its widely known original context, as asserted by the progenitor of the term, cisgender feminist Viv Smythe (Williams 2014a): "It was not meant to be insulting. It was meant to be a deliberately technically neutral description of an activist grouping. We wanted a way to distinguish TERFs from other RadFems with whom we engaged who were trans*-positive/neutral, because we had several years of history of engaging productively/substantively with non-TERF RadFems."

Absent this distinction, much has been written of the various ways in which "radical feminism" is critical of the trans experience. It is commonplace to find popular media outlets assert that "radical feminists" take issue with trans people. The *Globe and Mail* asserted (Wente 2014), "In fact, the most bitter battle in the LGBT movement today is between radical feminists and the transgender movement." The *New Yorker* recounted (Goldberg 2014) how a conference calling itself "Radfems Respond" was "going to try to explain why, at a time when transgender rights are ascendant, radical feminists insist on regarding transgender women as men, who should not be allowed to use women's facilities, such as public rest rooms, or to participate in events organized exclusively for women." The *National Post* said (Kay 2014) that radical feminism and Paul McHugh are of one mind when it comes to trans people: "True sex change is simply not possible; you end up as a 'feminized man' or a 'masculinized woman.' Which is exactly what the radical feminists believe."

Lost in these popular representations of radical feminism is its long and courageous trans inclusive history. These narratives don't tell us that Dworkin ensured that her 1980s-era prowoman legal activism was trans inclusive. Through these popular radfem vs. trans narratives, we also lose the reality that the sound of the 1970s-era women's music movement was engineered by an out trans woman because Olivia Records, the radical feminist lesbian separatist music collective, was itself trans inclusive, and we certainly don't hear that Olivia paid for trans medical care. Olivia, born out of the radical feminist lesbian collective The Furies, went on to become a "hugely successful recording company, marketing radical lesbian recordings and performances that soon defined the 'women's music' movement" (Morris 2015: 290).

When promoting the idea that TERF activism is radical feminism itself, it becomes difficult to clearly see the courage of the women of Olivia who endured months of threats of boycott and violence from TERF activists who demanded that the collective become trans exclusionary (Williams 2014b). When an armed group of TERF activists showed up at an Olivia show to murder out-trans woman and Olivia member Sandy Stone, it's important to note that this group's ideology was different from the radical feminism of Olivia. According to Stone, the threats of death and violence became common. "We were getting hate mail about me. . . . The death threats were directed at me, but there were violent consequences proposed for the Collective if they didn't get rid of me." Olivia and Stone were informed that a TERF group named The Gorgons asserted that they would murder Stone if Olivia's show came to Seattle. Stone said that the Olivia show was "probably the only women's music tour that was ever done with serious muscle security." Making good on their threats, armed Gorgons came to the show but were disarmed by Olivia security. Stone said, "In fact, Gorgons did come and they did have guns taken away from them. I was terrified. During a break between a musical number someone shouted out 'GORGONS!' and I made it from my seat at the console to under the table the console was on at something like superluminal speed. I stayed under there until it was clear that I wasn't about to be shot" (Williams 2014b).

Similarly, we need to acknowledge that there was an ideological difference between the radical feminism promoted at the largest lesbian gathering to date (Stryker 2008: 104) — the 1973 West Coast Lesbian Conference (WCLC) — and that of a group of TERF activists who attempted to rush the conference stage and bash out-trans woman and conference co-organizer Beth Elliott. When the radical feminists of WCLC stood in the way of the violent TERF activists — physically protecting a WCLC trans woman — and TERFs turned on those brave radical feminists and physically beat them instead, what does it say about the historical foundation of a contemporary TERF movement that consistently represents itself as radical feminism to the media? Robin Tyler, an early radical, feminist, lesbian women's music producer, was one of the women who protected Elliott from assault. "We defended Beth Elliott. Robin Morgan came up with this horrible speech and when Beth went on stage to play her guitar and sing, [TERFs] started threatening her. Patty [Harrison] and I jumped on stage and we got hit, because they came onto the stage to physically beat her" (Williams 2014c).

The obfuscation of the trans inclusive nature of radical feminism was apparent when TERF activist Sheila Jeffreys spoke at the Andrea Dworkin Commemorative Conference. While she credited Dworkin as being her inspiration and spoke at length about Dworkin's pioneering book, *Woman Hating*, she also denigrated the bodies of trans women and asserted trans medical care to be unnecessary. During her entire presentation, Jeffreys never once noted that — in the very book Jeffreys cited as being the inspiration for her activism — Dworkin advocated that trans people be given free access to trans medical care or that Dworkin viewed gender identity research as being subversive to patriarchy. Dworkin wrote (1974: 175), "Work with transsexuals, and studies of formation of gender identity in children provide basic information which challenges the notion that there are two discrete biological sexes. That information threatens to transform the traditional biology of sex difference into the radical biology of sex similarity." She went on to write, "Every transsexual is entitled to a sex-change operation, and it should be provided by the community as one of its functions" (186).

When confronted with the sex essentialism of TERF activists, pioneering radical feminist Catharine MacKinnon wrote (Williams 2015), "Male dominant society has defined women as a discrete biological group forever. If this was going to produce liberation, we'd be free. . . . To me, women is a political group. I never had much occasion to say that, or work with it, until the last few years when there has been a lot of discussion about whether transwomen are women." Moreover, MacKinnon said (*On Century Avenue* 2015), "I always thought I don't care how someone becomes a woman or a man; it does not matter to me. It is just part of their specificity, their uniqueness, like everyone else's. Anybody who identifies as a woman, wants to be a woman, is going around being a woman, as far as I'm concerned, is a woman." Stoltenberg echoed MacKinnon, saying, "Whatever individual trans folks' political views, their existence is threatening the conservatism of sex essentialism across a broad spectrum of sex-and-gender fundamentalists. And in this respect, I believe, trans folks are on today's front lines" (pers. comm., March 14, 2015).

It is my opinion that something intrinsic to radical feminism is lost when we characterize "radical feminism" as being locked in a bitter battle against trans people. Such assertions hide an exceptionally courageous history of radical trans inclusion. Moreover, conflating TERF ideology with radical feminism erases the voices of numerous radical feminist opinion leaders. Worse, when we fail to notice the voices of radical feminists who've stood by the trans community, we participate in diminishing the very feminism that braved violence and possible death to ensure that all women—even trans women—were included in their work toward the liberation of women.

Cristan Williams is a trans historian and activist, is the editor of the *TransAdvocate*, serves on the national steering body for the Urban Coalition for HIV/AIDS Prevention Services, and is the executive director of the Transgender Foundation of America.

Acknowledgments

I wish to express my profound gratitude to the two transgender historians who inspired my interest in researching trans history: Leslie Feinberg and Susan Stryker. Also, I wish to thank K. J. Rawson for their dedication to the preservation of transgender history. Lastly, I wish to thank those who helped care for the Houston Transgender Archive: Alexis Melvin, Monyque Starr, Koomah, Bethany Townsend, Daniel Williams, Carolyn Bosma, Robin Mack, and innumerable Trans Center volunteers.

References

Dworkin, Andrea. 1974. *Woman Hating.* New York: Penguin.

Goldberg, Michelle. 2014. "What Is a Woman?" *New Yorker,* August 4. www.newyorker.com /magazine/2014/08/04/woman-2.

Kay, Barbara. 2014. "Barbara Kay: Transgendered Advocacy Has Gone Too Far." *National Post,* August 6. www.news.nationalpost.com/full-comment/barbara-kay-transgendered -advocacy-has-gone-too-far.

Morris, Bonnie. 2015. "Olivia Records: The Production of a Movement." *Journal of Lesbian Studies* 19, no. 3: 290–304.

On Century Avenue. 2015. "Harm Is Harm, Hello." March 9. www.oncenturyavenue.org/2015/03 /harm-is-harm-hello/.

Stryker, Susan. 2008. *Transgender History.* Berkeley, CA: Seal.

Wente, Margaret. 2014. "The March of Transgender Rights." *Globe and Mail,* August 2. www .theglobeandmail.com/globe-debate/the-march-of-transgender-rights/article19888036/.

Williams, Cristan. 2014a. "TERF: What It Means and Where It Came From." *TransAdvocate,* March 15. www.transadvocate.com/terf-what-it-means-and-where-it-came-from_n_13066.htm.

———. 2014b. "TERF Hate and Sandy Stone." *TransAdvocate,* August 16. www.transadvocate .com/terf-violence-and-sandy-stone_n_14360.htm.

———. 2014c. "That Time TERFs Beat RadFems for Protecting a Trans Woman from Their Assault." *TransAdvocate,* August 17. www.transadvocate.com/that-time-terfs-beat-radfems -for-protecting-a-trans-woman-from-assault_n_14382.htm.

———. 2015. "Sex, Gender, and Sexuality: The TransAdvocate Interviews Catharine A. MacKinnon." *TransAdvocate,* April 7. www.transadvocate.com/sex-gender-and-sexuality -the-transadvocate-interviews-catharine-a-mackinnon_n_15037.htm.

Reconstructing the Transgendered Self as a Feminist Subject

Trans/feminist Praxis in Urban China

SHANA YE

Abstract This article explores the entangled relations between transgender lives and Chinese feminisms. It starts with a brief overview of how nonbinary genders have been addressed in both Chinese socialist and postsocialist feminisms. Then it outlines existing problems such as homophobia and remarginalization within the coalition of trans activists and feminists. By analyzing how grassroots trans/feminists negotiate such problems, this article argues that trans/feminist praxis transgresses subjective, intellectual, and political borders and calls for more critical feminist engagements in Chinese trans activism and knowledge production.

Keywords Chinese feminism, grassroots feminism, trans activism

> At least half of me is a woman . . . the woman I want to be is definitely not a "good" one. I am a queer bitch. I want to knock out all unearned "male privileges" I have been enjoying. I want to have a vagina, have menstruation, and be able to get pregnant; but I also want to share all risks of being a woman, especially a woman who is a "bitch." If I had a hymen, I would have already broken it before I turned twelve years old.
>
> —Interview with Piggy Kitty, February 2014 (translation mine)

Piggy Kitty (aka Zhuchuanmao Erbing 猪川猫二饼) is something of a celebrity in today's Chinese young grassroots feminist activism. A transgender queer who seeks not to pass on purpose, ze sees hirself as a parody of the heteronormative ideal of a real woman. Ze is a member of Slut International (Silate Guoji 斯拉特国际), a grassroots feminist group based in Beijing. In the feminist play *Ways of the Vagina* (阴道之道), inspired by Eve Ensler's *The Vagina Monologues*, Piggy Kitty performs a trans woman who desires to be a "slut."

TSQ: Transgender Studies Quarterly ∗ Volume 3, Numbers 1–2 ∗ May 2016   **259**
DOI 10.1215/23289252-3334475   © 2016 Duke University Press

Ze explains, "In a society where women are denigrated regardless, I want to embrace words such as 'slut' and 'bitch' thus reclaiming them. . . . I want to use my 'ridiculousness' to ridicule this sick world" (Piggy Kitty 2014).

As this quote makes plain, Piggy Kitty's gender work should be understood in terms of feminist political action, rather than being merely an expression of gender or self-identification. The "ideal" woman Piggy Kitty wants to be is a "failed" woman—a bitch or slut. On the one hand, this image challenges the patriarchal norm of chastity and virtuousness embodied in figures such as the virgin and the good wife; on the other hand, through performing a kitsch version of slut—masculine, with heavy body hair and a low-class drag hag style—ze disturbs the heteronormative male gaze that turns women's bodies into nothing but erotic objects. Through this twofold failure, Piggy Kitty seeks to queer dominant social and cultural structures of gender and sexuality.

Although Chinese trans/feminism as a field of study remains largely unarticulated, issues of nonbinary gender and gender variance have been taken up in women's studies and feminist praxis. In this article, I want to explore how recent grassroots trans/feminist work negotiates problems such as essentialization of gender, homophobia, and remarginalization in both trans activism and feminist knowledge production. I start with a brief overview of how transgender and gender variance are addressed in both socialist and postsocialist feminisms. Then I outline conundrums currently confronting Chinese transfeminism. Finally, by taking Piggy Kitty and hir grassroots peers as an example, I consider how transgender activism and feminist praxis can draw critical insights from each other.

Although the term *transgender* and discussions of trans issues did not gain popularity until late in the first decade of the twenty-first century in China, socialist and Maoist feminism since 1950s characterized gender equality in terms of "radical sameness" between women and men.[1] This concept of equality, predicated on a masculinist and androcentric norm, consequently viewed female masculinity embodied in figures such as the "iron girls" as a virtue that helped to promote socialist modernity (Evans 1997; Honig 2000, 2002; Jin, Manning, and Chu 2006). For example, the story of modern China's Hua Mulan,[2] Guo Junqing 郭俊卿, a woman solder who cross-dressed as a man in service of the Liberation Army in the 1950s, was applauded in state propaganda, inspiring several popular state-sponsored films and television series (Wang 2010). Female gender transgression was not only highly regarded but also encouraged when deemed useful for socialist purposes.

In the 1980s, Chinese feminists, such as Wang Zheng, Dai Jinhua and Li Jiaojiang, influenced by Western feminist thought, introduced the concept of "gender" to interrogate questions of structural inequality, the erasure of female subjectivity, and male dominance in state-sanctioned feminism (Song 2012). Their emphasis on gender differences and the valuing of femininity heralded profound changes in the outlook of postsocialist feminism and women's studies.

Against the backdrop of China's motive to move beyond political and economic impasses and restore its status in the global order after the Tian'anmen incident in 1989, the 1995 World Conference on Women was held in Beijing in the hope of changing China's international image, thereby regaining foreign investments and economic support. For Chinese feminists, the conference was also a turning point: it boosted the exchange of feminist thoughts and accelerated the development of gender studies in China. National and international funds initiated a vast number of programs to promote education about gender equality and women's emancipation and empowerment.[3]

Notably, the topic of sexuality gained increasing prominence in feminist scholarship and activism during this period. In the pre-1990s, by contrast, public discussion of sexuality was limited to the medical field and received scant feminist attention. In this context, the "lesbian tent" at the Beijing conference thus constituted an important moment in the recognition of lesbian issues as women's issues, helping to bridge discussions of gender and sexuality in Chinese feminist theorizing. In the late 1990s, discourses about sexual rights, sexual diversity, and queer theory were introduced by diasporic scholars and international LGBT activists,[4] and they were strategically appropriated by local scholars and activists alike to meet various political and academic ends. On the one hand, the vernacularization of Western feminist thoughts shows that Chinese feminists are not merely passive recipients; on the other hand, to some extent, the political usage leads to decontextualization and overgeneralization of these theories, thoughts, and concepts. For example, issues of homosexuality, LGBT, and queerness are often mashed into the umbrella of "gender and sexual diversity," overlooking historical, geopolitical, and class-based complicities and being treated with political abstraction.

It is interesting to note a prevailing difference of attitude regarding homosexuality between trans women and trans men: in my interviews and casual conversations, trans women often make clear distinctions between themselves, feminine gay men, and male cross-dressers, while trans men see their gender as more fluid, sharing an identity with masculine-gender-style lesbians—also called "T" lesbians in the Chinese "T-Po" system.[5] As the concepts of "transgender" and "trans men" have recently gained popularity, an increasing number of former T lesbians have found "trans men" to be a more suitable identity for themselves. On the contrary, there is a long history of denigrating and ostracizing male femininity within gay communities, owing to the social stigmatization and colonialist feminization of Asian/Chinese men. Feminine gays, transvestites, and cross-dressers are often the scapegoats of public homophobia in gay communities because it is widely believed that they contribute to the negative gay image held by the general public. While female masculinity was valued, as mentioned before, male femininity was and still is largely considered to be causing the weakness of the nation. In this context, trans women's embracing of femininity and insistence on their difference can be read as both an attempt to break from colonialist history and a critique of long-standing oppressions and transphobia within the gay community. However, these attempts to avoid being identified as gay men by asserting a real and essential womanhood may also be viewed as homophobic as well as gender conforming—to some extent it replicates the denigration of gay femininity and the idea of a "real and essential womanhood."

Despite the apparent inclusion of transgender in feminist and queer activism, transgender issues continue to be marginalized within LGBT communities and feminist movements. As Chinese feminist activists have been busy addressing denigrating public misunderstandings of feminism, structural sexism, and the lack of economic support for women, they have paid little attention to trans issues in complex and critical ways. Feminist attention to transgender issues is largely limited to commentary on transgender celebrities in the mass media. For example, the high-profile "coming out" in 2014 of prestigious feminist sociologist Li Yinhe and Da Xia, her transgender partner of over twenty years, has provided ample opportunities for spreading feminist ideas and for educating people about gender, sexuality, and hetero-patriarchy. On the one hand, sex/gender-variant people have gained unprecedented public visibility; on the other hand, the transgender person has become the poster child of current LGBT and queer politics in a gimmicky sort of way, thereby diverting attention from trans people's embodied life struggles. In addition, this celebrity model of LGBT and feminist praxis not only sidelines the experience of socioeconomically underprivileged queer subjects but also renders them pathological insofar as they do not pass as the "fully transitioned," "beautiful," and "monogamous and family-orientated" trans ideal.

Instead, the real-life struggles of trans people usually receives attention from nongovernmental organizations funded by human-rights-based or HIV/AIDS prevention programs. Much of their work focuses on the living conditions of transgender/transsexual sex workers, aiming for governmental and international policy changes. Such work, however, usually lacks a critical feminist perspective and tends to replicate the narrative of the "fallen woman" and the "victim in need of saving," thereby remarginalizing both transgender/transsexuals and sex workers (e.g., Asian Catalyst, Beijing Zuoyou Center, and Shanghai CSW and MSM Center 2015). Similar remarginalization also occurs in women's organizations. Grassroots trans-identified or pro-trans feminists who work for such organizations often found themselves compromising their radical political goals by replicating the logic of victims par excellence in order to obtain resources and monetary supports.[6]

Young feminist activists in urban China have been critically engaged with these aforementioned difficulties. To begin with, they have challenged the theory/practice divide and questioned what it means to claim "women" as the primary subject of feminist inquiry and praxis. The production of *Ways of the Vagina* is one such endeavor. Through including the specific experiences of trans women, the play questions the presumption of an essentialized, biologically determined female subject as the fundamental locus of empowerment, social movements, and solidarity. It does not deny that there are "women"; rather, it provides creative ways to interrogate identity politics by asking who "we" are, how this plural *we* has come to shape oppressions and desire through similar and different experiences of precarity, and how to build solidarity when the "we" is

Figure 1. Piggy Kitty (Zhuchuanmao Erbing). Courtesy of Xiao Meili and Zhuchuan

Figure 2. Piggy Kitty (Zhuchuanmao Erbing). Courtesy of Xiao Meili and Zhuchuan

heterogeneous. Such work further transforms the monolithic way of viewing the feminist subject in conventional Chinese feminism.

As shown in figure 1, Piggy Kitty juxtaposes hir self-described "ridiculous self" and "awkward and ugly body" with Snow White, an idealized, desirable role model for girls, in order to point to the artificiality of the cultural fantasy of perfect womanhood, and the failure inherent in any attempt to imitate such fantasies. The staging of the image makes Piggy Kitty appear as part of the background scene, delivering to the viewer a sense that ze is integrated into Snow White's fairy-tale world. This odd togetherness queers prevailing heterosexual and gender norms.

Piggy Kitty's "failed" cross-dressing not only disrupts the ideal of woman within heteronormative patriarchy but also questions a current trans politics in China that heavily relies on the experiences of people who conform to gender and class norms, who are conventionally physically "beautiful," who undergo so-called full transitions, or who are able to pass as straight and cisgender. In figure 2, Piggy Kitty's bad makeup, cheap wig, flat chest, and dirty tennis shoes counter such assimilative politics; they resist as well a normative trans aestheticism within both traditional Chinese expressions of androgyny and the contemporary commercial sex culture that caters to the heterosexual male gaze.[7]

Piggy Kitty's assertion of being a "trans slut by choice" parodies the oft-repeated trope of the "fallen sex worker" within the current frameworks of both trans activism and women's movements of empowerment and emancipation. Hir transgressions of gender identity and sexual expression push us to reexamine femininity, homophobia, and transphobia in both queer and feminist theory and praxis.

Conclusion

The history of Chinese feminisms is entangled with political and theoretical attentions to transgender, gender-variant, and nonbinary genders. Both socialist and postsocialist feminisms address gender transgression as a feminist issue, one that shapes how we imagine feminism's subject, agenda, and political outcomes. Although the intersections of trans and feminism remain largely unarticulated, grassroots trans/feminist practices are seeking new possibilities to destabilize "woman" as the basis of solidarity and social movement. Such work transgresses intellectual and political borders and expands both trans and feminist activism in China. It calls for more feminist engagement with knowledge production regarding transgender issues and more participation in trans/queer politics; at the same time, it summons trans people to engage more fully with feminism.

Shana Ye is a PhD candidate in feminist studies at the University of Minnesota Twin Cities. Her research interests lie in transnational queer and feminist studies, affect studies, and global studies. Her dissertation explores the relation between knowledge and memory production of the Chinese LGBTQ community and transnational power structures.

Notes

1. *Transgender* is translated into *kuaxingbie* 跨性别 in Mandarin. Although it has gradually gained popularity in academia and activism, it still remains unfamiliar to the public. Comparably, terms such as *bianxingren* 变性人 (transsexual), *renyao* 人妖 (lady boy), and *fanchuan* 反串 (cross-dresser) are more commonly used in mainland China.

2. A legendary woman warrior from ancient China who cross-dressed as a man to take her aged father's place and serve in the army.

3. Funding organizations included the Ford Foundation, UNDP programs, and Open Society Foundations.

4. One of the most famous scholars who discussed sexuality and homosexuality is Li Yinhe, who received her Phd from Pittsburg University.

5. *T* is from the word *tomboy*, referring to masculine-identified lesbians. *Po*, or simply *P* in Mandarin, refers to feminine-gender-style lesbians. As the T-P system has grown less rigid in recent years, *H*, indicating someone whose gender and sexuality falls between T and P, has become more widely adopted. See Kam 2014.

6. Based on my interviews with two trans-identified feminist activists in Beijing in January 2015.

7. China has a long history of androgynous aestheticism that can be dated back to the Shang dynasty (ca. sixteenth century–eleventh century BC). For androgynous aestheticism in modernity, see Kang 2009 and Chiang 2012.

References

Asian Catalyst, Beijing Zuoyou Center, and Shanghai CSW and MSM Center. 2015. *"My Life Is Too Dark to See the Light": A Survey of the Living Conditions of Transgender Female Sex Workers in Beijing and Shanghai*. www.asiacatalyst.org/wp-content/uploads/2014/09/Asia -Catalyst-TG-SW-Report.pdf (accessed October 7, 2005).

Chiang, Howard, ed. 2012. *Transgender China*. New York: Palgrave Macmillan.

Evans, Harriet. 1997. *Women and Sexuality in China: Female Sexuality and Gender since 1949*. New York: Continuum.

Honig, Emily. 2000. "Iron Girls Revisited: Gender and the Politics of Work in the Cultural Revolution." In *Re-drawing the Boundaries of Work, Households, and Gender*, edited by Barbara Gutwisle and Gail Henderson, 97–110. Berkeley: University of California Press.

———. 2002. "Maoist Mappings of Gender: Reassessing the Red Guards." In *Chinese Femininities/Chinese Masculinities*, edited by Susan Brownell and Jeffrey N. Wasserstrom, 255–68. Berkeley: University of California Press.

Jin, Yihong, Kimberley Ens Manning, and Lianyun Chu. 2006. "Rethinking the 'Iron Girls': Gender and Labour during the Chinese Cultural Revolution." *Gender and History* 18, no. 3: 613–34.

Kam, Lucetta Y. L. 2014. "Desiring T, Desiring Self: 'T-Style' Pop Singers and Lesbian Culture in China." *Journal of Lesbian Studies* 18, no. 3: 252–65.

Kang, Wenqing. 2009. *Obsession: Male Same-Sex Relations in China, 1900–1950*. Hong Kong: Hong Kong University Press.

Piggy Kitty [Zhuchuanmao Erbing]. 2014. Author interview, Beijing, January.

Song, Shaopeng. 2012. "Capitalism, Socialism, and Women: Why China Needs Marxist Feminist Critiques" (资本主义、社会主义和妇女—为什么中国需要重建马克思主义女权主义批判). *Open Times*, December. www.opentimes.cn/bencandy.php?fid =341&aid =1693.

Wang, Chong 王崇. 2010. "现代花木兰郭俊卿" ("The Modern Hua Mulan—Guo Junqing"). 党史楷模 *Dangshi Kaimo* (*Role Models in the Chinese Communist Party History*) 9. history.sina.com.cn/bk/ds/2013-12-03/094475611.shtml.

Mortal Life of Trans/Feminism

Notes on "Gender Killings" in Turkey

ASLI ZENGİN

Abstract This piece reflects on some ongoing tensions between cisgender women's and trans people's feminisms, suggesting specific frameworks to resolve these tensions into coalitional feminist organizing. To do that, the author draws on her ethnographic research and activist work in Turkey and proposes that a collective focus on the realm of death would bring feminist cis women and trans people together around a shared gender experience. In Turkey, the annual number of cis and trans women who are killed by cis men has been gradually increasing. This situation makes the availability of killing a shared gendered experience for cis women and trans people. Hence, organizing around the framework of "gender killings" would allow cis women and trans people to develop alliances to survive and transform the very material and symbolic conditions of their gender oppression.

Keywords death, gender killings, feminisms, Turkey

Since 2011, every International Women's Day March in Istanbul, Turkey, has been marked by tensions between feminist cisgender women and trans activists. In that year, when women and other feminist-identified individuals and groups were marching down Istiklal Street in the Beyoglu District to take back the night, a renowned senior feminist activist approached one participant and said, "Get out of the procession! Men are not allowed in this space." The person in question, bewildered and exasperated, responded that he had every right to participate in the march because he was a feminist trans man. The confrontation intensified as other feminists in the crowd got involved on both sides of the dispute. By transpiring publicly on the streets of Istanbul, the conflict between trans politics and feminism became sharply visible and engendered a series of intense conversations that have continued through the present day.

These recent conversations evoked long-standing biases rooted in earlier histories of miscommunication that often led to false conclusions by each party regarding the other's political demands. While for some feminists, trans politics has meant just another form of identity politics, and is thus not engaged in a

TSQ: Transgender Studies Quarterly ∗ Volume 3, Numbers 1–2 ∗ May 2016 **266**
DOI 10.1215/23289252-3334487 © 2016 Duke University Press

struggle to liberate women, trans activists often saw feminists as gender essentialists and gatekeepers of the category "woman." These exchanges have been characterized by questions now familiar to those of us at the intersection of feminism and trans activism: What is feminism? Whose feminism counts as feminism? Which demands herald a more feminist agenda? Who is a woman? What's the difference between having "feminine experience" and "compulsory feminine experience"? Why not a trans feminism? These questions emerged as urgent questions in the dialogue between the two groups. As a result of these conversations, the 2012 Women's Night March included trans activists and their allies carrying their own placards that read, "Transfeminists are here!"

The conflict at the trans/feminist intersection has been only partially resolved, and the full potential for coalitional politics is still far from maturity. In the Turkish context, the checkpoints at the border crossings of sex and gender remain closely guarded. What it means to have feminine experience has been vehemently challenged in the recent exchanges between trans and cis women feminists. Although these often tense dialogues are still evolving, the tensions between feminist and transgender politics have already generated a great deal of common language and common ground for political organizing, and for establishing alternative channels and relations of care and solidarity. Who is capable of being "the political actor of feminism" (a phrase coproduced by feminist cis women and trans people in Turkey) has become a central question. Through passionate debate, cis women and trans activists are collectively setting the terms and conditions of inclusivity in the spaces of feminist practice.

Ali, a dear friend and a pioneer in trans men's activism in Turkey, has been one of the key participants in these debates. During one of our conversations, he made a striking point:

> Some women argue that it's not experience as a woman in general, but experience as a woman in the streets in particular, that should be the common denominator for feminist politics. But I feel confused! Let's assume for a second I have grown a beard, and gained a deep voice and a muscular body due to taking testosterone, and I pass as an ordinary guy. Does the coerced feminine experience that I had to have until then slip from my mind, leak away from my body? Does it fade away? Do I start lacking feminine experience at that very moment? (pers. comm., 2010)

Thinking alongside Ali's provocative insights, this article addresses the question of trans/feminist experience in Turkey through ethnographic observation of two 2010 protests—sites where the intimate association of feminist and trans politics became clear. As a feminist cis woman and an ally to trans politics, everyday forms of violence in gender-nonconforming and sexually marginalized lives have significantly shaped my political and academic interests. The relations between feminist, queer, and trans politics and theory have guided me in my pursuit of such interests. Efforts to foster conversations and collaborations between these seemingly distinct yet close-knit realms of the political, in which many people simultaneously occupy more than one category, are of vital importance because heteronormativity, misogyny, and transphobia continue to cause troubling rates of death for cis women and queer and trans people across several countries, including Turkey.

In light of this deadly violence, there is a keen urgency to Paul Farmer's call for work that not only "relies on conversations with the living" but also "look[s] at the dead and those left for dead" (2004: 307). I suggest that we can approach death, as well as life lived under constant threat of killing, as a form of gender experience that provides us with one of the many possible common grounds for trans/feminism. In a masculinist and heteronormative society, the availability of killing becomes a shared gendered experience for cis women and trans people alike. I propose that the framework of "gender killings" will allow us to develop a coalitional trans/feminist politics that helps us survive and transform the very material and symbolic conditions of our gender oppression as cis women and trans people. To advance this framework, let us now revisit two political protests in Istanbul in 2010.

Protest 1

I am in the street with a large crowd of cis women, gathered together for a feminist protest against Valentine's Day. This is the first Valentine's Day after the decapitated and mutilated body of Münevver Karabulut, an eighteen-year-old cis girl from a working-class family, was discovered in pieces in a garbage bin—left there by her boyfriend. Feminists responded to Münevver's vicious murder, in addition to the killings of 108 other women that same year,[1] with a sense of urgency. Today in this march, I walk behind two women holding a large banner proclaiming a grievous fact: "Men's love kills three women every single day!" Our voices are rising in rebellion, anger, and outrage for those women who were killed by their husbands, boyfriends, lovers, sons, and brothers in the past few years. There is also frustration. Nothing has changed since an earlier, equally brutal murder set the stage for feminist organizing in 2004, when a cis woman named Güldünya was killed by her family in order to save their honor, after having discovered that she had been raped and impregnated by a male kin. In response to this murder, feminist groups in Turkey had rallied and called on the state to protect its female citizens from its male citizens. They demanded shelters, not graves. Yet cis men continued to kill women at an increasing pace.[2]

Protest 2

With rainbow flags, posters, and placards in our hands, we leave Istanbul LGBTT, a trans-majority LGBTQI rights center, to protest the killing of Sibel, yet another murdered trans woman sex worker. LGBTQ organizations in Turkey have recorded the murders of seventy trans women between 2002 and 2013 (KaosGL 2013). On this day in 2010, the same Beyoglu Street I marched down earlier to protest cis women's killings now welcomes a group of approximately forty people, the majority of whom are trans women. We stage a sit-in protest to call on the state to prevent the killing of trans women by their lovers and male clients. As we are subjected to a mix of bewildered and derisive looks by passers-by, we chant at the top of our voices, "Hate keeps killing us and the state is blind to it!"

For over a decade, I have participated in numerous similar protests organized by feminist and LGBTQ groups against these killings. In all such protests, the keywords and rallying cries remain the same: *hate, death, violence, exclusion, masculinity, patriarchy, men,* and *the state*. In both protests described above, the message is clear: misogyny and transphobia, two tightly coupled products of heteronormative and masculinist social and institutional life, kill both trans and nontrans women—it is their gendering that makes them available for killing.

The actors in each of these political spaces hold the state responsible for nearly all the murders, since the state's security forces and judicial institutions show little interest in finding and punishing the criminals. Even when the perpetrators are caught and sentenced, Turkish criminal law cultivates a culture of impunity, which fails to develop effective sanctions against perpetrators and often reduces the culprit's sentence. During the murder trials of the killers of some trans women, the request by the victim for intercourse deemed "homosexual" was used as a pretext for murder in the confessions of the perpetrators. Similar to Talia Mae Bettcher's discussion of the perpetrators' self-defensive accounts in the US context, the perpetrators in Turkey also often deploy a victim-blaming rhetoric of deception, betrayal, and pretension. An insistence on a "misalignment" between gender presentation (a gendered manifestation) and sexed body (the hidden, sexual reality) of the trans person becomes the source of this rhetorical device (Bettcher 2007).

Despite the overt display of a hate motive in these confessions, such accounts were considered mitigating factors in the commission of the crime, and the perpetrators received lesser punishments on the grounds of "undue provocation" (*haksız tahrik*). In the case of murdered cis women, some trials from 2008 and 2009 provide evidence of how even the most trivial issues could constitute undue provocation and thereby win judicial approval as adequate reasons for men to kill their wives: "She flirtatiously asked a man for the time," "She wore jeans and tights," "She cooked only pasta for a month," and "She didn't want to have sex with me and pushed me out of the bed" (Isci Cephesi 2011).

The logic of undue provocation, and the sexual and gender norms from which it derives its justification, demonstrate how particular lives are deemed more worthy of living, while others are deemed less worthy. In this social and legal matrix, cis and trans women's lives have less value. Hence, rather than being a uniform category equally available to all, life itself emerges as a contested domain. We must think about "the right to life" not as a universally applicable condition but, rather, as a very particular form of calculation that privileges and secures certain modes of life over others. "Who has the right to live?" and "What kinds of lives deserve to be given the right to live?" are constantly debated and contested zones of struggle in everyday life. From this perspective, undue provocation can be understood as a tool to generate various formulations of "the right to live."

Feminism in Turkey has a long history of struggle against sexual violence and the killing of cis women. Bringing this history of engagement and politicization together with activist responses to the killing of trans women, I suggest that "gender killings" offers a framework that allows us to think more capaciously about our shared experience as killable cis women and trans people. My understanding of gender killings emerges from intersections and exchanges between feminist and transgender politics. These intersections and exchanges open up fruitful avenues of analyzing the myriad ways of "doing gender," the complex meanings associated with the cis women's and trans people's enactment of their sense of gender, and the diverse ways in which they invest their bodies in gendering processes. Combining trans-political perspectives with feminism allows us to do a more refined work with the category of "gender," or "gender-based oppression," as necessary objects of analysis (Martin 1994). As we learn from both trans and feminist politics, the deployment of gender categories establishes a space for political action as well as frameworks by which women (both trans and nontrans) become intelligible to themselves and others.

Trans men and women, like cis women, do not benefit from heteronormativity, patriarchy, and misogyny. The same systems of sexual and gender oppression subject trans people to myriad forms of violence, including social exclusion and discrimination. Occupying our genders (whether trans or not) can pose a danger, an actual threat to our lives at certain times and under certain circumstances within the current masculinist and heteronormative organization of social life in many parts of the world. Hence, I see the claim to live trans lives as being a feminist claim. As Emi Koyama aptly put it, alliance between trans and cis women is essential to the liberation of both (2003). We, cis women and trans people, need each other. What kills us can also unite us. Our lives may well be contingent upon each other's care, support, and trust. Through our liberation and coalition work, we can transform the conditions of our oppression into new solidarities and emergent forms of politics.

Aslı Zengin is an Allen-Berenson postdoctoral fellow in women's, gender, and sexuality studies at Brandeis University. She is the author of "Sex for Law, Sex for Therapy: Pre-sex Reassignment Surgical Therapy Sessions of Trans People in Istanbul" (2014).

Acknowledgments
I wish to express my gratitude to Sema Semih, Maya Mikdashi, and the two anonymous reviewers for their valuable comments on earlier drafts of this essay.

Notes

1. These are official numbers, and feminist organizations' estimates of women's killings outnumber these statistics, making the number almost tripled (Kadin Cinayetlerini Durduracagiz Platformu 2013).
2. In 2010, independent and organized feminists in Istanbul founded a platform, "We Will Stop Women's Killings," to politicize and struggle against the killings. Their records demonstrate that men killed 210 women in 2012, 237 in 2013, and 294 in 2014. For further information see Kadin Cinayetlerini Durduracagiz Platformu 2015.

References

Bettcher, Talia Mae. 2007. "Evil Deceivers and Make-Believers: On Transphobic Violence and the Politics of Illusion." *Hypatia* 22, no. 3: 43–65.

Farmer, Paul. 2004. "An Anthropology of Structural Violence." *Current Anthropology* 45, no. 3: 305–25.

Isci Cephesi (Labor Front). 2011. "Haksiz Tahrik Nedir? Gercek Magduru Kimdir?" ("What Is Undue Provocation? Who Is the Real Victim?"). iscicephesi.net/kadin-sayfasi/hukuk-koeesi/642-haksiz-tahrik-nedir-gercek-magduru-kimdir (accessed April 5, 2013, page discontinued).

Kadin Cinayetlerini Durduracagiz Platformu (We Will Stop Women's Murders Platform). 2013. "2008–2012 Kadin Cinayeti Gercekleri" ("Reality Check for Women's Murders in 2008–2012"). www.kadincinayetlerinidurduracagiz.net/veriler/273/2008-2012-kadin-cinayeti-gercekler (accessed November 5, 2015).

———. 2015. "Veriler." www.kadincinayetlerinidurduracagiz.net/kategori/veriler (accessed November 5, 2015).

KaosGL. 2013. "LGBT Blok: Kurtulus Yok Tek Basina! Ya Hep Beraber Ya Hicbirimiz" ("LGBT Bloc: We Shall Not Be Free Alone! Either Altogether or None of Us!"). www.kaosgl.com/sayfa.php?id =14292 (accessed November 5, 2015).

Koyama, Emi. 2003. "The Transfeminist Manifesto." In *Catching a Wave*, edited by Rory Dicker and Elison Piepmeier, 244–59. Boston: Northwestern University Press.

Martin, Biddy. 1994. "Sexualities without Genders and Other Queer Utopias." *Diacritics* 24, nos. 2–3: 104–21.

African Trans Feminist Charter

Introduction by L. LEIGH ANN VAN DER MERWE

Background, August 2014

The African Trans Feminist Charter is crafted as an act of resistance and resilience, and mostly to position African trans women within feminist discourse on the continent and globally. We take a stand against exclusion of any kind and while we acknowledge that transgender women are often seen as enjoying some form of privilege, it is not true for every transgender woman. Intersectional factors like race, class and privilege, shape the realities of transgender women all over the African continent, and all over the world.

This document set forth the principles by which we engage with other groups of women in order to insert our voice in different spaces and linking our issue to a broader women's and feminist agenda. The idea for an African Trans Feminist Charter was born from the number of challenges facing African transgender women, including many different manifestations of violence. The history of the African transgender "movement" is that transgender persons on the masculine gender spectrum were leading the movement, including many different advocacy processes. Transgender women started organising themselves in 2010 and formed Social, Health and Empowerment Feminist Collective of Transgender Women of Africa as a feminist formation geared at crafting and advancing a feminist agenda for transgender women in Africa.

Social, Health and Empowerment has been involved in different feminist advocacy to ensure the inclusion of transgender women's voices, and we continue to include our voice and issues in feminist discourse and spaces.

* * *

We, the transgender women of Africa, who also identify ourselves as feminists, have united to draft a charter on transgender women's positioning and framing of a feminist agenda on the African continent.

TSQ: Transgender Studies Quarterly * Volume 3, Numbers 1–2 * May 2016 **272**
DOI 10.1215/23289252-3334511 © 2014 The African Trans Feminist Charter

We shall consider this document to be an official charter of African transgender women and our position on our own socio-cultural, political and economic context.

The charter shall elaborate on why we seek to position ourselves as African feminists and why it is critical for us to do so at this time.

The charter shall give guidance on regional advocacy priorities and engaging strategic spaces and/or people in our struggle to have our issues recognized as women's issues and the employment of a feminist framework to do our advocacy.

This framework is developed from a strong human rights approach to address the issues affecting transgender women on the African continent.

Our work as African trans feminists is built on the following values:

- Embracing diversity
- Cooperation
- Transparency
- Inclusivity
- Respect
- Dignity
- Openness
- Support
- Integrity
- Commitment
- Creativity
- Loyalty
- Acceptance
- Excellence
- Empathy
- Professionalism

* * *

The values, principles and behaviors of feminists are there to be a voice for all transwomen in Africa challenging sexist and discriminatory ways of operating. We are modelling feminist practice and we will be working with methods that are consistent with our politics and acknowledge transwomen's multiple roles. This is a space where one can respectfully challenge transwomen experience, support transwomen to identify their strength, value and nurture themselves and support transwomen's rights and decisions to determine how they live their lives.

We will safely challenge behavior that restricts transwomen's ability to take control over their lives. Working with important tools like professionalism, integrity and commitment to strengthen the power of transwomen and use effective forms of communications. We are embracing diversity and we stand in solidarity with other women. We promote transparency in both action and intention.

*   *   *

The charter will encourage the development of a feminist analysis of power in the face of hate legislation targeting sexual and gender minorities on the continent, and to gain an understanding of the impact of legal impediments on the lives of African transwomen.

It will develop an analysis of African "culture" and its manifestations in our lives as African transwomen—it will speak to issues of autonomy and agency over our lives and bodies.

The charter will be a living document to be reviewed when necessary and contextualized to our own situations and lives.

The charter will continue to serve generations of transwomen to come.

The charter will set out our priorities for advocacy and it will guide our documentation of the process in which we will engage relevant stakeholders and build alliances in order to create a more enabling environment, not only for transwomen, but also our allies who support our goals. Furthermore, to look at ways of supporting the work of our allies, particularly in relation to, but not limited to issues of abortion, child marriage, forced sterilization, female genital mutilation, and other issues pertaining to women's freedom, sexual and reproductive health and rights, and the full enjoyment of human rights. We take a feminist stance in the interrogation of power in any form, and the disruption of systems of oppression, and to also introspect with consciousness of our own power and privilege.

*   *   *

We recognize and acknowledge that this document is not cast in stone and that we will find ways to develop mechanisms to review and continuously update it.

*   *   *

At a meeting in Mellville, Johannesburg, during August 2014, transwomen from Namibia, Botswana, Zimbabwe, Zambia, Lesotho, Uganda, Kenya, Tanzania and South Africa have come together to plan and envision a movement driven by ourselves to articulate our politics and obtain conceptual clarity on working with feminist ideas. We have adopted the African Trans Feminist Charter at this momentous occasion.

L. Leigh Ann van der Merwe is a trans woman born in rural South Africa. She takes pride in her work as a feminist and women's rights activist. Leigh Ann is particularly interested in intersectional feminism(s). She is a journalist by training but also takes on the identities of leader, researcher, public health enthusiast, and social justice activist.

A Collective Editorial

THE *TIDE* COLLECTIVE

Following months of heated debate, the San Francisco chapter of the Daughters of Bilitis (DOB) voted against the inclusion of transsexual women on November 17, 1972, leading to the ouster of Beth Elliott, vice president of the chapter (and the subsequent protest resignation of the entire staff of Sisters, *the chapter's monthly newsletter). Cofounders of DOB, Del Martin and Phyllis Lyons, had argued for a compromise position, ultimately rejected, which excluded transsexual women but allowed an exception for Elliott in light of her long-standing involvement (Córdova 1972: 21). Articles both in defense of and against the inclusion of transsexual women had been written and circulated prior to the vote. These articles were also discussed by the Los Angeles–based Tide Collective, which held a vote on the issue and then sent a telegram to the San Francisco DOB the evening of the vote in San Francisco. The message of the telegram, along with summaries of the proinclusion/anti-inclusion arguments articulated in the articles, were published in a collective editorial in the* Lesbian Tide *(Tide Collective 1972). The document is important not only because it summarizes the main arguments on both sides, setting the stage for the controversy surrounding Elliott's performance at the Lesbian Conference in 1973, but also because it articulates a third position. Whereas the proinclusion arguments in San Francisco centered on traditional medical accounts of transsexuality, the proinclusion argument from the Tide Collective identified sex-role stereotypes as a common source of oppression. It can therefore be regarded as an early anticipation of the vision articulated by the transgender movement that arose in the United States in the early nineties.*
—*Editors*

In recent months the subject and matter of transsexuality has become once again a controversial issue among gay groups and organizations.

In the San Francisco chapter of the Daughters of Bilitis, the issue has threatened to split that organization in half. Insisting that transsexuals are "only synthetic women," who "should start trying to relate to each other and get out of

TSQ: Transgender Studies Quarterly * Volume 3, Numbers 1–2 * May 2016   **276**
DOI 10.1215/23289252-3334523   © 1972 *Tide* Collective courtesy Jeanne Córdova

our space," a number of S.F. D.O.B. members recently went on a campaign to oust two transsexual members of that organization. They stated "We don't like them voicing their opinions as lesbians. They are not lesbians. Even after surgery it would be hard to accept these people as lesbian women. There is no excuse for this 'passing.' These people should accept themselves for what they are. Their oppression is different than the lesbians' oppression."

Other D.O.B. members, in an article written from the standpoint that male-to-female transsexuals are women, and should therefore be allowed in D.O.B., have stated: "A transsexual is a woman who is born in a man's body or a man who is born in a woman's body, and who goes through reconstructive surgery to bring his or her body into harmony with her mind. . . . Actually the entire issue regarding transsexuals in D.O.B. really boils down to whether or not one accepts science's definition of a male-to-female transsexual as a woman; whether or not one accepts that any such woman who feels love for only women, who relates to only women, who identifies herself as a lesbian, is a lesbian."

They say further, "It is wrong to say that a lesbian woman in a male body is 'passing as a lesbian woman.' You don't 'pass' for something you ARE," and that "the true transsexual wants not just to be a woman (or man) inside, but also to have the physical body of their true sex. Despite all the disadvantages involved with being a woman and a lesbian, the transsexual woman, with the alignment of her body with her psyche, gains her self-identity and her self-esteem. And that is everything."

These statements appeared in articles recently sent to all members of S.F. D.O.B. in preparation for a vote on the issue. The proposal: "Any transsexual who considers her/himself to be a woman will be eligible for membership and participation in S.F. D.O.B."

The Tide Collective also received these articles. The matter was discussed and a vote of the collective was taken. A telegram was then sent to S.F. D.O.B. The words of that telegram are the essence of this editorial:

> Our common oppression is based on society's insistence that we perform certain roles: wife, husband, mother, father, masculine, feminine, etc. We cry out, "You cannot define us. WE DEFINE OURSELVES! Those who vote no tonight vote with our oppressors. Those who vote yes recognize that none of us is free unless all of us are free." Please advise our transsexual sisters that, if they are not welcome in the liberal city of San Francisco, they are most welcome in the city of Los Angeles.

Will the struggle for compassion and freedom please take one giant step backward.

References

Córdova, Jeanne. 1972. "D.O.B. Says No." *Lesbian Tide* 2, no. 5: 21, 31.
Tide Collective. 1972. "A Collective Editorial." *Lesbian Tide* 2, no. 5: 21, 29.

Radical Queen

An Interview with Tommi Avicolli Mecca

SUSAN STRYKER

Abstract Tommi Avicolli Mecca, born in Philadelphia in 1951, moved to San Francisco in 1991 and quickly established himself as a leading queer performance artist, playwright, and newspaper columnist as well as a leading housing rights and antigentrification activist. This interview is excerpted from an interview initially conducted by Susan Stryker, general coeditor of *TSQ: Transgender Studies Quarterly*, for the GLBT Historical Society on November 19, 1998, and edited in consultation with Mecca for publication in *TSQ*, to highlight content related to the interrelationships between feminism, drag culture, and gay liberation politics in Philadelphia in the 1970s. In what follows, Mecca discusses his early involvement with radical sexuality and gender politics with the Gay Liberation Front (GLF) at Temple University, his later involvement in the more assimilationist Gay Activist Alliance (GAA), the formation of the Radical Queens collective, and his alliance with the separatist lesbian feminist group DYKETACTICS.
Keywords Philadelphia, Radical Queens, Gay Liberation Front, Gay Activist Alliance, drag

Susan Stryker: *How did you get involved with gay liberation?*

Tommi Avicolli Mecca: I went to college in 1969 to avoid the draft. After I registered as a conscientious objector, I went to Temple University, which was the school that a lot of working-class kids went to. As a working-class kid, I thought that was the highest I could aspire to. My father wanted to keep me out of the service, and he was willing to scrape together some money to help me get through college—plus I had an almost full-time job to put myself through school. Nineteen-seventy, or 1971 I guess it was I discovered GLF. Once I got into Gay Liberation, I got into it big time. Within a few weeks I was the recording secretary of the group, and then before I knew it I was actually chairing the group. Temple GLF participated in the Black Panthers convention in 1970 that was held at the university. We also got into feminism early on. I remember first learning about feminism in GLF. We had consciousness-raising sessions once a week. We'd just get together and talk. We went to demonstrations to stop cuts to welfare. We'd be

TSQ: Transgender Studies Quarterly ★ Volume 3, Numbers 1–2 ★ May 2016 **278**
DOI 10.1215/23289252-3334535   © 2016 Duke University Press

marching over housing issues. So, we were multi-issues, and saw our issues as being part of other struggles. Oh, and another thing, there were a lot of people in GLF doing drag. Many of the guys in GLF did drag at some point. Genderfuck. I learned about genderfuck in GLF. There was this guy, Sweet Basil Razzle Dazzle, he called himself. Basil was very influential in helping me develop my drag identity, and to realize that that was part of me.

SS: *So that was new—you hadn't been a little tranny kid?*

TAM: Well, actually I had. I had been a little sissy. Absolutely. I used to put on my sister's clothes. She'd actually dress me up and we'd run around the house when my parents weren't home. Oh, yeah. Lots of fantasies about being a girl. But I kind of put all that aside by the time I got to high school. I kind of suppressed all that. Because it was hard. It was hard in my neighborhood to be effeminate. I got beat up a lot for it when I was a kid. So when I started having sex with guys I kind of put all that aside. At first I concentrated on the sex.

SS: *I'm interested in how you started thinking about gender in the context of gay liberation. I know there was a lot of genderfuck, and a lot of drag, and even a lot of transsexuals involved in early gay liberation, a relationship with hustling and the street queen culture, but there was also a real antipathy against all that as well.*

TAM: GLF definitely had a relationship with the street queens. Sure. We knew some of them, they knew us. Some of us went and hung on the streets. But when it came to our functions, a lot of the street queens didn't come to them because that just wasn't their thing. They didn't go to any of the political stuff.

SS: *Did you think of doing drag as "political stuff"?*

TAM: I think it began as a political thing, but it became a life. I started living in genderfuck, or in drag. As I got into it, and as I came to understand what it meant to defy gender in this country, it reinforced my radical politics. Because I came to see how ridiculous gender was, especially as I learned from feminists. And I learned a lot from feminists, and really began to see how gender roles functioned. There were all these people there to teach me.

SS: *Did you ever do hormones?*

TAM: No. But [my friend]—now let's see, was she on hormones that early? Probably not. But she was talking about it, and she was talking about a sex change. And I'm very clear at that point that that's not where I'm going. I wasn't exactly sure where I was going, but I was definitely clear that that was not where I wanted to go. I thought of myself as androgynous, male and female; I could have both.

SS: *So sex change just seemed like an option to change—not that it was an option for you personally, but that it was just one of the paths that someone might go down, just like "well, some people do, some don't, whatever"? There wasn't any negative political baggage associated with making that choice?*

TAM: No, not at all. I really considered it to be one of the things that we were fighting for—people's right to do that, just like people had a right to sleep with somebody of the same sex. It just seemed logical to me, that it extended to that. I mean, I thought [my friend] had a perfect right to change her body, to fit what she perceived as her real identity. But there was never any problem with that for me. Now, there was with some other people. Other gay activists. Obviously. But there was never for me.

SS: *Did you consciously think about any of the gender stuff you were doing as being an antiwar activity?*

TAM: Oh, yeah. I was involved with the antiwar movement. I was a member of SDS, Students for a Democratic Society, at Temple. I attended all the antiwar rallies. And I did see what we were doing, I think I wrote about it, though I'm not sure I published it, a piece about how men violating their gender role was revolutionary—because who could get serious about fighting if you're running around in mascara? Because if you spend all that time getting ready, who would then want to go on a battlefield and sweat? There was this whole thing about how we were going to break down the savagery of the human race because we were opening up a whole new area of male identity. It was kind of naive and idealistic when I look back on it now, but that was the era back then, it was the posthippie, or even still the hippie, era. But I guess some of us had the idea that if guys were running around in mascara then there wouldn't be war.

SS: *Genderfuck, don't fight?*

TAM: Yeah. Sort of. Make love not war, that kind of thing. But there was definitely a relationship, even though the antiwar movement wasn't necessarily crazy about us.

SS: *You've said you saw your gender expression somewhat in political terms—as being related to the antiwar movement, the radical movement. You also mentioned earlier that you were influenced by feminism, and that feminists attended GLF meetings, and that there was a lot of dialoguing going on.*

TAM: Yeah, especially at Temple. GLF had good working relations with Women's Liberation. I remember having long discussions with Laurie, who was heading up Women's Liberation and I was heading up GLF. And we had all these discussions about drag, because she was really curious about why I was suddenly wearing mascara and blue eye shadow to class, and doing all this sort of stuff. And wasn't this mocking women? No, I said, it's not about mocking women, it's about releasing something inside myself, and if anything it's mocking men. That male role, violating that male role, and so on and so forth. So we had these discussions and she was able to follow it all, and she came along with us and supported GLF. There was a great working relation between Women's Liberation and GLF. A total understanding of those of us in the group who were questioning the whole gender thing, and she saw that it was feminist, that it was the corollary to women wanting to get rid of the makeup.

I think it even carried over to GAA. When I started going to GAA, I'm not even sure what possessed me to stay in GAA because it wasn't as radical as GLF, but I stayed, and some other people from GLF stayed, and early on we got into conflict about drag stuff. Really serious conflicts about drag. Because there were people in GAA who felt we needed to put our best foot forward and that drag queens were an embarrassment. Queens were gonna stifle the development of the movement and limit the progress we could make because they embodied all the stereotypes and blah blah blah blah blah. You know that whole routine. We were there to say, "No No No No No—this is more than just the eye shadow. You don't understand. There is a whole liberation ideology behind this that you simply are not getting." And they didn't get it for the longest time, so that's why Cei Bell and I decided to start Radical Queens. We started it as part of GAA first.

SS: *So Radical Queens came out of GAA and not GLF? Because GLF was already totally hip to it, whereas GAA needed to be educated about it?*

TAM: Right. It would have been redundant in GLF. We started as a caucus. We did educational forums after meetings. They had this period after the meetings where you could present things. One week we did this thing where we took this working-class guy, this really nice guy, a real truck driver type, and we put him in drag right there in the room, right there in front of everybody. We totally transformed him. We showed everybody how we did the makeup, and turned him into looking like—well, probably, looking like his mother. He looked like this working-class woman. It was wonderful. People were like "Oh my god!" And the women—the women really got into it.

SS: *So GAA was a cogender group?*

TAM: Yes, although there were always more men than women. What eventually happened was that women were very dissatisfied with the male leadership and they formed a separate caucus, just like we had. So they had their little group within GAA too, and we started working together. They would bring a motion on the floor and we would support it. We would bring something up and they would support it. Same thing happened with the Black caucus, which my boyfriend at the time cofounded. They called themselves the Flaming Souls. So we had these three groups that were all disenfranchised that would form a voting bloc that was pretty powerful. It eventually led to me being elected president of GAA.

There really was a power that developed between the three caucuses that really started to change GAA, to change many of the policies of GAA, to broaden its issues, and to address women's issues, and to work with NOW [National Organization for Women] and other feminist groups. So when I ran the first time, I ran as a joke. We passed out red lipstick at the meeting and asked people to sign their ballots for me in lipstick. For all the high consciousness we had, there was also a trickster side to it. Kind of like the Sisters of Perpetual Indulgence. We could do some clownish sorts of things, just because it was fun, it was camp. I mean, we were still young. We were having fun.

But the following year, I guess that would have been 1975, I actually got elected. The power base was in place by then. Everybody wanted a radical change. Women were fed up. People of color were fed up. GAA was beginning to lose members. So one of my pledges was that I was going to bring people back into GAA, really make GAA what it used to be, and make it more inclusive. I started these community get-togethers—bring in all these groups in the city, get us at little tables in this big room, and they would put out their literature on the tables, and everybody would have a chance to come up to the microphone to have a chance to say a few words about their organizations, and it started to bring people back to GAA, and people started trusting us again, and being willing to work with us.

We started forging alliances with groups that hadn't been working with us, leftist-type groups. We were coming along pretty well. We were standing up for drag queens—bringing up those issues, talking about those issues. I remember once in a while street queens would come to meetings and say, "Oh, the cops were really harassing us last night. They came and raided and arrested so-and-so and so-and-so." And we would get our political committee to contact the cops and demand a meeting. This had never been done before—doing this for street queens. But this is all part of what I was trying to get GAA to do. More people were starting to trust us. This was really important to me.

SS: *Did you see any lesbian separatist reaction against being involved with GAA or GLF specifically because of their involvement with drag? Was it politicized that way in Philadelphia?*

TAM: Well, there was a lesbian separatist movement in Philadelphia. When I was GAA president, the most visible manifestation of it was a group called

DYKETACTICS, which was a group of lesbian feminist separatists who got involved with fighting for the gay rights bill before the City Council. They also took on the Archdiocese and various other institutions. They picketed a movie theater running snuff films in which a woman was supposedly murdered during sex. There was class consciousness there, too, because most of the women in DYKETACTICS were working class.

I had a really good relationship with them, because I knew some of the women. I mean, they were women who had been around and had been in other things. So I knew them and knew how to work with them. I was actually the only man—quote unquote "man" [laughing]—who was ever allowed to step into their house that they lived in, because they lived in this big collective house in Philly, and I was the only man allowed to come near that place. I mean, they wouldn't even allow a male from the electric company in to check the meter. But yet they didn't consider me a man. That's what they told me. They told me I didn't have male energy. It was amazing. And they respected Radical Queens. They did not trash drag. So there was never that sort of dialogue that happened in New York, that trashing and that kind of animosity between drag queens and lesbian feminists. Never had that happen in Philly. And I think that was because of Radical Queens, and the kinds of coalitions we formed early on. And because we worked to keep those alliances going.

SS: *Did you know Sylvia Rivera and Marsha Johnson from STAR—the Street Transvestite Action Revolutionaries? In New York?*

TAM: I met Sylvia, I guess it would have been late 1972, 1973. Because I would go to New York with friends occasionally, to go to the dances at the Firehouse. Anyway, we would go up there and they would have these dances. They were incredible—the place absolutely packed. So we would go up and I met Sylvia at one of those dances. I really liked Sylvia and Marsha, liked what they were trying to do, especially their idea of a drop-in center, a food program for street queens, safe places for people to go, legal help.

SS: *If you had to summarize the philosophy of Radical Queens in a few sentences, how would you do that?*

TAM: Gosh, I don't know. How would I do that? A group of people united by our belief that gender is a social construct and our dissatisfaction with the two-gender system. People wanting to free up other people's expectations about gender. A group of people who wanted other people to just leave us alone and let us be who we were. I don't know, it's hard to say in a few words.

SS: *But you did see it as an explicitly feminist thing to be doing?*

TAM: Yeah, I did. Well, it became that. I don't know if I saw that right at the beginning when I started doing drag, but it certainly became that as time went along, certainly by the time Radical Queens was formed. As GLF forged our alliances with women's groups, I certainly saw that what we were doing was feminist work. I think because I began to see how ridiculous gender was, by seeing how arbitrary it was, especially gender roles, and how easily you could totally change somebody's perception of gender, how you could walk down the street and be seen as somebody who was totally the other gender—I began to see just how fragile this whole thing was. And society puts so much weight on this, and there's so much prescription. And it seems like all of society is held up by these pillars, that the two genders are innate, and that, you know, they can't be violated, gender roles can't be violated. But they're not a solid foundation. They're a very shaky foundation.

Susan Stryker is associate professor of gender and women's studies and director of the Institute for LGBT Studies at the University of Arizona and general coeditor of *TSQ: Transgender Studies Quarterly*.

A Conversation with Jeanne Córdova

TALIA M. BETTCHER

Abstract This interview with long-time Los Angeles–based feminist, lesbian, and butch activist Jeanne Córdova, conducted by *TSQ: Transgender Studies Quarterly* guest editor and editorial board member Talia Bettcher in June and July 2015, explores the relationship between butch and transgender identities and the place of transgender issues in feminist and lesbian histories and cultures. It pays particular attention to the involvement of transsexual lesbian singer Beth Elliott at the 1973 Lesbian Conference organized by Córdova and others, which became a flashpoint in second-wave feminist dialogs about transsexual involvement in the women's movement and in lesbian feminism.

Keywords Jeanne Córdova, Beth Elliott, Los Angeles, lesbian, feminist, transsexual, transgender, butch

L os Angeles–based feminist, lesbian, and butch activist Jeanne Córdova was the founder and publisher of *The Lesbian Tide* (1971–80) and the *Gay and Lesbian Community Yellow Pages* (1982–99). She was a key organizer for several large conferences, including the first West Coast Gay Women's Conference (1971), the historic Lesbian Conference at the University of California, Los Angeles (UCLA, 1973), the founding convention of the National Lesbian Feminist Organization (1978), and the Butch Voices L.A. Conference (2010). She was president of the Los Angeles chapter of Daughters of Bilitis, the oldest lesbian organization in the United States (1971–72), founder and president of the Lesbian Center (1971), president of the Stonewall Democratic Club (1979–81), founder of the Los Angeles Gay and Lesbian Press Association (1983), and cofounder of LEX, the Lesbian Exploratory (2007–present). She campaigned against the "Briggs Initiative" (Proposition 6), which would have made it illegal for gays and lesbians to be school teachers in California (1978), served as media director for Stop Proposition 64, which opposed Lyndon LaRouche's proposed quarantine of people with AIDS (1986), and organized and participated in the Marry Us or Jail Us civil disobedience action following Proposition 8's ban on same-sex marriage in California (2009). She was also the author of three books, including the Lambda Literary Award

TSQ: Transgender Studies Quarterly * Volume 3, Numbers 1–2 * May 2016   **285**
DOI 10.1215/23289252-3334547   © 2016 Duke University Press

winning *When We Were Outlaws: A Memoir of Love and Revolution* (2011). Cordova died on January 10, 2016, after a long struggle with cancer. She is survived by her partner, Lynn Ballen. For further biographical information, see Córdova 2015.

The controversy surrounding transsexual singer Beth Elliott's performance at the 1973 Lesbian Conference introduced the "transsexual question" into lesbian feminist politics nationwide in the United States when many attendees objected to her presence. Elliott, former vice president of the San Francisco chapter of the Daughters of Bilitis, had been voted out of that organization a few months earlier solely because she was transsexual, prompting the resignation of some members, including the entire editorial staff of the chapter newsletter, *Sisters*. Although the conference organizing committee (Lesbian Activist Women), including Córdova, maintained a trans-positive position before, during, and after the conference, the San Francisco lesbian feminist separatist group the Gutter Dykes and others vehemently opposed the participation of transsexual women, as did keynote speaker Robin Morgan. Córdova and other organizers intervened, and the majority of those in attendance voted to allow Elliott to perform. Despite this support, the framing of Elliott as a man violating women's space first articulated what would become a standard antitransssexual accusation among many feminists in the decades ahead.

The following conversation about the conference, and trans and feminist politics more generally, was conducted on June 17 and July 1, 2015. The transcripts were merged and edited for style and length by the interviewer, Talia Bettcher, *TSQ: Transgender Studies Quarterly* general coeditor Susan Stryker, and Jeanne Córdova and Lynn Ballen. Bettcher has worked with Córdova on several projects, including serving as a panelist as part of the LEX exhibit *GenderPlay in Lesbian Culture* (2008), participating in the Marry Us or Jail Us action, and cofacilitating a workshop on transphobia and butchphobia for Butch Voices LA.

Talia M. Bettcher: *How do you see the relationship between butch politics and feminist politics?*

Jeanne Córdova: I don't think butch politics are necessarily feminist, but you can say that butch politics are an addition to feminist politics or feminist politics are an addition to butch politics. My butch politics run deeper, simply because my butch politics started at age four, and my feminist politics began at age twenty.

TMB: *What do you think about the relationship between butch politics and transgender politics?*

JC: Sometimes these years, I wonder whether the idea of butch has been interpreted more as a trans identity. Whereas before, butch was an identity in search of a politic and didn't have one. It was still a popular identity for many lesbians, including myself. I mean *butch* here as an umbrella term including *stud* as in black culture and *genderqueer* to some of the younger generations.

TMB: *Do you think that trans politics gave a political framework for butch?*

JC: Yes, in some ways. It does especially in this day and age when transgender politics are prominent. You could see the entire butch identity as a trans identity. It's not transgender in terms of going through all the hormones or surgeries, but it could certainly be seen as a type of gender-nonconforming identity. Right now I think there's some volleying back and forth between butch being a feminist politic and butch being a transgender politic, being part of the transgender scene or the feminist scene. We are in an age of transitory nomenclature.

TMB: *In your recent memoir, a pivotal chapter is entitled "The Rage of All Butches." It's obviously an allusion to lesbianism as "the rage of all women condensed to the point of explosion." What was it like as a young feminist activist in the 1970s, also being butch?*

JC: It was difficult. I did have to hide if I wanted to continue being the lesbian feminist leader that I was, especially at the beginning of the lesbian-feminist decade, the 1970s. It wasn't popular to be butch or femme, and it was seen, in the 1970s and 1980s, as aping heterosexual relationships. But the butch/femme dynamic within Lesbianville came about much earlier than any feminist politic at all.

TMB: *Let's talk about the Lesbian Conference in 1973. It has gone down in history as fairly controversial. One of the controversies was about Beth Elliott's participation, but there were other controversies that were a part of that conference. Can you speak to some of these other controversies?*

JC: Well, there was a controversy over feminism and whether lesbian separatism was to be the dominant discourse. Even though lesbian separatism espoused the same kind of politics as radical feminism, lesbian separatism was further seen by many as a lifestyle, a permanent separatism from men and even straight women. And others didn't want any part of its ideology. There was a big controversy over which way lesbian feminism should go. I wasn't a separatist because I knew that sooner or later men and the straight world would become part of what it meant to be a lesbian in this sexist and heteronormative society.

TMB: *Your politics have always been more coalition building. Perhaps more pragmatic in that sense?*

JC: Yes, I wanted it to be a national movement to effect political, societal change.

TMB: *Another debate at this conference involved a narrow definition of lesbian identity: as in, this is who I am romantically and sexually oriented toward versus a more political notion of lesbianism. At the conference Robin Morgan endorsed that broader notion. I imagine there was some discussion of that at the conference as well?*

JC: Yes, her identity as a political lesbian, that broader definition, was new, and shocked many at the time. She wanted to expand the definition of lesbianism irrespective of sexual attraction. She was married to a gay man, Kenneth, and it was quite well known. At the time she identified as a lesbian; she might be called bisexual today. She sought to widen the term *lesbian* to include women who were radical feminists but did not sleep with men or women!

TMB: *Did you see that as a co-option of lesbianism?*

JC: It was very pervasive at the time, and seen as politically correct. Later on, her version came into much controversy. I thought it was healthy for the movement (I was thinking always in terms of movement rather than my personal life) to have a wider definition than being only attracted to women. But I didn't personally agree that her definition would stick around. I thought you did have to be attracted to or sleep with women.

TMB: *Before the controversy around Beth Elliott's performance onstage at the conference, there was her ouster from DOB [Daughters of Bilitis] in San Francisco. There was a statement issued by the* Lesbian Tide *Collective the night of the DOB vote that read, "Those who vote no tonight [to the question of whether Elliott should be allowed to remain in the group] are voting with our oppressors. Those who vote yes vote that none of us are free until all of us are free. Please advise our transsexual sisters that if they are not welcome in the liberal city of San Francisco that they are most welcome in the City of Los Angeles" (Tide Collective 1972).[1]*

JC: I undoubtedly had a big part in that statement, yes. It was always my politic to include a lot of marginalized people in our lesbian feminist or gay movement. Yet that night six months later at the conference, I didn't realize that it was the same woman.

TMB: *At what point did you realize?*

JC: I suppose I knew it was Beth sometime later when I read some of the articles about the conference a few weeks after it. I should have known it was Beth. Maybe the organizer from Orange County, Linda (Tess) Tessier, did know. We organizers were loosely coordinated, with different subcommittees.

TMB: *Do you remember bringing Beth on as a correspondent [for the* Lesbian Tide*]?*[2]

JC: No. I might have written to Beth or had a phone call with her, maybe, but I don't remember anything further than that. If you look at the issues, she wasn't a very active correspondent. I mean she didn't send in many stories.

TMB: *The* Tide *had other trans women working for it later on?*

JC: Yes, definitely. Sue and Sheryl.[3] Sue Cooke was a photographer and a very good one. I didn't agree with any reason for excluding them. I thought the movement in general was about including marginalized people and transgender people along with intersexed, and that host of sexual minorities was part of who I thought we were. Take for instance myself being a butch lesbian—that adds another dimension to my feminism. One can even call it, as they did in the 1970s, counter to my feminism. But I didn't believe so. I remember Sue and Sheryl. You had to be a certain kind of feminist to be on the *Tide* Collective, deeper than liberal feminists. If you were, and you said that you were with a woman or had been, that was enough. We didn't ask further.

TMB: *How much of a leadership role did you play in developing that vision?*

JC: A big role.

TMB: *Let's go back to something you mentioned earlier. Even if some of the organizers, like Tess or Barb McLean, did know it was Beth, the DOB controversy was not well known, not very big.*

JC: San Francisco DOB, at the time, was small. In the LA DOB chapter the previous year or two we had sixty members coming to the meetings and maybe one hundred scattered around that didn't. It was very conservative, and I thought it was the same in San Francisco. These were DOB's dying-out years. I was no longer part of it in 1973. The *Lesbian Tide* began as LA DOB's official newsletter. We, on the *Tide* Collective, asked the membership of LA DOB to come together and vote the newsletter out of the organization. They did. They didn't like their own newsletter, big time, because they thought the *Lesbian Tide* was too radical.

TMB: *How was it too radical?*

JC: It talked about lesbian feminism a lot of different ways. Rape, abortion, marches, lesbians going to court and mostly losing, nonmonogamy, trying to change the country! All the new wave of youngsters like me were coming to the *Tide* and the organization called the Lesbian Feminists, not the LA DOB.

TMB: *The history books report that when you took the stage at the 1973 Lesbian Conference, you along with Reverend Freda Smith from Sacramento spoke "loud and strong in defense of Beth Elliott" (Candy Coleman, quoted in Stryker 2008: 103). You were cited as saying of her that she was both a feminist and a sister (Clendinen and Nagourney 1999: 166). You've already talked about the underlying personal and political convictions that led you to take a stance like that. It was also an extremely frightening moment that required courage. Can you talk about what you were feeling at the time when all this was going on?*

JC: Feelings are always part of politics. I was feeling afraid because there was a very large contingent of lesbians who wanted "that man" off the stage. I guess the most important part was I didn't want the conference to blow up and end on Friday. The fact that it was the opening night, with a long weekend ahead, was more than worrisome. The fear of the conference blowing up was very tangible and very threatening to me personally as well as the other conference organizers. We had spent months putting it together. It came as a big surprise, that particular issue over transsexuals. The issue itself was not one that we had given much thought to.

TMB: *Do you think that you were naïve about the conference?*

JC: I think the organizers all should have known that Beth would take the stage. We should have anticipated that the fighting in the San Francisco DOB would affect our conference. Or somehow known what Robin Morgan would say. Morgan's speech was very explosive. There was a certain undertone of "I belong here, you don't" to it. I was upset with the tone and rancor of the speech. It didn't imbue others with an inclusive feeling.

TMB: *In the end, on Friday night, a vote was held on whether Beth would be allowed to perform. You had to facilitate the vote, count the votes, even though you had proposed that there be a workshop instead. Ultimately, she was allowed to perform. Is there anything you regret about the way "the trans moment," as you later called it, was handled?*

JC: At the time, I of course regretted *any* issues that threatened to blow up the conference! I could say, "I wish this hadn't happened," but things do happen and they become part of our history. I'm glad that the majority voted the way it did—pro, that is. I still am glad. I remember one specific person who led the antitrans vote, a red-headed member of the Gutter Dykes. I think it was the same woman who has come to some of the butch conferences more recently. She now identifies as butch but did not identify as such at the time. She has created a lot of controversy and we do have different opinions. She is still proud of that moment, which in retrospect, was the first time the lesbian movement had to publicly deal with the transgender issue.

TMB: *Was there a sense of difference when you saw these radical Gutter Dykes? When they showed up and you saw the rage?*

JC: They were dressed more in flannel and khaki pants, with shorter hair—like crew cuts—than most lesbian feminists of LA who were androgynous yes, but not as angry looking. I was blown away by it at first. I was shocked at their vehemence. I thought most of their anger seemed to be going toward this person sitting on stage. I remember thinking this issue or person must be pretty important to engender all this rage.

TMB: *When you heard this new view that was coming out of San Francisco, did it alter your own views at all? Your own politics?*

JC: Besides the conference itself indirectly telling me to get out of organizing! I went into more writing, and into a journalism career. But no, I don't think my politics changed a great deal. I still believe in the same things and on the trans issue it didn't change me—it made me much, much more aware that it was an issue, and the last twenty years have made that clear! I have had many discussions with lesbian feminists who agree, and those who don't agree. I think there's a lot of hurt and anger on the part of lesbian feminists who disagree. Those who disagree don't recognize why the trans movement is kind of taking over some spaces, I mean both places and talk. It's the general dominant discourse. Some lesbian feminists don't like it. Take for instance when we watched the video of the undocumented trans woman [Jennicet Gutiérez] at the White House yelling at the president last week.[4] We, I mean Dykes, were once "those people," people like her, yelling because we were not heard. And before that it was gay men. I would have been on the side of the transgender woman even though a lot of gays started booing.

TMB: *Recently, Lisa Vogel announced that this will be the last year of the Michigan Womyn's Musical Festival. In 2013 you wrote a blog piece weighing in from a butch lesbian perspective in which you argued that her position was inconsistent. You thought that they ought to include trans women, and you questioned why they were including trans men. Rather than going over the old ground, I guess now that MichFest will be no more, the question is, where do we go from here?*

JC: I think the closing of Michfest is the end of an era, and the beginning of another era. I commend Lisa for bringing us all Michfest these many years. She has done a great service to her many communities. I think some trans festivals and other lesbian feminist types of festivals will start up, that speak to today's issues.

Reconciliation? There will always be some second wavers who feel antitrans. I don't think it will stay on the front burner much longer. I think as the trans movement matures more, then more lesbian feminists will understand it's the combination of feminism and trans and queer that has been the logical next step.

In some ways, I can understand the anger of some of the feminists who have labored for a long time and not gotten all the work, like the ERA [Equal Rights Amendment], done. But I've always looked at our social movements in the long term, and the arc of one movement may not be done when the arc of a new one begins. An individual has to interact with a trans person on a personal level and have something positive come out of that in order to be really protrans. I was lucky; I had that conversation. I began to realize, "maybe this is different than being gay, maybe this is deeper, or different." There are lots of different kinds of so-called gender dysphoria, including my own!

But I do wish that all young butch women growing up now could be more fully aware of the feminist alternative before they felt they had to choose. I wish all of us genderqueer and studs and butch women had been told they could either adopt the feminist alternative or transition their bodies. By "feminist alternative" I mean like my generation was told by feminism, "Look, you can be any kind of masculine-identified woman you want to be. You can be woman in your body and be masculine-of-mind or -dress—you can be *any* kind of woman." Or, you can change your body to be male or female. Many in the younger generations never hear this feminist alternative. They don't look at it, and never hear about it. Knowing you has been very good for me. It has taught me, verified, what I previously believed.

TMB: *One of the things happening recently in the United States is the increasing visibility of transgender politics. Laverne Cox appearing on the cover of* TIME *magazine under the caption "Transgender Tipping Point," for example. Do you have any thoughts on where you think the transgender movement might be headed? Or any advice you would give to transgender activists?*

JC: By the time any of our movements hit the cover of *Vanity Fair* or *TIME* or *Newsweek*, we have largely made it. I think the transgender movement is on the edge of being over, and successful. The first wave, anyway. I think there will be other waves and backlashes. It's over in that you've won a lot. It's now just beginning to be okay to be trans in the workplace, housing, and other areas. But that's where the battle still is, in people's consciousness. That's where the roots of trans bashing are.

I wonder what it means to question the categories "man" and "woman"; the definition of what is man and what is woman has been a long time coming, and that's one of the positive lessons that the transgender movement will have to teach us.

Talia M. Bettcher is a professor of philosophy at California State University, Los Angeles, and she currently serves as chair. Some of her articles include "Evil Deceivers and Make-Believers: Transphobic Violence and the Politics of Illusion" (*Hypatia*, summer 2007), "Trapped in the Wrong Theory: Re-thinking Trans Oppression and Resistance (*Signs*, winter 2014), and "When Selves Have Sex: What the Phenomenology of Trans Sexuality Can Teach about Sexual Orientation" (*Journal of Homosexuality*, April 2014). With Ann Garry, she coauthored the *Hypatia* special issue "Transgender Studies and Feminism: Theory, Politics, and Gender Realities" (summer 2009).

Acknowledgments

Special thanks to my research assistant, Bree Lacey, for her invaluable transcription work.

Notes

1. For a report on the vote, see Córdova 1972.
2. Beth Elliott is credited as San Francisco correspondent for the *Tide* from July 1972 until April 1973, after which correspondents were discontinued. She is also a contributor to the "Special West Coast Lesbian Conference Commemorative Issue" (May–June 1973).
3. Sue Cooke is credited with layout for the *Tide* from March/April 1979 until May/June 1980. She also did much uncredited photography, according to Córdova. I could not find credits for Sheryl. But Córdova notes that not all staff were credited.
4. Gutiérez interrupted President Obama's speech during a White House LGBT reception on June 24, 2015. She said, "President Obama, release all LGBTQ detention centers! President Obama, stop the torture and abuse of trans women in detention centers! President Obama, I am a trans woman. I'm tired of the abuse" (Democracy Now! 2015).

References

Clendinen, Dudley, and Adam Nagourney. 1999. *Out for Good: The Struggle to Build a Gay Rights Movement in America*. New York: Simon and Shuster.

Córdova, Jeanne. 1972. "D.O.B. Says No." *Lesbian Tide* 2, no. 5: 21, 31.

———. 2013. "Michigan: A Butch Feminist Responds." *This Lesbian World* (blog), April 25. www .thislesbianworld.blogspot.com/.

———. 2015. Jeanne Córdova. www.jeannecordova.com/ (accessed July 9, 2015).

Democracy Now! 2015. "Headlines, June 25, 2015." www.democracynow.org/2015/6/25/headlines.

Stryker, Susan. 2008. *Transgender History*. Berkeley, CA: Seal.

Tide Collective. 1972. "A Collective Editorial." *Lesbian Tide* 2, no. 5: 21, 29.

Another Dream of Common Language

An Interview with Sandy Stone

SUSAN STRYKER

Abstract Sandy Stone's "Posttranssexual Manifesto" is often regarded as the principal point of departure for transgender studies. In this 1995 interview, portions of which first appeared in *Wired* magazine, Stone discusses her various careers in telecommunications, medical research, recording engineering, consumer electronics, and cultural studies of media and performance. The interview has been edited to highlight Stone's persistent attention to questions of language and communication, and the relationship of these concerns to feminist and transgender theorizing.
Keywords computers, music industry, cyberspace, language, cultural studies

T his interview with venerable transfeminist foremother Sandy Stone, whose field-founding "Posttranssexual Manifesto" responded, in part, to her experience of exclusion from lesbian feminist culture and politics in the late 1970s and early 1980s, was conducted by *TSQ: Transgender Studies Quarterly* general coeditor Susan Stryker in Austin, Texas, over the Labor Day weekend in 1995. Portions of the interview were published in *Wired* magazine (vol. 4, no. 5, May 1996) as "Sex and Death among the Cyborgs." Excerpts from this same interview have been edited for publication in *TSQ*, in consultation with Sandy Stone, on August 1–3, 2015.

Susan Stryker: *Sandy, you were a child prodigy. You graduated early from high school, and then worked at Bell Labs while still a teenager, audited classes at MIT [Massachusetts Institute of Technology], did medical research at the NIH [National Institutes of Health] and the Menninger Clinic, and wound up being a recording engineer for a while. When were you at Bell Labs?*

Sandy Stone: That was about 1955. I was fresh out of high school. I was there for two years, in the special systems development department. We were building among the very first solid-state digital computers. They were clumsy, yet they

TSQ: Transgender Studies Quarterly ★ Volume 3, Numbers 1–2 ★ May 2016 **294**
DOI 10.1215/23289252-3334559 © 2016 Duke University Press

demonstrated the principles that could be done on computers in the future, the technology that could be developed. I arrived just as they were beginning to put the ball into play with digital telephony. We were building touch-tone. It was at a primitive level—are the keys going to be in a circle like a dial, or are they going to be in a simpler shape?

Stryker: *When you were at MIT, you sat in on classes with some of the first-generation cyberneticists. Can you talk a little bit about what it was like to be at MIT at that time?*

Stone: Those people were the legends of modern computer technology, who jammed on what all this was about in a very basic way. How can we build simple models of neurons? What is a computer going to be? How are these things going to affect our lives? The idea of associated circuits was new, and the idea of networks hadn't really come into being. Even at that time they were called hackers. It was partly a derogatory term, but partly a very laudatory term. It just meant a kind of thrashing, trying to understand how these things worked and how to get them to do what you wanted them to do.

Stryker: *So you were a hacker?*

Stone: It was our way of playing with the computers. The idea of computer games hadn't happened yet. Spacewar wasn't written until 1961, maybe later. So the idea that people played with computers was not yet really around.

Stryker: *Where was the fun in what you were doing?*

Stone: Well, the fun was just the thrill of basically perverting, diverting, subverting the technology.

Stryker: *Tell me about some of your medical research.*

Stone: I did a series of experiments with implants. These for me were one of the most fascinating things I had ever done. I did neurological implants in cats. I brought the electrode out to a miniature stereo FM transmitter which I attached to the cat's collar. I would let the cats wander around outside in the fields. I would put on the stereo headphones and "become" a cat and hear myself walking through the grass. Cats don't hear like humans. You can hear every grass blade. You can hear every insect walking and, of course, you can hear the field mice off in the distance, in stereo. I came to understand something about feline subjectivity. That for me was the beginning of my experience with communication prosthetics. Not just human/machine, but species/machine.

Stryker: *Trans-species.*

Stone: Yes. And then, around this time, I discovered the Beatles and moved on into rock-and-roll. I went to work for some recording studios in Manhattan.

Stryker: *How did you become a recording engineer?*

Stone: I went to New York, walked into the Record Plant [studio], right when they were beginning to do their first dates. I didn't understand anything about the recording industry. Gary, the owner, desperately needed maintenance people. He took me into the other room and they had the state-of-the-art machine at that point, which was a Scully twelve-track. Here was this machine that wasn't working right, and Gary said, "Can you fix that?" I said, "Yeah sure, I've seen stuff like that before, no problem," which was a total lie. "But, it looks slightly different from the ones I'm used to working with. Let me see your manual." And I speed-read it.

I proceeded to walk over to the Scully and fix it. It took me about two minutes, and the thing worked, and Gary's jaw fell open. He hired me on the spot. For three weeks, I literally lived in the Record Plant. I had no place to go in New York. I was utterly in another world, no social networks, no idea how to find an apartment, no nothing. But I knew how to sleep, so I slept in the basement. Actually, I slept on Jimi's old capes. I spent every waking moment in the control room. When there wasn't anybody in there, I would fix things. When they were, I would watch what they did and absorb it. As soon as they left I would sit down at the board and mix the tapes that they had just recorded. I was getting really good at it really quickly.

Stryker: *When you say you "slept on Jimi's old capes," you mean Jimi Hendrix, right? What was it like to mix him?*

Stone: The third week that I was doing this, the engineer turned around to me and said, "I'm sick. You have to take over this date." He got up and left. He had the flu or something. I sat down in the seat at the control console, like Captain Kirk. I put my hands on the controls, and I did Jimi. I was shaking with the energy. I didn't really care about Jimi's aura as Jimi Hendrix. All I cared about was the fact that I loved the kind of music he made. Anyway, there I was sitting at the board, shaking because I had my hands on the controls, on this connection to Jimi. Without me there, it was not really happening. The music was both of us. Jimi picked up on that. Other people could see that blue energy that crackled off me when I had my hands on the console. That was one of the reasons that I got gigs. I got the gigs from the people who could see the kind of energy that surrounded me.

Stryker: *So besides Hendrix, who else did you work with?*

Stone: Crosby, Stills, and Nash. Van Morrison. The Dead at one point, but the Dead had many, many engineers. Marty Balin in various incarnations, briefly with the Airplane. Johnny Winter, Todd Rundgren. I worked with Ultraviolet. I can go on.

Stryker: *It seems like a bit of a jump, Jimi Hendrix to Olivia. How did that happen?*

Stone: Let me give you more context here. Gary wanted to start a whole other subsidiary company. They wanted me to do that, but it meant not doing the music. I said, "Gary, I want to mix. That's who I am. That's what I do." Gary said, "You do this, or else." I resigned. I would have been a millionaire. I moved to Woodstock. I was in Bethel for the Woodstock festival, where I hung out back-stage. After the festival, I went to an event called the First Alternative Media Conference. The first day of that was great. The "alternative media" at that point was individuals doing alternative newspapers here and there. None of these people really knew each other. We looked at each other and said, "Holy shit, there are a lot of us. We're a community. How do we use this community to build a political agenda? How can we work together?" The second day, Holding Together showed up. Holding Together was the group organized to get Tim Leary out of jail. With a big grin, a person whose name I cannot remember opened an attaché case. It was full to the top with Golden Sunshine. By the end of the second day, it was a totally different conference. Quicksilver Messenger Service showed up, Dr. John, Ram Dass. It turned into a huge party. Party is not the right word. At one point, Larry Yurdin said, "Anyone who wants to go to California, raise your hand and come over here." So I raised my hand and went over there. We got on a bus and we went to the airport in Brattleboro. We got on a charter jet plane, took off, flew with many interesting things en route, landed, and the next thing I knew I was sitting on the curb at the San Jose Airport, coming off the acid. I knew one person in San Jose. I called her up and she drove to the airport, took me in my slightly bemused state to her house, fed me tea, put me up on the couch to sleep. I became part of her extended family. I moved into the backyard and lived in a tent for about six months, maybe a year. That's how I got to California. Then I did all the other stuff.

Stryker: *At some point before you get to Olivia you came out as transsexual and started to transition. As long as we're doing context, why don't you tell me something about that?*

Stone: After I got to California, I got on the phone and tried to find how to get information about transsexuality. I didn't have the faintest idea who to call. I had done nothing like this in New York, nothing. So the first group I called was Mattachine Society because that's the only group I'd heard of. They said well, we don't do anything like this but why don't you call so and so. After about half a dozen of these phone calls, I came up with the transsexual counseling project.

Stryker: *The Erickson Foundation?*

Stone: No, it was run by the police department.

Stryker: *Oh, the National Transsexual Counseling Unit. That was funded by the Erickson Foundation, but administered by the San Francisco Police Community Relations Unit. It was run by Officer Elliot Blackstone, and a variety of transsexual peer counselors.*

Stone: Right, Elliot Blackstone and Jan Maxwell. I walked in and there was Jan, the first live transie I had really ever met. She tried to talk me out of transitioning, took me on a tour of the Tenderloin. It was like Dante in the inner circles of hell. She showed me people who had gotten stuck, people with bad surgery, electrolysis-scarred faces. People who had dead-ended, gone crazy. Unbelievable poverty, despair. Visiting apartments with no furniture and bare red lightbulbs hanging from strings nailed to the ceiling, people who were not identifiable as a particular sex or gender, sitting on the floor, strung out on smack and sewing their own brassieres. I was supposed to be terrified. I was furious. I said to Jan, "Why aren't you helping them?" She said, "There is nothing I can do to help them." She just walked on ahead of me and walked out of the hotel and back to her office. She said, "You still want to do this?" I said yes, I know there's a dark side, but I still want to do this. I started transition, but then I had a bad automobile accident and was in the hospital for three months. I had twenty-seven broken bones. It took me a year to walk. This interfered with transition. Eventually I went through electrolysis.

I started a business in Santa Cruz, worked for myself. I just couldn't work for other people. Actually, when I first arrived in Santa Cruz I had gotten a job with a home electronics chain store, which fired me when I started transition. I scuttled across the street and rented a storefront and started my own electronics business, called the Wizard of Aud, and within two years I had put the chain store out of business. Schadenfreude is so sweet. Mostly I fixed stereos. It seemed easy. It put me in a public place where I could transition around other people and get their reactions. I couldn't be fired. It was an interesting adventure. I didn't know what was going to happen.

Stryker: *I do want to hear the Olivia Records story, but I'm fascinated with Santa Cruz. It seems to be on the margins of all these different sets of influences—it's on the* *fringe of the San Francisco Bay Area queer culture, as well as all the high-tech stuff in Silicon Valley. The city of Santa Cruz itself is an old resort town, a place to play, with the boardwalk. It's had a significant psychedelic counterculture. It's one of the primary places where surfing culture first established itself in the United States. The University of California, Santa Cruz, was a hotbed of early chaos theory. It has the History of Consciousness Department in critical cultural studies. And yet Santa Cruz is a relatively secluded little place, a very small geographical community. Almost like a big playground or laboratory, situated at the intersection of some fascinating and transformative social, cultural, political, and economic trends.*

Stone: Santa Cruz is the crack between the worlds. Many, many senses of that. It was a place where I could transition, open a store for $250, and be running a successful business within thirty days. When I opened the store I had nothing, one old oscilloscope. By the end of the month I was hiring people to help. By the third month we were just roaring, full scale. Shortly thereafter a woman called and said, "We would like to talk to you about doing an album with us." I said oh good, and this group of women appeared at my door shortly thereafter. It was Linda Tillery and Judy Dlugacz and several other people. They were from the Olivia collective. I knew that these people were lesbian separatists, and that I would eventually say something that was obviously politically incorrect. Apparently this didn't bother anyone much because they asked me if I would like to work with them. I said fine. I did the Be'be K'roche album with them. We enjoyed each other's company. We worked very well together. But I didn't understand the politics. We went through a period of getting to know each other during which I would say totally incorrect things like, "Well if she can't play, we should get somebody who can." Then they'd say, "Sit down, and shut up." We'd do take after take after take and I'd be going oh, what am I doing here. Eventually we would get something and move on.

I remembered the first time I ever heard an Olivia record was when I had been really down, and was having some problems, during transition. A friend of mine said "here, lie down" and she put me on her couch, put these headphones on me, and played *The Changer and the Changed*. I remember thinking, oh this music is beautiful but Jesus, the mix is horrible, and the musicianship is so indifferent. If this had been done by, say, Jefferson Airplane, it would have been transcendent. It would have been selling millions. I thanked her from the bottom of my heart and I told her how wonderful it was, which it was, and how it had changed my life, which it did, and I went off. I didn't realize that Olivia was the company that had made that record until fairly late in the game, after we were working together. Then it began to dawn on me that I had entered the recording industry at the top, and that everything I had done had been with the best musicians in the business. Now I had to adjust to the fact that I was doing something else, that I was making music and politics at the same time. And the genders were different. I had to learn that being the highest-quality musician was not the important thing here, but rather that supporting other women was the important thing. Learning the spirit of sisterhood was more important than technical perfection. So we did that album, and it was good. They invited me to come down and visit them at Olivia House in Los Angeles. I was stunned at the way in which they mixed community and friendship and professional life in music and business. All in the same house. This was the early days, the collective days. One person would cook, and then rotate. I thought this was what I've been trying to do for my whole life.

Stryker: *I've read this next part of the story in your* TranSisters *interview. Next comes Janice Raymond and all the high drama—your being outed in Raymond's* The Transsexual Empire, *and the threatened boycott of Olivia because the collective included a transsexual, all the stuff that becomes the background and motivation for "The* Empire *Strikes Back: A Posttranssexual Manifesto." But I want to focus on the continuities, rather than the breaks. I see in you such a powerful desire for connection, and an understanding of the body as a means of connecting to others, a technologically transformable means of connection. I see that desire to connect in your work as a recording engineer, as well as in your involvement with the Olivia collective, and in following a transsexual path in life. I see it in your making a home in the crack between the worlds we call Santa Cruz. And I see it in your eventual move into the History of Consciousness Department. Had you read Donna Haraway by that time?*

Stone: Yes. I had read "Manifesto for Cyborgs." I had first gone up to HistCon to meet Donna, I also met Billie Harris, who was at that time the administrative assistant. I got to know her and we liked each other. Sometime later I was standing in line at Straw Hat Pizza and Billie came in, very distraught, and I walked back to see her and I said, "Hey, how are you doing?" She said, "You don't happen to know anyone who could TA for a course in history of film, do you?" There weren't enough graduate students for all the teaching assistant positions, and they were desperate. Just absolutely out of the blue with no particular purpose or anything I said, "How about me?" She said, "You? Do you really think you could? I said, "Yeah, sure I could, just give me some idea of how it needs to look and I'll do it." So the next day they gave me the job. The next thing I knew I was in the class, sitting on the steps of the auditorium listening to a lecture. At one point I was walking between classes, thinking about the professor, thinking about the students I adored, thinking about how gorgeous the sun was; I could see cows in the fields, there was a soft breeze blowing. All of a sudden, I had a vision. I saw my entire life, everything I had done passing before me in the form of a circus train. Each car was a different career. Each car was a different aspect of my life, complete in itself with all of its little adventures painted in bright colors on the side. As it disappeared in the distance, I said, "Bye-bye. I'm home now." It had taken me a long time to get there. I had actually thought about doing a doctorate earlier, on issues of patriarchal language and memory. The project was to remember and reinvent the essentialist female language. By reinventing that language, women would be able to speak in a way that would bring into being a new consciousness. It would crystallize not just a new episteme but a new kind of being in the world that would cause the patriarchal type to wither away.

Stryker: *This sounds like something straight out of a Monique Wittig novel.*

Stone: Well, shortly thereafter I met Monique, and we had some interesting conversations about this. And of course Adrienne Rich wrote *The Dream of a Common Language* around this time. There was a lot of this stuff happening, it was something in the air. Part of the process was speaking the language to other women and seeing what happened with them. I was not doing this alone. There were many of us. We imagined a magic ur-time when the images that had become associated with a set of syllables were understood in the same way by very different groups. The language grew out of that, and we could actually speak it to each other. Anyway, it was a very high time. But I then had some very hard experiences being repudiated by some of the feminist scholars I wanted to work with. I felt everything that I had dreamed of in my life quite suddenly shatter. The cracks in the universe got bigger and bigger and crumbled away, the whole thing falling down. That's how the idea of going back to the university became utterly repugnant to me. That's why I didn't go back until much later on.

Stryker: *Let's talk about your book,* The War of Desire and Technology at the Close of the Mechanical Age. *What's it about?*

Stone: The erotization of technology. People sense the computer as a vague and somewhat troubling intelligence. A quasi-intelligence and quasi-life in which they can interact in a way one does not interact with a simple machine. By speaking to it in code we cause the machine to speak back. It speaks back in ways that are powerful and quirky and productive and potent, in the sense of opening up to new arenas of experience and consciousness, and from there to new forms of subjectivity. Which I think is what is behind a fair amount of that attraction. I think it's the tension between the obvious rupture in epistemes that this technology produces, the tension between that epistemic rupture and the change in subjectivity that that rupture produces. The change in subjectivity is just hovering at the edges of consciousness as it were, as something *in potentio*. The tension of that subjective change, I think, produces the eroticization. Desire emerges from that.

Stryker: *You see something really useful coming out in play, don't you?*

Stone: Absolutely. I think all learning is play. I don't think that learning needs to be work. But I think that the way in which almost the entire edifice of learning in Western civilization has been set up has an intent to recreate the aura of work.

Stryker: *The university as a factory?*

Stone: Yeah, right, as a production machine. But saying that learning should be fun implies that people should pursue it for their own pleasure because they want to do it, because they are intrigued by the things that they learn for the sake of learning them, not for the sake of . . . whatever, but for the sake of the knowledge itself and the sheer joy of discovery. But that implies an entire world that doesn't really exist in the United States. Nevertheless, I think it is the most natural state for humans. If learning were in fact treated as play, as joy, we wouldn't rank people. If we stopped ranking people, how do we know who is going to be fit for what job? I'm being ironic when I say that. If we stop ranking people, civilization would fall apart. Or it would be a different kind of civilization.

Stryker: *When you found cultural studies as an academic interdiscipline, through HistCon, you seemed to settle into something. At last you've arrived at a place you want to be. Why this place?*

Stone: Because it was big enough to hold me. Because I could be in love with the many different things that I am under the umbrella of cultural studies. When I was doing this and that, I always had the sense that there was a ceiling on whatever discipline I was pursuing. I would go up to a certain level and then my interest would stop. The other parts of me would be wasted there. I needed to engage other parts of myself. There was too much stuff not being used. When I hit cultural studies I found that I could bring so much into play—my experience with neurology and telephony, with sound recording and computer programming, with my studies of classics, with my brief encounters with theory. I could take all of those things and find ways in which they fit together. That's one reason why. The other reason is that cultural studies is part of the solution, one of the possible solutions, to the dilemma of the university system.

Stryker: *I see it being necessary to create spaces for dialogues to happen between different disciplines. That it's necessary for all of the disciplines to be in conversation, but that you run a risk in doing so. When you try to link psychoanalysis to history of science, or whatever, what you risk doing is becoming unintelligible to people outside the interdisciplinary conversation. It thwarts the purpose of doing what you're trying to do.*

Stone: I know what you mean, but the only other solution is staying away from it entirely. In that sense I'm still searching for that common language. I think performativity, or performance, if you will, is very close to that kind of a common language, because when you're performing, you're using a great deal more language than you would if you were simply putting words on a page, or even speaking. People respond to your facial expressions, for example.

Stryker: *I want to talk more about embodiment. One of the things I'm always hearing people talking about when talking about virtual reality and the Internet is that it's a disembodied space. We're never disembodied. We never get out of the meat part, we're just performing ourselves in different spaces. I want to hear you talk about the question of embodiment and disembodiment, about where subjectivity happens. Remember that story you told in your book, about the person who has multiple personalities, and some of the alters manifest only online? Where do those alter-subjects go when the body isn't connected to its performative media?*

Stone: This is one of those "where does the candle flame go when it goes out" questions. As long as we analyze it in those terms, we're not going to get anywhere. The best analogy would be quantum theory. They appear and they disappear. They go from virtual to real, from real to virtual and they cross back and forth over those boundaries, sometimes predictably and usually not. It is a transactional identity, a riff on quantum mechanics. So when you ask, where is this identity when it's off the Net? Basically, an easily speakable, easily intelligible answer to that question is that it becomes virtual during that time. Now we have to deal with the problem of what we mean by "virtuality," because the existence of the prosthesis in the network is what makes the virtual persona become real. We still need a little bit of language, a more powerful and complex language to describe this.

Stryker: *Transgender studies. Is that going to be a field for exploring this set of issues?*

Stone: Uh-huh.

Stryker: *I see gender as the language through which you communicate the reality of your identifications and desires to other people. Not just verbally and visually, but with your whole body, in a language of movement and smell and sound. It's a very full language with many realms and registers. I think of transsexuality as an instrumentalization of that language—of the language that makes the world real. I like your term* posttranssexual. *Historically, transsexuality has been conservative in the sense that, out of the desire to communicate, we're taking on a language that is already being* *spoken by other people. It's like any other language—the transmission of meaning relies on a shared structure. But, on the other hand, what we've seen happening the last five or six years or so is that there is a new critical mass of transsexuals. Transsexuality itself is now another gender possibility, another site of identification, a place, a space where you have the luxury of obtaining and coining new words, making neologisms. Those new words, the knowledges and the desires they represent, they're beginning to have some communicational efficacy—you can say them to new people who are going to have some idea of what you're talking about, like, "Oh yeah, that thing you just said, I call it this." They know what you're talking about, and whole new discussions come about. This is not just about transsexuality. I think in a lot of ways, transsexuality—the way it has been stigmatized and pathologized, or eroticized in a very suspect way—is really just a powerful mechanism for containing the transformative potential of human existence. As we do the political work to depathologize it, to make it sexy to be what being transsexual represents, to pull people out of conventional human existence, we're going to see it become something very different than it's been before. We really can't even see what that is very clearly yet. Part of this work is pulling transsexuality out of the discourse of homosexuality where it's been embedded for so long, and into a whole new network of ways of talking about embodiment and desire and pleasure and identity.*

Stone: Yes. This is what I've been calling "transsubjectivity," precisely because I want to move away from the sexuality model for very much those reasons. The body as an instrumentality for involvement, consciousness trying to evolve that richer, deeper language. We're at the pidgin stage right now. Using that as a guideline, we can look and see that the next stage will be the creole stage, which I think we're getting ready to move into, to where we do have analogies and similar structures, but also words that are composed of combinations of other languages so that they remain intelligible—what are called boundary objects, things which are visible on both sides, a translational process. From there we move on to the next stage, which has its own grammar and syntax and has gone on to involve a richer, deeper set of meanings of its own. We're definitely embarked on that. We're aware that the language that we're currently using to describe this kind of subjectivity is the language of the oppressor culture. When we actually get down to it, it is because societies tend to perpetuate themselves by preserving—by fixing—their identities and keeping those identities intact. We're talking about something which is quite alien. I think it's important to understand that transgender is not so much about sex or gender as it is about a new subjectivity.

Stryker: *The flip side of that coin is that, paradoxically, change happens because you're trying to perpetuate patterns over time. Transcription error, mutation, sustainable divergences—that's the motor of change. Flux and stasis go together. Part of* *the big political picture is to contest whatever discourses and practices emerge to outlaw nomadic subjectivity.*

Stone: Yes. Transsexuality is not the end. It's just a place to gather your energies so that you can go on to the next thing.

Susan Stryker is associate professor of gender and women's studies and director of the Institute for LGBT Studies at the University of Arizona and general coeditor of *TSQ: Transgender Studies Quarterly.*

Unapologetically Rain

Interview with Fashion Model Rain Dove Dubilewski

TANIA HAMMIDI

The fashion section for issue 3.1–2 of TSQ: Transgender Studies Quarterly *features two interviews conducted by Tania Hammidi, who currently represents a central voice in all things trans* and queer in the fashion world. Tania Hammidi is the founder of Queerture: Queer + Couture, an organization highlighting LGBTQIA fashion design, illustration, modeling, and style innovation. Hammidi also writes about fashion and dance, curates fashion shows, and participates as a model in the fashion industry. Hammidi's guest curation of the fashion section features interviews with designer Vanessa Craig and agender model Rain Dove; both interviews highlight the various politics of embodiment, representation, and production that readers of TSQ's fashion section can expect to learn more about in issues to come.*
—Editor

> I always tell people that clothing is your bird, your feathers, your scales in the animal world. It is a way for you to really tell the world how you want to be treated and what you want to be in that environment.
> —Rain Dove Dubilewski

There's so much to say about agender supermodel Rain Dove Dubilewski, since her fabulous splash onto the fashion runway at New York Fashion Week in 2014. For one, Dubilewski broke into modeling by losing a bet with a friend, which is kind of hot as well as a pleasant reminder that "success" does not unfold in a linear fashion. For two, she likes animals and uses her visibility as a model to bring awareness to social issues she finds important enough to research, sometimes at

TSQ: Transgender Studies Quarterly ∗ Volume 3, Numbers 1–2 ∗ May 2016
DOI 10.1215/23289252-3334571 © 2016 Duke University Press

the United Nations. Applying her agender philosophy to work, Dove broke onto the scene by walking both men's and women's wear for designers Malan Breton, Vivienne Hu, and Rochambeau as her debut.

At 6'2" with dark eyes and strong cheek lines, Dove's dreamy tall, dark, and handsomeness creates alluring representations of normative state power through fashion imagery. But Dove unsettles the dust by calling attention to these constructions of gender and power. And handsome masculinity is not her only look. Dove walked one of haute couture designer Vivienne Hu's "super femme" black dresses, briefcase, and work boots down the New York runway in 2015 without ado. Dove's first runway modeling job was in a pair of Calvin Klein (CK) briefs for a designer who presumed she was a cis-gendered male. As the story goes, she walked down the runway topless and in the CK briefs, to the designer's confusion. This unanticipated public explication of gender's constructed nature in relation to clothing and fashion started her rolling.

As the only agender model in the world, Dove uses her voice as well as her body to confront normative ideas about gender identity and its relationship to clothing, style, and fashion design. I first saw Rain Dove walk Auston Björkman's designs for SIR New York down the queer runway at "(un)Heeled: A Fashion Show for the Unconventionally Masculine," conceived by Anita Dolce Vita, presented by *DapperQ*, and hosted at the Brooklyn Museum in December 2014. But it wasn't until I saw her work it with gender-queer model Corey Wade at the 2015 "Queer Fashion Week" in Oakland, California (the brainchild of Miz Chris, presented by fiveTEN Oakland Events), and speak on a panel at "Rainbow Fashion Week" 2015 (produced by fashion designer E. Jaguar Beckford of Jag and Co.), that I understood the expansive range of Dove's abilities on the runway.

From the looks of things from the outside, her agency, Major Models New York, as well as designers like Vivienne Hu, Calvin Klein, Ace Rivington, Rochambeau, SIR New York, and more are giving Dove the opportunity to express and create more complicated images of gender and sexuality, within the framework of commercial, brand-driven fashion advertising.

Tania Hammidi: *Hi Rain! I am interested in how the fashion industry is handling your ability to rock both menswear and women's wear as a professional model.*

Rain Dove: Hi! The only thing that makes someone male or female is the anatomical value that the specific clothing was tailored to when it was designed. The only thing that means anything in clothing are those anatomical values. They change the structure of the clothing and how it fits on your body. More room in the pants. Higher sitting on the waist for hips. For butts, you have the curve. So certain clothing is tailored to be more flattering for anatomy. Otherwise, social trends dictate whether you should be wearing something based on if you have a penis or not. You know? [laughs]

TH: *Who were your heroes in entertainment or music growing up?*

RD: I never questioned my gender, ever. But I did go through isolation. Right up to high school, I thought I was a very ugly woman. You know? So I knew I would not be a sorority girl, but I might be like Sigourney Weaver from *Aliens*. [The focus was on] action.

I listened to music that told me there was going to be a time that was better. Kids feel trapped in their environment. But once you get out of high school you can choose to put yourself in an environment where people love you 100 percent. Get through. Listen to positive music, maybe some death metal.

TH: *How would you characterize this particular moment in the fashion industry? Is this revolution really happening, or just another trend?*

RD: In the past, things have been a trend I think. But now in the age of information, we are smarter than we used to be. We have access to a lot of information and can find things out for ourselves. We know when we are being duped. There are so many brands out there and so many companies to be loyal to. And most people are loyal to reflections of themselves. The companies realize that they can't trick people anymore. Like if you wear their clothes all of a sudden you are going to be 6'2". People don't want to try to be anything other than themselves, or a slightly nicer version of themselves [in ad campaigns]. We are starting to see a trend of "real models" that are emulating real people.

TH: *Are we seeing buyers who are buying from the LGBTQ designers?*

RD: They are slowly integrating. International companies can be progressive in the United States, but this is not the case around the world. I was talking to another magazine about this, recently. The reason it is not so in your face [internationally] is because there is a huge fear that there is not enough money in the gay community—consumer power—to compensate for the loss of clientele that the company would incur to represent that community. It is business!

If we want to see a change as people, we need to show those companies that there are consumers who will buy. Those companies are not obligated to be a social movement. They don't have to be the space of change. They don't have to say, "We want to do something different." They are not obligated, any more than we are. They have to have incentive.

TH: *Has modeling in the fashion industry led you to discover a femininity or masculinity in yourself that you didn't know about?*

RD: Yes, this has been a really good journey. I used to think I was just an ugly woman! Fashion has allowed me to explore sides of myself that I never gave myself permission to be. It has allowed me to take that high-fashion female Cruella Deville vibe, and also to [model in ways] that are more masculine and unapologetic. The amount of feedback has been phenomenal! Just to see that there are so many ways to construct yourself, and it is all done through clothing is incredible.

I always tell people that clothing is your bird, your feathers, your scales in the animal world. It is a way for you to really tell the world how you want to be treated and what you want to be in that environment. Do you want to be a poisonous caterpillar? Or do you want to be a jaguar or a blending-in chameleon? It is something that we use to reflect what is on the inside. It has been really great.

TH: *Have kids come up to you and given feedback?*

RD: This is the difficult thing. I have an interesting view on the trans* community. And it has a lot to do with fashion. I think there are two kinds of being trans. First we have to understand that there is sex, which is a biological thing. Genitalia hanging off our body or your ability to or not to have a baby. There is gender which is the constructed definition of how we treat that sex or what that sex is or is not. Which is interesting. My opinion on the trans community is that there are people who are bodily dysmorphic. It is a physical thing. But I think that there is a lot of social dysmorphia too. A lot of this has to do with the fashion world. So some people might not want to change their biology, but they want to be treated like a different sex, if that makes sense. And so there has been a lot of crossover with that world. A mom wrote to me recently she is giving hormone therapy to their seven-year old child. I said, "That is amazing! What were the signs?" She said her daughter doesn't like wearing men's clothes, she likes pink and ponies. All I heard [in that response] were socially constructed things. I didn't hear that this child was looking in the mirror every day and was saying, "Why do I have a penis? I don't want this."

I think it is very important that we give each other permission to be however we want in our society you know and there should not be a gender-specific construct. Clothing should not be gender specific. It is so stupid—I mean, really, it is the least of our worries. You know?

TH: *Who are your favorite designers right now?*

RD: I have a ton of different favorites because I have a ton of different sides. So certain designers accent different parts of what I want to express. If I were to go on my casual boy side, I started loving this menswear company ACE Rivington out of California. They do casual clothing, upscale sweaters, et cetera. I am working with them, and when we met, [founder and president Beau Lawrence] was still developing the branding for his company. He said, "You know I really don't care who wears my clothing as long as they feel comfortable in it." He decided to incorporate that idea into his new campaign. That is the concept: if people love it they should buy it and they shouldn't be ashamed to wear it. I really like them as far as comfort goes.

TH: *The public seems to really like what you are doing! Do you feel tokenized?*

RD: I don't think there is another agender model in the world at this current moment. I think the final frontier is yourself—your identity. No one else can explore it but you. I think that the difference is that I talk a lot. Not a lot of models talk, or are vocal. So, definitely I get added to lists because I talk! [laughs]

TH: *Any pleasant surprises from your journey thus far?*

RD: There is diversity in high fashion. One thing I was surprised about is the way that [haute couture designers] value gender—it is something I never knew was possible. Great designers have used all kinds of people because they want their art to be expressed! But commercial fashion has very little diversity in it. Haute couture designers like Alexander Wang, Jean Paul Gaultier use very diverse models, but since they are not in the commercial market, we don't see them as much.

TH: *Thank you for your words and hard work, Rain!*

Tania Hammidi is a visiting faculty member at the San Francisco Art Institute and founder of Queerture: Queer + Couture. She was voted "100 Most Stylish DapperQ's 2015" by *DapperQ Magazine*. Her recent publication, "Harrison House: Sacred Proportions" (2014), appears in *Conversations across the Field of Dance Studies*.

She Ain't Taking It
Interview with Suit Consultant Vanessa Craig

TANIA HAMMIDI

I'm so happy this movement is taking place and to be a part of it. It's been too long and I think queers are just like, "We're not gonna take it anymore."
—Vanessa Craig

Vanessa Craig is a suit consultant, fashion designer, and queer-events curator working it for two decades out of Los Angeles. Craig has a wicked taste for disco balls and uses her skateboard for pretty much everything. Her clothing lines include Sew-Gay and X-Killer, both design concepts utilizing silk screen, fashion design, and queer-community embodiments and knowledges. Through art, satire, and that special savoir faire, Craig creates queer, trans*, and lesbian public sites for dialogue, dance, and other forms of community participation. Craig, a surfer, was featured in *Curl Girls*, a Logo reality TV show chronicling the friendship of a group of lesbian surfers in 2007.

Tania Hammidi: *What is your preferred gender pronoun?*

Vanessa Craig: Vanessa, or "She," or "Sir" if I am in the checkout line at Vons.

TH: *How is it to be a part of community-based art projects and the commercial world simultaneously?*

VC: I don't consider myself a part of the commercial world. I put my heart, soul, and vision into and therefore don't really see my work, in particular, as being commercial. I approached a recent stylist position at clothier Sharpe Suiting as a design project, curating the look and feel, collaborating with the community, using my network to spread the word. I gave it my heart and did not think about the end result. I was mostly concerned with creating something awesome and hopefully the people would get it and jump on board. I think people can tell when you are only out for profit, especially the queer community. Your aesthetic, reputation, product, and business will suffer.

Although I do believe commerce is essential, I feel my role is and my desire has always been community. Being a queer person, naturally I want to involve the queer community in everything. I've collaborated with Maricon Collective, an [Los Angeles] LA-based Chicano art and dj collective and RobinsonABC, an eco-friendly waxed-canvas goods co. I asked our friends from [the band] Hi Fashion to use their music for Sharpe Suiting's Kickstarter video. These artists are friends of mine, whose work and vision I deeply admire. I always want to promote other artists' work in everything I do.

TH: *How do you identify? Artist, barber, hair stylist, visual artist, conceptual artist, painter, model, coach, mentor, hustler, tailor, anthropologist, poet, seamstress, stylist, on a journey...*

VC: That's a tough one. I tried to write a resume the other day and totally cracked. Let's just go with conceptual artist.

I am currently compiling all my work onto a new website called "vanessacraigslist.com." It will look just like craigslist.com, but will have most of my work on it. It's the only way I know how to showcase all of my strange and varied talents.

TH: *How has the current energy directed at queer, masculine-of-center, gender-queer, and trans* folk in the fashion industry effected your thoughts, practices, or self-imaginings?*

VC: One thing you can always count on with most masculine-of-center women as well as trans men, is their horrible encounters with trying to find traditional menswear that fits their bodies. You'll hear stories of the horrible dress they had to wear to their sister's wedding because they couldn't find a suit that fit and didn't want to be mocked again for being the awkward, ill-fitted queer at the wedding. Or on the flip side, a huge and bulky oversized sport coat with mismatched pants because that's "all there was." I can totally relate. It's time we had more options and outlets to buy clothing that fits *us* better. That's why I went to fashion school in the first place, to start making clothes that fit me and how I wanted to dress because there weren't any. Nothing looks better than confidence, and I believe when people are in the clothes they want and clothes that fit, they will embody that no matter how they identify. I'm so happy this movement is taking place and to be a part of it. It's been too long and I think queers are just like, "We're not gonna take it anymore."

TH: *How would you characterize this moment you see the fashion world and queer communities are in?*

VC: This is an interesting question. I think queerness is beautifully morphing into so many different tangents and things I never imagined growing up. I believe queer and trans people are always at the forefront of fashion, whether it is in and of itself being queer or trans, or whatever style one possesses on that big gay spectrum.

Once the basics are established, that is, clothes that actually fit (or purposely made to not fit), the possibilities are endless. Even now I see queer fashion taking a more modern, futuristic, and high-fashion approach. I believe there is a whole frontier beyond the dapper movement and I can't wait to see it, or maybe even design a few things myself. It's a very inspiring time!

TH: *How does your practice as an artist cross over with the work you may or may not be doing in fashion?*

VC: In my Sew-Gay T-shirt line, I used subversive images to make a commentary on a number of issues: prop. 8, gays in the military, and overall lack of gay visibility. I wanted the shirts to be fun and campy, but to still deliver a message. I gave a nod to gays in the military with an army shirt that read "Mary," an ode to tops 'n' bottoms with "Private Parts" and "Major Ass," and a heads-up to [Frank] Zappa with the 1980s neon lesbian fave: "Titties 'n' Beer," which on the back read "Thank God I'm Queer." The beauty of this line was that not only was it a hit with queers, but a lot straight people bought them too.

Aside from suits and parties, I make disco ball art. I have adorned boom boxes, BBQs, crosses, armbands, a bed frame, and even a low-rider bike. I don't know what it is about these magical mirrored squares, but I'm mesmerized by them and want to put them on everything!

Currently I'm refreshing my pattern making and sewing skills to develop some really amazing, cutting-edge suits aimed at masculine-of-center women and trans men!

TH: *Is this real? Meaning: are we doing all the work we need to do as queer and trans* folks to support the boom in fashion modeling, advertising? Are we asking the right questions? If not, what do you see being left out?*

VC: I think a lot is being done on this new frontier. I say "new" because never before have so many specifically queer and trans brands been popping up. It's a new wave and everyone is riding it. From bloggers to models to designers, everyone is excited, and it definitely feels like a movement. So many doors have been opened, so much more visibility has been gained, so many new jobs are being created. Even though there may not be a lot of money behind this movement just yet, most people are just happy to be involved, and that's really touching and what I believe sets it apart.

I feel like there will be companies, small or large that will continue to pop up as I'm seeing everyday now. Bravo to all of them. I feel it just adds to the Army of Us. In numbers, we can transform mainstream shopping, and more importantly, mainstream thinking.

TH: *What is exciting to you in the fashion world today?*

VC: I think we are totally headed to a super postmodern fashion state, and I'm excited about that. I think there will be less and less rules and structure, more free form and more freedom. Fashion will always swing like a pendulum, so don't worry, whatever style you are pining over will be back in some way, whether you like it or not. Although this time, some queer designer may actually design it to actually fit you.

Personally, I'm going to be working on a goth children's line specifically for babies of queer parents. Look, a new category already!

Cheers and thank you, Tania!

Tania Hammidi is a visiting faculty member at the San Francisco Art Institute and founder of Queerture: Queer + Couture. She was voted "100 Most Stylish DapperQ's 2015" by *DapperQ Magazine*. Her recent publication, "Harrison House: Sacred Proportions" (2014), appears in *Conversations across the Field of Dance Studies*.

Venezuelan Beauties

JOSÉ QUIROGA

*Queen for a Day: Transformistas, Beauty Queens, and the Performance
of Femininity in Venezuela*
Marcia Ochoa
Durham, NC: Duke University Press, 2014. 282 pp.

Queen for a Day dazzlingly sashays from the tulle and satin dresses of the Miss
Venezuela beauty contest to the very specific sites in Caracas where sex and desire
transform, reimagine, and reorder the city. The spectacular story of modern
Venezuela may not be familiar to many in the United States, more attuned to
issues of revolution (Cuba), dictatorship (Argentina, Chile, and others), and
US proxy wars in Central America and other parts of the region. But this fast-
paced story, which begins in the 1950s, takes us to a time when a country looking
at its present and past could see only a future of brilliant transformation in a
city intended to be one of the modern centers of the continent. In Venezuela, the
wealth produced by petroleum financed progress as an attainable dream: extraordinary abstract art and dazzling architectural feats; publishing houses that nur-
tured a continental, and not simply a national, readership; a communications
powerhouse ruled by televisual spectacle and advertising; and a metropolis connected by highways that intended to glue economic disparities. That this latter
aim was never achieved is the main reason why the Bolivarian revolution erupted
in the latter years of the twentieth century and the initial decade of this century
led by the charismatic figure of Hugo Chávez, who put an end to what used to be
called the most stable democracy in South America.

As all stories crafted for an age in which mass media and visuality rule,
there are grand events and minor acts of resistance and survival. Marcia Ochoa
takes note of them all: the most humble stage connects to a future and possible
glory, just as a drag queen today may be walking the Avenida Libertador and find

TSQ: Transgender Studies Quarterly ∗ Volume 3, Numbers 1–2 ∗ May 2016   **315**
DOI 10.1215/23289252-3334595   © 2016 Duke University Press

herself roaming Italian medieval plazas, only to be deported back to a territory forcibly gendered by the state. All the different strands that Ochoa offers for a study of femininity and gender in Venezuela that is not simply a study of "gendered behavior" can be seen as unrelated to each other, but one of the most important underpinnings of Ochoa's book is that it is rightly founded upon a faith in connection, in communication, across social classes spread throughout the country of Venezuela. All the pieces are found together, despite the fact that they form a shape we may not immediately recognize, but, then again, this speaks more to our difficulty with understanding or accepting contradiction than to the impossibility of a national cohesion.

As the book unfolds, it becomes clear (at least to this reader) that in order to "explain" Venezuela, one needs to choose between metaphor or metonymy. In other words, one can deconstruct the contradictions of modern Venezuela by focusing on a major event, such as one of the state funerals for Hugo Chávez, and use it as a metaphor whose ultimate referent may always be elusive. But conversely, one may actually go further by working with discrete units—the route of metonymy. The latter is the kernel for Ochoa's unfolding analysis, and it seems to me important to repeat it here. It is a minor detail—an inconsequential incident—that put a spell on Ochoa, and it works its magic on us when we read about it in the opening pages of the book.

Ochoa boards a plane at the San Antonio de Táchira provincial airport, and just before the plane departs, a flight attendant—"tall, gaunt, and arduously stylized"—proceeds to (explain? illustrate? act out?) the airline safety procedures in a way that turns the (honest, responsible, inquisitive, curious) cultural critic into a poststructuralist mess—but one with her feet on the ground. Ochoa does not mourn the lack of "authenticity" evident in the performance of a flight attendant repeating for the umpteenth time the same safety rules—a performance that no disgruntled traveler really pays attention to. On the contrary, she is going to be fascinated and enthralled, and she is going to fall for those lips "dripping with a mocha-tinged red" and the skin coated with a foundation "the color of café con leche" (1).

Without that recognition, without that image of the critic seduced, floored even (one could say "transported," but let's recall that Ochoa is not flying Air France, and she is not even in "economy comfort class"), by the unfolding spectacle, *Queen for a Day* would have been a solid contribution; but we have here an extraordinary book that tackles the complexity of the present Venezuelan moment with an academic rigor that does not discount the intuitive or the improvisational "hunch" pursued to its ultimate consequences. It is true that, in part, Ochoa's reaction is the product of a different historical moment, for at another point in time, the flight attendant's lack of authenticity would have been read differently—for example, as an anguished performance of the explicit demands of femininity as a system of oppression, one that maintains her in a state of false consciousness and keeps her indebted to a reactionary notion of an always similar gendered subject in the social sphere. Ochoa does not necessarily disavow this reading, nor should she—just as she does not merely celebrate the flight attendant's gestural complexity as a triumph of glamour over the actually existing conditions of labor and of life that produce that momentary escape from reality, a flight that can also represent an act of defiance. Ochoa is haunted by that image, and that image haunts us in turn. The flight attendant reappears at other points in the book, most notably when Ochoa discusses a fundamental contradiction that is not necessarily resolved in the book. (There is no need to resolve it, to tame its extraordinary pull.) It is stated succinctly in the following manner: "The perversions of modernity that seek to normalize, or perhaps extinguish, our messy bodies are also those in which we produce our own perverse, colored, and queer existences" (75). And here again, the flight attendant reappears: "She, with her jangling baubles, what is she doing?" (75). She is casting an aura of glamour over her captive audience, and she is engaging in imaginary travel, transporting herself to another runway, somewhere else.

Escaping may be thought of as a tool for negotiating a landscape of contradiction. "In Venezuela cannibalist cosmopolitanism takes the form of glamour—both in the ways the nation of Venezuela and queer and trans Venezuelans make space for themselves in the world" (75). There is much to unpack in this sentence. What fascinates Ochoa is the possibility (or the reality) of self-fashioning, but I think we can push this idea further (and I think Ochoa would agree with me, or perhaps not) and stress the political importance of flight, of escape—of flight as political praxis—without in any way implying that self-delusion is a necessary component of that flight. During that brief moment in time, arrested and suspended within the laborious displacements around her where everything moves, everything travels, everything is translated, the flight attendant has control, and she knows it. That such authority can be produced by an act in which the performer in essence "escapes" or "flees," projecting herself into a different context, renders the act a political one—even if the flight attendant herself may have the "reactionary" politics that is explored elsewhere in the book.

Ochoa's notion of spectacle derives from, but also distinguishes itself from, Guy Debord's *Society of the Spectacle* while keeping it as a point of reference. As Ochoa states, although Debord talks about the "harsh logic of spectacle" (204), Ochoa brings its very material facticity to the forefront. For Ochoa (and I think this is an illuminating critique), Debord ignores or pays little attention to labor (204). In contrast, Ochoa focuses on how desire here entails energy, preparation, and coordination. For in order to produce an illusion that is, or may be, the performance of femininity in Venezuela, one has to keep in mind the space that supports it and that does not merely serve as background but as a factor that determines much of what can be found as conventional or unconventional (or radical) within it. Labor, in other words, is an integral part of the spectacle, and it contributes its own kind of weight to the final overall product. The self-possession and sense of ambition and drive that make young women work sometimes beyond what is humanly possible in order to be "Misses" (or "queens") underscore an ethics that Ochoa can at no point dismiss or minimize. For all the kitschy glamour entailed in the soft-focus lens that registers the victorious queen, Ochoa is above all the one who seeks to understand both the mechanics and rationale that drive these spectacles. There is nothing pathological here, but it is evident that only hard work may, in the end, pay off.

If *Queen for a Day* stages the relationship between femininity in Venezuela and the national passion for beauty contests, the second part stages how subjects survive on the street—specifically, a street that functions as a runway (*pasarela*) along the Avenida Libertador in Caracas. Here, Ochoa enters the dangerous urban, nocturnal territory of the *transformistas* (allow us for a moment to leave the word untranslated). These "night workers" claim different corners, streets, and zones of the city, but in particular the *pasarelas*—perhaps imagined as red carpets—along Avenida Libertador where *transformistas* offer something more than just physical beauty. Like the Misses, they display a certain "feminine" essence, a manufactured product that is spectacular and illusory at the same time. As such, it is not unrelated to the logic that prevailed in the construction of the Avenida Libertador in itself, which is not solely an avenue but the very model of what the Venezuelan state thought modernity should be. Apprehended at this point as an object that lives in its own time, in its own "future past," Avenida Libertador is where Venezuelan modernity put on its high heels. As if responding precisely to this fact, "at this site on the juncture of power and modernity in late twentieth century Caracas, transformistas have carved out a persistent place to project themselves onto the national imaginary" (152). One may not know when it happened or who was wearing the first high pumps while strutting down the street, but there the *transformistas* defend and define their own parcel and resistance, as well as their labor, which Ochoa recognizes as complicated and multifaceted: they are constantly looking for tricks, fleeing from the police, and fighting, if not for the territory, then at least for their recognition as citizens.

That one small part of the urban rendition of the Venezuelan modernist dream is now an open-air nightly habitus for *transformistas* forces Ochoa to excavate that dream to its very foundations, in addition to her very dangerous fieldwork in the *transformista* scenario at night. As Ochoa notes, on Avenida

Libertador, both client and worker engage in coded transactions in which illusion defines the very human need for physical contact and release. If the street in no way resembles the artificial, air-conditioned, and superbly coiffed microclimate of femininity that can be seen in the beauty contests, then what links them both is a notion of a subject whose praxis is constantly enacted, as if the subject were always managing to look like she was in front of a television camera. It is not that Ochoa finds similar behavior in two different places, but that a common logic sustains what certain aspects of the person's inflection, the "gestuality," and the bodily movement want to enforce: an attention to the self that goes beyond physical beauty and that includes open and implicit understandings of social structure and behavior, of presentation vis-à-vis an Other, in order to craft a self that allows social upward mobility and success.

Queen for a Day also stages, in its final part, Venezuela's complex politics after the death of Hugo Chávez. It is important to note that, although she takes note of political processes that occur beyond the realm of the visual—with its constant visual reminders of scarcities of all kinds, and citizens taking to the street to protest the way in which the government has seemingly occupied all oppositional spaces—Ochoa is at her best when she captures what is happening "on the street." With concrete and asphalt as foundational leveling factors for new iterations of Venezuelan culture, the book accomplishes its riskier moves, putting the Misses and the *travestis* back together. It is a dazzling combination pursued in the final parts of the book, which includes a coda, or epilogue. The book as a whole does come together at this point, and despite the persistence of social clashes in the thoroughly modern and urban context of Caracas, I think Ochoa sees great opportunities in the almost complete upheaval that the country is experiencing at this moment. As Ochoa herself states, she did not seek to write a book on the Bolivarian revolution, but the revolution did happen, and it changed some things in unexpected ways, and it left others seemingly intact. In terms of those elements that changed, she mentions the process of citizenship, one that has been gained by all Venezuelans, who see themselves, for good or bad, as belonging to a broader collective, one in which the state—any state, as a matter of fact, whether inefficient, corrupt, imperfect—emerges as the guarantor or advocate of the rights of all citizens.

As one reads Ochoa's *Queen for a Day*, one becomes aware of how Venezuela still is, amazingly, one of the most understudied Latin American political and social scenarios for US Latin American studies. Within transgender, gender, and sexuality studies, no other author comes close to approximating the sheer feat of creating a book about a "national" deployment of gender that at the same time manages not to repeat national platitudes in the midst of what has been surely the most contested period in recent Venezuelan history, in which competing visions of gendered nationalism skew the conversation toward zones of dispute. Ochoa has thankfully avoided the temptation to write a book in which representations of feminism (or feminism itself) become the traveling companion to ideology. That this is an unimaginative mode of addressing an issue can immediately be ascertained by following Ochoa, who keeps the focus on performativity and mass media. This reader welcomed this approach, for it joined fields that have also produced, in Venezuela and elsewhere, marvelous interlocutors.

For the reader who knows little of Venezuela, it may seem unreal that such serious politics originate, or are inscribed within, the banalities that can be seen on television. But bear in mind that, whereas the structures that defined Venezuelan nationality may have tottered and collapsed during the Bolivarian revolution, the beauty pageant lives on. The fact that so many millions adore, worship, and revere the replicant product crowned at the end of the show may surely seem like an academic exaggeration. Be very afraid: it is not. Ochoa guides us at various points of the book through the history of this monstrous spectacle (monstrous in the sense of producing wonder), from the fascinating account of the first Miss Venezuela, an almost savage beauty who refused to be tamed by the corporatist system, to the multifaceted, varied industry of the Misses that permeates the high and low, the poor, rich, and middle-class residents of Venezuela and members of the Venezuelan diaspora.

That the performances of femininity these events produce are eminently "readable" proves how the citational aspect of gender is the most normativized way of constructing the intimate technologies of glamour. It also served to clarify that the hard work of the contestants, as well as that of the *transformistas* that adopt that same citational construct, may employ a register of self-possession evident in each and every detail of its composition—its modes of speech, the composed way in which it gives itself over to the public and the audience—all of these served to project authority on the one hand, while on the other it rendered evident the fact that the authority itself was elsewhere, that the gendered, articulate subject was responding to a call, to a form of interpellation that came from someplace else. It is in the process of responding to it that the subject constructs herself as an "emblem" of Venezuelan femininity.

José Quiroga is professor of comparative literature at Emory University. His recent published books include *Mapa Callejero* (2010) and *Law of Desire: A Queer Film Classic* (2009). At present, he is completing an edited collection for Duke University Press titled *The Havana Reader* and a book of dissident practices in Cuba and Argentina, for which he was awarded a Guggenheim Fellowship for the year 2010–11.

Still Here

Gender, Ballroom, and HIV/AIDS

RINALDO WALCOTT

Butch Queens Up in Pumps:
Gender, Performance, and Ballroom Culture in Detroit
Marlon Bailey
Ann Arbor: University of Michigan Press, 2013. 296 pp.

Queer family is real. And indeed, the realness of queer family has as its counterpoint the hegemonic notion of family as based in blood. While all family formations are political, queer family formations ask that we think the politics of family as an always already problematic formation. The existence of queer family, then, highlights how other family forms necessarily exceed the normative definition and practice of hegemonic family claims. Of course, hegemonic practices of family have evolved beyond the logic of blood, but one might argue that a notion of "blood relations" is still very much the basis of how even families made through adoption are generally understood. Unconditional love and commitment comes to stand in for blood as a way to perpetuate normative codes for the hegemonic family form in patriarchal white supremacist capitalism.

Interestingly, one might say that for a certain generation of gay men, blood, too, has been a kind of familial bind: if not blood, then semen; if not semen, then fluid(s). By the latter I mean to signal how HIV/AIDS has worked to produce "familial" relations among gay men, as a kind of cement, working in a similar fashion as blood did for the hegemonic family form. Blood and semen have come to mark and make possible the "familial relations" of the discourse of family central to the politics of contemporary queer life, but this is family politics with a difference: it is a family politics launched against hegemonic normative family claims, if you wish. The emergency of the ongoing HIV/AIDS pandemic

TSQ: Transgender Studies Quarterly ★ Volume 3, Numbers 1–2 ★ May 2016   **321**
DOI 10.1215/23289252-3334607   © 2016 Duke University Press

for black families is central to rethinking the hegemonic family form as we know it. Indeed, black families have been since slavery queer family forms. However, black queer family forms further complicate an already queer dynamic because the black family form exists on the margins of all other family forms as the deficit and or excess of hegemonic claims of the family. Thus the black family form might also be the most policed and reviled family form.

Marlon Bailey's *Butch Queens Up in Pumps: Gender, Performance, and Ball Culture in Detroit* begins with the trope of "family" to explain how he entered into and came to understand the work that his book seeks to do. Bailey retells the story of his "brother" who seroconverted at age nineteen and how, as nonblood brothers, the bond forged through that "event" became central to the kind of book and research he was able to undertake in its aftermath. As Bailey recounts the story of his brother's diagnosis and twenty-five years or more now of living his life with HIV, an intimacy of the kind that is generally thought to frame hegemonic familial relations is revealed. The way in which Bailey leads the reader to consider such familial intimacy is a political maneuver meant to unhinge family from old blood relations but that also works to produce family as something more than just choice. By so doing, Bailey immediately orients the reader to an unfolding of family that, while it will not be surprising for many contemporary readers, nonetheless asks us to (re)consider what and how family works, and what it means and how it is enacted for us. Bailey proffers an ethics of family that requires us to pay attention to the consequences of familial claims. Of course, one cannot write a book about ballroom culture without engaging the question of family, given that family is central to the houses of ball culture. However, I want to suggest that Bailey has given us something more as well. His delineation of the gender system in the houses and its reference to traditional familial relations and order both retains and jettisons the family form as we know it. Indeed, one of the most significant aspects of Bailey's work might be a reminder of how to live with contradiction.

Butch Queens Up in Pumps is more than a study of ballroom culture. To make such a claim is not to take anything away from the significant ethnographic and archival work that Bailey engages to produce this study of ball culture. The "something more" of this study is the way in which familial politics and fluids or blood have shaped ball culture in Detroit. Bailey's attention to these kinship networks provides us with a difficult and devastating picture of fractured black (queer) family and how black queers—most but not all of whom were assigned male at birth and articulate a wide range of gender identifications—have worked to re-create families of love, care, and support in the face of racist-homophobia. By "racist-homophobia," I mean the ways in which white supremacy attempts to limit, and often succeeds at limiting, the life chances of black queer people, and the way in which black heteronormativity or homophobia is often enacted against black queer people. The combined force of racist-homophobia places black queer people in a unique position from which to assess contemporary queer culture and its many claims, and this is what Bailey's work offers us. Especially when it comes to HIV/AIDS, black queer people arguably occupy a vantage point from which to access a historical present that is utterly unique and that complicates the "new" queer settlement, marriage, drug cocktails, and all the other elements of our present moment.

Bailey provides readers with a detailed description of ballroom's gender signs and order. However, the book does not investigate these signs and orders as much as it seeks to diagnose how gender-nonconforming queer black people make lives through using ballroom as a significant life-affirming resource. Bailey's nuanced articulation of gender is positioned through a nexus of race, gender, and sexuality that resists privileging either gender or sexuality in favor of mapping blackness as the foundational marker of the exclusions and resistances he seeks to document. Bailey's work thus sets a template for further discussions concerning gender nonconformity in black queer studies and, more broadly, in transgender studies. A significant contribution of this work lies in Bailey's respect for the gender fluidity that arises when persons whose gender performances and identifications move between the ballroom and other social and cultural spaces; in crossing contexts, gender emerges as simultaneously indeterminate, often already assured and situational.

These folks produce gender fluidity as a way of life, and even as a way of navigating a racist, homophobic, and transphobic world. Through Bailey's lens, it might be argued that ballroom gives us one of the most complicated gender systems of any contemporary queer formation we have witnessed.

This past February (2015), I participated in an event celebrating twenty-five years of Jenny Livingston's *Paris Is Burning* (Livingston [1991] 2005). The audience was the whitest one I have seen in recent memory for a film that featured black lives. The cult status of Livingston's film is in direct opposition to the status that black queer people are accorded in contemporary queer culture. Given the context that I was in, I could not help but move the end of my written comments to the beginning of my talk. I began, then, with calling out the names of all those in the film who had passed on. I insisted that the audience repeat their names. I was not engaging in some form of domination, but I wanted the audience to share in the intimacy of saying those names in the hope that something about knowing a name and uttering it might produce a different relation to the person being called out. Indeed, contemporary queer culture is full of black creativity without being able to name the black persons responsible for the creative contributions.

Unfortunately and ambivalently, it is now almost impossible to come to ballroom culture without going through *Paris Is Burning*. *Paris Is Burning* has left in its wake a relation to black queer culture that is both sadly nuanced and madly spectacular. In its aftermath one cannot think of balls without *Paris Is Burning*'s proliferating imagery and pageant. But what is often missing from *Paris Is Burning* is a sustained engagement with the lives lost. The carnage that HIV/AIDS and racist-homophobia wreaked on the subjects of that film remains one of the most unobserved aspects of the aftermath of the film in white queer culture. Almost all the film's subjects are gone now. Similarly, the way in which the subjects of the film offered us their unapologetically trans lives and desires, without recourse for respectability, remains unmatched still in contemporary queer culture. Indeed, Livingston was allowed extraordinary access, and we have benefited from that access as viewers. Yet what continues to rankle is how a film so celebrated and loved by white queers does not lead to forms of engagement with black queer life that is meaningful. Indeed, the HIV/AIDS pandemic continues to devastate black lives, a point noted in the film, but a point that could be the basis of a more complex relationship between black and other queers, which has yet to occur.

Butch Queens Up in Pumps is neither a counterpoint nor an extension of *Paris Is Burning*. Bailey's book sits alongside the film offering readers a different kind of intimacy. While Livingston gives us the outside-in look, Bailey gives us the inside-out-inside look, a way of seeing that is both about belonging and being outside simultaneously, conditioned by familial intimacy and love. Bailey's work is constituted through a politics of love that grapples with and recognizes the stakes of racist-homophobia for black queer life. The work asks it readers to recognize the limits of the hegemonic black family form at the same time that it asserts new ways of being family in the context of ongoing discourses and material practices that seek to pathologize and even make black families of all kinds impossible. *Butch Queen Up in Pumps*, then, is a book that in part maps the ways in which black family forms persist despite an array of forces meant to invalidate black personhood.

Indeed, the story of *Butch Queen Up in Pumps* can be read as a story of survival. Bailey's "family" in the pages of this book not only survive the rejection of hegemonic families, homophobic communities, an antiblack national culture, and so on; they also make meaningful lives while doing so. Bailey documents a ball culture concerned with raising funds for HIV/AIDS organizations. Utilizing his concept of "housework," Bailey offers readers an account of ballroom activism around HIV/AIDS that is sobering and necessary, all the while demonstrating the creative energies of black queer subjecthood. It is this aspect of Bailey's work that makes its most original contribution, his thinking through HIV/AIDS and ball culture. It is somewhat startling that, twenty-five years after *Paris Is Burning*, Bailey's intervention is so necessary—HIV/AIDS was the unspoken backdrop to that very popular film and remains a crisis today.

The link between members of the ball scene and HIV/AIDS service pro-viders is especially important, given how the balls function as gathering places for a population that safer-sex advocates wish to reach. Bailey's work brings him into conversation with the many in Detroit who work across the two contexts. Bailey's work documents how successful such cross-fertilized contexts can be and how such contexts can sometimes not work as well. Indeed, the ongoing epidemic of HIV/AIDS in black communities and among the ball community is evidence of the complicated context of the problem. But Bailey also skillfully points out that those who are closest to the actual lives of those affected are often not listened to as well. What Bailey documents is the work that racist-homophobia does to impede the lives of black queers. Thus the analysis offered by Bailey of HIV prevention efforts and their lack of impact fits a longer historical pattern of the state's disregarding black people's views, understandings, and assessments of their lives. The consequences of such disregard are always dire for black populations, and HIV/AIDS is our contemporary condition of such disregard.

It is precisely the disregard for black queer life that makes *Butch Queen Up in Pumps* an important book. Bailey offers readers insight into how black queers (re)make and make selves fashioned in-between and against an array of forces. *Butch Queens up in Pumps* ask us to consider our ethical relation to black queer people, their lives and their deaths. Bailey complicates how black queers work within, across, and against gender performance to create worlds in which their lives might have some value. The forms of creative deconstruction, renovation, and invention that black queer people produce have much to teach us about how it might be possible to imagine new worlds, put them into place, and make them viable, even as those worlds are surrounded by forces hostile to their very existence. The ballroom scene is a glimpse into such worlds. Indeed, Bailey offers us crucially important insights into how black queer life is a necessary life of creative destruction and invention but also one that is fulfilling in ways that hegemonic contemporary queer culture can't seem to notice or can only notice at the site of entertainment, like Rupaul's drag race. Instead, *Butch Queens Up in Pumps* reveals to us pleasure, death, and life as creative forces shaping everyday existence always slightly ahead of that which seeks to drag us into the abyss.

Rinaldo Walcott is the director of the Women and Gender Studies Institute at the University of Toronto. He works on themes of masculinity, queerness, coloniality, and freedom.

Reference

Livingston, Jennie, dir. (1991) 2005. *Paris Is Burning*. Offwhite Productions, 71min. DVD. Burbank, CA: Miramax Home Entertainment.

Rearward Trajectories

HELEN HOK-SZE LEUNG

A View from the Bottom:
Asian American Masculinity and Sexual Representation
Nguyen Tan Hoang
Durham, NC: Duke University Press, 2015. 287 pp.

A View from the Bottom is bookended by references to two trends on gay male sex cruising websites: the "douchebags of Grindr" who routinely express preferences like "no fats, no femmes, no Asians" on their profiles and the resilient GAMS (gay Asian men) who recycle racist epithets into online handles that they adopt without shame. This move from abjection's violence to its potential utility parallels the book's own trajectory. Drawing from a diverse range of visual media, author Nguyen Tan Hoang compiles an eclectic "archive of bottomhood" to show us how "the threatening force of bottom-as-abjection" (21) can be received and transformed rather than disavowed.

Nguyen approaches his material from highly original perspectives and with intriguing points of focus. In chapter 1, the "rise and fall" and subsequent comeback of gay Asian American porn star Brandon Lee provide the lens through which Nguyen observes the racial dynamics of 1990s West Hollywood porn flicks. While Lee has been touted as the first Asian top in North American porn, Nguyen argues that his topness is constructed at the expense of Asian costars who perform as his racialized other. By contrast, Lee's postcomeback roles as not only a bottom but one with a bad accent illustrate what Nguyen calls "accented pornography." Adapting Hamid Naficy's notion of "accented cinema" and Yiman Wang's "yellow yellow face," Nguyen argues that this "mode of porn performance and reception" allows actors as well as viewers to inhabit a toxic racial stereotype with self-awareness and irony. Similarly, in the following chapter, Nguyen views the supporting role of Philippine houseboy Anacleto in *Reflections in a Golden Eye* (dir.

John Huston; 1967) as much more than just a dehumanizing and cartoonish portrayal of a hissy screaming queen. Adopting Anacleto's "view from below," Nguyen shows how the character "upends the heteronormative constructions of gender, race, sexuality, and nation" by "embracing femininity and racial castration" (73). An equally adventurous reading in chapter 3 of *The Lover* (dir. Jean Jacques Annaud; 1992) highlights the camera's gaze on actor Tony Leung's "gorgeous ass." Nguyen shows how this "unabashed specularity" on his penetrable and receptive behind creates an alliance of bottomhood in colonial Vietnam between the aristocratic Chinese heterosexual man and his white-trash French lover. In the final and most intimate chapter, Nguyen contrasts gay Asian documentaries that reject bottomhood as exploitation with the playful and ironic works of experimental queer Asian video artists, including those by the author himself, that try to mine those exploitative images for pleasures and agency.

The book is written with nuance and theoretical sophistication, in a clear and lively style that is at once personable and playful. Nguyen even manages to line his impeccably elegant academic prose with occasional sexual innuendo that is by turn funny and smutty. As Nguyen describes, he is "reading as a bottom": a methodology that he characterizes as a combination of Eve Sedgwick's "paranoid mode" and "reparative mode" of analysis (24). His inventive readings remind us that ideologically problematic material can feel viscerally pleasurable. Nguyen chooses to explore (rather than dismiss, hide, or ignore) such pleasures, guided by "a politics of the behind, the outmoded, the embarrassing" (25). He shows that receptivity to humiliating and painful representations can expose the structure of power and reshuffle its hierarchies in unexpected and unpredictable ways.

The gendered nature of the racial abjection that Nguyen examines presents a conundrum that the book grapples with throughout. The racialization of Asian men in North America has depended on their feminization and a conflation of femininity with gayness and sexual bottomhood. Such a representation valorizes white, heteronormative, phallic masculinity and projects attributes it imagines as opposites onto Asian bodies. In turn, resistant strategies against this racist and homophobic imaginary from many Asian American and gay male discourses attempt to remasculinize the Asian and gay male body as virile and butch. While Nguyen understands the political contexts that produce these counternarratives, he argues that their readiness to delink from femininity and bottomhood unwittingly reproduces the masculinist logic they are resisting in the first place. However, Nguyen's own project does not try to redeem bottomhood as necessarily subversive. Citing Heather Love's critique of queer criticism's "compulsion" to disavow a shameful and injurious past, Nguyen demonstrates alternative ways of confronting social abjection (20).

Nguyen deftly mobilizes feminist and queer-of-color critiques to reexamine queer Asian bottomhood. While there is no explicit engagement with trans studies, the potential for doing so surfaces throughout the book. For example, Nguyen illustrates with vivid examples the deep-seated anxiety over femininity that is found not only in racist discourse about gay Asian men but also in counternarratives that try to remasculinize gay Asian bodies. Nguyen approaches this anxiety as a form of sexist femmephobia over male effeminacy, which he understands primarily as a gay male gender role. Yet, as expressed quite literally by one of the "douchebags of Grindr" who is "scared about getting old and having to date a young Asian ladyboy" (2), it is actually a form of transphobia that fears the slippage between male effeminacy and trans femininity. The racialized nature of this transphobia views Asian bodies to be especially susceptible to this slippage. Even more troubling, a similar anxiety is reproduced in gay male theoretical discourse, which Nguyen points out is premised on a post-Stonewall "homo-ideal of a straight-acting Euro-American gay man" (79). The examples he cites include Vito Russo's understanding of stereotypical effeminacy as a gay man's "assumption of a female role," Alan Sinfeld's characterization of the sexoloigcal type of "passive homosexuality" as a man who "wants to be female . . . (who) may be said to have a woman's soul in a man's body" (quoted on 74), and David Halpern's distinction between "prehomosexual models" that favor hierarchical gender roles and "modern" homosexuality that is based on "sameness and mutuality" (78). While these texts may not belong in the same category of douchery as the phobic expressions found on Grindr, their language certainly betrays a similar anxiety over male effeminacy's proximity to trans femininity. It seems to me that the "archive of bottomhood" Nguyen compiles is far more than a corpus of gay male representations, as it is sometimes characterized in the book. The very marginalization and abjection of these representations within gay male discourse, not to mention in everyday gay male sexual culture, as being essentially "too trans" speaks to the need to also explore their significance as trans phenomena.

Even though Nguyen does not explicitly examine his archive as trans phenomena, his critical strategy relinks gender variance with sexual subjectivity, an association that narratives of modern homosexuality have been anxious to disavow. Nguyen explains that his "insistence on reattaching gender deviance (i.e., effeminacy) with homosexuality" in his formulation of bottomhood is meant as an affront to this "oppressive and tyrannical" narrative of Eurocentric gay male subjectivity (80). There is much to explore between Nguyen's critical move here and recent scholarship in trans studies that questions the globalizing category of "transgender" in similar ways, such as David Valentine's critique of *transgender* as an umbrella term adopted in scholarship, policy, and community contexts that distinguishes gender identity absolutely from expression of desire and sexual identity (2007) as well as decolonial scholarship that details the colonial and globalizing construction of "transgender" as a regulatory category that reclassifies practices and identities in the non-West (Aizura et al. 2014). It seems fitting and timely at this juncture to read gay studies and trans studies together through these self-reflexive critiques of the fields' foundational categories and attend to phenomena that cannot be adequately understood as distinctly gay or transgender.

It is perhaps no accident that Nguyen concludes the last of his main chapters with two visual texts that feature trans protagonists. True to his "politics of the behind," Nguyen is inspired by these figures' defiance of politically and aesthetically "correct" queer styles. First, the "drag superheroine" Iron Pussy in the eponymous series of films directed and performed by Thai artist Michael Shaowanasai is an ironic composite of both the Western gay stereotype of the muscle queen and the traditional Thai gender role of *kathoey*. In the films, "getting fucked is business as usual" (182), and Iron Pussy performs the sexual labor routinely offered up by women, gay men, and *kathoey* to benefit a state that in turn stigmatizes them. Nguyen identifies critical potential in Iron Pussy's over-the-top and hyperenthusiastic performance to provide an ironic commentary on the exploitation while also embodying a modicum of pleasure that exceeds such forces of exploitation. Second, the boy-dyke protagonist in Korean American artist Erica Cho's experimental video *We Got Moves* embraces a "femme-fag aesthetic" from 1970s and 1980s male teen idols. The video re-creates (or recovers) the homoerotic and intergenerational bond from the film *The Karate Kid* with a boy-dyke hero who replays the humiliation sequences over and over without ever reaching the redemption arc of the Hollywood film. Nguyen locates "rearward trajectories" in these texts to show how they embrace putatively "backward" embodiments to interrupt the developmental narratives of resistance that insist on a move from shame to pride, objectification to empowerment, stereotype to identity, and backwardness to modernity. Along the same rearward trajectory, the book reclaims the messy, frequently disavowed, yet affectively powerful link between gender-variant presentation and sexual subjectivity, despite the imperative in identity politics, institutional formations, and intellectual trends to do otherwise. *A View from the Bottom* is certainly well positioned to provoke new conversations—even realignments of boundary—between gay studies and trans studies.

Helen Hok-Sze Leung is associate professor of gender, sexuality, and women's studies at Simon Fraser University. She is the author of *Undercurrents: Queer Culture and Postcolonial Hong Kong* (2008) and *Farewell My Concubine: A Queer Film Classic* (2010).

References

Aizura, Aren Z., et al., eds. 2014. "Decolonizing the Transgender Imaginary." Special issue, *TSQ* 1, no. 3.

Valentine, David. 2007. *Imagining Transgender: An Ethnography of a Category*. Durham, NC: Duke University Press.

Printed and bound by CPI Group (UK) Ltd, Croydon, CR0 4YY

13/04/2025

14656482-0002